JAMES MADISON
CRITICAL THINKING COURSE

Written by
William O'Meara, Ph.D
Daniel Flage, Ph.D

Edited by
William J. Hawk, Ph.D
Catherine Connors-Nelson

Graphic Design by
Annette Langenstein
Trisha Dreyer • Danielle West

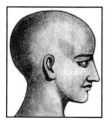

© 2011
THE CRITICAL THINKING CO.™
(Bright Minds™)
www.CriticalThinking.com
Phone: 800-458-4849 • Fax: 831-393-3277
P.O. Box 1610 • Seaside • CA 93955-1610
ISBN 978-1-60144-145-4

Mixed Sources
Product group from well-managed
forests and other controlled sources
www.fsc.org Cert no. SW-COC-002283
© 1996 Forest Stewardship Council

Table of Contents

About the Authors

William O'Meara is a Professor of Philosophy. He received his Ph.D. in philosophy from Loyola University, 1969, and is now (2010-11) in his fortieth year of teaching at James Madison University. He was selected the 2008-09 Distinguished Teacher of the Year for the College of Arts and Letters at James Madison University. He has written articles on 19th and 20th century European and American philosophers. He is one of the authors of the *James Madison Critical Thinking Test*.

Daniel Flage is a Professor of Philosophy. He received his Ph.D. in philosophy from the University of Iowa in 1977. He taught at Illinois State University, the University of Wisconsin-La Crosse, and the University of Texas at Austin before coming to James Madison University, where he has taught for the past twenty years. He was a National Endowment for the Humanities Fellow in 1988-89 and was selected the 2000-01 Madison Scholar for the College of Arts and Letters at James Madison University. His eight books and more than fifty articles cover issues in 17th and 18th century European philosophy, logic, and critical thinking. He is one of the authors of the *James Madison Critical Thinking Test*.

About the James Madison Critical Thinking Course

Critical thinking is identifying and evaluating evidence to guide decision making. It is a set of skills you use to guide you in deciding whether a claim is, or probably is, true or false. Some of those skills concern individual words and claims. To determine whether a claim is true or false, you need to know what is being claimed, and sometimes that is not as obvious as you might wish. Other skills concern collections of claims. If certain claims are true, when will they allow you to conclude that some other claim is true? How strong is the evidence supporting the truth of that claim? When an event occurs, what will explain why or how that event came to be?

Each chapter in this book focuses on a skill or set of skills involved in making an informed decision. Through short, clear explanations of the principles involved, combined with vivid examples and numerous exercises, you will learn to ask questions of what you read and write. It presents a very practical way for you to learn to think clearly and reason precisely.

Each chapter begins with the most basic concepts and principles, and builds slowly and systematically, step-by-step toward the more complicated issues involved. The sequential building assures that you will master one element of a topic before going on to the next. It also allows instructors to choose the desired depth of instruction.

Within limits, the book itself is arranged in the same way. The first four chapters involve basic concepts and principles. Because of this, we believe it would be most beneficial to examine the opening chapters before proceeding to the last four. The order in which you examine the issues in the final four chapters is less important, and instructors occasionally might find it useful to focus on one or another of them to fulfill specific needs of an individual class.

Chapter 1 is a basic introduction to critical thinking. It focuses on the questions critical thinkers ask and the qualities critical thinkers deem important.

Chapter 2 focuses on the distinction between facts and opinions. Facts are states of the world. Claims of fact are claims about the world. Claims are either true or false, and there are methods you usually can follow to decide whether a factual claim is true or false. Opinions, however, are beliefs about something. The problem with opinions is that there is no good way to prove that they are true or false.

Chapter 3 looks first at some of the hazards commonly encountered when attempting to determine what is claimed by a descriptive sentence. Some words and sentences are ambiguous; that is, they can be understood to have more than one meaning. Some words are vague. They have no precise meaning. The opening sections of the chapter explore ways to determine what is probably meant by ambiguous or vague words or sentences. The chapter continues by examining more extensive descriptions; that is, passages that answer the questions Who? What? When? Where? and How? It concludes with a discussion of explanations, passages that answer the questions: Why is something the way it is? How did it come to be the way it is? How do you do something?

Chapter 4 is an introduction to arguments. An argument is a group of claims of which one or more of these claims (the premises) intend to provide support for one of the other claims (the conclusion). Arguments are central to critical thinking. The chapter distinguishes between inductive and deductive arguments. It focuses on the form or structure of those arguments. The form or structure of a valid deductive argument guarantees that if its premises are true, then so is its conclusion.

Chapter 5 examines deductive arguments whose validity depends upon the relationship between the truth-values of claims. This is commonly known as sentential or propositional logic. Most of the deductive arguments you find in everyday life are arguments of this sort. The chapter focuses on identifying valid argument forms, and it devotes some space to logically equivalent claims; that is, claims that are true under exactly the same circumstances (alternative ways to make the same claims).

Chapter 6 investigates categorical syllogisms. Categorical claims assert relations among sets of things. Categorical syllogisms are arguments composed solely of categorical claims. The chapter begins with categorical claims and categorical syllogisms in their purest forms—what are known as standard form categorical claims and categorical syllogisms. Next we examine two ways to determine whether categorical syllogisms are valid, and proceed to examine the various hazards you encounter when examining categorical syllogisms in ordinary English.

Chapter 7 focuses on inductive arguments. It examines arguments by analogy, generalizations, and arguments to the best explanation (reasoning with hypotheses). Inductive arguments can only give evidence for the probable truth of a conclusion. This chapter gives you practice in determining what evidences can make for a more probable conclusion.

Chapter 8 discusses "Informal Fallacies," common ways in which arguments in everyday life fail. This chapter gives you practice in identifying and evaluating typical mistakes such as hasty generalization, fallacious appeal to authority, begging the question, and avoiding the issue.

Any student who works through the entire book should be well-grounded in the issues that constitute critical thinking. But the development of one's critical thinking skills is a lifelong odyssey. So, while the authors believe that you can expect a significant improvement (7-10 percent) on such standard assessment tests as the James Madison Test of Critical Thinking or the Cornell Critical Thinking Test, a thorough mastery of critical thinking is the task of a lifetime.

Our book will help you learn the skills needed for the *James Madison Test of Critical Thinking*. For example you will learn to:

- recognize ambiguity and lack of clarity in claims;
- distinguish between arguments and explanations;
- distinguish premises and conclusions in arguments;
- distinguish deductive and inductive arguments;
- evaluate deductive arguments as valid or invalid;
- evaluate specific reasons that make an inductive argument stronger or weaker; and
- evaluate common fallacies in reasoning.

So, turn now to the adventures of Detective Stephanie Wise of the Los Angeles Police Department as she reasons her way through various cases. And, as you reason with her, you will begin your own intellectual adventures.

CHAPTER 1

- Questions and Practices of Critical Thinkers
- Qualities of Critical Thinkers
- Review

Overview

Critical thinking is identifying and evaluating evidence to guide decision making.   Critical thinkers ask questions about the meaning of claims and the evidence that supports claims. Critical thinkers are open-minded, curious, know the limits of their knowledge, and try to find connections among pieces of evidence.

| **CASE 1** | City of Los Angeles Police Department |

¹It is Sunday afternoon. ²Detective Stephanie Wise of the Los Angeles Police Department (LAPD) is taking her dog, Killer, for a walk in the park. ³Detective Wise is dressed in jeans and a sweatshirt reading, "UCLA (when the smog lifts)." ⁴Her dog is a twelve-year-old Shetland sheep dog, who is nearly deaf and blind and has trouble walking.

⁵A stranger approaches her. ⁶He says, "Can you give me $20 to feed my homeless family?" ⁷The stranger is dirty, alone, and smells of alcohol, but he seems sober and genuinely concerned.

⁸Detective Wise is a nice person and is considering helping the stranger. ⁹She also knows several people in the park have been mugged. ¹⁰The victims reported that the mugger was an apparently homeless man about 5 feet, 8 inches tall. ¹¹The guy in front of her is between five-seven and five-nine. ¹²What should she do? ¹³Detective Wise asks the stranger if he knows anything about the muggings. ¹⁴The stranger looks nervously into Detective Wise's eyes and denies having any knowledge of any muggings. ¹⁵He claims he just arrived in town this morning.

1.1 Questions and Practices of Critical Thinkers

> **What Is Critical Thinking?**
> **Critical thinking is identifying and evaluating evidence to guide decision making.**

In Case 1, Detective Wise is considering three possibilities:
1. The stranger is the mugger so she should arrest him.
2. The stranger could be the mugger so she should take him in for questioning.
3. The stranger is not the mugger so she should consider helping him.

As a critical thinker, Detective Wise will identify and evaluate each piece of evidence in this case to try to find out if the stranger is involved in the park muggings. By examining the evidence, Detective Wise hopes to learn the facts of the case. Learning the facts will tell Detective Wise what is true, what is false, and what is unknown without more evidence.

As a critical thinker, how would you help Detective Wise? First, you need to identify and evaluate the evidence of the case.
1. What does each person involved in the case claim to be true?
2. After reading the case, what do you know to be true, false, or unknown?

What you and others claim to know or believe about the case are all considered claims. Some examples of claims in Case 1 are:
1. The stranger claims he was not involved in the park muggings.
2. The stranger claims he has a homeless family.
3. Detective Wise claims the stranger is between five-seven and five-nine inches tall.
4. Detective Wise claims the stranger is dirty and smells of alcohol.

These are a few claims surrounding this case that should be examined to identify and evaluate the available evidence. When examining a claim, a critical thinker asks three basic questions:

> **Three Questions to Ask About a Claim**
> 1. **What does the claim mean?**
> 2. **What evidence is there to support or deny a claim?**
> 3. **How strong is the evidence to support or deny the truth of the claim?**

1. What does the claim mean?
If you cannot understand the meaning of a claim, it is more difficult—and sometimes impossible—to try to decide if the claim is true, false, or unknown without more information.

Examples of claims that are clear in Case 1:

a.	It is Sunday afternoon.
b.	Detective Stephanie Wise of the Los Angeles Police Department (LAPD) is taking her dog, Killer, for a walk in the park.

Examples of claims that are not clear in Case 1:

a.	In sentence 6, does "family" mean the man and his immediate family and other relatives, or does it mean the man and a group of people he calls family?
b.	Sentence 8 states that Detective Wise is a "nice person." How is she nice? Is she nicer than most people?

1.2   Exercise Each claim below is about Case 1. Circle the best answer for each claim.

1. **Example:**
    Detective Wise has a small dog.
    a. The meaning of the claim is clear.
    (b.) **The claim is unclear because the meaning of "small" is not clear.**
    c. The claim is unclear because the meaning of "dog" is not clear.
    d. The claim is unclear because the meaning of "detective" is not clear.

2. "My family is over there," said the stranger, waving his hand.
    a. The meaning of the claim is clear.
    b. The claim is unclear because the meaning of "hand" is not clear.
    c. The claim is unclear because the meaning of "stranger" is not clear.
    d. The claim is unclear because the meaning of "over there" is not clear.

3. The stranger is dirty and alone.
    a. The meaning of the claim is clear.
    b. The claim is unclear because the meaning of "stranger" is not clear.
    c. The claim is unclear because the meaning of "dirty" is not clear.
    d. The claim is unclear because the meaning of "alone" is not clear.

4. The stranger wants money for his family in the park.
    a. The meaning of the claim is clear.
    b. The claim is unclear because the meaning of "money" is not clear.
    c. The claim is unclear because the meaning of "family" is not clear.
    d. The claim is unclear because the meaning of "park" is not clear.

5. The stranger seems sober but smells of alcohol.
    a. The meaning of the claim is clear.
    b. The claim is unclear because the meaning of "stranger" is not clear.
    c. The claim is unclear because the meaning of "sober" is not clear.
    d. The claim is unclear because the meaning of "smells of alcohol" is not clear.

6. Muggers are dangerous criminals.
    a. The meaning of the claim is clear.
    b. The claim is unclear because the meaning of "muggers" is not clear.
    c. The claim is unclear because the meaning of "dangerous" is not clear.
    d. The claim is unclear because the meaning of "criminals" is not clear.

7. Detective Wise is a smart woman.
    a. The meaning of the claim is clear.
    b. The claim is unclear because the meaning of "smart" is not clear.
    c. The claim is unclear because the meaning of "woman" is not clear.
    d. The claim is unclear because the meaning of "detective" is not clear.

8. In the police station, Detective Wise often discusses crimes.
   a. The meaning of the claim is clear.
   b. The claim is unclear because the meaning of "discusses" is not clear.
   c. The claim is unclear because the meaning of "crimes" is not clear.
   d. The claim is unclear because the meaning of "crimes in the police station" is not clear.

9. The stranger is a middle-sized man.
   a. The meaning of the claim is clear.
   b. The claim is unclear because the meaning of "stranger" is not clear.
   c. The claim is unclear because the meaning of "middle-sized" is not clear.
   d. The claim is unclear because the meaning of "man" is not clear.

10. The stranger said, "Just last week, I killed a rat in my pajamas."
    a. The meaning of the claim is clear.
    b. The claim is unclear because the meaning of "last week" is not clear.
    c. The claim is unclear because the meaning of "killed" is not clear.
    d. The claim is unclear because the meaning of "rat in my pajamas" is not clear.

2. What evidence is there to support or deny a claim?

Evidence gives us a reason to believe a claim is true or false. Evidence either supports that a claim is true or supports that a claim is false.

Examples of questions of evidence in Case 1:

a.	"The stranger is homeless." **Evidence for:** 1. He says he wants money for his homeless family (sentence 6). 2. He dresses like a homeless person (sentence 7). **Evidence against:** There is no evidence against.
b.	"The stranger is the park mugger." **Evidence for:** 1. The mugger was described as a homeless man and the stranger appears to be homeless (sentences 6, 7, and 10). 2. The stranger is the approximate height of the mugger (sentences 10 and 11). **Evidence against:** There is no evidence against, but the evidence is not strong enough to conclude that the stranger is the mugger.
c.	"Detective Wise's dog, Killer, is probably not dangerous." **Evidence for:** 1. Shetland sheep dogs are usually gentle. 2. The dog is old and not in great health (sentence 4). **Evidence against:** There is no evidence against.
d.	"The stranger wants money to feed his family." **Evidence for:** 1. That's why the stranger asked for money (sentence 6). 2. The stranger seems sober and genuinely concerned (sentence 7). **Evidence against:** 1. The stranger smells of alcohol (sentence 7). 2. The family is not with him (sentence 7).

1.3 Exercise Use the evidence in Case 1 to make the best judgement about each claim and then list the sentence with the best evidence to support your answer.

1. **Example:**

   Detective Wise's dog is not in good health.

   (True:) _____ sentence 4 _____

   False: _____

2. The stranger has a family.

   True: _____

   False: _____

3. Stephanie Wise is a police officer.

   True: _____

   False: _____

4. Detective Wise is wearing a police uniform.

   True: _____

   False: _____

5. Detective Wise has a sense of humor.

   True: _____

   False: _____

6. The stranger was about 5 feet, 8 inches tall.

   True: _____

   False: _____

7. The stranger drinks nothing stronger than tea.

   True: _____

   False: _____

(Continued)

8. The stranger has a regular job.

    True: _____

    False: _____

9. Several people recently have been mugged in the park.

    True: _____

    False: _____

10. The stranger showers regularly.

    True: _____

    False: _____

3. How strong is the evidence to support or deny the truth of the claim?

There are 3 steps to judging the strength of evidence of a claim.

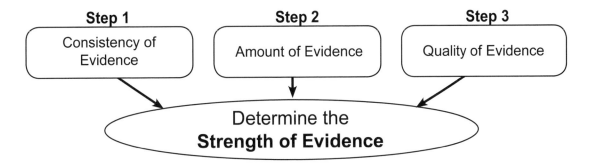

Step 1: Evaluate the consistency of evidence.

Since evidence either supports or denies a claim, if <u>all</u> the evidence supports a claim, then the evidence is consistent. If <u>all</u> the evidence denies a claim, then the evidence is consistent. If some evidence supports the claim and some evidence denies the claim, the evidence is inconsistent. Inconsistent evidence for a claim usually shows that the evidence for the claim is weak.*

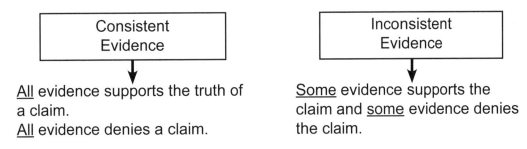

*Evaluating evidence is the principal focus of later chapters of this book.

1.4   Exercise Each claim below is about Case 1. Circle the best answer and supply sentence evidence when needed.

1. **Example**:
    Detective Wise's dog, Killer, is a puppy.
    a. The claim is consistent with the evidence, but no sentences show (prove) that the factual claim is true.
    b. The claim is consistent with the evidence and sentence(s) _____ tend(s) to show that the factual claim is true.
    (c.) **The claim is not consistent with the evidence. Sentence(s) __4__ tend(s) to show that the factual claim is false.**

2. Detective Wise is on a picnic in the park.
    a. The claim is consistent with the evidence, but no sentences show (prove) that the factual claim is true.
    b. The claim is consistent with the evidence and sentence(s) _____ tend(s) to show that the factual claim is true.
    c. The claim is not consistent with the evidence. Sentence(s) _____ tend(s) to show that the factual claim is false.

3. The stranger wants to feed his homeless family.
    a. The claim is consistent with the evidence, but no sentences show (prove) that the factual claim is true.
    b. The claim is consistent with the evidence and sentence(s) _____ tend(s) to show that the factual claim is true.
    c. The claim is not consistent with the evidence. Sentence(s) _____ tend(s) to show that the factual claim is false.

4. Killer is a lively dog.
    a. The claim is consistent with the evidence, but no sentences show (prove) that the factual claim is true.
    b. The claim is consistent with the evidence and sentence(s) _____ tend(s) to show that the factual claim is true.
    c. The claim is not consistent with the evidence. Sentence(s) _____ tend(s) to show that the factual claim is false.

5. Detective Wise is wearing a University of California, Los Angeles sweatshirt.
    a. The claim is consistent with the evidence, but no sentences show (prove) that the factual claim is true.
    b. The claim is consistent with the evidence and sentence(s) _____ tend(s) to show that the factual claim is true.
    c. The claim is not consistent with the evidence. Sentence(s) _____ tend(s) to show that the factual claim is false.

6. Detective Wise is in the park to try to solve the park-muggings case.
    a. The claim is consistent with the evidence, but no sentences show (prove) that the factual claim is true.
    b. The claim is consistent with the evidence and sentence(s) _____ tend(s) to show that the factual claim is true.
    c. The claim is not consistent with the evidence. Sentence(s) _____ tend(s) to show that the factual claim is false.

7. Detective Wise is a police officer.
    a. The claim is consistent with the evidence, but no sentences show (prove) that the factual claim is true.
    b. The claim is consistent with the evidence and sentence(s) _____ tend(s) to show that the factual claim is true.
    c. The claim is not consistent with the evidence. Sentence(s) _____ tend(s) to show that the factual claim is false.

8. Detective Wise will give the stranger $20.
    a. The claim is consistent with the evidence, but no sentences show (prove) that the factual claim is true.
    b. The claim is consistent with the evidence and sentence(s) _____ tend(s) to show that the factual claim is true.
    c. The claim is not consistent with the evidence. Sentence(s) _____ tend(s) to show that the factual claim is false.

9. The stranger is neatly dressed.
    a. The claim is consistent with the evidence, but no sentences show (prove) that the factual claim is true.
    b. The claim is consistent with the evidence and sentence(s) _____ tend(s) to show that the factual claim is true.
    c. The claim is not consistent with the evidence. Sentence(s) _____ tend(s) to show that the factual claim is false.

10. The stranger drinks nothing stronger than tea.
    a. The claim is consistent with the evidence, but no sentences show (prove) that the factual claim is true.
    b. The claim is consistent with the evidence and sentence(s) _____ tend(s) to show that the factual claim is true.
    c. The claim is not consistent with the evidence. Sentence(s) _____ tend(s) to show that the factual claim is false.

Step 2: Evaluate the amount of the evidence.

Evidence is stronger if the amount of evidence is greater. For example, the evidence is stronger in a situation where 25 of 30 eyewitnesses identify the accused mugger versus a situation where only 3 of 30 eyewitnesses identify the accused mugger.

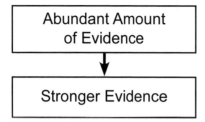

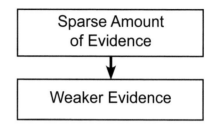

1.5   Exercise Each claim below is about Case 1. Circle the (strongest evidence) for the claim.

1. **Example:**
   The mugger is 5 feet, 8 inches tall.
   a. **Ten victims say the mugger is about 5 feet, 8 inches tall.**
   b. No victims can remember how tall the mugger was.
   c. Five victims say the mugger is about 5 feet, 8 inches tall.

2. The stranger wants to feed his homeless family.
   a. Only the stranger says this.
   b. Five hungry children who accompany the stranger say the same thing.
   c. The stranger looks well fed.

3. The stranger is the mugger.
   a. One victim says so.
   b. All the victims say so.
   c. Five eyewitnesses and all the victims say so.

4. The stranger just arrived in town today.
   a. Twenty people in the park have never seen this person.
   b. Thirty people in the park have never seen this person.
   c. Forty people in the park have never seen this person.

5. The stranger just arrived in town today.
   a. Twenty people in the park have not seen this person in the last three weeks.
   b. Twenty people in the park have not seen this person in the last week.
   c. Twenty people in the park have not seen this person in the last two weeks.

6. The detective's dog is nearly blind and deaf.
   a. Detective Wise says so.
   b. Three veterinarians say so.
   c. Four veterinarians say that the dog has perfect eyesight and hearing.

7. Detective Wise is generous.
   a. Detective Wise says so.
   b. Her five brothers say that she is not generous.
   c. Her two sisters say that she is generous.

8. Detective Wise works for the LAPD.
   a. Detective Wise says so.
   b. The mayor of LA says that she does not work for the city.
   c. The Chief of Police and his assistant say that she works for the LAPD.

9. There have been muggings in the park.
   a. A radio station said so.
   b. Two newspapers say so.
   c. One TV station and two newspapers say so.

Step 3: Evaluate the quality of evidence.

Evidence is stronger when the quality of evidence is better. For example, medical evidence supplied by a medical doctor is stronger than medical evidence supplied by someone with little or no medical education. A medical doctor's experience and knowledge in medicine makes his or her medical testimony more likely to be true.

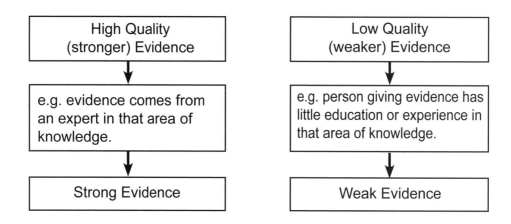

Examples of determining the strength of the evidence for claims in Case 1:

a.	"The stranger is the mugger." The stranger fits the description of the mugger (sentences 10-11), but there are many homeless men who are about 5 feet, 8 inches tall. So, the evidence is weak.
b.	"The stranger is homeless." The stranger's actions and appearance are consistent with his being a homeless man (sentences 6-7). There is no evidence against it. So, it is likely the stranger is a homeless man.
c.	"The stranger has a family." The stranger says he has a family (sentence 6), but the supposed family is not with the stranger (sentence 7). We have no way to know whether the stranger is telling the truth. So, the evidence is weak.
d.	"Detective Wise is wearing a police uniform." She is wearing jeans and a sweatshirt (sentence 3), which is not a police uniform. It is not consistent with the evidence. So the evidence shows that the claim is false.

1.6   Exercise Each claim below is about Case 1. Circle the highest quality of evidence for the claim.

1. **Example:**
   The mugger is 5 feet, 8 inches tall.
   (a.) **A photo of the mugger shows that the top of his head is exactly where a street sign begins at 5 feet, 8 inches.**
   b. Someone from 200 yards away says that the mugger is that height.
   c. Five victims say the mugger is about 5 feet, 8 inches tall.

2. Which statement provides the best evidence for the claim that the stranger needs to feed his homeless family?
   a. Only the stranger says this.
   b. A medical doctor who examines the children affirms that they are suffering from malnutrition.
   c. The stranger looks well fed.

3. Which statement provides the best evidence for the claim that the stranger is the mugger?
   a. One victim says so.
   b. All the victims say so.
   c. DNA evidence confirms that the stranger is the mugger.

4. Which statement provides the best evidence for the claim that the stranger just arrived in town today?
   a. The stranger himself says so.
   b. No one has ever seen the stranger in the park before.
   c. The stranger has a credit card receipt for an airplane ticket in his own name from Chicago to Los Angeles, arriving today.

5. The stranger just arrived in town today.
   a. The stranger has an official record of being released from jail in San Francisco yesterday.
   b. One person in the park has never seen this person in the last week.
   c. One person in the park has never seen this person in the last two weeks.

6. Detective Wise's dog is nearly blind and deaf.
   a. Detective Wise says so.
   b. A veterinarian reached that conclusion.
   c. An optometrist said, "Killer could read none of the letters on the eye chart."

7. Detective Wise is generous.
   a. Detective Wise says so.
   b. Her five brothers say that she is not generous.
   c. Detective Wise has won an award from the UCLA School of Social Work for the most generous person in city employment.

(Continued)

8. Detective Wise works for the LAPD.
   a. Detective Wise says so.
   b. The mayor of LA says that she does not work for the city.
   c. The Chief of Police says that she does work for the city.

9. There have been muggings in the park.
   a. Detective Wise says so.
   b. Two newspapers say so.
   c. The Chief of LAPD Detectives says so.

| **CASE 2** | City of Los Angeles Police Department |

[1]There was a fire at the Hair Today! beauty parlor on Sunset Boulevard. [2]The body of Jorge Sanchez, the owner of Hair Today!, was found in the remains. [3]The fire inspector determined the fire was started with gasoline and a match. [4]It was no accident. [5]Detective Wise interviewed the employees.

[6]"Danny McGwynn torched it," said Martha Mendez. [7]"He's a redhead, and redheads are all hot-tempered firebugs." [8]Detective Wise had talked with Danny McGwynn at Cedars-Sinai Hospital. [9]He had been in an auto accident and was in emergency surgery at the time of the fire.

[10]Aisha Samos cried, "Jorge was such a wonderful man! [11]I bet Lucy Roma had a hand in it. [12]She and Jorge had a big fight on the day of the fire."

[13]"Jorge was my husband," said Lucy Roma. [14]"We were married three years ago, but we didn't tell the others. [15]We didn't want our personal relationship to change things. [16]Of course there were some jealousies. [17]Aisha seemed to have a thing for Jorge. [18]Yes, we had a disagreement on the day of the fire. [19]Eddie Schmidt—owner of Shears Delight—and a few of our employees had been pressuring Jorge to sell Hair Today! [20]Jorge didn't want to sell, but I figured we'd make enough to retire to a small village in Italy. [21]We got a little loud when we disagreed."

[22]Detective Wise considered what she had learned. [23]Was Sanchez dead or unconscious before the fire started? [24]How badly had Roma wanted to sell? [25]Who was working with Schmidt to try to buy Hair Today!?

1.7 Four Qualities of Critical Thinkers

> **Four Qualities of Critical Thinkers**
> 1. **Critical thinkers are open-minded.**
> 2. **Critical thinkers are curious.**
> 3. **Critical thinkers know the limits of their knowledge.**
> 4. **Critical thinkers try to find connections between pieces of evidence.**

1. Critical thinkers are open-minded.

They do not reject claims of fact without examining the evidence for and against them. Rejecting claims before examining the available evidence is less reliable than making a decision based on the available evidence.

Open-minded people are willing to consider evidence before judging whether a claim is true or false. In particular, they attempt to set aside their emotions and prejudices to let their evaluation of the available evidence guide their decision.

Examples of claims that require an open-minded examination of the evidence in Case 2:

a.	"Danny McGwynn torched it" (sentence 6). Martha is prejudiced against redheads (sentence 7).
b.	"I bet Lucy Roma had a hand in it" (sentence 11). There is some evidence that Aisha Samos was jealous of Lucy (sentence 17).
c.	"Sanchez torched his business to collect the insurance." It does not fit the evidence well since he died in the fire.
d.	"Lucy Roma burned the business to cover the fact she had murdered her husband." This claim might explain what happened, but there's no evidence to support it.

1.8   Exercise Each claim below is about Case 2. Circle the answer that best explains why each claim should be questioned.

1. **Example:**
   Shears Delight is a big corporation. So, they did the deed to take over the business.
   a. **This reflects a prejudice against big business.**
   b. This reflects a prejudice against hair salons.
   c. Corporations and their employees never commit crimes.
   d. There is no reason to question the claim.

2. Danny McGwynn said, "Lucy is a fine woman. So, she couldn't have done it."
   a This reflects a prejudice against Lucy.
   b. This reflects a prejudice in favor of Lucy.
   c. This reflects a prejudice in favor of women.
   d. There is no reason to question the claim.

3. "I hate Schmidt. He did it."
   a. This reflects a prejudice against Schmidt.
   b. This reflects a prejudice in favor of Schmidt.
   c. This reflects a prejudice against other hair salons.
   d. There is no reason to question the claim.

4. "Lucy's Italian. So she must have connections to organized crime."
   a. This reflects a prejudice against Lucy.
   b. This reflects a prejudice against Italians.
   c. This reflects a prejudice against organized crime.
   d. There is no reason to question the claim.

5. "Aisha is so lovely. She couldn't have had a hand in it."
   a. This reflects a prejudice against Aisha.
   b. This reflects a prejudice in favor of lovely people.
   c. This reflects a prejudice with respect to women.
   d. There is no reason to question the claim.

6. "The marriage partner is always the suspect, since he or she often has a motive and often gains by the death."
   a. This reflects a prejudice against married people.
   b. This reflects a prejudice against people with motives to commit crimes.
   c. This claim would be a problem only if it prevented the police from looking at other suspects.
   d. There is no reason to question the claim.

7. "Sanchez was a Mexican. So he had no right to own the business."
   a. This reflects a prejudice against foreigners.
   b. This reflects a prejudice against Mexicans.
   c. This reflects a prejudice against business owners.
   d. There is no reason to question the claim.

(Continued)

8. "Hair Today! is a wonderful place! It couldn't have burned down!"
    a. This reflects a prejudice against Hair Today!
    b. This reflects a prejudice in favor of Hair Today!
    c. This reflects a tendency to allow one's emotions to blur the facts.
    d. There is no reason to question the claim.

9. "Given its location, a lot of criminal activity probably went on at Hair Today!"
    a. This reflects a prejudice against a certain area of the city.
    b. This reflects a prejudice against Hair Today!
    c. This reflects a prejudice against criminal activity.
    d. There is no reason to question the claim.

10. "Female detectives can't be trusted."
    a. This reflects a prejudice against detectives.
    b. This reflects a prejudice against females.
    c. This reflects a prejudice in favor of female detectives.
    d. There is no reason to question the claim.

2. Critical thinkers are curious.
Curiosity can lead to new evidence or information relevant to the case.

Examples of questions to ask regarding Case 2:

a.	Was Sanchez dead or unconscious before the fire started (sentence 23)?
b.	How badly had Roma wanted to sell (sentence 24)?
c.	Who was working with Schmidt to take over the business (sentence 25)?

1.9 **Exercise** Each claim below states a fact about Case 2. Circle the question following each claim that is most likely to lead to evidence or information relevant to the case.

1. **Example:**
   Lucy was married to Jorge Sanchez, and they had a fight (sentences 12, 13, 18, and 21).
   (a.) **Could the fight have resulted in Lucy wanting to hurt or murder her husband?**
   b. How long had Lucy worked at Hair Today!?
   c. Did Jorge own Hair Today! before he married Lucy?

2. Lucy wanted to sell the business and retire to Italy (sentence 20).
   a. Does Lucy like Italian food?
   b. What would Lucy do to have her way on this issue?
   c. Would Lucy be satisfied if she retired to Greece?

3. Aisha was jealous of Lucy (sentences 16 and 17).
   a. Does Aisha own a gun?
   b. Has Aisha worked at Hair Today! longer than Lucy?
   c. Would Aisha hurt Jorge or the business to hurt Lucy?

4. Shears Delight wanted to take over the business (sentence 19).
   a. Is Shears Delight a candy store?
   b. When Shears Delight tried to take over other salons, what did it do?
   c. How much is a share of Shears Delight?

5. Danny McGwynn had been in an auto accident and was in surgery at Cedars-Sinai Hospital when the fire was reported (sentence 9).
   a. What make of car did Danny drive?
   b. What kinds of injuries did Danny suffer in the accident?
   c. Could the fire have been set before Danny's accident?

6. The fire was started with gasoline and a match (sentence 3).
   a. Could Jorge have set the fire himself?
   b. What brand of gasoline was used?
   c. Were book matches or kitchen matches used to set the fire?

7. Jorge Sanchez's body was found in the remains of the fire (sentence 2).
   a. What was the cause of Jorge's death?
   b. How did the medical examiner identify Jorge's body?
   c. What clothes was Jorge wearing when the fire started?

8. There were jealousies among the employees (sentence 16).
   a. Was Aisha in love with Jorge?
   b. How many employees were jealous of Jorge's Ford Mustang?
   c. Could the jealousies have resulted in violent actions?

9. Several employees were interested in selling the business (sentences 19 and 20).
    a. What would those interested in selling do to guarantee a sale?
    b. Would the business sell for more than $500,000?
    c. Would Shears Delight have remodeled the salon?

10. As his wife, Lucy probably will be Jorge's primary heir (sentence 13).
    a. Did Jorge leave any money to charity?
    b. How anxious was Lucy to gain control of the money?
    c. Was Jorge's will hand-written?

3. Critical thinkers know the limits of their knowledge.

A person educated and experienced to do a job will likely be an expert about that type of work. For example, an experienced zoologist would likely be an expert on animals. A critical thinker might have expertise in one or a few jobs, but will not be an expert in all jobs. It is, therefore, important for a critical thinker to recognize the limits of his or her knowledge and other people's knowledge. For example, an experienced emergency room doctor is usually an expert in treating patients with cuts and broken bones, but is rarely trained or has experience in brain surgery. Therefore, an emergency room doctor is likely to be an expert in a case involving emergency room treatment, but not likely to be an expert in a case about a brain surgery.

Examples of knowing the limits of one's knowledge in Case 2:

a.	Detective Wise investigates crimes. She does not investigate the causes of fires. (sentences 3-4) So she should get an expert to help determine the cause of the fire rather than make an uneducated guess.
b.	The medical examiner determines the cause of death, not the detective who investigates (sentence 23). Therefore, Detective Wise should get expert help to determine the cause of Jorge Sanchez's death.

1.10 Exercise The first part of each problem describes a character in Case 2. The second part is a claim made by that character. Based on the evidence in the case, determine if the person is speaking within the limits of his or her knowledge. Circle the best answer.

1. **Example:**
   Eddie Schmidt is a hairdresser.
   He said, "Jorge was dead before the fire started."
   a. He should know this.
   b. **He should not know this.**
   c. He should know, but there are reasons to question his testimony.

2.   Lucy Roma is a hairdresser who had appeared in some TV commercials.
   She said, "Short people who wear their hair long and straight look taller than they are."
   a. She should know this.
   b. She should not know this.
   c. She should know, but there are reasons to question her testimony.

3.   Dennis Bray is the fire inspector.
   He said, "Mr. Sanchez was not dead when the fire started."
   a. He should know this.
   b. He should not know this.
   c. He should know, but there are reasons to question his testimony.

4.   Dr. Maria Mendez is the medical examiner.
   She said, "Mr. Sanchez was killed by a blow to his head."
   a. She should know this.
   b. She should not know this.
   c. She should know, but there are reasons to question her testimony.

5.   Aisha Samos was an explosives expert in the army.
   She said, "With a cell phone attached to a can of gas, they could have started the fire from a pay phone."
   a. She should know this.
   b. Beyond her limited knowledge.
   c. She should know, but there are reasons to question her testimony.

6.   Danny McGwynn had served three years in prison for breaking and entering before becoming a hairdresser.
   He said, "The fire inspector is wrong: The fire was an accident."
   a. He should know this.
   b. He should not know this.
   c. He should know, but there are reasons to question his testimony.

(Continued)

7.   Jorge Sanchez was an accomplished businessman.
     He said, "After expenses—including my salary—the business makes more in eight months than Shears Delight wanted to pay for it."
a. He should know this.
b. He should not know this.
c. He should know, but there are reasons to question his testimony.

8.   Manfred J. Mordici is a professional streetperson.
     He said, in a slightly slurred voice, "I was in the alley enjoying a libation when I saw two men run out of Hair Today! Then the whole place burst into flames."
a. He should know this.
b. He should not know this.
c. He should know, but there are reasons to question his testimony.

9.   Eddie Schmidt is president of Shears Delight.
     He said, "We talked with Mr. Sanchez several months ago. When it became clear he was uninterested in selling, we dropped all contact."
a. He should know this.
b. He should not know this.
c. He should know, but there are reasons to question his testimony.

10.   Big Al is head of the local street gang.
     He said, "Me and the guys, we had nothin' to do with it. If we did, there wouldn't 'a' been no loose ends."
a. He should know this.
b. He should not know this.
c. He should know, but there are reasons to question his testimony.

4. Critical thinkers try to find connections between pieces of evidence.
They look to see if one piece of evidence supports or is inconsistent with another.

Examples of connections between pieces of evidence in Case 2:

a.	Both Aisha and Lucy said that Lucy and Jorge had a fight on the day of the fire. Since the testimony agrees, there is better evidence that Lucy and Jorge had a fight.
b.	The fire was discovered while Danny McGwynn was in surgery. Since the fire was started with gasoline and a match, Danny could not have set it.
c.	There are no clear connections between the claims because the two following claims are totally unrelated, "There was a fire at the Hair Today! beauty parlor on Sunset Boulevard" (sentence 1) and "Jorge was my husband" (sentence 13).

1.11 Exercise Each problem contains three claims about Case 2. Evaluate the evidence and circle the best answer.

1. **Example:**

   (A) Lucy was Jorge's wife. (B) Lucy inherited more than five million dollars from her late husband. (C) Lucy should be a suspect.

   a. If (A) and (B) are true, (C) must be true.
   b. If (A) and (B) are true, (C) is probably true.
   c. If (A) and (B) are true, (C) must be false.
   d. If (A) and (B) are true, (C) is probably false.
   e. (A) and (B) provide no reasons to believe that (C) is either true or false.

2. (A) Eddie Schmidt was at Ricco's Restaurant when the fire was reported. (B) Ricco's Restaurant is in Chicago, Illinois. (C) Eddie set the fire.

   a. If (A) and (B) are true, (C) must be true.
   b. If (A) and (B) are true, (C) is probably true.
   c. If (A) and (B) are true, (C) must be false.
   d. If (A) and (B) are true, (C) is probably false.
   e. (A) and (B) provide no reasons to believe that (C) is either true or false.

3. (A) The fire was started with gasoline and a match. (B) Two men were seen running from Hair Today! shortly before the fire was reported. (C) The two men seen running from Hair Today! started the fire.

   a. If (A) and (B) are true, (C) must be true.
   b. If (A) and (B) are true, (C) is probably true.
   c. If (A) and (B) are true, (C) must be false.
   d. If (A) and (B) are true, (C) is probably false.
   e. (A) and (B) provide no reasons to believe that (C) is either true or false.

4. (A) If Jorge Sanchez died of a massive heart attack, then he might have set the fire himself. (B) Jorge Sanchez died of a massive heart attack. (C) Jorge Sanchez might have set the fire himself.

   a. If (A) and (B) are true, (C) must be true.
   b. If (A) and (B) are true, (C) is probably true.
   c. If (A) and (B) are true, (C) must be false.
   d. If (A) and (B) are true, (C) is probably false.
   e. (A) and (B) provide no reasons to believe that (C) is either true or false.

5. (A) Jorge was killed before the fire started. (B) Jorge was killed in MacArthur Park. (C) Jorge set the fire.

   a. If (A) and (B) are true, (C) must be true.
   b. If (A) and (B) are true, (C) is probably true.
   c. If (A) and (B) are true, (C) must be false.
   d. If (A) and (B) are true, (C) is probably false.
   e. (A) and (B) provide no reasons to believe that (C) is either true or false.

6. (A) Either the fire was deliberately set or Hair Today! was both a beauty parlor and a gas station. (B) Hair Today! was not both a beauty parlor and a gas station. (C) The fire was deliberately set.

    a. If (A) and (B) are true, (C) must be true.
    b. If (A) and (B) are true, (C) is probably true.
    c. If (A) and (B) are true, (C) must be false.
    d. If (A) and (B) are true, (C) is probably false.
    e. (A) and (B) provide no reasons to believe that (C) is either true or false.

7. (A) Aisha learned that Lucy was married to Jorge. (B) Aisha is a very jealous, violent person. (C) Aisha killed Jorge.

    a. If (A) and (B) are true, (C) must be true.
    b. If (A) and (B) are true, (C) is probably true.
    c. If (A) and (B) are true, (C) must be false.
    d. If (A) and (B) are true, (C) is probably false.
    e. (A) and (B) provide no reasons to believe that (C) is either true or false.

8. (A) If Danny McGwynn didn't set the fire, then Eddie Schmidt had a hand in the affair. (B) If Eddie Schmidt had a hand in the affair, then Eddie hired someone to set the fire. (C) If Danny McGwynn didn't set the fire, then Eddie hired someone to set the fire.

    a. If (A) and (B) are true, (C) must be true.
    b. If (A) and (B) are true, (C) is probably true.
    c. If (A) and (B) are true, (C) must be false.
    d. If (A) and (B) are true, (C) is probably false.
    e   (A) and (B) provide no reasons to believe that (C) is either true or false.

9. (A) Shears Delight would do anything to own Hair Today! (B) Jorge Sanchez refused to sell the business. (C) Shears Delight arranged to have Jorge killed.

    a. If (A) and (B) are true, (C) must be true.
    b. If (A) and (B) are true, (C) is probably true.
    c. If (A) and (B) are true, (C) must be false.
    d. If (A) and (B) are true, (C) is probably false.
    e. (A) and (B) provide no reasons to believe that (C) is either true or false.

10. (A) The local street gang—the Chrome Sharks—collected "protection money" from all the businesses in the neighborhood. (B) Jorge Sanchez had refused to pay "protection money" for six weeks before the fire. (C) The Chrome Sharks did not torch Hair Today!

    a. If (A) and (B) are true, (C) must be true.
    b. If (A) and (B) are true, (C) is probably true.
    c. If (A) and (B) are true, (C) must be false.
    d. If (A) and (B) are true, (C) is probably false.
    e. (A) and (B) provide no reasons to believe that (C) is either true or false.

CASE 3	City of Los Angeles Police Department

[1]She was lying on a tombstone in Forest Lawn Cemetery. [2]She was beautifully dressed and perfectly groomed. [3]Except for the dagger in her chest, one would have thought she was taking a nap.

[4]Dr. Mendez, the medical examiner, was at the scene when Detective Wise arrived at 9:22 a.m. "[5]The body is cold—air temperature. [6]So, she has been dead for a while," Dr. Mendez remarked. "[7]And there's no blood anywhere. [8]So, either she was killed elsewhere and carefully cleaned, or the dagger was added as a decoration. [9]I should be able to tell you the cause of death in a couple of days."

[10]The body had been found by a gardener, Charley Kahn. [11]He said, "I was mowing at about 7:30 this morning when I saw a woman lying on a tombstone. [12]We've had a little trouble with kids breaking in and drinking lately. [13]First I thought one of them had passed out. [14]Then I saw the dagger and called the police."

[15]Mort Tician, the president of the cemetery association, commented, "We lock the gates every night at 6:00 and open at 8:00 a.m. [16]When the body was discovered, I called Sam Smiley, our head of security. [17]Sam checked all the entrances. [18]There was no sign that anyone had broken in."

[19]The body was identified as Amanda Smith. [20]Her fingerprints were in the national fingerprint registry. [21]She had served five years for armed robbery in Nebraska.

[22]Two days after the body was discovered, Dr. Mendez phoned Detective Wise and said, "She was poisoned. [23]Someone injected a large dose of nicotine into her right thigh. [24]Given the condition of the body, I suspect she'd been dead for about two days before she was found."

[25]Detective Wise pondered the facts.

1.12 Review Exercise Each claim below is about Case 3. Circle the best answer for each claim.

1. **Example:**
   The body was found near the main entrance to the cemetery.
   a. The meaning of the claim is clear.
   b. The claim is unclear because the meaning of "body" is not clear.
   (c.) **The claim is unclear because the meaning of "near" is not clear.**
   d. The claim is unclear because the meaning of "cemetery" is not clear.

2. Charley Kahn said, "On a tombstone I saw the body."
   a. The meaning of the claim is clear.
   b. The claim is unclear because the meaning of "on" is not clear.
   c. The claim is unclear because the meaning of "saw" is not clear.
   d. The claim is unclear because the meaning of the "body" is not clear.

3. The victim was an old woman.
   a. The meaning of the claim is clear.
   b. The claim is unclear because the meaning of "victim" is not clear.
   c. The claim is unclear because the meaning of "old" is not clear.
   d. The claim is unclear because the meaning of "woman" is not clear.

4. Sam Smiley said, "At 6:00 all the gates were locked."
   a. The meaning of the claim is clear.
   b. The claim is unclear because the meaning of "6:00" is not clear.
   c. The claim is unclear because the meaning of "gates" is not clear.
   d. The claim is unclear because the meaning of "locked" is not clear.

5. A track was within twenty feet of the victim's body.
   a. The meaning of the claim is clear.
   b. The claim is unclear because the meaning of "track" is not clear.
   c. The claim is unclear because the meaning of "twenty feet" is not clear.
   d. The claim is unclear because the meaning of "the victim's body" is not clear.

6. If the dagger had killed her, the body would have been swimming in blood.
   a. The meaning of the claim is clear.
   b. The claim is unclear because the meaning of "dagger" is not clear.
   c. The claim is unclear because the meaning of "the body" is not clear.
   d. The claim is unclear because the meaning of "swimming in blood" is not clear.

7. The signs indicate that the victim had been dead for almost a day.
   a. The meaning of the claim is clear.
   b. The claim is unclear because the meaning of "victim" is not clear.
   c. The claim is unclear because the meaning of "almost a day" is not clear.
   d. The claim is unclear because the meaning of "dead" is not clear.

(Continued)

8. The victim looked older.
    a. The meaning of the claim is clear.
    b. The claim is unclear because the meaning of "the victim" is not clear.
    c. The claim is unclear because the meaning of "older" is not clear.
    d. The claim is unclear because the meaning of "dressed" is not clear

9. Detective Wise applauded Dr. Mendez's discovery of the cause of death.
    a. The meaning of the claim is clear.
    b. The claim is unclear because the meaning of "applauded" is not clear.
    c. The claim is unclear because the meaning of "discovery" is not clear.
    d. The claim is unclear because the meaning of "cause of death" is not clear.

10. Mort Tician remarked, "It's a dark day at Forest Lawn Cemetery."
    a. The meaning of the claim is clear.
    b. The claim is unclear because the meaning of "remarked" is not clear.
    c. The claim is unclear because the meaning of "dark day" is not clear.
    d. The claim is unclear because the meaning of "Forest Lawn Cemetery" is not clear.

1.13 Review Exercise Each claim below is about Case 3. Circle true or false and then identify the sentence(s) that provide the best evidence that the claim is true or false.

1. **Example:**

   The woman was killed by being stabbed in the chest.

       True:

       (False:)   Sentences <u>22, 23</u>

2. The woman died a significant amount of time before her body was found.

       True:

       False: Sentences ___ ___ ___

3. The dead woman committed suicide.

       True:

       False: Sentences ___ ___ ___

4. The woman did not die where the body was found.

       True:

       False: Sentences ___ ___

5. The victim used to live in Nebraska.

    True:

    False: Sentence ___

6. The woman was killed by someone with keys to the cemetery.

    True:

    False: Sentence ___

7. Young people had recently broken into the cemetery.

    True:

    False: Sentence ___

8. The gates to the cemetery had been locked the night before.

    True:

    False: Sentences ___ ___

9. No one had broken into the cemetery.

    True:

    False: Sentence ___

10. The dagger was added as a decoration.

    True:

    False: Sentences ___ ___ ___

1.14 Review Exercise Each claim below is about Case 3. What is the strength of the evidence for each factual claim? Circle the best answer and supply the best sentence(s) evidence when needed.

1. **Example:**
    The woman was killed by being stabbed in the chest.
    a. The claim is consistent with the evidence, but no sentences tend to show that it the factual claim is true.
    b. The claim is consistent with the evidence and sentence(s) ___ ___ ___ ___ tend(s) to show that the factual claim is true.

    c. **The claim is not consistent with the evidence. Sentence(s)** <u>7, 8, 22, 23</u> **show(s) that the factual claim is false.**

(Continued)

2. The victim had been dead for a time.
    a. The claim is consistent with the evidence, but no sentences tend to show that the factual claim is true.
    b. The claim is consistent with the evidence and sentence(s) ___ ___ ___ tend(s) to show that the factual claim is true.
    c. The claim is not consistent with the evidence. Sentence(s) ___ ___ ___ show(s) that the factual claim is false.

3. The dead woman did not commit suicide.
    a. The claim is consistent with the evidence, but no sentences tend to show that the factual claim is true.
    b. The claim is consistent with the evidence and sentence(s) ___ ___ ___ tend(s) to show that the factual claim is true.
    c. The claim is not consistent with the evidence. Sentence(s) ___ ___ ___ show(s) that the factual claim is false.

4. The victim's name was Amanda Smith.
    a. The claim is consistent with the evidence, but no sentences tend to show that the factual claim is true.
    b. The claim is consistent with the evidence and sentence(s) ___ ___ tend(s) to show that the factual claim is true.
    c. The claim is not consistent with the evidence. Sentence(s) ___ ___ show(s) that the factual claim is false.

5. Dr. Mendez has a medical degree.
    a. The claim is consistent with the evidence, but no sentences tend to show that the factual claim is true.
    b. The claim is consistent with the evidence and sentence(s) ___ tend(s) to show that the factual claim is true.
    c. The claim is not consistent with the evidence. Sentence(s) ___ show(s) that the factual claim is false.

6. Sam Smiley should know whether the gates to the cemetery were locked.
    a. The claim is consistent with the evidence, but no sentences tend to show that the factual claim is true.
    b. The claim is consistent with the evidence and sentence(s) ___ ___ tend(s) to show that the factual claim is true.
    c. The claim is not consistent with the evidence. Sentence(s) ___ ___ show(s) that the factual claim is false.

7. The victim was an adult.
   a. The claim is consistent with the evidence, but no sentences tend to show that the factual claim is true.
   b. The claim is consistent with the evidence and sentence(s) ___ tend(s) to show that the factual claim is true.
   c. The claim is not consistent with the evidence. Sentence(s) ___ show(s) that the factual claim is false.

8. Charley Kahn knows how to run a lawnmower.
   a. The claim is consistent with the evidence, but no sentences tend to show that the factual claim is true.
   b. The claim is consistent with the evidence and sentence(s) ___ tend(s) to show that the factual claim is true.
   c. The claim is not consistent with the evidence. Sentence(s) ___ show(s) that the factual claim is false.

9. Young people had recently broken into the cemetery.
   a. The claim is consistent with the evidence, but no sentences tend to show that the factual claim is true.
   b. The claim is consistent with the evidence and sentence(s) ___ tend(s) to show that the factual claim is true.
   c. The claim is not consistent with the evidence. Sentence(s) ___ show(s) that the factual claim is false.

10. The victim had been poisoned.
   a. The claim is consistent with the evidence, but no sentences tend to show that the factual claim is true.
   b. The claim is consistent with the evidence and sentence(s) ___ tend(s) to show that the factual claim is true.
   c. It is not consistent with the evidence. Sentence(s) ___ show(s) that the factual claim is false.

1.15 Review Exercise Circle the statement that provides the greatest amount of evidence for the claim.

1. **Example:**
   The victim was poisoned by nicotine.
   a. **Three medical tests show this point.**
   b. No medical tests show this point.
   c. One medical test shows this point.

2. The victim had been dead for a time.
   a. The body was the temperature of the surrounding air.
   b. Two medical examiners concluded that the victim had been dead for almost two days.
   c. Detective Wise found no blood near the body.

(Continued)

3. The body is that of Amanda Smith.
   a. Her driver's license says so.
   b. Her fingerprints say so.
   c. Both a and b make up stronger evidence because of the amount of evidence.

4. The victim had been dead for about two days before she was found.
   a. The victim's body temperature was that of a body dead for two days.
   b. There was a newspaper under the dead body dated two days ago.
   c. Both a and b make up stronger evidence because of the amount of evidence.

5. The victim had served five years for armed robbery in Nebraska.
   a. The prison in Nebraska has a record of this punishment and the chief of police from her hometown in Nebraska has called to confirm this point.
   b. The prison in Nebraska has a record of this punishment.
   c. The chief of police from her hometown in Nebraska has called to confirm this point.

6. The cemetery had not been broken into.
   a. Detective Wise checked one gate of the cemetery which was properly locked.
   b. Mort Tician, the president of the cemetery association, affirms that they lock the gates every night.
   c. Sam Smiley, the head of Security, checked all the gates which were properly locked.

7. The victim was not killed in the cemetery.
   a. Dr. Mendez and Detective Wise both agree on the point.
   b. Dr. Mendez agrees on the point.
   c. Sam Smiley, the head of Security, concludes that the victim was killed in the cemetery.

8. The gates of the cemetery are locked every night.
   a. Detective Wise has a hunch that the gates are locked every night.
   b. Sam Smiley, the head of Security, locks the gates every night.
   c. Both statements a and b together provide stronger evidence.

9. She was poisoned by a needle injection.
   a. Detective Wise has found a discarded hypodermic needle.
   b. The medical examiner has found poison in the victim's body.
   c. Both statements a and b together provide stronger evidence.

1.16 Review Exercise Circle the statement that provides the highest quality of evidence for the claim.

1. **Example:**
   The victim was poisoned by nicotine.
   (a.) **One medical test shows this point.**
   b. No medical tests show this point.
   c. The detective has a hunch that nicotine was the cause of death.

2. The victim had been dead for a time.
   a. The gardener says so.
   b. Detective Wise says so.
   c. Medical Examiner Mendez says so.

3. The body is that of Amanda Smith.
   a. Her driver's license says so.
   b. Her fingerprints say so.
   c. Her purse has a letter addressed to Amanda Smith.

4. The victim had been dead for about two days before she was found.
   a. The victim's body temperature was that of a body dead for two days.
   b. There was a newspaper under the dead body dated two days ago.
   c. The victim's sister had not had a phone call from her for four days.

5. The victim had served five years for armed robbery in Nebraska.
   a. The prison in Nebraska has a record of this punishment and the chief of police from her hometown in Nebraska has called to confirm this point.
   b. A newspaper report from five years ago said that the victim was convicted of a crime.
   c. The victim's sister says that the victim was framed for the crime of armed robbery.

6. There was no evidence that the cemetery had been broken into.
   a. Mort Tician, the president of the cemetery association, affirms that they lock the gates every night.
   b. Detective Wise believes what Mort Tician has said.
   c. Sam Smiley, the head of Security, checked all the gates which were properly locked.

7. The victim was not killed in the cemetery.
   a. Dr. Mendez has found no evidence of blood at the cemetery.
   b. Mort Tician is afraid for the reputation of the cemetery if it were proven that someone was killed at the cemetery.
   c. Sam Smiley, the head of Security, concludes that the victim was not killed in the cemetery.

(Continued)

8. The gates of the cemetery are locked every night.
    a. Detective Wise has a hunch that the gates are locked every night.
    b. Sam Smiley, the head of Security, says that he locks the gates every night.
    c. Mort Tician, the president of the cemetery association, says that it is the policy to lock all gates at night.

9. She was poisoned by a needle injection.
    a. Detective Wise has found a discarded hypodermic needle.
    b. The medical examiner found poison in the victim's body and evidence of a needle puncture.
    c. A newspaper reporter has a hunch that this crime is similar to another cemetery murder in which a victim was poisoned by a needle injection.

1.17 Review Exercise Each claim below is about Case 3. Circle the answer that best explains why each claim should be questioned.

1. **Example:**
    "The victim had a jail record. So, she was killed by a criminal gang."
    a. **This reflects a prejudice against persons with criminal records.**
    b. This reflects a prejudice against criminal gangs.
    c. This reflects a prejudice in favor of criminals.
    d. There is no reason to question the claim.

2. "Charlie Kahn is a German. So, he probably had a hand in the murder."
    a. This reflects a prejudice against murderers.
    b. This reflects a prejudice against Germans.
    c. This reflects a prejudice against gardeners.
    d. There is no reason to question the claim.

3. "Female doctors don't have the stomach to figure out the causes of murders."
    a. This reflects a prejudice against women.
    b. This reflects a prejudice against doctors.
    c. This reflects a prejudice against medical personnel.
    d. There is no reason to question the claim.

4. "Detective Wise is only about thirty-five. So, she doesn't have enough experience to figure out who the killer was."
    a. This reflects a prejudice against detectives.
    b. This reflects a prejudice against women.
    c. This reflects a prejudice against fairly young people.
    d. There is no reason to question the claim.

5. "Mort Tician will want to cover up the murder so Forest Lawn won't look bad."
   a. This reflects a prejudice against business owners.
   b. This reflects a prejudice against cemetery workers.
   c. This reflects a prejudice against men.
   d. There is no reason to question the claim.

6. "It's Los Angeles. So, you'd expect strange crimes."
   a. This reflects a prejudice against cemeteries.
   b. This reflects a prejudice against big cities.
   c. This reflects a prejudice against Los Angeles.
   d. There is no reason to question the claim.

7. "Devil-worshipers had been hanging around the cemetery lately. So, they probably did it."
   a. This reflects a prejudice against devil-worshipers.
   b. This reflects a prejudice against people who hang around cemeteries.
   c. This reflects a prejudice against anyone who spends time in a cemetery.
   d. There is no reason to question the claim.

8. "The rent-a-cops who patrol Forest Lawn are strange people. They can't be trusted."
   a. This reflects a prejudice against police.
   b. This reflects a prejudice against people who carry guns.
   c. This reflects a prejudice against security personnel.
   d. There is no reason to question the claim.

9. "No one who works at a cemetery should be trusted."
   a. This reflects a prejudice against people who work at cemeteries.
   b. This reflects a prejudice against grave diggers.
   c. This reflects a prejudice against cemetery owners.
   d. There is no reason to question the claim.

10. "Sam Smiley never smiles. I bet he has criminal connections."
   a. This reflects a prejudice against Sam Smiley.
   b. This reflects a prejudice against serious people.
   c. This reflects a prejudice against security officers.
   d. There is no reason to question the claim.

1.18 Review Exercise Each fact below is about Case 3. Circle the question that is the most relevant to the fact and the investigation.

1. **Example:**
   The body was found shortly before the cemetery opened.
   (a.) **Was the body there when the cemetery closed the night before?**
   b. When did the cemetery open?
   c. Was there a burial in the vicinity yesterday?

(Continued)

2. The dagger did not kill the victim.
   a. Were there jewels on the dagger's handle?
   b. Are there other recent cases in which a dagger was just a "decoration"?
   c. Was the dagger purchased at a pawn shop?

3. When the body was found, it was well-dressed and carefully groomed.
   a. Were the clothes purchased at a designer store?
   b. Was the victim wearing heels?
   c. Was the killer a professional hairstylist?

4. All the employees at the cemetery have a key to at least one gate.
   a. Are the gates all padlocked at night?
   b. Do any employees have keys to all the gates?
   c. Did any of the employees know the victim?

5. The body was found on the tombstone of a well-known criminal.
   a. Is there some connection between the victim and the criminal?
   b. Was the criminal the head of a crime family?
   c. Was the tombstone made of granite or marble?

6. Nicotine is a poison found in many insecticides.
   a. Did the victim smoke?
   b. Is nicotine more common in fly sprays than in sprays for other kinds of insects?
   c. Was the poison that killed the victim taken from an insecticide container in the cemetery?

7. The body was found in a cemetery, but the victim probably wasn't killed there.
   a. Where was the victim killed?
   b. Was the body left in Forest Lawn because the victim was a famous person?
   c. Why didn't the killers just bury the victim in the cemetery?

8. Charley Kahn has a criminal record.
   a. Was Charley sent to prison in California?
   b. Are there any connections between Charley and the victim?
   c. Does Charley drive a blue Mustang?

9. Amanda Smith was also known as Amelia Smit and Alice Smyth.
   a. Were Amanda Smith or Amelia Smit or Alice Smyth connected with any criminal organizations?
   b. Why did the victim use the same initials in each of her aliases?
   c. Which name was on her birth certificate?

10. Amanda Smith was seen three days ago having dinner with Mort Tician.
    a. What did they have for dinner?
    b. Could Mort Tician have played a role in the victim's death?
    c. Did Mort pay for the dinner, or did they go Dutch treat?

1.19 Review Exercise The first part of each problem describes a character in Case 3. The second part is a claim made by that character. Based on the evidence in the case, determine if the person is speaking within the limits of his or her knowledge. Circle the best answer.

1. **Example:**

    Dr. Mendez is the medical examiner.

    She said, "The nicotine that killed Amanda Smith probably came from an insecticide."

    a. **She should know this.**
    b. She should not know this.
    c. She should know, but there are reasons to question her testimony.

2. Sam Smiley is the head of Security at the cemetery.

    He said, "The victim almost certainly had a history of taking drugs."

    a. He should know this.
    b. He should not know this.
    c. He should know, but there are reasons to question his testimony.

3. Mort Tician runs the cemetery.

    He said, "None of my employees could have had a hand in the murder."

    a. He should know this.
    b. He should not know this.
    c. He should know, but there are reasons to question his testimony.

4. Brad Smith is the victim's brother.

    He said, "Amanda always hung out with people of questionable morals."

    a. He should know this.
    b. He should not know this.
    c. He should know, but there are reasons to question his testimony.

5. Charley Kahn is a gardener.

    He said, "We regularly used nicotine-based insecticides."

    a. He should know this.
    b. He should not know this.
    c. He should know, but there are reasons to question his testimony.

6. Mort Tician runs the cemetery.

    He said, "This is the first time in its history that Forest Lawn has been associated with a murder."

    a. He should know this.
    b. He should not know this.
    c. He should know, but there are reasons to question his testimony.

(Continued)

7.   George Mott is chief of police.
        He said, "This case is similar to a murder that occurred in Evergreen Cemetery three years go."
   a. He should know this.
   b. He should not know this.
   c. He should know, but there are reasons to question his testimony.

8.   Dr. Mendez is the medical examiner.
        She said, "This is the third time in the last two years that someone in the city was killed by nicotine poisoning."
   a. She should know this.
   b. She should not know this.
   c. She should know, but there are reasons to question her testimony.

9.   Sam Smiley is head of Security at Forest Lawn Cemetery.
        He said, "The cause of death couldn't have been nicotine poisoning."
   a. He should know this.
   b. He should not know this.
   c. He should know, but there are reasons to question his testimony.

10.   Lolita Lowe is head gardener at Forest Lawn.
        She said, "Two gallons of insecticide are missing from our gardening supplies."
   a. She should know this.
   b. She should not know this.
   c. She should know, but there are reasons to question her testimony.

1.20 Review Exercise Each problem contains three claims about Case 3. Evaluate the evidence and circle the best answer.

1. **Example:**
   (A) Either the dagger killed the victim, or the dagger was just a decoration. (B) The dagger did not kill the victim. (C) The dagger was just a decoration.
   a. **If (A) and (B) are true, (C) must be true.**
   b. If (A) and (B) are true, (C) is probably true.
   c. If (A) and (B) are true, (C) must be false.
   d. If (A) and (B) are true, (C) is probably false.
   e. (A) and (B) provide no reasons to believe that (C) is either true or false.

2. (A) The body was the temperature of the air, about 78°F. (B) The temperature of a corpse drops an average of one and a half degrees Fahrenheit every hour after death until it reaches the temperature of the air around it. (C) The victim has been dead for at least twelve to fifteen hours.

   a. If (A) and (B) are true, (C) must be true.
   b. If (A) and (B) are true, (C) is probably true.
   c. If (A) and (B) are true, (C) must be false.
   d. If (A) and (B) are true, (C) is probably false.
   e. (A) and (B) provide no reasons to believe that (C) is either true or false.

3. (A) Amanda Smith was seen on Sunset Boulevard three days ago. (B) Amanda's body was found this morning. (C) Amanda was killed two days ago.

   a. If (A) and (B) are true, (C) must be true.
   b. If (A) and (B) are true, (C) is probably true.
   c. If (A) and (B) are true, (C) must be false.
   d. If (A) and (B) are true, (C) is probably false.
   e. (A) and (B) provide no reasons to believe that (C) is either true or false.

4. (A) If all the gates were locked at 6:00 last night and there was no break-in, then it had to be an inside job. (B) It didn't have to be an inside job. (C) Either not all the gates were locked at 6:00 last night or there was a break-in.

   a. If (A) and (B) are true, (C) must be true.
   b. If (A) and (B) are true, (C) is probably true.
   c. If (A) and (B) are true, (C) must be false.
   d. If (A) and (B) are true, (C) is probably false.
   e. (A) and (B) provide no reasons to believe that (C) is either true or false.

5. (A) Amanda had a criminal record. (B) Amanda was seen having dinner with Mort Tician three days ago. (C) Mort Tician has a criminal record.

   a. If (A) and (B) are true, (C) must be true.
   b. If (A) and (B) are true, (C) is probably true.
   c. If (A) and (B) are true, (C) must be false.
   d. If (A) and (B) are true, (C) is probably false.
   e. (A) and (B) provide no reasons to believe that (C) is either true or false.

6. (A) Mort Tician claims he never met the victim. (B) Mort Tician had dinner with the victim three days ago. (C) Mort Tician is not telling the truth.

   a. If (A) and (B) are true, (C) must be true.
   b. If (A) and (B) are true, (C) is probably true.
   c. If (A) and (B) are true, (C) must be false.
   d. If (A) and (B) are true, (C) is probably false.
   e. (A) and (B) provide no reasons to believe that (C) is either true or false.

(Continued)

7. (A) Charley Kahn said there were five gallons of insecticide in the storeroom last night. (B) This morning, there were only four gallons of insecticide in the storeroom. (C) Charlie stole a gallon of insecticide.

    a. If (A) and (B) are true, (C) must be true.
    b. If (A) and (B) are true, (C) is probably true.
    c. If (A) and (B) are true, (C) must be false.
    d. If (A) and (B) are true, (C) is probably false.
    e. (A) and (B) provide no reasons to believe that (C) is either true or false.

8. (A) Three years ago Amanda Smith was an inmate in the Nebraska Correctional Center for Women. (B) Three years ago Sam Smiley was a guard at the Nebraska Correctional Center for Women. (C) Amanda Smith and Sam Smiley knew one another.

    a. If (A) and (B) are true, (C) must be true.
    b. If (A) and (B) are true, (C) is probably true.
    c. If (A) and (B) are true, (C) must be false.
    d. If (A) and (B) are true, (C) is probably false.
    e. (A) and (B) provide no reasons to believe that (C) is either true or false.

9. (A) The fingerprints of the victim matched those of Amanda Smith. (B) There was no evidence that the fingerprints of the victim had been modified. (C) The victim was probably Amanda Smith.

    a. If (A) and (B) are true, (C) must be true.
    b. If (A) and (B) are true, (C) is probably true.
    c. If (A) and (B) are true, (C) must be false.
    d. If (A) and (B) are true, (C) is probably false.
    e. (A) and (B) provide no reasons to believe that (C) is either true or false.

10. (A) As little as 60 milligrams of nicotine can kill a human being. (B) Dr. Mendez determined that more than 1,000 milligrams of nicotine had been injected into the victim's body. (C) Nicotine poisoning was the cause of the victim's death.

    a. If (A) and (B) are true, (C) must be true.
    b. If (A) and (B) are true, (C) is probably true.
    c. If (A) and (B) are true, (C) must be false.
    d. If (A) and (B) are true, (C) is probably false.
    e. (A) and (B) provide no reasons to believe that (C) is either true or false.

Chapter 1 Quiz

Choose the best answer for each of the following questions.

1. A person who is open-minded:
   a. accepts any claim as true.
   b. accepts religious beliefs as true.
   c. tries not to make judgments based on prejudices and emotions.
   d. tries not to make judgments based on the best evidence available.

2. If two claims are inconsistent:
   a. no more than one of them can be true.
   b. one claim is true and the other is false.
   c. both claims are false.
   d. both claims can be true.

3. Knowing that one claim is true:
   a. can help one show that any other claim is false.
   b. can never help one determine whether some other claim is true or false.
   c. can help one determine whether any other claim is true.
   d. can sometimes help one determine whether another claim is true.

4. The meaning of a claim can be unclear if:
   a. one of the words in a sentence has several meanings.
   b. the structure of the sentence allows the claim to be understood in more than one way.
   c. the meaning of one or more words is imprecise.
   d. all of the above

5. A critical thinker should base decisions on:
   a. an evaluation of emotions and facts.
   b. a strong piece of evidence.
   c. an evaluation of the people involved.
   d. an evaluation of available evidence.

6. Some evidence:
   a. is better than other evidence.
   b. is independent of the claim for which it may be taken as evidence.
   c. is based on emotion alone.
   d. is no reason to believe that a claim is true or false.

7. Evidence consists of:
   a. reasons to believe it would be nice if a claim were true.
   b. reasons to believe that a claim is true or false.
   c. emotional responses to situations.
   d. reasons to reject claims.

(Continued)

8. Critical thinkers ask questions to:
   a. obtain information about the topic being examined.
   b. hear themselves talk.
   c. appear to be well-versed in many areas.
   d. show that their prejudices are justified.

9. In looking for connections among claims, a critical thinker will recognize that:
   a. sometimes two claims cannot both be true.
   b. sometimes the truth of one claim shows that another claim must be true.
   c. sometimes the truth of one claim shows that another claim is probably true.
   d. all of the above

10. An English teacher is most qualified to talk about:
    a. politics and government.
    b. items in the news.
    c. English grammar and literature.
    d. grammatical structures that apply across languages.

CHAPTER 2

- Facts
- Claims of Fact
- Opinions
- Review

Overview

A critical thinker strives to base arguments upon facts rather than upon mere opinions. We will examine key differences between facts and mere opinions. We will also examine different kinds of evidence used to support claims of fact:

1. observational evidence based upon direct perception of a claimed fact.

2. mathematical evidence based upon conclusive proof from mathematical reasoning.

3. scientific evidence based upon confirmed experiments and scientific principles.

4. conclusive evidence from a correct definition of a claim.

| CASE 4 | City of Los Angeles Police Department |

[1]Detective Wise of the LAPD is investigating an apparent murder. [2]Elmo Smith appears to have been shot twice at close range with a small-caliber pistol. [3]Detective Wise questioned Smith's neighbor, Sadie Gonzalez. [4]Ms. Gonzales was in jail two years ago for armed robbery.

[5]Ms. Gonzalez said, "I was taking a bath at about 10:30 last night when I heard a couple of pops. [6]I thought it was a car backfiring. [7]I was shocked when I looked out the window a few minutes later and saw Elmo sprawled on the ground. [8]He was such a good neighbor, such a fine man. [9]The neighborhood just won't be the same without him," she sobbed.

[10]"I need facts ma'am, just facts." said Detective Wise.

[11]Detective Wise also questioned another neighbor, Tyrone Brown. [12]Mr. Brown is the president of the neighborhood association. [13]He works at the local video store.

[14]Mr. Brown said, "I got home at about 11:00 last night. [15]The ambulance and police were already on the scene. [16]So, I can't tell you anything about how Smith died. [17]Smith kept pretty much to himself. [18]I don't know what he did for a living. [19]He used to be seen regularly with Sadie Gonzalez. [20]For the past few weeks, a red sports car was often parked in front of Smith's place. [21]I saw the driver once. [22]She was a real knockout! [23]I think Sadie killed Smith."

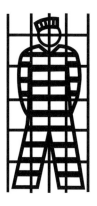

2.1 Facts and Opinions

Facts are the ways things really are. They are independent of what anyone believes. True claims correspond to facts.

Examples of facts in Case 4:

a.	Detective Wise is an LAPD detective (sentence 1).
b.	Elmo Smith is dead (sentences 1, 2).
c.	Sadie Gonzalez was Smith's neighbor (sentence 3).
d.	Sadie Gonzalez was in jail two years ago (sentence 4).
e.	Mr. Brown is the president of the neighborhood association (sentence 12).
f.	Mr. Brown works at the local video store (sentence 13).

A *claim of fact* is a statement that something is a fact.

Examples of claims of fact in Case 4:

a.	Ms. Gonzalez was taking a bath at 10:30 (sentence 5).
b.	Ms. Gonzalez heard two pops while she was taking a bath (sentence 5).
c.	Ms. Gonzalez saw Smith's body sprawled on the ground (sentence 7).
d.	Mr. Brown got home at about 11:00 last night (sentence 14).
e.	The police were already on the scene when Mr. Brown got home (sentence 15).
f.	Mr. Brown saw the driver of a red sports car that parked in front of Smith's house (sentence 21).

Most claims of fact can be proven. Evidence is used to prove claims of fact true or false. In Case 4, Mr. Brown claimed he got home at about 11:00, but we only have his word for it. If he was seen by one of the neighbors at that time, then that would be evidence that his claim is true.

Not every claim in Case 4 was a fact or claim of fact. Case 4 also includes some opinions.

An **opinion** is a belief that cannot be proven true or false due to the unscientific nature of the claim or a claim supported by little or no evidence.

Examples of opinions that cannot be proven true or false due to their unscientific nature in Case 4:

a.	Mr. Smith was a good neighbor (sentence 8).
b.	Mr. Smith was a wonderful man (sentence 8).
c.	The neighborhood will not be the same without Mr. Smith (sentence 9).
d.	The driver of the red sports car was a real knockout (sentence 22).
e.	I think Sadie murdered Mr. Smith (sentence 23).

Ms. Gonzalez claimed that Mr. Smith was a good neighbor, but there are no accepted *criteria* or standards for determining what makes someone a good neighbor. Mr. Brown and Ms. Gonzalez could have very different opinions as to whether Mr. Smith was a good neighbor because they could have very different standards as to what makes someone a good neighbor. Similarly, Mr. Brown's opinion that the driver of the sports car was a knockout tells us that he thought she was attractive, but there is no one acceptable definition of a "knockout" so his claim is nonfactual and cannot be proven true or false.

An example of an opinion (belief) supported with little or no evidence can be found in a new person, Mr. Robertson, who is not an eyewitness but has had a dream about the murder. Mr. Robertson calls up Detective Wise and says that in his dream a woman kills Elmo Smith. Mr. Robertson's claim is an opinion for which he has little or no evidence. Perhaps evidence will be discovered later that will support the claim strongly, but a dream is not strong evidence for a factual claim.

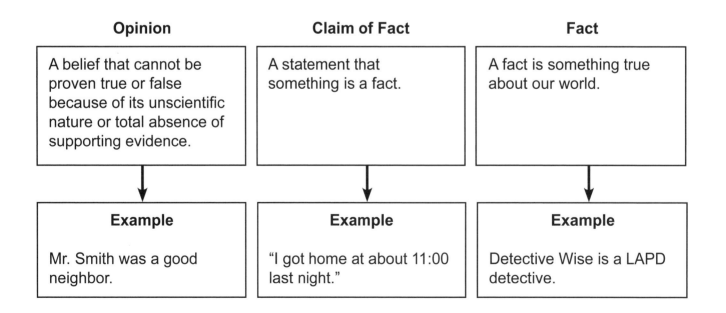

Opinion	Claim of Fact	Fact
A belief that cannot be proven true or false because of its unscientific nature or total absence of supporting evidence.	A statement that something is a fact.	A fact is something true about our world.
Example	**Example**	**Example**
Mr. Smith was a good neighbor.	"I got home at about 11:00 last night."	Detective Wise is a LAPD detective.

2.2 Exercise Each claim below is about Case 4. Circle which claims are claims of fact and which are opinions. A claim of fact may be true or false.

1. **Example:**
    Detective Wise is a beautiful woman.
    (a.) **Opinion***
    b. Claim of fact
    *Standards of beauty are difficult to state

2. **Example**:
    Smith died sometime between 10:30 and 10:45.
    a. Opinion
    (b.) **Claim of fact***
    *It describes when this event happened.

3. Mr. Brown saw Mr. Smith die.
    a. Opinion
    b. Claim of fact

4. The sports car driver was 5 feet, 10 inches tall, weighed about 130 pounds, and had long blond hair.
    a. Opinion
    b. Claim of fact

5. Red sports cars are the coolest cars around!
    a. Opinion
    b. Claim of fact

6. "Elmo Smith" was the name on the victim's birth certificate.
    a. Opinion
    b. Claim of fact

7. "Elmo Smith" was 30 years old when he died.
    a. Opinion
    b. Claim of fact

8. Ms. Gonzalez is a strange woman.
    a. Opinion
    b. Claim of fact

9. Mr. Smith moved into the neighborhood three years ago.
    a. Opinion
    b. Claim of fact

10. Mr. Smith was lying on his back when his body was found.
    a. Opinion
    b. Claim of fact

(Continued)

11. Murder is the worst of all crimes.
    a. Opinion
    b. Claim of fact

12. Mr. Smith was having dinner with the sports car driver when he died.
    a. Opinion
    b. Claim of fact

CASE 5	City of Los Angeles Police Department

[1]Detective Wise was vacationing at the MGM Grand in Las Vegas. [2]At 2:30 a.m., she was awakened by loud noises from the next room. [3]She glanced at the clock and fell back to sleep a few minutes later. [4]As she headed to breakfast later that morning, she saw crime-scene tape across the door to the neighboring room. [5]She approached the officer in charge, introduced herself as an LAPD detective, and asked, "What happened?"

[6]He replied, "It was a robbery. [7]The call was logged in at 4:41 this morning. [8]Mr. and Mrs. Jones said that two masked men broke into their room at 4:15 and made off with nearly $50,000 in jewelry. [9]You can see the mess they made. [10]Mr. Jones was injured when a chair was broken over his shoulder. [11]The Joneses were bound with duct tape. [12]It took almost half an hour for Mrs. Jones to work herself loose and call."

[13]Detective Wise replied, "Something's wrong. [14]My room's next door. [15]I heard some loud noises at 2:30. [16]I thought it was a domestic dispute. [17]I'm a light sleeper. [18]If this kind of damage occurred at 4:15, I would have heard it. [19]If anyone is being robbed, I suspect it is the insurance company."

2.3 Claims of Fact

A **claim of fact** is true if what it claims is fact. A claim of fact is false if what it claims is not fact.

Examples of true claims of fact in Case 5:

a.	Detective Wise was vacationing in Las Vegas (sentence 1).
b.	Mr. and Mrs. Jones said they were robbed (sentence 8).
c.	Detective Wise talked with the officer outside the room next to hers (sentences 5-19).

Examples of false claims of fact in Case 5:

a.	Detective Wise's room was below the Joneses' room (sentence 2).
b.	Detective Wise did not wake up during the night (sentence 2).
c.	The officer said Mrs. Jones had a table broken over her head (sentences 6-12).

2.4   Exercise Each claim below is about Case 5. Circle the correct answer and best supporting sentence evidence for each factual claim.

1. **Example:**
    Detective Wise is vacationing in France.
    a. True
    (b.) **False, sentence 1**
    c. True, sentence 4
    d. False, sentence 18

2. Detective Wise heard noises in the next room at 4:15.
    a. True. sentence 4
    b. True, sentence 6
    c. False, sentence 18
    d. False, sentence 19

3. The officer says the Joneses were killed during a robbery.
    a. True, sentence 1
    b. True, sentence 3
    c. False, sentence 19
    d. False, sentence 8

4. According to the officer, the Joneses said they were robbed of nearly $50,000 in jewelry.
    a. True, sentence 8
    b. True, sentence 9
    c. False, sentence 10
    d. False, sentence 11

5. Detective Wise heard noises in the next room at 2:30.
    a. True, sentence 18
    b. True, sentence 15
    c. False, sentence 12
    d. False, sentence 14

6. Detective Wise stayed up until 3:00 a.m.
    a. True, sentence 1
    b. True, sentence 2
    c. False, sentence 3
    d. False, sentence 17

7. The room in which the robbery supposedly occurred was neat and tidy.
    a. True, sentence 6
    b. True, sentence 7
    c. False, sentence 8
    d. False, sentence 9

(Continued)

8. Detective Wise found out about the supposed robbery while on her way to breakfast.
   a. True, sentence 4
   b. True, sentence 5
   c. False, sentence 6
   d. False, sentence 7

9. Detective Wise works for the Las Vegas Police Department.
   a. True, sentence 1
   b. True, sentence 3
   c. False, sentence 5
   d. False, sentence 7

10. Detective Wise did not sleep after 2:30.
    a. True, sentence 15
    b. True, sentence 16
    c. False, sentence 17
    d. False, sentence 3

2.5 Evidence

Evidence gives us a reason to believe a claim is true or false. Sometimes though, because there is not sufficient (enough) evidence, we may not know that the claim is true. We may only have some reason to believe that it is true. The claim may actually be false. What is sufficient evidence to decide the truth of a claim of fact isn't always clear and is frequently debated.

Examples of claims of fact for which there is some evidence of truth in Case 5:

a.	Detective Wise woke up at 2:30. The evidence that the claim is true is that she saw the time on her clock (sentences 2-3).
b.	The Joneses were robbed at 4:15. The evidence that the claim is true is that the Joneses said so (sentence 8). There is some reason to believe that it is true, but there is not enough evidence in Case 5 to know that it is true. The claim made by the Joneses that they were robbed may actually be false.
c.	The police logged in a call regarding a robbery at 4:41 (sentence 7). The evidence that the claim is true is that this was the time logged in (written down) at the police station (sentence 7).

Examples of claims of fact for which there is some evidence of falsehood in Case 5:

a.	The room next to Detective Wise's is neat and tidy. The evidence that the claim is false is that both the officer in charge and Detective Wise saw a messy room (sentences 9 and 18).
b.	The Joneses were robbed at 4:15. The evidence that the claim is false is that Detective Wise is a light sleeper and would have heard the noise next door if it had happened (sentences 14-18).
c.	The police have solved the case. The evidence that the claim is false is that a police officer is still at the scene (sentences 4-5).

2.6   Exercise Each claim below is about Case 5. Circle the correct answer and best sentence evidence for each claim.

1. **Example:**
   Detective Wise is an LAPD detective.
   a. **True, sentence 5***
   b. True, sentence 2
   c. False, sentence 3
   d. False, sentence 17
   *The evidence that the claim is true is that she introduced herself as an LAPD detective and, perhaps, showed the officer her badge.

2. Detective Wise was awake at 3:00 a.m.
   a. True, sentence 1
   b. True, sentence 2
   c. False, sentence 3
   d. False, sentence 17

3. Two masked men broke into the Joneses' room at 4:15 and robbed them.
   a. True, sentence 13
   b. True, sentence 11
   c. False, sentence 18
   d. False, sentence 17

4. The room next to Detective Wise's was blocked by crime-scene tape.
   a. True, sentence 4
   b. True, sentence 5
   c. False, sentence 6
   d. False, sentence 7

5. The Joneses had been bound with ropes.
   a. True, sentence 15
   b. True, sentence 16
   c. False, sentence 17
   d. False, sentence 11

6. It was a quiet night in the room next to Detective Wise's.
   a. True, sentence 1
   b. True, sentence 3
   c. False, sentence 19
   d. False, sentence 15

7. There is no crime in Las Vegas.
   a. True, sentence 1
   b. True, sentence 2
   c. False, sentence 3
   d. False, sentence 4

8. Detective Wise works for the Las Vegas Police Department.
   a. True, sentence 1
   b. True, sentence 5
   c. False, sentence 5
   d. False, sentence 13

9. Nearly $100,000 in jewelry was reported as stolen.
   a. True, sentence 4
   b. True, sentence 6
   c. False, sentence 8
   d. False, sentence 10

10. Mr. and Mrs. Jones were having an argument at 2:30.
   a. True, sentence 16
   b. True, sentence 17
   c. False, sentence 18
   d. False, sentence 19

2.7 Observational Evidence

Evidence that shows a claim of fact is true or probably true is said to *verify* the claim. Evidence is often based on what one observes (sees, hears, smells, tastes, or touches). This is called **observational evidence.**

Examples of claims of fact supported by observational evidence in Case 5:

a.	There was a scuffle in the room next to Detective Wise's at 2:30 (sentence 2).
b.	Mr. and Mrs. Jones said they were robbed (sentence 8).
c.	Mr. and Mrs. Jones' room is a mess (sentences 9 and 18).

Not all evidence is verifiable by observational evidence.

Examples of claims of fact not verifiable by observational evidence:

a.	Detective Wise is 36 years old. This could not be known by observation. We might be able to judge her approximate age – "She appears to be in her mid-thirties" – but her exact age could be known only by calculations based on her birth date.
b.	Detective Wise was born in Coos Bay, Oregon. This could not be known by observation except by those actually present at her birth. Most people would need to examine a legal document such as her birth record which lists where she was born, ask Detective Wise where she was born, or interview someone present at her birth.

2.8   Exercise Each claim of fact below is about Case 5. Evaluate the evidence and circle the correct answer. Supply the best sentence evidence for your answer when asked.

1. **Example:**
   Detective Wise is over 5 feet tall.
   a. Verified in Case 5 by sentence _____.
   b. **Verifiable, but no observational evidence in Case 5.**
   c. Not verifiable with observational evidence.

2. **Example:**
   Detective Wise is 36 years old.
   a. Verifiable in Case 5 by sentence _____.
   b. Verifiable, but no observational evidence.
   c. **Not verifiable by any observational evidence.**

3. The room where the robbery happened smells of lilacs.
   a. Verifiable in Case 5 by sentence _____.
   b. Verifiable, but we need more observational evidence.
   c. Not verifiable by any observational evidence.

4. A chair in the room was broken.
   a. Verifiable in Case 5 by sentence 10.
   b. Verifiable, but we need more observational evidence.
   c. Not verifiable by any observational evidence.

5. Someone recently smoked a cigar in the room.
   a. Verifiable in Case 5 by sentence _____.
   b. Verifiable, but we need more observational evidence.
   c. Not verifiable by any observational evidence.

6. The missing jewelry is worth nearly $50,000.
   a. Verifiable in Case 5 by sentence 8.
   b. Verifiable, but we need more observational evidence.
   c. Not verifiable by any observational evidence.

7. The officer at the scene is taller than Detective Wise.
   a. Verifiable in Case 5 by sentence _____.
   b. Verifiable, but we need more observational evidence.
   c. Not verifiable by any observational evidence.

8. The officer at the scene is shorter than Mrs. Jones.
   a. Verifiable in Case 5 by sentence _____.
   b. Verifiable, but we need more observational evidence.
   c. Not verifiable by any observational evidence.

(Continued)

9. Mr. Jones is older than Mrs. Jones.
   a. Verifiable in Case 5 by sentence _____.
   b. Verifiable if there is a big age difference, but we need more observational evidence.
   c. Not verifiable by any observational evidence.

10. Mr. and Mrs. Jones were robbed by two masked men at 4:15.
    a. Verifiable in Case 5 by sentence _____.
    b. Verifiable, but we need more observational evidence.
    c. Not verifiable by any observational evidence.

11. The officer at the scene is older than Detective Wise.
    a. Verifiable in Case 5 by sentence _____.
    b. Verifiable if there is a big age difference, but we need more observational evidence.
    c. Not verifiable by any observational evidence.

12. Mrs. Jones was buying duct tape at a drug store at 3:22 a.m.
    a. Verifiable in Case 5 by sentence _____.
    b. Verifiable, but we need more observational evidence.
    c. Not verifiable by any observational evidence.

2.9 Conclusive Evidence

The truth of certain claims of math and science can be proven conclusively. **Conclusive evidence** is evidence that guarantees the truth of a claim.

Note: The claim "The robbers stole a $25,000 diamond necklace and a $15,000 diamond bracelet which totaled $40,000" is true only if the value of each of item is correct. If the diamond necklace's value was really $10,000, then the claim would be false on two counts. The value of the necklace would be false and the total value of the two stolen items would be false.

Examples of claims of fact for which there is conclusive mathematical evidence in Case 5:

a.	If the value of items stolen were a $25,000 diamond necklace, a $15,000 diamond bracelet, and two rings valued at $5,500 and $4,350, then the jewelry stolen was worth $49,850 (conclusively true).
b.	If the date Detective Wise talked with the officer outside the room was July 13, 2008, and Detective Wise was born on April 11, 1972, then Detective Wise is 36 years old (conclusively true).
c.	If the value of items stolen were a $25,000 diamond necklace, a $15,000 diamond bracelet, and two rings valued at $5,500 and $4,350, then the jewelry stolen was worth $51,850 (conclusively false).
d.	If the date Detective Wise talked with the officer outside the room was July 13, 2008, and Detective Wise was born an April 11, 1972, then Detective Wise is 26 years old (conclusively false).

Claims of fact that correctly define a word or concept are conclusively true (by definition). Claims of fact that incorrectly define a word or concept are conclusively false (by definition).

Examples of claims that are conclusively true or conclusively false by definitions in Case 5:

a.	If Detective Wise is a woman, then Detective Wise is a human being (conclusively true). Part of what it means to be a woman is to be a human being.
b.	If the officer outside the room is a bachelor, then the officer outside the room is unmarried (conclusively true). Part of what it means to be a bachelor is to be unmarried.
c.	If Detective Wise is a woman, then she is a male (conclusively false).
d.	If the Joneses were robbed, they willingly gave away their jewelry (conclusively false).

Claims of fact based on principles of science are conclusively true. Claims of fact that are inconsistent with principles of science are conclusively false.

Examples of claims of fact that are conclusively true or conclusively false on the basis of science principles in Case 5:

a.	If Mrs. Jones had jewelry, it was composed of atoms and molecules (conclusively true).
b.	If Mrs. Jones owned real diamonds, then she owned carbon compounds (conclusively true).
c.	If the Joneses' jewelry is missing, it might have just flown away (conclusively false).
d.	If the Joneses are human beings, then they produce their own food by photosynthesis (conclusively false).

2.10 Exercise Circle the best answer that is proven conclusively for each claim of fact about Case 5.

1. **Example:**
   If the Joneses were robbed of their jewelry, then they had jewelry before the robbery.
   a. Conclusively true by mathematics
   (b.) **Conclusively true by definition***
   c. Conclusively true by principles of science
   d. Conclusively false by mathematics
   e. Conclusively false by definition
   f. Conclusively false by principles of science
   *By definition, you cannot take something someone doesn't have.

2. **Example:**
   If the Joneses owned three rings that were each worth $850, then altogether the three rings were worth $1,700.
   a. Conclusively true by mathematics
   b. Conclusively true by definition
   c. Conclusively true by principles of science
   (d.) **Conclusively false by mathematics ($850 x 3 = $2,550)**
   e. Conclusively false by definition
   f. Conclusively false by principles of science

3. If there was water in the Joneses' room, then there was a compound of hydrogen and oxygen in their room.
   a. Conclusively true by mathematics
   b. Conclusively true by definition
   c. Conclusively true by principles of science
   d. Conclusively false by mathematics
   e. Conclusively false by definition
   f. Conclusively false by principles of science

4. If the Joneses were born in 1950 and 1952, they are both over 50 years old.
   a. Conclusively true by mathematics
   b. Conclusively true by definition
   c. Conclusively true by principles of science
   d. Conclusively false by mathematics
   e. Conclusively false by definition
   f. Conclusively false by principles of science

5. If Mr. Jones was hit by a chair, the chair did not move faster than the speed of light.
   a. Conclusively true by mathematics
   b. Conclusively true by definition
   c. Conclusively true by principles of science
   d. Conclusively false by mathematics
   e. Conclusively false by definition
   f. Conclusively false by principles of science

(Continued)

6. If Detective Wise's room cost $450 per night, but they gave her a Las Vegas discount of $300 per night, then she paid $150 per night (plus applicable taxes).
    a. Conclusively true by mathematics
    b. Conclusively true by definition
    c. Conclusively true by principles of science
    d. Conclusively false by mathematics
    e. Conclusively false by definition
    f. Conclusively false by principles of science

7. If Mr. Jones' DNA was found on a chair, then Mr. Jones probably came into contact with the chair.
    a. Conclusively true by mathematics
    b. Conclusively true by definition
    c. Conclusively true by principles of science
    d. Conclusively false by mathematics
    e. Conclusively false by definition
    f. Conclusively false by principles of science

8. If Mr. and Mrs. Jones had a domestic dispute (loud argument) at 2:30, then they were hugging and kissing at that time.
    a. Conclusively true by mathematics
    b. Conclusively true by definition
    c. Conclusively true by principles of science
    d. Conclusively false by mathematics
    e. Conclusively false by definition
    f. Conclusively false by principles of science

9. If Detective Wise was going to breakfast at 8:00, then she had not eaten breakfast at 8:00.
    a. Conclusively true by mathematics
    b. Conclusively true by definition
    c. Conclusively true by principles of science
    d. Conclusively false by mathematics
    e. Conclusively false by definition
    f. Conclusively false by principles of science

10. If broken furniture was spread around the room, then the room was a mess.
    a. Conclusively true by mathematics
    b. Conclusively true by definition
    c. Conclusively true by principles of science
    d. Conclusively false by mathematics
    e. Conclusively false by definition
    f. Conclusively false by principles of science

11. If Detective Wise is vacationing in Las Vegas, then she went to Las Vegas to help investigate a crime.
    a. Conclusively true by mathematics
    b. Conclusively true by definition
    c. Conclusively true by principles of science
    d. Conclusively false by mathematics
    e. Conclusively false by definition
    f. Conclusively false by principles of science

12. If Mr. Jones' fingerprints are on the table, then Mr. Jones probably touched the table.
    a. Conclusively true by mathematics
    b. Conclusively true by definition
    c. Conclusively true by principles of science
    d. Conclusively false by mathematics
    e. Conclusively false by definition
    f. Conclusively false by principles of science

13. If the missing jewelry is worth $51,652, then less than $50,000 worth of jewelry is missing.
    a. Conclusively true by mathematics
    b. Conclusively true by definition
    c. Conclusively true by principles of science
    d. Conclusively false by mathematics
    e. Conclusively false by definition
    f. Conclusively false by principles of science

14. If Detective Wise was asleep during the reported robbery, then she was not awake.
    a. Conclusively true by mathematics
    b. Conclusively true by definition
    c. Conclusively true by principles of science
    d. Conclusively false by mathematics
    e. Conclusively false by definition
    f. Conclusively false by principles of science

15. If type B blood was found at several places in the room and Mrs. Jones has type A blood, then some of the blood found in the room was probably Mrs. Jones'.
    a. Conclusively true by mathematics
    b. Conclusively true by definition
    c. Conclusively true by principles of science
    d. Conclusively false by mathematics
    e. Conclusively false by definition
    f. Conclusively false by principles of science

(Continued)

16. If the Joneses are thieves, then not everything they have is rightfully theirs.
    a. Conclusively true by mathematics
    b. Conclusively true by definition
    c. Conclusively true by principles of science
    d. Conclusively false by mathematics
    e. Conclusively false by definition
    f. Conclusively false by principles of science

17. Detective Wise is more than 1,000 years old.
    a. Conclusively true by mathematics
    b. Conclusively true by definition
    c. Conclusively true by principles of science
    d. Conclusively false by mathematics
    e. Conclusively false by definition
    f. Conclusively false by principles of science

18. If the Joneses make it look as if they were robbed so they could collect on the insurance, then they are thieves.
    a. Conclusively true by mathematics
    b. Conclusively true by definition
    c. Conclusively true by principles of science
    d. Conclusively false by mathematics
    e. Conclusively false by definition
    f. Conclusively false by principles of science

19. Mr. and Mrs. Jones had a fight at 2:30 a.m., then the sun was visible at the time.
    a. Conclusively true by mathematics
    b. Conclusively true by definition
    c. Conclusively true by principles of science
    d. Conclusively false by mathematics
    e. Conclusively false by definition
    f. Conclusively false by principles of science

20. If Detective Wise's room was next to the Joneses' room, then it was a floor below the Joneses' room.
    a. Conclusively true by mathematics
    b. Conclusively true by definition
    c. Conclusively true by principles of science
    d. Conclusively false by mathematics
    e. Conclusively false by definition
    f. Conclusively false by principles of science

2.11 Knowing or Sufficient Evidence

To know that a claim of fact is true, there must be enough evidence to prove that it is true. To know that a claim of fact is false, there must be enough evidence to prove that it is false.

Note: People often disagree about what is enough (sufficient) evidence needed to know that a factual claim is true. We will examine some of these issues in later chapters.

Examples of claims of fact known to be true in Case 5:

a.	Detective Wise woke up at 2:30 (sentence 2).
b.	When Detective Wise went to breakfast, the room next door was a mess. The evidence is that she saw the room (sentences 4, 9, and 18).
c.	The Las Vegas police received the call that a crime had been committed at 4:41. The police officer reports this, and there is no reason to believe he would not correctly report the fact (sentence 7).

Examples of claims of fact known to be false in Case 5:

a.	Detective Wise believes the Joneses were robbed at 4:15 that morning. Detective Wise gave reasons to believe that the crime could not have happened as it was reported. So, she *does not* believe they were robbed at 4:15. She questions whether they were robbed at all (sentences 13-19).
b.	The Las Vegas police do not suspect that a crime was committed in the hotel. The police are present and they say there was a robbery, so you can be certain they believe that a crime *was* committed (sentences 4 and 6-12).
c.	Detective Wise was vacationing in New York City. This is inconsistent with the factual claim that she was vacationing in Las Vegas. So, if you know that Detective Wise was vacationing in Las Vegas, it must be false that she was vacationing in New York City (sentence 1).

Examples of claims of fact that might be true but lack sufficient (enough) evidence to be "known" truths in Case 5:

a.	The Joneses were robbed at 4:15. The Joneses claimed they were robbed at 4:15. This provides *some* evidence that they were robbed. However, there is also evidence that they might not have been robbed. Detective Wise states that if there had been a noisy fight at 4:15, she would have heard it. So we do not *know* if the Joneses were robbed at 4:15 (sentences 8 and 14-18).
b.	The Joneses had a noisy argument at 2:30. Detective Wise heard loud noises coming from the next room at 2:30. Her *guess* was that the people in the room were having an argument (a domestic dispute). This would explain why she heard what she heard, but it remains no more than a hypothesis (sentences 2, 15, and 16).
c.	The Joneses themselves stole the jewelry so they could collect money from the insurance company. This is Detective Wise's theory. It would explain why she heard no noise at 4:15, but there is insufficient evidence to know the truth of the theory (sentences 17-19).

2.12 Exercise Circle the best answer for each claim of fact from Case 5. Then supply the number of the sentence that best supports your answer when asked.

1. **Example:**
   There was crime-scene tape over the door to the room next to Detective Wise's room when she went to breakfast.
   (a.) **Known truth with evidence from sentence 4.**
   b. Known falsehood with evidence from sentence _____.
   c. Cannot be proven true or false with evidence from Case 5.

2. **Example:**
   The room where the robbery supposedly happened was neat and tidy.
   a. Known truth with evidence from sentence _____.
   (b.) **Known falsehood with evidence from sentence 9.***
   c. Cannot be proven true or false with evidence from Case 5.
   *Both Detective Wise and the police officer saw it was a mess.

3. **Example:**
   Mrs. Jones bought duct tape at a convenience store at 3:32.
   a. Known truth with evidence sentence _____.
   b. Known falsehood with evidence from sentence _____.
   (c.) **Cannot be proven true or false with evidence from Case 5.**

4. Mr. and Mrs. Jones both served time in jail.
   a. Known truth with evidence from sentence _____.
   b. Known falsehood with evidence from sentence _____.
   c. Cannot be proven true or false with evidence from Case 5.

5. If there was a robbery, it happened while Detective Wise was asleep.
   a. Known truth with evidence from sentence 18.
   b. Known falsehood with evidence from sentence _____.
   c. Cannot be proven true or false with evidence from Case 5.

6. The Joneses said they were robbed by two masked men.
   a. Known truth with evidence from sentence 8.
   b. Known falsehood with evidence from sentence _____.
   c. Cannot be proven true or false with evidence from Case 5.

7. Detective Wise is a sound sleeper.
   a. Known truth with evidence from sentence _____.
   b. Known falsehood with evidence from sentence 17.
   c. Cannot be proven true or false with evidence from Case 5.

8. Detective Wise was once an officer in the Marine Corps.
   a. Known truth with evidence from sentence _____.
   b. Known falsehood with evidence from sentence _____.
   c. Cannot be proven true or false with evidence from Case 5.

(Continued)

9. The Joneses said the robbers had taken several thousand dollars in cash.
    a. Known true with evidence from sentence _____.
    b. Known falsehood with evidence from sentence 8.
    c. Cannot be proven true or false with evidence from Case 5.

10. The Las Vegas police asked Detective Wise to consult on the case.
    a. Known truth with evidence from sentence _____.
    b. Known falsehood with evidence from sentence _____.
    c. Cannot be proven true or false with evidence from Case 5.

11. The officer at the scene of the crime was a woman.
    a. Known true with evidence from sentence _____.
    b. Known falsehood with evidence from sentence 6.
    c. Cannot be proven true or false with evidence from Case 5.

12. Detective Wise sleeps with her gun under her pillow.
    a. Known truth with evidence from sentence _____.
    b. Known falsehood with evidence from sentence _____.
    c. Cannot be proven true or false with evidence from Case 5.

13. The broken chair was three feet from the wall, and the foot of the bed was two and a half feet from the chair.
    a. Known truth with evidence from sentence _____.
    b. Known falsehood with evidence from sentence _____.
    c. Cannot be proven true or false with evidence from Case 5.

14. Detective Wise stayed at the Sands Hotel in Las Vegas.
    a. Known truth with evidence from sentence _____.
    b. Known falsehood with evidence from sentence 1.
    c. Cannot be proven true or false with evidence from Case 5.

15. Mr. Jones was injured during a robbery in his room.
    a. Known truth with evidence from sentence _____.
    b. Known falsehood with evidence from sentence _____.
    c. Cannot be proven true or false with evidence from Case 5.

16. The officer on the scene was 5 feet, 10 inches tall.
    a. Known truth with evidence from sentence _____.
    b. Known falsehood with evidence from sentence _____.
    c. Cannot be proven true or false with evidence from Case 5.

17. Mr. Jones told the truth when he said he was robbed.
    a. Known truth with evidence from sentence _____.
    b. Known falsehood with evidence from sentences 17-18.
    c. Cannot be proven true or false with evidence from Case 5.

18. Detective Wise is convinced that the Joneses were robbed by two masked men.
    a. Known truth with evidence from sentence _____.
    b. Known falsehood with evidence from sentence 19.
    c. Cannot be proven true or false with evidence from Case 5.

19. The officer Detective Wise meets at the scene of the crime is a member of the Los Angeles Police Department.
    a. Known truth with evidence from sentence _____.
    b. Known falsehood with evidence from sentence 1.
    c. Cannot be proven true or false with evidence from Case 5.

20. The Joneses faked a robbery so they would not have to pay for the furniture they broke during an argument.
    a. Known truth with evidence from sentence _____.
    b. Known falsehood with evidence from sentence _____.
    c. Cannot be proven true or false with evidence from Case 5.

CASE 6	City of Los Angeles Police Department

[1]The robbery at 1st National Bank was dramatic. [2]The robbers announced themselves by shooting at the wall above the tellers' cages. [3]No one was hurt. [4]They collected money from each of the ten tellers. [5]"Don't be in a hurry to leave," said one of the robbers, "or you'll all be blown to bits." [6]As they left the bank, the robbers attached a black box to each of the bank's doors.

[7]Detective Wise arrived after the bomb squad left. [8]The "bombs" were black cardboard boxes. [9]Each box contained only a printed card saying, "Have a nice day! ☺ The robbers."

[10]Detective Wise talked with the tellers. [11]The first teller said, "There were five of them. [12]They each wore a black ski mask, a black shirt, and black pants. [13]They were carrying some kind of machine guns."

[14]The second teller said, "There must have been eight or nine of them. [15]They were such nasty men."

[16]The third teller said, "I know guns. [17]All six of them were packing AK-47 assault rifles."

[18]All the tellers agreed that the robbers were dressed in black, that they carried "big guns," and that there were somewhere between four and ten robbers.

[19]Detective Wise asked each of the tellers about how much money was stolen. [20]They reported: less than $6,000, no more than $10,000, about $4,500, around $3,000, no more than $8,000, less than $5,000, about $3,500, only about $2,000, perhaps as much as $6,500, about $8,300.

[21]An examination of the wall behind the tellers' cages found no bullet holes. [22]"Did they shoot blanks?" Detective Wise asked herself.

[23]At a news conference later in the day, the bank president reported, "The robbers got away with over a half-million dollars in cash." [24]Detective Wise was puzzled.

2.13 Review Exercise Each claim of fact below is about Case 6. Circle whether the claim is a claim of fact or an opinion.

1. **Example:**
   1ˢᵗ National Bank was robbed.
   a. Opinion
   (b.) **Claim of fact**

2. **Example:**
   The robbery at 1ˢᵗ National Bank was dramatic.
   (a.) **Opinion**
   b. Claim of fact

3. Two of the robbers were killed during the robbery.
   a. Opinion
   b. Claim of fact

4. Guns were fired during the robbery.
   a. Opinion
   b. Claim of fact

5. The robbers were nasty men.
   a. Opinion
   b. Claim of fact

6. One of the robbers said that anyone leaving the bank would be killed in an explosion.
   a. Opinion
   b. Claim of fact

7. Robbers live interesting lives.
   a. Opinion
   b. Claim of fact

8. The robbers were sweet and gentle guys.
   a. Opinion
   b. Claim of fact

9. There were bullet holes in the wall behind the tellers.
   a. Opinion
   b. Claim of fact

10. Some things that are called bombs are not really bombs.
    a. Opinion
    b. Claim of fact

(Continued)

11. Being a bank teller can be exciting.
    a. Opinion
    b. Claim of fact

12. Bank robberies are uninteresting.
    a. Opinion
    b. Claim of fact

13. What the tellers said was stolen was not the same amount of money that the bank president said was stolen.
    a. Opinion
    b. Claim of fact

14. The robbers were wearing masks.
    a. Opinion
    b. Claim of fact

15. There's nothing like a good robbery to spice up one's day.
    a. Opinion
    b. Claim of fact

2.14 Review Exercise Each claim of fact below is about Case 6. Evaluate the evidence and circle the best answer.

1. **Example:**
   All the robbers were midgets.
   a. Verified in the story.
   (b.) **Verifiable, but no observational evidence in Case 6.**
   c. Not verifiable with any observational evidence.

2. The robbers were all dressed in black.
   a. Verified in the story.
   b. Verifiable, but no observational evidence in Case 6.
   c. Not verifiable with any observational evidence.

3. The robbers carried guns.
   a. Verified in the story.
   b. Verifiable, but no observational evidence in Case 6.
   c. Not verifiable with any observational evidence.

4. The robbers collected money from each of the tellers.
    a. Verified in the story.
    b. Verifiable, but no observational evidence in Case 6.
    c. Not verifiable with any observational evidence.

5. All the robbers were well under 6 feet tall.
    a. Verified in the story.
    b. Verifiable, but no observational evidence in Case 6.
    c. Not verifiable with any observational evidence.

6. There were five male and five female tellers.
    a. Verified in the story.
    b. Verifiable, but no observational evidence in Case 6.
    c. Not verifiable with any observational evidence.

7. The robbers drove to the bank in a black Rolls-Royce.
    a. Verified in the story.
    b. Verifiable, but no observational evidence in Case 6.
    c. Not verifiable with any observational evidence.

8. The black boxes were not bombs.
    a. Verified in the story.
    b. Verifiable, but no observational evidence in Case 6.
    c. Not verifiable with any observational evidence.

9. The robbers were all born in California.
    a. Verified in the story.
    b. Verifiable, but no observational evidence in Case 6.
    c. Not verifiable with any observational evidence.

10. The bank president was much taller than the oldest teller.
    a. Verified in the story.
    b. Verifiable, but no observational evidence in Case 6.
    c. Not verifiable with any observational evidence.

11. The robbers left a note wishing everyone a nice day.
    a. Verified in the story.
    b. Verifiable, but no observational evidence in Case 6.
    c. Not verifiable with any observational evidence.

12. The robbers each had a college education.
    a. Verified in the story.
    b. Verifiable, but no observational evidence in Case 6.
    c. Not verifiable with any observational evidence.

(Continued)

13. According to the tellers, the robbers stole nearly $57,000.
    a. Verified in the story.
    b. Verifiable, but no observational evidence in Case 6.
    c. Not verifiable with any observational evidence.

14. One of the tellers wore perfume.
    a. Verified in the story.
    b. Verifiable, but no observational evidence in Case 6.
    c. Not verifiable with any observational evidence.

15. One robber was taller than all the other robbers.
    a. Verified in the story.
    b. Verifiable, but no observational evidence in Case 6.
    c. Not verifiable with any observational evidence.

2.15 Review Exercise Each claim of fact below is about Case 6. Evaluate the evidence and circle the best answer that is proven conclusively.

1. **Example:**
    If the tellers' figures are correct, then less than $60,000 was stolen.
    a. **Conclusively true by mathematics***
    b. Conclusively true by definition
    c. Conclusively true by principles of science
    d. Conclusively false by mathematics
    e. Conclusively false by definition
    f. Conclusively false by principles of science
    *$6,000 + $10,000 + $4,500 + $3,000 + $8,000 + $5,000 + $3,500 + $2,000 +$6,500 + $8,300 = $56,800, which is less than $60,000

2. If Lulu was a teller at 1st National Bank, then she worked in a bank.
    a. Conclusively true by mathematics
    b. Conclusively true by definition
    c. Conclusively true by principles of science
    d. Conclusively false by mathematics
    e. Conclusively false by definition
    f. Conclusively false by principles of science

3. If a robber dropped the money, it floated to the ceiling of the bank.
    a. Conclusively true by mathematics
    b. Conclusively true by definition
    c. Conclusively true by principles of science
    d. Conclusively false by mathematics
    e. Conclusively false by definition
    f. Conclusively false by principles of science

4. If the tellers' account of the amount of money taken in the robbery is correct, then the bank president's claim is incorrect.
    a. Conclusively true by mathematics
    b. Conclusively true by definition
    c. Conclusively true by principles of science
    d. Conclusively false by mathematics
    e. Conclusively false by definition
    f. Conclusively false by principles of science

5. If there was a robbery at 1st National Bank, nothing was taken.
    a. Conclusively true by mathematics
    b. Conclusively true by definition
    c. Conclusively true by principles of science
    d. Conclusively false by mathematics
    e. Conclusively false by definition
    f. Conclusively false by principles of science

6. Paper money is composed of natural elements.
    a. Conclusively true by mathematics
    b. Conclusively true by definition
    c. Conclusively true by principles of science
    d. Conclusively false by mathematics
    e. Conclusively false by definition
    f. Conclusively false by principles of science

7. Robbers are honest people.
    a. Conclusively true by mathematics
    b. Conclusively true by definition
    c. Conclusively true by principles of science
    d. Conclusively false by mathematics
    e. Conclusively false by definition
    f. Conclusively false by principles of science

8. If the tellers' figures are correct, then over half a million dollars was stolen.
    a. Conclusively true by mathematics
    b. Conclusively true by definition
    c. Conclusively true by principles of science
    d. Conclusively false by mathematics
    e. Conclusively false by definition
    f. Conclusively false by principles of science

(Continued)

9. If the tellers' figures are correct, then more money was taken from some tellers' cages than from other tellers' cages.
    a. Conclusively true by mathematics
    b. Conclusively true by definition
    c. Conclusively true by principles of science
    d. Conclusively false by mathematics
    e. Conclusively false by definition
    f. Conclusively false by principles of science

10. If paper money is green, then it is a plant.
    a. Conclusively true by mathematics
    b. Conclusively true by definition
    c. Conclusively true by principles of science
    d. Conclusively false by mathematics
    e. Conclusively false by definition
    f. Conclusively false by principles of science

11. If Detective Wise is a police officer, then she works for a police department.
    a. Conclusively true by mathematics
    b. Conclusively true by definition
    c. Conclusively true by principles of science
    d. Conclusively false by mathematics
    e. Conclusively false by definition
    f. Conclusively false by principles of science

12. If no one was hurt in the robbery, then some of the tellers were injured.
    a. Conclusively true by mathematics
    b. Conclusively true by definition
    c. Conclusively true by principles of science
    d. Conclusively false by mathematics
    e. Conclusively false by definition
    f. Conclusively false by principles of science

13. If the black boxes had contained nitroglycerine, then they could have exploded.
    a. Conclusively true by mathematics
    b. Conclusively true by definition
    c. Conclusively true by principles of science
    d. Conclusively false by mathematics
    e. Conclusively false by definition
    f. Conclusively false by principles of science

14. If one of the robbers carried an AK-47 assault rifle, then the robber carried a gun.
    a. Conclusively true by mathematics
    b. Conclusively true by definition
    c. Conclusively true by principles of science
    d. Conclusively false by mathematics
    e. Conclusively false by definition
    f. Conclusively false by principles of science

15. The robbers who stole the money were criminals.
    a. Conclusively true by mathematics
    b. Conclusively true by definition
    c. Conclusively true by principles of science
    d. Conclusively false by mathematics
    e. Conclusively false by definition
    f. Conclusively false by principles of science

2.16 Review Exercise Each claim below is about Case 6. Circle the correct answer. Supply the number of the sentence that supports your answer when asked.

1. **Example:**
There was a robbery at 1ˢᵗ National Bank.
    (a.) **Known truth with evidence from sentence 1.**
    b. Known falsehood with evidence from sentence _____.
    c. Cannot be proven true or false with evidence from Case 6.

2. There were more than two robbers.
    a. Known truth with evidence from sentence 18.
    b. Known falsehood with evidence from sentence _____.
    c. Cannot be proven true or false with evidence from Case 6.

3. The bank's president was involved in the robbery.
    a. Known truth with evidence from sentence _____.
    b. Known falsehood with evidence from sentence _____.
    c. Cannot be proven true or false with evidence from Case 6.

4. The same amount of money was taken from each of the tellers.
    a. Known truth with evidence from sentence _____.
    b. Known falsehood with evidence from sentence 20.
    c. Cannot be proven true or false with evidence from Case 6.

5. The black boxes the robbers put on each door were dangerous.
    a. Known truth with evidence from sentence _____.
    b. Known falsehood with evidence from sentence 9.
    c. Cannot be proven true or false with evidence from Case 6.

(Continued)

6.   Detective Wise drives a red Corvette.
     a. Known truth with evidence from sentence _____.
     b. Known falsehood with evidence from sentence _____.
     c. Cannot be proven true or false with evidence from Case 6.

7.   The bank's president said more money was stolen than the tellers said was stolen.
     a. Known truth with evidence from sentences 20, 23.
     b. Known falsehood with evidence from sentence _____.
     c. Cannot be proven true or false with evidence from Case 6.

8.   The robbers all used AK-47 assault rifles.
     a. Known truth with evidence from sentence _____.
     b. Known falsehood with evidence from sentence _____.
     c. Cannot be proven true or false with evidence from Case 6.

9.   Two of the robbers were injured during the robbery.
     a. Known truth with evidence from sentence _____.
     b. Known falsehood with evidence from sentence _____.
     c. Cannot be proven true or false with evidence from Case 6.

10. The robbers shot bullets into the wall.
     a. Known truth with evidence from sentence _____.
     b. Known falsehood with evidence from sentence 21.
     c. Cannot be proven true or false with evidence from Case 6.

11. The robbers carried handguns.
     a. Known truth with evidence from sentence _____.
     b. Known falsehood with evidence from sentence 18.
     c. Cannot be proven true or false with evidence from Case 6.

12. The tellers agreed with each other regarding the number of robbers.
     a. Known truth with evidence from sentence _____.
     b. Known falsehood with evidence from sentence 18.
     c. Cannot be proven true or false with evidence from Case 6.

13. The robbers threatened to injure the bank employees.
     a. Known truth with evidence from sentence 5.
     b. Known falsehood with evidence from sentence _____.
     c. Cannot be proven true or false with evidence from Case 6.

14. The robbers shot at the wall above the tellers' cages.
     a. Known truth with evidence from sentence 2.
     b. Known falsehood with evidence frin sentence _____.
     c. Cannot be proven true or false with evidence from Case 6.

15. Detective Wise was a member of the bomb squad.
   a. Known truth with evidence from sentence _____.
   b. Known falsehood with evidence from sentence 7.
   c. Cannot be proven true or false with evidence from Case 6.

| CASE 7 | City of Los Angeles Police Department |

[1]There was a pileup on Wilshire Boulevard. [2]Normally accidents are jobs for patrol officers, but there was a small hole in the windshield of one car and a corresponding hole in the driver's forehead. [3]It was no ordinary accident. [4]Detective Wise got the call at 5:31 p.m.

[5]When Detective Wise arrived, Officer Baker briefed her on what they'd found. [6]He said, "Six cars were involved. [7]This time of day, Wilshire's little more than a parking lot. [8]The victim must have been shot just after crossing South Vermont. [9]He hit the gas and plowed into the car in front of him, which set off a chain reaction. [10]The other drivers were just shaken up. [11]The victim's driver's license says he's Victor O'Toole from Chicago. [12]We found a loaded Colt .45 automatic in his glove box. [13]The serial number was filed off the gun. [14]So, I don't think this guy was an angel."

[15]There were several witnesses. [16]Edith Taylor had been in a car following the victim's. [17]She said, "Just as the victim's car surged ahead, I saw someone running along the sidewalk. [18]It must have been that young hooligan who shot him."

[19]Norma Hernandez said, "I saw a flash of light coming from that tree just before the accident."

[20]Homer Price said, "It was just terrible! [21]I was jogging along the sidewalk when it happened. [22]I heard this crack and saw the guy jolt back into his seat. [23]Then his car surged ahead and smashed into the one ahead of him."

[24]Detective Wise considered the evidence. [25]Only the medical examiner can say for sure, but I'd guess the shooter was in the tree. [26]The angle does not seem to be right for a shot from the sidewalk.

2.17 Review Exercise Circle whether the claim is a claim of fact or an opinion from Case 7.

1. **Example:**
   There was an automobile crash on Wilshire Boulevard.
   a. Opinion
   (b.) **Claim of fact**

2. The accident was terrible.
   a. Opinion
   b. Claim of fact

3. The person running along the sidewalk was a hooligan.
   a. Opinion
   b. Claim of fact

4. The shooter was in a tree.
   a. Opinion
   b. Claim of fact

5. The man in the car that started the chain reaction had a heart attack.
   a. Opinion
   b. Claim of fact

6. Detective Wise got the call at 5:31 p.m.
   a. Opinion
   b. Claim of fact

7. The victim's driver's license said he was from Chicago.
   a. Opinion
   b. Claim of fact

8. The victim was not a good guy.
   a. Opinion
   b. Claim of fact

9. A gun was found in the glove compartment of the victim's car.
   a. Opinion
   b. Claim of fact

10. The victim's name was Victor O'Toole.
    a. Opinion
    b. Claim of fact

2.18 Review Exercise Circle whether a claim of fact is true or false from Case 7.

1. **Example:**
   There was a small hole in the windshield of one car and a corresponding hole in the driver's forehead.
   a. True, sentence 2
   b. True, sentence 8
   c. False, sentence 5
   d. False, sentence 6

2. When Officer Baker arrived, Detective Wise briefed her on what they'd found.
   a. True, sentence 7
   b. True, sentence 8
   c. False, sentence 5
   d. False, sentence 6

3. The victim was Victor O'Toole from Chicago.
   a. True, sentence 11
   b. True, sentence 13
   c. False, sentence 14
   d. False, sentence 15

4. There were several witnesses.
   a. True, sentences 6, 7, and 8
   b. True, either sentence 15 or sentences 15-23
   c. False, sentence 9
   d. False, sentence 10

5. Detective Wise got the call at 5 a.m.
   a. True, sentence 7
   b. True, sentence 8
   c. False, sentence 4
   d. False, sentence 16

6. James Taylor had been in a car following the victim's.
   a. True, sentences 6-9
   b. True, sentences 10-15
   c. False, sentences 16-24
   d. False, sentences 25-27

7. Sixteen cars were involved in the pileup.
   a. True, sentences 6-9
   b. True, sentences 10-15
   c. False, sentence 6
   d. False, sentences 25-27

8. The accident took place on Wilshire Boulevard.
    a. True, sentence 1
    b. True, sentence 6
    c. False, sentence 11
    d. False, sentence 16

9. Norma Hernandez was one of the witnesses.
    a. True, sentences 6-9
    b. True, sentences 16-24
    c. False, sentences 1-5
    d. False, sentences 25-27

10. No gun was found in the victim's car.
    a. True, sentence 7
    b. True, sentence 9
    c. False, sentence 11
    d. False, sentence 12

2.19 Review Exercise Circle the best answer for each claim of fact written about Case 7.

1. **Example:**
    There was a small hole in the windshield of one car and a corresponding hole in the driver's forehead.
    (a.) **Verified in the story.**
    b. Verifiable, but no observational evidence in Case 7.
    c. Not verifiable with observational evidence.

2. The victim's driver's license said he was Victor O'Toole from Chicago.
    a. Verified in the story.
    b. Verifiable, but no observational evidence in Case 7.
    c. Not verifiable with observational evidence.

3. Edith Taylor wore glasses.
    a. Verified in the story.
    b. Verifiable, but no observational evidence in Case 7.
    c. Not verifiable with observational evidence.

4. A gun was found in the victim's car.
    a. Verified in the story.
    b. Verifiable, but no observational evidence in Case 7.
    c. Not verifiable with observational evidence.

(Continued)

5. Detective Wise had not yet eaten supper.
    a. Verified in the story.
    b. Verifiable, but no observational evidence in Case 7.
    c. Not verifiable with observational evidence.

6. The victim had false teeth.
    a. Verified in the story.
    b. Verifiable, but no observational evidence in Case 7.
    c. Not verifiable with observational evidence.

7. The victim had been daydreaming just before the accident.
    a. Verifiable, sentence 6.
    b. Verifiable, but we need more observational evidence.
    c. Not verifiable by any observational evidence.

8. There were several witnesses to the pileup.
    a. Verified in the story.
    b. Verifiable, but no observational evidence in Case 7.
    c. Not verifiable with observational evidence.

9. The victim, Victor O'Toole, was going to turn himself to the police in for bank robbery.
    a. Verified in the story.
    b. Verifiable, but no observational evidence in Case 7.
    c. Not verifiable with observational evidence.

10. Only the medical examiner can say for sure what the angle of the shot was and where it came from.
    a. Verified in the story.
    b. Verifiable, but no observational evidence in Case 7.
    c. Not verifiable with observational evidence.

2.20 Review Exercise Circle the best answer for each Case 7 claim of fact. Supply the best sentence evidence for your answer if asked.

1. **Example:**
    The victim's name was Victor O'Toole.
    (a.) **Proven true with sentence 11 as evidence.**
    b. Proven false with sentence _____ as evidence.
    c. Cannot be proven true or false with the evidence in Case 7.

2. Six cars were involved in the pileup.
    a. Proven true with sentence 6 as evidence.
    b. Proven false with sentence _____ as evidence.
    c. Cannot be proven true or false with the evidence in Case 7.

3. The victim was dead when the police arrived.
    a. True with evidence from sentence _____ as evidence.
    b. False with evidence from sentence _____ as evidence.
    c. Cannot be proven true or false with evidence from Case 7.

4. The victim's car surged ahead, causing the pileup.
    a. Proven true with sentences 9, 23 as evidence.
    b. Proven false with sentence _____ as evidence.
    c. Cannot be proven true or false with the evidence in Case 7.

5. There was a pileup of nine cars late in the afternoon on Wilshire.
    a. Proven true with sentence _____ as evidence.
    b. Proven false with sentence 6 as evidence.
    c. Cannot be proven true or false with the evidence in Case 7.

6. There were three witnesses to the pileup.
    a. Proven true with sentences 15-20 as evidence.
    b. Proven false with sentence _____ as evidence.
    c. Cannot be proven true or false with the evidence in Case 7.

7. Detective Wise did not come to the accident scene.
    a. Proven true with sentence _____ as evidence.
    b. Proven false with sentence 5 as evidence.
    c. Cannot be proven true or false with the evidence in Case 7.

8. Detective Wise trusts the medical examiner.
    a. Proven true with sentence 25 as evidence.
    b. Proven false with sentence _____ as evidence.
    c. Cannot be proven true or false with the evidence in Case 7.

9. Two witnesses saw the victim's car surge ahead, causing the pileup.
    a. Proven true with sentences 17, 23 as evidence.
    b. Proven false with sentence _____ as evidence.
    c. Cannot be proven true or false with the evidence in Case 7.

10. Three persons were dead in the pileup.
    a. Proven true with sentence _____ as evidence.
    b. Proven false with sentence 10 as evidence.
    c. Cannot be proven true or false with the evidence in Case 7.

11. Victor O'Toole has three children.
    a. Proven true with sentence _____ as evidence.
    b. Proven false with sentence _____ as evidence.
    c. Cannot be proven true or false with the evidence in Case 7.

(Continued)

12. Detective Wise arrived at 6 a.m. to see the crime scene.
   a. Proven true with sentence _____ as evidence.
   b. Proven false with sentence 4 as evidence.
   c. Cannot be proven true or false with the evidence in Case 7.

2.21 Review Exercise Which of these Case 7 claims of fact can be proven conclusively true or conclusively false by definition or principles of mathematics?   Circle the correct answer.

1. **Example:**
   If three shots were fired from the tree, then at least one shot was fired from the tree.
   (a.) **Conclusively true by mathematics**
   b. Conclusively true by definition
   c. Conclusively false by mathematics
   d. Conclusively false by definition

2. If three shots were fired from the tree, then at least two shots came from the direction of the tree.
   a. Conclusively true by mathematics
   b. Conclusively true by definition
   c. Conclusively false by mathematics
   d. Conclusively false by definition

3. If Homer Price was jogging, then he was moving.
   a. Conclusively true by mathematics
   b. Conclusively true by definition
   c. Conclusively false by mathematics
   d. Conclusively false by definition

4. If Stephanie Wise is a police detective, then she works for a police department.
   a. Conclusively true by mathematics
   b. Conclusively true by definition
   c. Conclusively false by mathematics
   d. Conclusively false by definition

5. If Detective Wise works for the LAPD, then she is a police officer.
   a. Conclusively true by mathematics
   b. Conclusively true by definition
   c. Conclusively false by mathematics
   d. Conclusively false by definition

6. If there were three witnesses, five survivors of the accident, and three police officers on the scene, then there were at least eleven people on the scene.
   a. Conclusively true by mathematics
   b. Conclusively true by definition
   c. Conclusively false by mathematics
   d. Conclusively false by definition

7. If six people were involved in the accident and only one was killed, then five people survived the accident.
   a. Conclusively true by mathematics
   b. Conclusively true by definition
   c. Conclusively false by mathematics
   d. Conclusively false by definition

8. If Norma Hernandez saw a flash of light before the accident, then the accident occurred after the flash of light.
   a. Conclusively true by mathematics
   b. Conclusively true by definition
   c. Conclusively false by mathematics
   d. Conclusively false by definition

9. If a shooter was in the tree, then a gun shot from the tree would make some sound or have a flash of light.
   a. Conclusively true by mathematics
   b. Conclusively true by definition
   c. Conclusively false by mathematics
   d. Conclusively false by definition

Chapter 2 Quiz

Choose the best answer for each of the following questions.

1. Claims of fact:
   a. are neither true nor false.
   b. are always expressed by declarative sentences.
   c. are either true or false, even if it is unknown whether they are true or false.
   d. are always either true or false, and one always knows the truth value of a claim.

2. If I know that Detective Wise works for the Los Angeles Police Department, then:
   a. she works for the Los Angeles Police Department.
   b. she works for the Los Angeles Police Department and there is no evidence that she works for the Los Angeles Police Department.
   c. there is evidence that she works for the Los Angeles Police Department even if she does not work for the Los Angeles Police Department.
   d. she drives an unmarked car.

3. It is just my opinion that Detective Wise is a remarkable person because:
   a. I have never met Detective Wise.
   b. Detective Wise solves most of her cases.
   c. I do not have enough evidence to show that she solves most of her cases.
   d. there are no clear criteria for determining what makes a person remarkable.

4. If a mathematical claim is true:
   a. it tells you things about the observable world without having to make observations.
   b. it provides reasons to believe that your opinions are true.
   c. it only states someone's opinion.
   d. it is always true.

5. If it is a fact that Detective Wise lives on Venice Boulevard, then:
   a. there can be evidence that she lives on Venice Boulevard.
   b. someone must believe she lives on Venice Boulevard.
   c. it is only someone's opinion that she lives on Venice Boulevard.
   d. someone has to know that she lives on Venice Boulevard.

6. If the claim, "Sadie Gonzalez shot Elmo Dubcek," is true now:
   a. it will always be true in the future.
   b. it always has been true.
   c. its truth depends on mathematical considerations.
   d. its truth is known by observation.

7. Observational evidence is:
   a. always known to be true.
   b. usually supported by mathematical evidence.
   c. rests upon the meanings of words.
   d. based on seeing, hearing, touching, tasting, and smelling.

8. If two claims are inconsistent, then:
    a. both claims can be true.
    b. both claims must be false.
    c. at most, one of the two claims is true.
    d. at most, one of the two claims is false.

9. If there is evidence that a claim is true, then:
    a. the claim is true.
    b. there is some reason to believe the claim is true, even if the claim is false.
    c. there is some reason to believe that the claim is false.
    d. the truth of the claim is known.

10. If there is some evidence that Victor O'Toole was the victim of a shooting, then:
    a. there always will be evidence that Victor O'Toole was the victim of a shooting.
    b. Victor O'Toole was the victim of a shooting.
    c. there could be other evidence that Victor O'Toole was not the victim of a shooting.
    d. there always has been evidence that Victor O'Toole was the victim of a shooting.

CHAPTER 3

- Ambiguity
- Descriptions
- Explanations
- Review

Overview

A critical thinker strives for clarity and avoids ambiguity.

A critical thinker strives for accurate descriptions of facts and events in the world.   Who is involved? What happened?

A critical thinker strives to arrive at the best explanation for an event in the world.

CASE 8

City of Los Angeles Police Department

[1]When she got home from shopping at 8:30 a.m., Mrs. Green found this note where her dog should have been. [2]Print from a newspaper had been glued to a piece of paper.

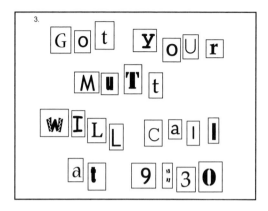

3.
Got Your
MuTt
WILL call
at 9:30

[4]Mrs. Green called the police. [5]Detective Wise arrived at the Green residence at 9:05 a.m.

[6]Mrs. Green was a 5 foot, 90-year-old woman. [7]The missing dog, Fluffy, was a 5-year-old Rottweiler. [8]Mrs. Green cried, "It's just terrible! [9]There are two sentences, but there are no subject terms, no periods, and they use *got* rather than *have*! [10]To what is the world coming?"

[11]Detective Wise, a bit puzzled, comforted the elderly woman as they waited for the call. [12]By shortly after 10:00 Detective Wise concluded the call was not coming. [13]"Perhaps they meant 9:30 tonight," she said.

[14]Before she left, Detective Wise examined the scene of the crime. [15]Fluffy lived in a large doghouse. [16]It was surrounded by tightly packed dirt. [17]There were neither fingerprints nor footprints.

[18]The call came at 9:31 p.m. [19]A voice said, "We want $25,000 in small unmarked bills. [20]Leave it in a brown paper bag along 6th Street in MacArthur Park at 10:00 tomorrow night. [21]No cops or the dog is dead!"

[22]Mrs. Green replied, "I don't have $25,000 in small bills. [23]All my small bills—and most of my large ones—are marked 'Paid.' [24]Slip a cashier's check for $30,000 through my mail slot by noon tomorrow and then I'll talk about taking the dog back." [25]She slammed down the receiver.

[26]She explained, "Fluffy is my daughter, Sheila's, dog. [27]She left Fluffy here for the weekend—more than four and a half years ago. [28]That monster almost ate me out of house and home! [29]And they want me to *pay* to get it *back*? [30]I'm tired of young punks trying to pull my chain!"

[31]Detective Wise was speechless.

3.1 Ambiguity and Vagueness

To determine whether a claim of fact (factual claim) is true or false, you must understand what is claimed. This can be difficult if the claim is ambiguous or vague.

A word or phrase is *ambiguous* if it has more than one meaning and we do not know which meaning is intended. We are talking about words such as light, race, left, or hot. For example, if Jim says, "Sally is hot," does he mean she is great looking or does he mean she is physically hot? What we have here is a mix-up of meaning. The same thing can happen with phrases.

Examples of ambiguous words and phrases in Case 8:

a.	In the note, *9:30* could mean 9:30 a.m. or 9:30 p.m.
b.	*Bills* could mean paper money or claims of money owed.
c.	*Pulling my chain* could be taken as pulling on an actual chain or as trying to make someone do something.

3.2   Exercise Each claim below is written about Case 8 and contains an ambiguous word or phrase (underlined). Circle two possible meanings of the ambiguous word or phrase.

1. **Example:**
   What is missing is a <u>real dog</u>.
   (a.) **A four-legged animal that barks**
   (b.) **Something of inferior quality**
   c. A cat that eats dog food

2. Fluffy is a little <u>monster</u>.
   a. Naughty animal
   b. Friendly animal
   c. Frightening creature

3. Mrs. Green has a <u>short fuse</u>.
   a. Small garden hose
   b. Piece of electrical equipment
   c. Quick temper

4. Mrs. Green is an <u>animal</u>.
   a. Cartoon character
   b. Living being
   c. Wild character

5. Mrs. Green kept Flossy <u>on a short leash</u>.
   a. Short rope or strap to restrain a dog
   b. Restricted from doing many things
   c. Small vegetable

6. Mrs. Green was an <u>English teacher</u>.
   a. A bilingual teacher
   b. English citizen who is a teacher
   c. A person who teaches English

7. Fluffy was usually <u>in the doghouse</u>.
   a. Small outside structure for a dog
   b. Small kitchen
   c. Being punished

8. Fluffy was <u>free</u>.
   a. Able to move without restriction
   b. No money was paid to own the animal
   c. Unable to move

9. The thieves discovered that Mrs. Green was <u>mad</u>.
    a. Deaf
    b. Angered
    c. Crazy

10. Detective Wise said, "I want to <u>see the thieves in jail</u>."
    a. Catch them and imprison them
    b. Catch and release them
    c. Visit them in the jail

Sometimes the *context* of a claim can provide clues to the intended meaning.

Examples of ambiguous words and phrases in Case 8:

a.	In the note, *9:30* could mean 9:30 a.m. or 9:30 p.m. In this case it was impossible to tell whether the writer of the note meant 9:30 a.m. or 9:30 p.m., as Detective Wise discovered.
b.	*Bills* could mean paper money or claims of money owed. The thieves (sentence 19) wanted paper money; that's the typical desire of thieves. Mrs. Green's reply (sentences 21-22) sounds as if the concern was with claims of money owed.
c.	*Pulling my chain* could be taken as pulling on an actual chain or as trying to make someone do something. Given Mrs. Green's reply to the thieves, she almost certainly meant she did not want the thieves to tell her what to do.

3.3 **Exercise** Each claim below is about Case 8 and contains an ambiguous word or phrase (underlined). Using the context of Case 8, circle the most likely meaning.

1. **Example:**
   What is missing is a <u>real dog</u>.
   a. **A four-legged animal that barks**
   b. Something of inferior quality
   c. A cat that eats dog food

2. Fluffy is a little <u>monster</u>.
   a. Naughty animal
   b. Friendly animal
   c. Frightening creature

3. Mrs. Green has a <u>short fuse</u>.
   a. Small garden hose
   b. Piece of electrical equipment
   c. Quick temper

4. Mrs. Green is an <u>animal</u>.
   a. Cartoon character
   b. Living being
   c. Wild character

5. Mrs. Green kept Fluffy <u>on a short leash</u>.
   a. Short rope or strap to restrain a dog
   b. Restricted from doing many things
   c. Small vegetable

6. Mrs. Green was an <u>English teacher</u>.
   a. A bilingual teacher
   b. English citizen who is a teacher
   c. A person who teaches English

7. Fluffy was usually <u>in the doghouse</u>.
   a. Small outside structure for a dog
   b. Small kitchen
   c. Being punished

8. Mrs. Green received Fluffy for <u>free</u>.
   a. Able to move without restriction
   b. No money was paid to own the animal
   c. Unable to move

(Continued)

9. The thieves discovered that Mrs. Green was <u>mad</u>.
   a. Deaf
   b. Angered
   c. Crazy

10. Detective Wise said, "I want to <u>see the thieves in jail</u>."
    a. Catch them and imprison them
    b. Catch and release them
    c. Visit them in the jail

A *sentence* is **ambiguous** if it can be understood to make more than one claim. This is usually caused by a mistake in grammar, punctuation, faulty word order, or insufficient information (context).

Examples of ambiguous sentences in Case 8:

a.	"Detective Wise and Mrs. Green were looking in the doghouse." Were they outside the doghouse looking into it, or were they in the doghouse while looking? There is no way to tell. **Notice** that the problem is with the word *in*. Sometimes by changing a word (using *into* rather than *in*) or by adding a word one can eliminate the ambiguity.
b.	"Mrs. Green was sitting on a sofa with tired eyes." It probably means "Mrs. Green, with tired eyes, was sitting on a sofa." It could be taken to mean that the sofa has tired eyes, but sofas do not have eyes.
c.	Detective Wise told Mrs. Green that she made a mistake. Who made the mistake? Detective Wise or Mrs. Green?

3.4   Exercise Each ambiguous claim below is about Case 8. Using the context of Case 8, circle the most likely meaning.

1. **Example:**
    "The thieves stole the dog with some difficulty."
    a. **The thieves had trouble stealing the dog.**
    b. The dog the thieves stole was ill.

2. "The thieves wanted the money in MacArthur Park."
    a. The thieves wanted the money delivered to MacArthur Park.
    b. The thieves wanted the money people had lost in MacArthur Park while walking in the park.

3. "Riding in the back seat, the thieves drove the dog to their hideout."
    a. The thieves were in the back seat.
    b. The dog was in the back seat.

4. "Mrs. Green talked with the detective who was 90 years old."
    a. Mrs. Green is 90 years old.
    b. The detective is 90 years old

5. "Fluffy rode with the thieves with bared teeth."
    a. The dog bared its teeth.
    b. The thieves bared their teeth.

6. "Detective Wise looked at the doghouse with a puzzled expression."
    a. The doghouse had a puzzled face painted on it.
    b. The detective looked puzzled.

7. "While driving down Wilshire Boulevard, Fluffy attacked the thieves."
    a. The dog was driving the car.
    b. The thieves were driving the car.

8. "The thief muzzled Fluffy with a long beard."
    a. The thief had a beard.
    b. The dog had a beard.

9. "Mrs. Green celebrated the theft of her dog at 10:00 a.m."
    a. The dog was stolen at 10 a.m.
    b. The woman celebrated at 10 a.m.

10. "Detective Wise talked about Fluffy's disappearance in Mrs. Green's house."
    a. The dog disappeared in the house.
    b. Detective Wise and Mrs. Green talked together in the house about the dog's disappearance.

A word or phrase is *vague* if it has no *precise* meaning, but it has a blurry or fuzzy meaning instead. For example, the word "old" is vague. When do we label someone "old?" To a child seven years old, someone who is thirty is old, but to someone thirty, "old" might best describe someone sixty-five and older.

Vague words often concern imprecise size, measurements, distance, location, length, or anything else that can be measured exactly.

Sometimes being very precise is important. For example, if a witness knows that the dog was stolen between 8:00 and 8:30 in the morning but tells detective Wise, "The dog was stolen in the morning," the witness' statement is vague because it does not tell the precise time of the theft.

Examples of vague words in Case 8:

a.	"Shortly after 10:00" in sentence 12 is vague. One does not know how long after 10:00.
b.	"Fluffy lived in a large doghouse" (sentence 15). *Large* is vague.
c.	"Leave it [the money] in a brown paper bag along 6th Street in MacArthur Park at 10:00 tomorrow night" (sentence 20). *Along 6th Street* is vague: It does not tell one exactly where to leave the money.

Example of a word both ambiguous and vague:

a.	"Fluffy is a slow dog." The word "slow" is ambiguous in so far as it could mean slow in speed or mentally slow. It is vague because if Fluffy is slow in speed, then how slow is Fluffy? Or, if Fluffy is mentally slow, then how mentally deficient is she?

3.5   Exercise Each claim below is written about Case 8 and contains a vague word or phrase (underlined). Using the context of Case 8, circle the most likely meaning.

1. **Example:**
   The doghouse is <u>close</u> to the house.
   (a.) **Close could mean within a yard or within ten yards.**
   b. Close could mean inside the kitchen or in the basement.

2. Fluffy had been living with Mrs. Green for a <u>long time</u>.
   a. Long time could mean one year or 10 years.
   b. Long time could mean one minute or ten minutes.

3. Mrs. Green is an <u>old</u> woman.
   a. Old could mean 50 years old or 80 years old.
   b. Old could mean ancient Greece or ancient Rome.

4. The robbers wanted <u>a lot of</u> money.
   a. A lot of could mean $5.00 or $10.00.
   b. A lot of could mean $5,000.00 or $100,000.00.

5. Mrs. Green is not <u>tall</u>.
   a. Tall could mean 3'6" or 4'6".
   b. Tall could mean 5'10" or 6'2".

6. Fluffy had been tied to the doghouse by a <u>long</u> chain.
   a. Long could mean two feet or three feet.
   b. Long could mean 15 feet or 30 feet

7. <u>Many</u> detectives are careful reasoners.
   a. Many could mean eight or nine.
   b. Many could mean 50 or 100.

8. Detective Wise is <u>intelligent</u>.
   a. Intelligent could mean 100 or 105 IQ.
   b. Intelligent could mean 120 or 150 IQ.

9. Officer Parker was in the <u>doghouse</u>.
   a. Doghouse could mean a house for a dog.
   b. Doghouse could mean in trouble with someone.

10. Detective Wise is on another <u>hot</u> case.
    a. Hot could mean a high profile case.
    b. Hot could mean active, things are happening quickly.

CASE 9	City of Los Angeles Police Department

¹Nora Bates was dead. ²Her body was found in Silver Lake Reservoir. ³Whenever a dead body is found, a detective is called to investigate. ⁴Detective Wise arrived at 10:32 a.m.

⁵Nora Bates was 26. ⁶She was 5 feet, 3 inches tall and weighed about 120 pounds. ⁷She had lived at 10234 North Hobart Blvd. ⁸Her boyfriend, Jorge Gomez, had reported her missing about a week ago.

⁹At one time, Nora Bates probably had been attractive. ¹⁰But the left side of her face was crushed, and there were bruises on her arms and legs. ¹¹A week of decay had not helped, even if the water had slowed it. ¹²The officers at the scene were able to identify the body only because she had a tattoo on her left arm.

¹³Detective Wise called headquarters to see if there had been any recent boating accidents on Silver Lake Reservoir. ¹⁴None had been reported. ¹⁵She concluded that Nora had been the victim of foul play.

3.6 Descriptions

Claims of fact (factual claims) *describe* the world. They answer the questions Who? What? When? Where? and sometimes How? (they tell you how something is).

Descriptions often involve more than one claim. A description is *accurate* to the extent that it is composed of true claims. Accuracy is a matter of degree. One description of an event can be more accurate than another description of the same event.

Examples of descriptive claims in Case 9:

a.	"Nora Bates was dead" (sentence 1). This sentence tells one who is dead. It also tells one how Nora is (or what Nora's state of health is).
b.	"Detective Wise arrived at 10:32 a.m." (sentence 4). This sentence tells one who arrived and when she arrived.
c	"Her body was found in Silver Lake Reservoir" (sentence 2). This sentence tells one where Nora's body was found.

3.7 **Exercise** Answer the following questions about Case 9. Circle the best answer.

1. **Example:**
   Whose body was found in Silver Lake Reservoir?
   (a.) **Nora Bates's body was found in Silver Lake Reservoir.**
   b. Stephanie Wise's body was found in Silver Lake Reservoir.

2. How old was Nora Bates?
   a. Nora was 22.
   b. Nora was 26.

3. How tall was Nora Bates?
   a. Nora was 6 feet, 3 inches tall.
   b. Nora was 5 feet, 3 inches tall.

4. How many pounds did Nora Bates weigh?
   a. Nora weighed about 110 pounds.
   b. Nora weighed about 120 pounds.

5. Where did Nora Bates live?
   a. She had lived at 10234 North Hobart Blvd.
   b. She had lived at 10243 South Hobart Blvd.

6. What was the condition of Nora's body when it was found?
   a. The left side of her face was crushed, and there were bruises on her arms and legs.
   b. The right side of her face was crushed, and there were bruises on her arms and legs.

7. What was Nora's boyfriend's name?
   a. His name was Paul Gomez.
   b. His name was Jorge Gomez.

8. About how long had Nora been missing?
   a. She has been missing about a month.
   b. She had been missing about a week.

9. What was the condition of Nora's body when it was found?
   a. There were bruises on her arms and legs.
   b. The left side of her face was crushed, and there were bruises on her arms and legs.

10. How did the police identify the body?
    a. The police identified her body from the engraved bracelet on her wrist.
    b. The police identified her body from the tattoo on her left arm.

CASE 10	City of Los Angeles Police Department

[1]There was a robbery at the 7-Eleven at 1913 Colorado Blvd. [2]The robber, 20-year-old Dan Nelson, pulled a gun on the cashier and demanded cash. [3]The store's owner, Jeff Lee, was in the restroom when the robbery occurred. [4]He came out, saw what was happening, pulled a gun, and shot the robber with a tranquilizer dart. [5]Nelson collapsed and was taken away by the police minutes later. [6]No one was injured.

[7]Detective Wise tried to understand why Nelson had pulled the robbery. [8]Usually robbers need money. [9]Often they live in one of the poorer parts of the city. [10]Nelson was a junior at UCLA. [11]His family's home was in Beverly Hills, and he had more than $15,000 in his checking account. [12]There was no evidence he was a drug user. [13]Did he pull it just for the thrill? [14]Or was it part of something bigger?

[15]Within ten minutes of the time Nelson hit the 7-Eleven, there were robberies at 20 convenience stores in the area. [16]All the robbers were described as young. [17]The other two robbers who were caught were also UCLA students. [18]While the police were responding to those calls, there was a robbery at Union Bank of California at 6301 N Figueroa. [19]The robbers got away with more than two million dollars in cash and securities. [20]Could there have been an elaborate plot? [21]Could the robberies at the mom-and-pop stores have been a distraction?

[22]Nelson and the others refused to speak.

3.8 Explanations

Explanations answer the questions "Why is something as it is?" or "How did something come to be?" or "How does one do something?"

Explanations search for the *cause* of an event. To provide an explanation, you try to uncover why or how the event occurred. Often there are several possible explanations of an event. In these cases, it is important to figure out the real (true) explanation.

There are several types of explanations including scientific, behavioral, and religious. Scientific explanations usually appeal to natural laws to explain events. Some explanations about human action appeal to the purpose, objective, or motive of a human being.

What counts as an acceptable explanation in a religious context usually will *not* count as an adequate explanation in a scientific context. What counts as an acceptable explanation must *always* be based on true explanatory claims.

Note: We examine explanations in greater detail in Chapter 7.

Examples of explanations in Case 10:

a.	"Jeff Lee shot the robber with a tranquilizer dart to stop the robbery" (sentences 3-4). This explains why Jeff shot the robber.
b.	"Dan Nelson could have pulled the robbery because he needed the money" (sentence 8). This is a possible explanation of why Dan robbed the 7-Eleven. Detective Wise rejected the explanation (sentence 11).
c.	When Dan Nelson explained why he had pulled the robbery, he said, "The devil made me do it." The police probably will not take this as an acceptable explanation, since there is not enough evidence for the existence of the devil. If there is good evidence that Dan really believes that the devil made him pull the robbery, the police probably will conclude that he has mental problems.
d.	"The neurons in Dan's brain caused reactions in the nerves and muscles of his body, which resulted in the gun pointing at the cashier." This is a rough scientific explanation of how Dan pointed the gun at the cashier.

3.9 Exercise The explanations below are written about Case 10. Circle the best answer.

1. **Example:**
   Dan Nelson robbed the 7-Eleven to obtain money to support his drug habit.
   a. Acceptable explanation because it would be a good motive for the robbery.
   (b.) **Unacceptable explanation because there is no evidence Dan was a drug user.**

2. Dan Nelson pulled the robbery just for the thrill of it.
   a. Acceptable explanation because it would be a good motive for the robbery.
   b. Unacceptable explanation because the robberies at the mom-and-pop stores were probably a distraction for the big bank robbery.

3. Jeff Lee shot Dan Nelson because Jeff wanted to kill Dan.
   a. Acceptable explanation because Jeff Lee was upset that his store was being robbed.
   b. Unacceptable explanation because Jeff Lee was only using a tranquilizer dart gun.

4. Union Bank of California was robbed because a UCLA club wanted to pull a prank.
   a. Acceptable explanation because many UCLA students were involved.
   b. Unacceptable explanation because robberies are crimes and much more serious than pranks.

5. Detective Wise was investigating the robberies because someone had called the police.
   a. Acceptable explanation because detectives are the ones called to investigate robberies.
   b. Unacceptable explanation because only patrol officers are the ones that investigate robberies.

6. Dan Nelson had more than $15,000 in his checking account because his family was well-to-do.
   a. Acceptable explanation because the wealth of the family would explain how a college student could have so much money.
   b. Unacceptable explanation because rich people always have excuses for having too much money in their bank accounts.

7. The robbery at Union Bank of California was successful because the police were responding to robberies at convenience stores.
   a. Acceptable explanation that links together all the evidence.
   b. Unacceptable explanation that shows prejudice against college students.

8. Dan Nelson's attempted robbery failed because the owner of the 7-Eleven gave him the evil eye.
   a. Acceptable explanation that gives a possible motive for stopping the robbery.
   b. Unacceptable explanation that introduces something that does not fit the evidence of a store owner defending his store.

9. The robbery at Union Bank of California was successful because each of the robbers carried a lucky silver dollar.
    a. Acceptable explanation because good luck could explain anything.
    b. Unacceptable explanation because good luck could explain anything.

10. The convenience store robberies were planned to keep police away from the robbery at Union Bank of California.
    a. Acceptable explanation because it fits with the evidence of all the robberies occurring about the same time.
    b. Unacceptable explanation because it assumes that events are causally connected simply because they occur about the same time.

CASE 11

City of Los Angeles Police Department

¹When Omar McGruder unlocked his jewelry store on Monday morning he noticed that his display cases were bare. ²They had been full when he closed on Saturday night. ³He called the police to report a robbery. ⁴It was Detective Wise's job to figure out who did it and how. ⁵So, after the crime scene investigators (CSI) gathered the evidence, she sat down to think.

⁶McGruder had an elaborate alarm system. ⁷He had only fifteen seconds after unlocking the door to disable the system. ⁸If anyone had tried to break in through the doors or windows, the alarm would have sounded, but it didn't. ⁹So, it's unlikely there was a break-in through the doors or windows. ¹⁰CSI also found no marks on the windows or doors, and there should have been marks if it was a typical burglary.

¹¹McGruder's building is similar to one on South Main where there was a burglary last year. ¹²There, the bad guys rented a room upstairs and came down through the air vents. ¹³There is an empty room above McGruder's store, and it wouldn't have taken more than a skeleton key to get into it. ¹⁴There'd be no marks of illegal entry, and the air vent could have been replaced after the job. ¹⁵But that still doesn't explain the alarm—breaking into the display cases should have triggered the alarm. ¹⁶The backs of the display cases had been shattered.

¹⁷Either it was a break-in, or it was an inside job. ¹⁸The facts about the alarm system spoke against a break-in. ¹⁹If it was an inside job, then either McGruder or one of his two employees, Freddy Fiero or Joyce Sanchez, had a hand in it. ²⁰They all had keys to the store and knew the code to disable the alarm. ²¹But Joyce was out. ²²She was in the middle of a two-week vacation at the Royal Lahaina Resort on Maui. ²³A quick investigation by the Hawaiian police gave good reason to believe she hadn't left the island. ²⁴Freddy Fiero, however, was missing. ²⁵He didn't show up for work. ²⁶His landlady hadn't seen him since late Saturday night, and his car was missing. ²⁷So, Freddy became Detective Wise's prime suspect.

²⁸Three days later, Freddy Fiero's body was found in his crumpled car in a canyon near Malibu. ²⁹It did not take the medical examiner to conclude that he'd been there for a while. ³⁰And McGruder was missing. ³¹Detective Wise revised her conclusion.

3.10 Arguments

An **argument** is a group of claims of which one or more of these claims (the premises) intend to provide support for one of the other claims (the conclusion).

Note: We will examine arguments in detail in the following chapters.

Examples of arguments in Case 11:

a.	**Premise:** If anyone had tried to break in through the doors or windows, the alarm would have sounded (sentence 8). **Premise:** The alarm did not sound (sentence 8). **Conclusion:** It is unlikely there was a break-in through the doors or windows (sentence 9).
b.	**Premise:** Either it was a break-in, or it was an inside job (sentence 17). **Premise:** It was not a break-in (sentence 18). **Conclusion:** It was an inside job.
c.	**Premise:** McGruder's building is similar to one on South Main where there was a burglary last year (sentence 11). **Premise:** In the South Main robbery the bad guys rented a room upstairs and came down through the air vents (sentence 12). **Premise:** There was an empty room above McGruder's store (sentence 13). **Conclusion:** There is some reason to believe the robbers came through the air vents from the room upstairs.
d.	**Premise:** If McGruder robbed his own store, that would explain all the facts. **Premise:** No other hypothesis we have now will explain all the facts. **Conclusion:** McGruder robbed his own store.

3.11 Exercise Each of the following is an argument about Case 11. Given the two premises, circle the conclusion that is supported.

1. **Example:**
   Premise: If it was an inside job, then either McGruder or Fiero or Sanchez did it.
   Premise: It was an inside job.
   Conclusion:
   (a.) **Either McGruder or Fiero or Sanchez did it.**
   b. Fiero did it.

2. Premise: Either McGruder or Fiero or Sanchez robbed the store.
   Premise: Sanchez didn't rob the store and it is unlikely that McGruder robbed the store
   Conclusion:
   a. Sanchez robbed the store.
   b. Fiero robbed the store.

3. Premise: If it was a break-in, then the alarm sounded; and if it was an inside job, then the alarm didn't sound.
   Premise: Either it was a break-in or it was an inside job
   Conclusion:
   a. Either it was an inside job or an outside job.
   b. Either the alarm sounded or it didn't sound.

4. Premise: If Sanchez was in Hawaii, then she didn't do the job.
   Premise: If Sanchez didn't do the job, then Fiero probably did the job.
   Conclusion:
   a. If Sanchez was in Hawaii, then Fiero probably did the job.
   b. If Fiero probably did the job, then Sanchez was in Hawaii.

5. Premise: If McGruder is innocent, then he's not missing; and if Fiero committed the crime, then he's not dead.
   Premise: Either McGruder is missing or Fiero is dead.
   Conclusion:
   a. Either McGruder is innocent or Fiero committed the crime.
   b. Either McGruder is not innocent or Fiero did not commit the crime.

6. Premise: The robbery at McGruder's store is like a robbery at a store on Wilshire.
   Premise: The robbery on Wilshire was committed by the owner.
   Conclusion:
   a. The robbery at McGruder's store was committed by its owner.
   b. The robbery at McGruder's store was not committed by its owner.

7. Premise: If Sanchez committed the crime, then she was in town over the weekend.
   Premise: Sanchez was not in town over the weekend.
   Conclusion:
   a. Sanchez committed the crime.
   b. Sanchez did not commit the crime.

8. Premise: Detective Wise is puzzled and McGruder is missing.
   Premise: If McGruder is missing, then he is the primary suspect.
   Conclusion:
   a. Detective Wise is the primary suspect.
   b. McGruder is the primary suspect.

9. Premise: If either McGruder or Sanchez committed the crime, then it was an inside job.
   Premise: It was not an inside job.
   Conclusion:
   a. Either McGruder or Sanchez committed the crime.
   b. Neither McGruder nor Sanchez committed the crime.

10. Premise: Either Sanchez committed the crime, or if it was an inside job, then McGruder committed the crime.
    Premise: Sanchez did not commit the crime, and it was an inside job.
    Conclusion:
    a. McGruder committed the crime.
    b. McGruder did not commit the crime.

CASE 12	City of Los Angeles Police Department

[1]Detective Wise was investigating a case. [2]She knew the following facts about the case: [3]Juan Ruiz is dead. [4]He had a small hole in the middle of his forehead. [5]No weapon had been found near the body. [6]Dr. Mendez, the medical examiner, had found no bullet during the autopsy. [7]A spike-heeled shoe with blood of the same type as the victim's was found in the alley near the victim's home. [8]Except on the body, no blood was found in the victim's apartment. [9]The hole in the forehead matched the shape of the shoe's heel. [10]The position of the body and the shape of the wound were similar to those of Gabriel Hernandez, who had been killed two weeks ago. [11]Hernandez had not been killed by a bullet.

[12]Given that Juan Ruiz is dead, and given that there was a hole in his forehead, his death was either an accident or suicide or murder.

[13]Since there was no blood in his apartment except on the body, we may conclude that it was not an accident. [14]For if it had been an accident, then there would have been blood somewhere in the apartment other than on his body.

[15]Given that Ruiz's death was not accidental, it follows that it was either suicide or murder. [16]But it couldn't have been suicide, since no weapon was found near the body. [17]So, it had to be murder.

[18]If the death was caused by a gunshot to the head and there was no exit wound, then a bullet should have been recovered at the autopsy. [19]There was no exit wound, but no bullet was recovered at the autopsy. [20]Therefore, it was not caused by a gunshot to the head.

[21]Since a spike-heeled shoe was found that had the victim's blood type on it, and since the heel matches the hole in the victim's head, it follows that the shoe was probably the murder weapon.

[22]Because the position of Ruiz's body was similar to the position of Hernandez's body, and inasmuch as the holes in their foreheads were similar in shape, and given that neither was killed by a bullet, it is likely that both were killed by the same person.

3.12 Recognizing Arguments: Finding Premises and Conclusions

There are words that *tend* to show that a claim is the premise or conclusion of an argument.
These are known as premise indicators and conclusion indicators.

Common Premise Indicators
since
because
for
as
due to
in light of
given (that)
assuming (that)
in view of the fact that
inasmuch as
insofar as

Argument

1. Juan Ruiz is dead.

2. It is given that there is a hole in
the middle of his forehead.

3. It follows that his death
was an accident, suicide, or
murder.

**Common
Conclusion Indicators**
therefore
thus
ergo that
hence
so
it is likely
consequently
accordingly
we may infer
I conclude that
proves that
as a result
for this reason
it follows that
is a reason to believe that*
is a reason to hold that*

*often preceded
by the premise

Indicator-words can identify an argument, but be careful, they are not always used. Sometimes indicator words are used in sentences that have nothing to do with argument; for example, they can also be used in explanations.

Since can refer to a past time.
  "Since she joined the LAPD, Stephanie Wise has become a detective."

Because can refer to a cause.
  "Stephanie Wise joined the police force because she wanted to make L.A. a safer place."

Important: Arguments are not explanations. Unlike explanations, arguments try to provide something; so, the premises intend to provide support for the conclusion. An explanation, however, explains why something is the way it is, how something came to be, or how we do something. There are no premises or conclusion. Sometimes, though, arguments and explanations overlap such as in the case of an *argument to the best explanation* (example a). We will look at this type of argument in more detail in Chapters 4 and 7.

Examples of arguments with indicator words noted in Case 12:
(premise-indicators are in boxes, conclusion-indicators are circled, and the conclusion is underlined)

a.	[Given] that Juan Ruiz is dead, and [given] that there was a hole in his forehead, <u>his death was either an accident or suicide or murder</u> (sentence 12). The premises provide reasons to believe that Ruiz either died accidentally or committed suicide or was murdered. It is *also* an explanation: Each of the three possible causes of death could explain how Ruiz died. It is an argument to the best explanation.
b.	[Since] there was no blood in his apartment except on the body, (we conclude) that <u>the death was not an accident</u>. [For] if it had been an accident, then there would have been blood somewhere in the apartment other than on his body (sentences 13-14).
c.	[Insofar as] the cause of Ruiz's death was either an accident or suicide or murder, and [given] that Ruiz's death was not an accident, (it follows) that <u>it was either suicide or murder</u> (the conclusion of the previous argument plus sentence 15).

3.13 Exercise Box the premise indicators, circle the conclusion indicators, and underline the conclusions for each argument about Case 12.

1. **Example:**

   (Therefore) it must have been a murder, [because] the shoe was not found near the body.

2. It couldn't have been suicide, since no weapon was found near the body.

3. Since it was either suicide or murder, and it wasn't suicide, hence, it was murder.

4. Assuming that Ruiz was awake when he was killed, there should have been signs of a struggle. Since there were no signs of a struggle, we must infer that Ruiz was not awake when he was killed.

5. Assuming Ruiz was killed in his sleep, it is likely that he died in bed.

6. If it is given that Ruiz died in bed, but his body was propped against the fireplace, we must conclude that the murderer moved the body.

7. As the law requires that an autopsy be performed if a doctor cannot declare the death was from a disease, and Dr. Mendez performed an autopsy, there is reason to believe that the death was not from a disease.

8. If the death was caused by a gunshot to the head and there was no exit wound, then a bullet should have been recovered at the autopsy. There was no exit wound, but no bullet was recovered at the autopsy. Therefore, it was not caused by a gunshot to the head.

9. Since a spike-heeled shoe was found that had blood of the victim's type on it, and since the heel matches the hole in the victim's head, it follows that the shoe was probably the murder weapon.

10. Because the position of Ruiz's body was similar to the position of Hernandez's body, and inasmuch as the holes in their foreheads were similar in shape, and given that neither was killed by a bullet, it is likely that both were killed by the same person.

CASE 13	City of Los Angeles Police Department

[1]On January 25, Hernando Garcia, president of Moyra Plastics, worked late in his office on the twenty-fifth floor of Wimberley Towers. [2]At 11:45, two men wearing ski masks entered his office. [3]"Get up and put your hands behind your head," said one of the men. [4]Before rising, Garcia hit a silent alarm button on his desk.

[5]The alarm sounded at the security center in the basement of the building. [6]Immediately the security team moved to lock down the building. [7]They turned off the elevators, moved to secure the four stairwells, and called the LAPD. [8]By 11:47, the twenty-fifth floor was sealed. [9]Anyone attempting to enter the stairwells would be greeted by four heavily armed security officers. [10]By 12:02, the building was swarming with police. [11]Detective Wise was the officer in charge.

[12]Detective Wise talked with DeForest Smidts, head of building security. [13]She asked, "How tight is after-hours security in this building?"

[14]Smidts replied, "It's good. [15]The Towers were built with security in mind. [16]After 6:00, anyone entering the building has to sign in in the lobby. [17]There are both key and key-pad locks on the stairwell doors to each floor and the door to the roof. [18]Even the heating ducts have six-inch-spaced steel bars every twelve feet. [19]And there are motion-sensors in the halls on each floor that are turned on at 6:00. [20]If anyone moves in the hall without disabling the sensors, we get a signal. [21]Cameras allow us to observe every inch of the halls."

[22]"What about the cleaning crew?" Detective Wise asked.

[23]At 12:16 a call came though to the security center. [24]The caller said, "We're the Blue Brigade. [25]We have Garcia. [26]You will transfer $100 million to a bank account number I shall give you. [27]You will fly us by helicopter to the L.A. Airport, and provide an executive jet to fly us to a destination I'll set once we're off the ground. [28]If the money isn't in place by 5:00, we'll blow up the building."

[29]Detective Wise knew something about the Blue Brigade. [30]In the last three months, they had kidnapped the heads of eight major corporations and demanded multi-million-dollar ransoms. [31]They hadn't taken hostages and stayed in a building. [32]This didn't fit the pattern. [33]Could it have been a kidnapping gone bad?

3.14 Review Exercise In each of the following sentences there is either an ambiguous word, a vague word, or the sentence itself is ambiguous. Circle the analysis of the sentence that removes the ambiguity in the sense most probably intended.

1. **Example:**
   Wimberley Towers is a tall building.
   a. **Wimberley Towers is thirty-five stories tall.**
   b. Wimberley Towers is a single-family home.

2. Members of the Blue Brigade thought their actions would be arresting.
   a. Members of the Blue Brigade thought their actions would put them in jail.
   b. Members of the Blue Brigade thought their actions would gain attention.

3. The building was swarming with police.
   a. The police were flying around like honey bees.
   b. The building was crowded with police milling about.

4. Mr. Garcia is on the 25th story.
   a. Mr. Garcia is on the 25th short story of a collection of short stories.
   b. Mr. Garcia is on the 25th floor of the building.

5. The person breaking into the room approached the man wearing a ski mask.
   a. The person breaking into the room wore a ski mask.
   b. The other person wore a ski mask.

6. Mr. Garcia and the masked men were on the floor.
   a. Mr. Garcia and the masked men were lying down on the floor.
   b. Mr. Garcia and the masked men were there on the 25th floor.

7. There is good security in Wimberley Towers.
   a. There are good locks in the building.
   b. There is not only a secret alarm system, but also a good response to the alarm system in the building.

8. Several members of the Blue Brigade were holding Mr. Garcia hostage.
   a. Several members of the Blue Brigade were holding Mr. Garcia by his hands.
   b. Several members of the Blue Brigade had made Mr. Garcia their captive.

9. Smidts reached forward for a light.
   a. Smidts reached forward to turn on a light switch.
   b. Smidts reached forward for a cigarette lighter or match.

10. Smidts came toward the detective with the building plans.
    a. Smidts had the building plans in his hands.
    b. The detective had the building plans in her hands.

(Continued)

11. Mr. Garcia stared at the masked man raising his hands.
    a. The masked man raised his hands.
    b. Mr. Garcia raised his hands.

12. Numerous police officers were in the building.
    a. Precisely how many police officers were in the building?
    b. Precisely how many police officers were on each floor of the building?

13. Detective Wise sat in a chair with legs crossed.
    a. Detective Wise crossed her legs as she sat.
    b. The legs of the chair were criss-cross.

14. Mr. Garcia stayed cool when the masked men came into his office.
    a. Mr. Garcia's body temperature did not rise.
    b. Mr. Garcia maintained his emotional calmness.

15. Mr. Garcia and the masked men are close to one another.
    a. Mr. Garcia and the masked men were physically within two feet of each other.
    b. Mr. Garcia and the masked men are blood relatives.

3.15 Review Exercise Read each question and circle the correct answer.

1. **Example:**
    When did the masked men approach Garcia?
    a. January 25 at 11:45 p.m., sentences 1 and 2
    b. February 4 at noon, sentence 5

2. Of what company was Hernando Garcia president?
    a. Moyra Plastics, sentence 1
    b. Flexible Plastics, sentence 2

3. Where was Hernando Garcia's office?
    a. 26th floor of Wimberly Towers, sentence 1
    b. 25th floor of Wimberly Towers, sentence 1

4. Who is head of security in the building?
    a. Samuel Smidts, sentence 10
    b. DeForest Smidts, sentence 12

5. How long did it take the security people to isolate the twenty-fifth floor?
    a. Five minutes, sentences 2 and 5
    b. Two minutes, sentences 2 and 8

6. Who was the police officer in charge of the police investigation?
    a. Detective Wise, sentence 11
    b. Detective Jones, sentence 23

7. Who heard the alarm?
    a. Detective Wise at the police station, sentence 15
    b. Security center in the basement, sentence 5

8. How did the members of the Blue Brigade want to leave the building?
    a. By helicopter, sentence 27
    b. By ropes, sentence 27

9. How large a ransom did the Blue Brigade demand?
    a. $10 million, sentence 30
    b. $100 million, sentence 26

10. How did the Blue Brigade want to collect the ransom?
    a. Transfer to a numbered bank account, sentence 26
    b. In $100 bills, sentence 26

3.16 Review Exercise The explanations below are written about Case 13. Circle the best answer.

1. **Example:**
    The masked men were able to get into Garcia's office because they'd stayed in the halls on the twenty-fifth floor after the building closed.
    a. Acceptable explanation because it tells how the masked men got into Garcia's office.
    (b.) Unacceptable explanation because the masked men would have been detected by the motion sensors.

2. The masked men got onto the twenty-fifth floor by posing as cleaning people.
    a. Acceptable explanation because a cleaning crew would have access to the building and its floors, whereas there seems to be no other way for the masked men to get into the building.
    b. Unacceptable explanation because it assumes there is no other way to get into the building and the 25th floor.

3. The masked men got into the building by shooting their way past the guard on the first floor.
    a. Acceptable explanation because it fits with the evidence of Case 13.
    b. Unacceptable explanation because it contradicts the clear evidence that there are no dead bodies.

(Continued)

4. The masked men were friends of Mr. Garcia and he gave them passes to the building. That's how they got onto the twenty-fifth floor.
    a. Acceptable explanation because it could explain how they got in without being detected.
    b. Unacceptable explanation because it doesn't fit with the evidence of Mr. Garcia sounding the silent alarm as soon as the masked men came into his office.

5. The masked men had no trouble getting into the building because Security Chief DeForest Smidts is part of the plot.
    a. Acceptable explanation because it would explain how the masked men escaped detection.
    b. Unacceptable explanation because it merely surmises what could have happened without any evidence that it did happen.

6. The masked men got into the building by stealing the photo identification cards of the twenty-fifth floor cleaners.
    a. Acceptable explanation because it fits with the evidence so far analyzed.
    b. Unacceptable explanation because it assumes that this explanation is the easiest way to explain how the masked men got into the building.

7. The masked men got into the building by kidnapping the twenty-fifth floor cleaners, stealing their photo identification cards, and putting their own pictures in the place of the cleaners' pictures.
    a. Acceptable explanation because it fits with the evidence so far analyzed.
    b. Unacceptable explanation because it assumes that this explanation is the easiest way to explain how the masked men got into the building.

8. The masked men had no trouble getting into the building because the whole thing is part of a security drill.
    a. Acceptable explanation because it fits with the evidence, especially with all the police swarming about.
    b. Unacceptable explanation because it does not fit with the evidence about high-profile kidnappings that have been occurring and because the masked men demand ransom money.

9. The masked men got onto the twenty-fifth floor by crawling through the heating ducts.
    a. Acceptable explanation because it explains how the masked men escaped detection.
    b. Unacceptable explanation because it doesn't fit with the evidence of the heating ducts having six inch bars every twelve feet that would block people from moving through the ducts.

10. The masked men got onto the twenty-fifth floor by climbing up the outside of Wimberley Towers and breaking through a window.
    a. Acceptable explanation because it explains how the men escaped detection so easily.
    b. Unacceptable explanation because there is no evidence of a broken window.

3.17 Review Exercise Each of the following is an argument about Case 13. Given the premises, circle the conclusion that is supported.

1. **Example:**
   Premise: Either it's the Blue Brigade or it's not.
   Premise: If it is the Blue Brigade, then it's unlikely they'd use explosives.
   Premise: If it's not the Blue Brigade, then we have no idea what we're up against.
   Conclusion:
   (a.) **Either it's unlikely they'd use explosives or we have no idea what we're up against.**
   b. The Blue Brigade does not use explosives.

2. Premise: It is unlikely that the Blue Brigade set up its raid over a period of more than a year.
   Premise: If the masked men had executive positions with some business in the building, the Blue Brigade would have had to plan the raid for more than a year.
   Conclusion:
   a. The masked men had executive positions with some business in the building.
   b. The masked men did not have executive positions with some business in the building.

3. Premise: The two people who clean the twenty-fifth floor were hired three weeks ago.
   Premise: If the two people who clean the twenty-fifth floor were hired three weeks ago, there might be a connection between the cleaners and hostage situation.
   Conclusion:
   a. The two people who clean the twenty-fifth floor were not hired three weeks ago.
   b. There might be a connection between the cleaners and hostage situation.

4. Premise: All activities of the Blue Brigade are illegal activities.
   Premise: Some kidnappings are activities of the Blue Brigade.
   Conclusion:
   a. All illegal activities are kidnappings.
   b. Some kidnappings are illegal activities.

5. Premise: No kidnappers are gentle people.
   Premise: Some members of the Blue Brigade are kidnappers.
   Conclusion:
   a. Some members of the Blue Brigade are not gentle people.
   b. Some gentle people are not members of the Blue Brigade.

6. Premise: No kidnappers are explosives experts.
   Premise: All members of the Blue Brigade are kidnappers.
   Conclusion:
   a. All members of the Blue Brigade are explosive experts.
   b. No members of the Blue Brigade are explosive experts.

(Continued)

7. Premise: At least one member of the Blue Brigade is a sharpshooter.
    Premise: Every sharpshooter always carries a gun.
    Conclusion:
    a. At least one member of the Blue Brigade always carries a gun.
    b. At least one member of the Blue Brigade does not always carry a gun.

8. Premise: No one who works late at his or her office expects to be kidnapped by terrorists.
    Premise: Mr. Garcia worked late at his office.
    Conclusion:
    a. Mr. Garcia did not expect to be kidnapped by terrorists.
    b. Mr. Garcia did expect to be kidnapped by terrorists.

9. Premise: If the Blue Brigade planned to kidnap Mr. Garcia, then the members of the Blue Brigade did not expect tight security at Wimberley Towers.
    Premise: If the Blue Brigade did not expect tight security at Wimberley Towers, then they were taken by surprise when the twenty-fifth floor was isolated.
    Conclusion:
    a. If the Blue Brigade planned to kidnap Mr. Garcia, then the members of the Blue Brigade were taken by surprise when the twenty-fifth floor was isolated.
    b. If the Blue Brigade planned to kidnap Mr. Garcia, then the members of the Blue Brigade were not taken by surprise when the twenty-fifth floor was isolated.

10. Premise: If DeForest Smidts is head of security and Detective Wise is on the case, then we can expect Mr. Garcia to be released.
    Premise: DeForest Smidts is head of security and Detective Wise is on the case.
    Conclusion:
    a. We can expect Mr. Garcia to be released.
    b. We cannot expect Mr. Garcia to be released.

3.18 Review Exercise Box the premise indicators, circle the conclusion indicators, and underline the conclusions for each argument about Case 13.

1. **Example:**
    Since we would have seen activity on the roof if they had landed on the roof, and we saw no activity on the roof, (it follows) that they did not land on the roof.

2. In each past case, the Blue Brigade kidnapped its victim. These people claim to be members of the Blue Brigade, but they are not kidnapping their victim. So it seems to follow that either they are not members of the Blue Brigade or it is a kidnapping that has gone bad.

3. Since the hostage situation is like the Blue Brigade kidnappings in numerous ways, and because they say they are the Blue Brigade, we may conclude that it is likely that the Blue Brigade took Mr. Garcia hostage.

4. Insofar as Detective Wise is on the case, it follows that the LAPD is interested in the outcome of the crisis. For Detective Wise is on the case only if the LAPD is interested in the outcome of the crisis.

5. There is a hostage crisis at Wimberley Towers. Therefore, the LAPD is on high alert, inasmuch as the LAPD is on high alert whenever there is a hostage crisis.

6. We must assume that if there were enough explosives in Wimberley Towers to destroy the building, cleaners on some of the floors would have reported finding them. But none of the cleaners reported finding explosives. Therefore, there are not enough explosives in Wimberley Towers to destroy the building.

7. Due to the fact that the masked men are isolated on the twenty-fifth floor, we may infer that they are desperate men, for there is no way for them to escape.

8. Desperate men often take big risks. Hence, Mr. Garcia is in a dangerous situation, in light of the fact that he is being held by desperate men.

9. Assuming the Blue Brigade is holding the hostage, it seems to follow that it is a kidnapping that was interrupted, for the Blue Brigade always kidnapped its hostages.

10. From the fact that it is unlikely that the masked men can blow up the building, and as there is only one person held hostage, we may infer that the masked men will not get a helicopter ride to the Los Angeles Airport.

Chapter 3 Quiz

Choose the best answer for each of the following questions.

1. A word is ambiguous if it:
    a. has more than one meaning.
    b. is nonsensical.
    c. has no clear meaning.
    d. states a precise quantity.

2. A word is vague if it:
    a. has more than one meaning.
    b. is nonsensical.
    c. is precise.
    d. has no clear meaning.

3. In an argument:
    a. the conclusion is known or assumed to be true before the premises are known to be true.
    b. the premises are known or assumed to be true before the conclusion is known to be true.
    c. at least two people disagree with each other.
    d. the event to be explained must be clearly described.

4. The words since, because, and for are:
    a. words used to show locations in time.
    b. words used to describe events.
    c. conclusion-indicators.
    d. premise-indicators.

5. If a paragraph tells how something is, it is:
    a. an argument.
    b. an explanation.
    c. a description.
    d. an emotional claim.

6. If a paragraph tells how something came to be, it is:
    a. an argument.
    b. an explanation.
    c. a description.
    d. a factual claim.

7. Before one can determine whether a claim is true or false, one needs to:
    a. determine the meanings of ambiguous words.
    b. clarify the meanings of vague words.
    c. determine which of several claims might be meant by an ambiguous sentence.
    d. all of the above

8. An explanation tells one:
    a. what or how something is.
    b. who or where someone is.
    c. when something happened, where someone or something is, or how something is.
    d. why something is as it is, how to do something, or how something came to be as it is.

9. The premises of an argument:
    a. give evidence that some claim, the conclusion, is true.
    b. explain why some event occurred.
    c. are always true claims.
    d. both a and c

10. Words that are sometimes called conclusion-indicators:
    a. are words that follow the premises of an argument.
    b. are words that appear only in arguments.
    c. are words that sometimes occur before the conclusion of an argument.
    d. are words that always can be used to find the conclusion of an argument.

CHAPTER 4

- Valid Arguments
- Invalid Arguments
- Review

Overview

An argument is valid if its conclusion must be true when its premises are true.

An argument is invalid if its conclusion could be false when its premises are true.

CASE 14

City of Los Angeles Police Department

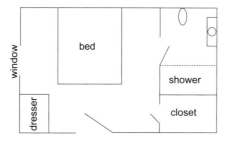

¹Emily Dorn was the victim of foul play. ²She had been attacked. ³Her valuables had been stolen from her room. ⁴But it appears that no one could have broken into her room.

⁵Emily Dorn had been a guest at the Clarke Mansion. ⁶Since the party the previous evening had lasted into the wee hours of the morning, no one was surprised by her absence at brunch. ⁷When she still had not appeared by late in the afternoon, her fiancé, John Clarke, became concerned. ⁸He found that the door to her room was locked and bolted from the inside. ⁹Repeated knocks on the door yielded no response. ¹⁰Giles, the butler, took a ladder and climbed to her third-floor window. ¹¹The window was locked. ¹²He saw that Ms. Dorn was tied to a chair, apparently unconscious. ¹³The room was a mess. ¹⁴Giles returned to the house and called the police.

¹⁵After Detective Wise arrived, the patrol officers forced open the door to the room. ¹⁶Ms. Dorn's breathing and heartbeat were slow but regular. ¹⁷Attempts to revive her were unsuccessful. ¹⁸She was rushed by ambulance to Cedars-Sinai Hospital.

¹⁹There had been a robbery. ²⁰The room had been ransacked. ²¹Her wallet and credit cards were missing. ²²The diamond and emerald necklace Ms. Dorn had worn at the party was nowhere in the room.

²³Dr. Andrea Schmidt reported her medical findings to Detective Wise. ²⁴"Ms. Dorn had been given a large dose of flurazepam. ²⁵She should be coming around within the next few hours."

²⁶"Either it was a robbery or she faked the theft," Detective Wise reasoned. ²⁷"Since she couldn't have bound herself to the chair and the syringe that administered the drug was not found in the room, she couldn't have faked the theft. ²⁸So, it had to be a robbery. ²⁹But if it was a robbery, someone had to enter the room. ³⁰But the room was locked and bolted from the inside. ³¹So, no one could get in. ³²So, it couldn't have been a robbery."

³³"One of my premises has to be false," concluded Detective Wise.

4.1 Valid and Invalid Arguments

Valid Arguments

Every argument is either valid or invalid. An argument is **valid** if it is impossible for all its premises to be true and its conclusion false. Any argument that is not valid is **invalid**.

Valid arguments have a perfect form because whenever all their premises are true, their conclusions are true.

If an argument is valid, it does not guarantee the argument's conclusion is true. A valid argument only guarantees that if all the premises are true, then the argument's conclusion is true.

Invalid Arguments

An argument's invalidity does *not* show that the argument provides no evidence for its conclusion. Many of the arguments we use every day—including many of the arguments in the sciences—are invalid. An argument's invalidity means *only* it is possible that all the argument's premises are true and its conclusion is false. Some invalid arguments provide *very good evidence* for the truth of their conclusions—but they do not guarantee the truth of the conclusion.

Valid arguments

An argument is valid if its conclusion must be true when its premises are true.

Example

Premise 1: If it is a whale, then it has a tail.
Premise 2*: It is a whale.
Conclusion: So, it has a tail.

*The standard practice is to separate the premises from the conclusion by drawing a line.

Invalid Arguments

An argument is invalid if it is possible for all its premises to be true and its conclusion false.

Example

Premise 1: Robins are birds.
Premise 2: Robins can fly.
Conclusion: So, all birds can fly.

Examples of valid and invalid arguments in Case 14:

a.	All suspects are people who were at the party. All the Clarke Mansion servants are suspects. So, all the Clarke Mansion servants are people who were at the party.	The argument is *valid* and its premises are true.
b.	No suspects attended the party. All the Clarke Mansion servants are suspects. So, no Clarke Mansion servants attended the party.	The argument is *valid* but the first premise and the conclusion are false.
c.	If John Clarke committed the crime, then he knew of a secret way into the room. John Clarke committed the crime. So, John Clarke knew of a secret way into the room.	The argument is *valid*. We do not know whether the second premise is true. So, we do not know whether the conclusion is true.

(Continued)

d.	The Clarke Mansion is like the Heath Mansion. They were designed by the same architect who is known for designing secret passages within most of his homes. They were both built in the nineties in the hills outside of L.A. The Heath Mansion contains secret passages. ——— So, the Clarke Mansion contains secret passages.	The argument is *invalid*. Even if the premises are true, they do not guarantee the truth of the conclusion. The evidence that the mansions are alike in some ways does not guarantee they are alike in others.
e.	John Clarke went to the party, and he is wealthy. Emily Dorn went to the party, and she is wealthy Judith St. James went to the party, and she is wealthy. Claus Hernandez went to the party, and he is wealthy. ——— So, everyone who went to the party is wealthy.	The argument is *invalid*. Even if the premises are true, they do not guarantee the truth of the conclusion. The evidence that several wealthy people went to the party does not guarantee that everyone who went to the party was wealthy.

4.2   Exercise Are the following arguments valid or invalid? Assume the premises are true. Circle the correct answer.

1. **Example:**
   If Emily Dorn was found unconscious in her room, then she was robbed.
   Emily Dorn was found unconscious in her room.
   So, Emily Dorn was robbed.
   (a.) **The argument is valid.**
   b. The argument is invalid.

2. John Clarke was at the party, and he was not robbed.
   Giles, the butler, was at the party, and he was not robbed.
   Mary, the maid, was at the party, and she was not robbed.
   So, no one at the party was robbed.
   a. The argument is valid.
   b. The argument is invalid.

3. If Emily Dorn was bound to a chair, then she didn't commit the crime.
   Emily Dorn was bound to a chair.
   So, Emily Dorn didn't commit the crime.
   a. The argument is valid.
   b. The argument is invalid.

4. If there was a secret entrance into Emily's room, that would explain how
   the robber got into and out of what appears to be a locked room.
   So, it is likely that there is a secret entrance into Emily's room.
   a. The argument is valid.
   b. The argument is invalid.

5. If John Clarke knows about the secret passages in the house, then he can move around
   without being seen.
   If John Clarke can move around without being seen, then he could have committed
   the crime.
   So, if John Clarke knows about the secret passages in the house,
   then he could have committed the crime.
   a. The argument is valid.
   b. The argument is invalid.

6. None of the Clarke Mansion servants had access to the guest rooms after 9:30 on the
   night of the party.
   Mary, the maid, is one of the Clarke Mansion servants.
   So, Mary, the maid, did not have access to the guest rooms after 9:30 on the night of
   the party.
   a. The argument is valid.
   b. The argument is invalid.

(Continued)

7. Giles, the butler, and Mary, the maid, are similar insofar as they both work for John Clarke.
    Giles, the butler, looked into Emily Dorn's room while standing on a ladder.
    So, Mary, the maid, looked into Emily Dorn's room while standing on a ladder.
    a. The argument is valid.
    b. The argument is invalid.

8. John Clarke lives in Clarke Mansion, and he attended the party.
    Giles, the butler, lives in Clarke Mansion, and he attended, the party.
    Mary, the maid, lives in Clarke Mansion, and she attended the party.
    So, everyone who lives in Clarke Mansion attended the party.
    a. The argument is valid.
    b. The argument is invalid.

9. If John Clarke committed the crime, then he owns Clarke Mansion.
    John Clarke owns Clarke Mansion.
    So, John Clarke committed the crime.
    a. The argument is valid.
    b. The argument is invalid.

10. If John Clarke knew how to get into Emily's locked room, then he committed the crime; and if Mary, the maid, knew how to get into Emily's locked room, then she committed the crime.
    Either John Clarke did not commit the crime or Mary, the maid, did not commit the crime.
    So, either John Clarke or Mary, the maid, did not know how to get into Emily's locked room.
    a. The argument is valid.
    b. The argument is invalid.

4.3 Argument Forms

The form of an argument is its structure. The form of argument is like the design of a house. Many houses have the same design. Similarly, many arguments have the same form.

Argument A:
Either Joe went to the store or Bob went to the store.
Joe did not go to the store.
Therefore, Bob went to the store.

Argument's form:

> Either p or q.
> Not p.
> q.

We replace the argument's claims with letters (variables) to represent the argument's form.

Argument with the same form as argument A:
Either the murderer will get away with the crime or Detective Wise will solve the crime.
The murderer will not get away with the crime.
Therefore, Detective Wise will solve the crime.

> Either p or q.
> Not p.
> q.

Argument B:
If Emily Dorn faked the robbery, then she could have tied herself to the chair.
She could not have tied herself to the chair.
Therefore, Emily Dorn did not fake the robbery.

> If p, then q.
> Not q.
> Not p.

Argument of the same form as argument B:
If Giles committed the robbery, then he knew of a secret passage into the room.
Giles did not know of a secret passage into the room.
Therefore, Giles did not commit the robbery.

> If p, then q.
> Not q.
> Not p.

Argument C:
Both Emily and John were at the party last night.
Therefore, Emily was at the party last night.

p and q.
p.

Argument of the same form as argument C:
Both John and Giles were present for brunch.
Therefore, John was present for brunch.

p and q.
p.

Valid Argument

Remember, validity is a property of an argument's **form**. An argument is valid if its conclusion must be true when its premises are true.

Sound Argument

A valid argument with true premises is known as a **sound argument**. An argument is **unsound** if it is invalid, or one or more of its premises is false, or both.

Sound Arguments	Unsound Arguments	
All valid arguments with true premises	Valid arguments with a false premise	All invalid arguments

Deduction and Induction

A **deductive argument** is just another term for a valid argument. An **inductive argument** is an invalid argument. The strength of an invalid (inductive) argument is measured by the ability of its premises to support its conclusion.

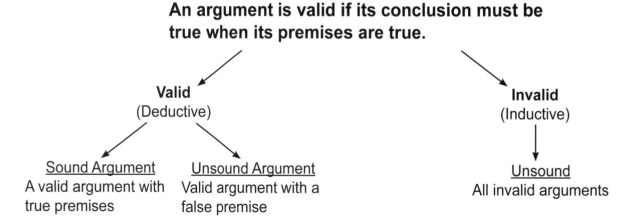

An argument is valid if its conclusion must be true when its premises are true.

Valid
(Deductive)

Invalid
(Inductive)

Sound Argument
A valid argument with true premises

Unsound Argument
Valid argument with a false premise

Unsound
All invalid arguments

4.4 Exercise Circle the argument form that best represents each argument. Writing the form of the argument is often helpful, but it is not required.

1. **Example:**
   If there is a secret passage into the room, then the dresser hides a staircase.
   There is a secret passage into the room.
   So, the dresser hides a secret staircase.

   If p, then q.
   p.
   —
   q.

   (a.) **If p, then q.**
   p.
   —
   q.

   b. If p, then q.
   Not q.
   —
   Not p.

   c. If p, then q.
   q.
   —
   p.

   d. If p, then q.
   Not p.
   —
   Not q.

2. If it was a murder, then someone entered the room.
   No one entered the room.
   —
   So, it was not a murder

   a. If p, then q.
   p.
   —
   q.

   b. If p, then q.
   Not q.
   —
   Not p.

   c. If p, then q.
   q.
   —
   p.

   d. If p, then q.
   Not p.
   —
   Not q.

3. If the case provides a locked-room problem,
   then there is a secret passage into the room.
   If there is a secret passage into the room,
   then not everything is as it appears to be.
   —
   So, if the case provides a locked-room problem,
   then not everything is as it appears to be.

   a. If p, then q.
   If not q, then not r.
   —
   If p, then not r.

   b. If p, then q.
   If q, then r.
   —
   If r, then p.

   c. If p, then q.
   If r, then q.
   —
   If p, then q.

   d. If p, then q.
   If q, then not r.
   —
   If p, then not r.

(Continued)

4. Detective Wise is on the case.
   Emily Dorn is dead.
   So, Detective Wise is on the case and Emily Dorn is dead.

   a. *p.*
      q.
      p or *q.*

   b. *p.*
      q.
      If *p*, then *q.*

   c. *p.*
      q.
      p and *q.*

   d. *p.*
      q.
      p if and only if *q.*

5. Detective Wise has an idea how the robber got into the room.
   Therefore, either Detective Wise has an idea how the robber got into the room or the murderer will get away with the crime.

   a. *p.*
      p and *q.*

   b. *p.*
      If *q*, then *p.*

   c. *p.*
      p or *q.*

   d. *p.*
      If *p*, then *q.*

6. John Clarke robbed his fiancée and Detective Wise will solve the crime.
   So, John Clarke robbed his fiancée.

   a. *p* and *q.*
      q.

   b. *p* and *q.*
      If *p*, then *q.*

   c. *p* and *q.*
      Either *p* or *q.*

   d. *p* and *q.*
      p.

7. If Detective Wise solves the crime, then the thief will go to prison; and if Detective Wise does not solve the crime, then someone in the house will get away with robbery.
Either Detective Wise solves the crime or she doesn't.
So, either the robber will go to prison or someone in the house will get away with robbery.

a. If *p*, then *q*; and if not *p*, then *r*.
Either *p* or not *p*.
Either *q* or *r*.

b. If *p*, then *q*; and if not *p*, then *r*.
Either not *q* or not *r*.
Either *p* or not *p*.

c. If *p*, then *q*; and if not *p*, then *r*.
Either *p* or not *p*.
If *q*, then *r*.

d. If *p*, then *q*; and if not *p*, then *r*.
If *p*, then not *p*.
Either *q* or *r*.

8. If the butler did it, then playing with the ladder was just for show; and if John Clarke did it, then he really wasn't concerned about his fiancée.
Either playing with the ladder was not just for show or John Clarke really was concerned about his fiancée.
Therefore, either the butler did not do it or John Clarke did not do it.

a. If *p*, then *q*; and if *r*, then not *s*.
Either *p* or *r*.
Either *r* or not *s*.

b. If *p*, then *q*; and if *r*, then not *s*.
Either not *q* or *s*.
Either not *p* or not *r*.

c. If *p*, then *q*; and if *r*, then not *s*.
If *q*, then not *s*.
Either not *p* or not *r*.

d. If *p*, then *q*; and if *r*, then not *s*.
If *p*, then *r*.
If *q*, then not *s*.

(Continued)

9. Either the butler did it or Clarke did it,
but they didn't both do it.
The butler did it.
Therefore, Clarke didn't do it.

a. Either *p* or *q*.
p.
q.

b. Either *p* or *q*.
Not *p*.
q.

c. Either *p* or *q*, and not both *p* and *q*.
p.
q.

d. Either *p* or *q*, and not both *p* and *q*.
p.
Not *q*.

10. If Emily Dorn faked the robbery, then John Clarke
did not commit the robbery.
Emily Dorn did not fake the robbery.
Thus, John Clarke committed the robbery.

a. If *p*, then not *q*.
Not *p*.
q.

b. If *p*, then not *q*.
p.
Not *q*.

c. If *p*, then not *q*.
q.
Not *p*.

d. If *p*, then not *q*.
Not *p*.
Not *q*.

4.5   Exercise Identify the argument that matches each argument form. Circle the correct
          answer.

1. **Example:**
   If *p*, then *q*.
   p.
   ___
   q.

   a. **If Detective Wise solves the case, then the robber will be caught.**
      Detective Wise solves the case.
      _____
      So, the robber will be caught.
   b. If Detective Wise solves the case, then the robber will be caught.
      The robber will be caught.
      _____
      So, Detective Wise solves the case.
   c. If Detective Wise solves the case, then the robber will be caught.
      Detective Wise does not solve the case.
      _____
      So, the robber will not be caught.
   d. If Detective Wise solves the case, then the robber will be caught.
      Detective Wise does not solve the case.
      _____
      So, the robber will be caught.

2. If *p*, then *q*.
   Not *q*.
   ___
   Not *p*.

   a. If Detective Wise solves the case, then the robber will be caught.
      Detective Wise solves the case.
      _____
      So, the robber will be caught.
   b. If Detective Wise solves the case, then the robber will be caught.
      The robber will be caught.
      _____
      So, Detective Wise solves the case.
   c. If Detective Wise solves the case, then the robber will be caught.
      Detective Wise does not solve the case.
      _____
      So, the robber will not be caught.
   d. If Detective Wise solves the case, then the robber will be caught.
      The robber will not be caught.
      _____
      So, Detective Wise does not solve the case.

(Continued)

3. Either *p* or *q*.
    Not *p*.
    ___
    q.

    a. Either the room has a secret entrance or Detective Wise has solved the crime.
        Detective Wise has not solved the crime.
        _____
        Thus, the room has a secret entrance.
    b. Either the room has a secret entrance or Detective Wise has solved the crime.
        The room has a secret entrance.
        _____
        Thus, Detective Wise has solved the crime.
    c. Either the room has a secret entrance or Detective Wise has solved the crime.
        The room does not have a secret entrance.
        _____
        Thus, Detective Wise has solved the crime.
    d. Either the room has a secret entrance or Detective Wise has solved the crime.
        If the room has a secret entrance, then it's a mansion worthy of a mystery; and if
        Detective Wise has solved the crime, then Detective Wise will be promoted to captain.
        _____
        Thus, either it's a mansion worthy of a mystery or Detective Wise will be promoted
        to captain.

4. If *p,* then *q*.
    If *q,* then *r*.
    ___
    If *p,* then *r*.

    a. If it is a mansion worthy of a mystery, then there is a secret entrance into the room.
        If the butler committed the robbery, then there is a secret entrance into the room.
        _____
        So, if it is a mansion worthy of a mystery, then the butler committed the robbery.
    b. If there is a secret entrance into the room, then it is a mansion worthy of a mystery.
        If the butler committed the crime, then it is a mansion worthy of a mystery.
        _____
        So, if there is a secret entrance into the room, the butler committee the crime.
    c. If it is a mansion worthy of a mystery, then there is a secret entrance into the room.
        If there is a secret entrance into the room, then Clarke would know about the entrance.
        _____
        So, if Clarke would not know about the entrance, it is not a mansion worthy of a
        mystery.
    d. If it is a mansion worthy of a mystery, then there is a secret entrance into the room.
        If there is a secret entrance into the room, then Clarke would know about the entrance.
        _____
        So, if it is a mansion worthy of a mystery, then Clarke would know about the entrance.

5. p and q.
    p.

    a. Both the servants and the guests at the party are suspects in the crime.
       Therefore, the servants are not suspects in the crime.
    b. Both the servants and the guests at the party are suspects in the crime.
       Therefore, the guests at the party are suspects in the crime.
    c. Both the servants and the guests at the party are suspects in the crime.
       Therefore, the servants are suspects in the crime.
    d. Both the servants and the guests at the party are suspects in the crime.
       Therefore, the guests are not suspects in the crime.

6. p.
    q.
    p and q.

    a. Detective Wise works for the LAPD.
       Sergeant McCorkel works for the LAPD.
       So, Detective Wise works for the LAPD, but Sergeant McCorkel does not work for the LAPD.
    b. Detective Wise works for the LAPD.
       Sergeant McCorkel works for the LAPD.
       So, Detective Wise works for the LAPD.
    c. Detective Wise works for the LAPD.
       Sergeant McCorkel works for the LAPD.
       So, both Detective Wise and Sergeant McCorkel work for the LAPD.
    d. Detective Wise works for the LAPD.
       Sergeant McCorkel works for the LAPD.
       So, neither Detective Wise nor Sergeant McCorkel works for the LAPD.

7. p.
    p or q.

    a. Clarke Mansion is a spooky place.
       So, Clarke Mansion is a spooky place and Detective Wise is puzzled.
    b. Clarke Mansion is a spooky place.
       So, either Clarke Mansion is a spooky place or Norman Bates has a home in Beverly Hills.
    c. Clarke Mansion is a spooky place.
       So, if Clarke Mansion is a spooky place, then Detective Wise is puzzled.
    d. Clarke Mansion is a spooky place.
       So, if Clarke Mansion is not a spooky place, then Norman Bates has a home in Beverly Hills.

(Continued)

8. If *p*, then *q*.
    _____
    If *p*, then both *p* and *q*.

    a. If Emily Dorn was drugged, then she was robbed.
        Emily Dorn was drugged.
        _____
        So, Emily Dorn was both drugged and robbed.
    b. If Emily Dorn was drugged, then she was robbed.
        _____
        So, if Emily Dorn was not robbed, she was not drugged.
    c. If Emily Dorn was drugged, then she was robbed.
        _____
        So, if Emily Dorn was drugged, then she was both drugged and robbed.
    d. If Emily Dorn was drugged, then she was robbed.
        _____
        So, if Emily Dorn was drugged, then she was both drugged and not robbed.

9. If *p*, then *q*; and if *r*, then *s*.
    Either *p* or *r*.
    _____
    Either *q* or *s*.

    a. If there was a robbery at Clarke Mansion, then the servants are suspects; and if there
        was a murder at Clarke Mansion, then the party guests are suspects.
        Either the servants are not suspects or the party guests are not suspects.
        _____
        So, either there was not a robbery at Clarke Mantion or there was not a murder at
        Clarke Mansion.
    b. If there was a robbery at Clarke Mansion, then the servants are suspects; and if there
        was a murder at Clarke Mansion, then the party guests are suspects.
        Either there was a robbery at Clarke Mansion or there was a murder at Clarke Mansion.
        _____
        So, either the servants are suspects or the party guests are suspects.
    c. If there was a robbery at Clarke Mansion, then the servants are suspects; and if there
        was a murder at Clarke Mansion, then the party guests are suspects.
        If the servants are suspects, then the butler did it; and if the party guests are
        suspects, then John Clarke did it.
        _____
        So, if there was a robbery at Clarke Mansion, then the butler did it; and if there was a
        murder at Clarke Mansion, then John Clarke did it.
    d. If there was a robbery at Clarke Mansion, then the servants are suspects; and if there
        was a murder at Clarke Mansion, then the party guests are suspects.
        Either there was a robbery at Clarke Mansion or the servants are not suspects.
        _____
        So, either the servants are suspects or there was not a murder at Clarke Mansion.

10. If *p*, then *q*; and if *r*, then *s*.
    Either not *q* or not *s*.
    _____
    Either not *p* or not *r*.

    a. If there was a robbery at Clarke Mansion, then the servants are suspects; and if there
       was a murder at Clarke Mansion, then the party guests are suspects.
       Either the servants are not suspects or the party guests are not suspects.
       _____
       So, either there was not a robbery at Clarke Mansion or there was not a murder at
       Clarke Mansion.
    b. If there was a robbery at Clarke Mansion, then the servants are suspects; and if there
       was a murder at Clarke Mansion, then the party guests are suspects.
       Either there was a robbery at Clarke Mansion or there was a murder at Clarke
       Mansion.
       _____
       So, either the servants are susptects or the party guests are suspects.
    c. If there was a robbery at Clarke Mansion, then the servants are suspects; and if there
       was a murder at Clarke Mansion, then the party guests are suspects.
       If the servants are suspects, then the butler did it; and if the party guests are suspects,
       then John Clarke did it.
       _____
       So, if there was a robbery at Clarke Mansion, then the butler did it; and if there was a
       murder at Clarke Mansion, then John Clarke did it.
    d. If there was a robbery at Clarke Mansion, then the servants are suspects; and if there
       was a murder at Clarke Mansion, then the party guests are suspects.
       Either there was a robbery at Clarke Mansion or the servants are not suspects.
       _____
       So, either the servants are suspects or there was not a murder at Clarke Mansion.

11. Either *p* or *q*, and not both *p* and *q*.
    p.
    _____
    Not *q*.

    a. Either Detective Wise is perplexed or the robbery has been solved.
       Detective Wise is not perplexed.
       _____
       Therefore, the robbery has been solved.
    b. Either Detective Wise is perplexed or the robbery has been solved, but it is not the
       case that both Detective Wise is perplexed and the robbery has been solved.
       The robbery has not been solved.
       _____
       Therefore, Detective Wise is perplexed.
    c. Either Detective Wise is perplexed or the robbery has been solved, but it is not the
       case that both Detective Wise is perplexed and the robbery has been solved.
       Detective Wise is perplexed.
       _____
       Therefore, the robbery has not been solved.
    d. Either Detective Wise is perplexed or the robbery has been solved, but it is not the
       case that both Detective Wise is perplexed and the robbery has been solved.
       Detective Wise is perplexed.
       _____
       Therefore, the robbery has been solved.

Categorical Syllogisms

Some valid (deductive arguments) concern the relations between sets of objects. The simplest of these are concerned with the relations between three sets. These types of arguments are **categorical syllogisms**.

A categorical syllogism has three claims (two premises and a conclusion) and each claim begins with either 'all,' 'no,' or 'some.' The three sets are represented by three terms. The variables S, P, and M represent the three specific terms as follows:

S = Subject Term of the conclusion
P = Predicate Term of the conclusion
M = The Middle Term which is the term found in both of the premises but not the conclusion

When written in standard form, the claims of the categorical syllogism are listed in a specific order. The major premise, which contains the predicate term, is listed first. The minor premise, which contains the subject term, is listed second. And finally, the conclusion is listed.

Examples of categorical syllogisms:

	Categorical Syllogisms	Form	Terms
a.	All robbers are criminals. All people who steal are robbers. Thus, all people who steal are criminals.	All M are P. All S are M. All S are P.	S: people who steal P: criminals M: robbers

By replacing each variable with a new term, you produce another categorical syllogism of the same form.

All detectives are intelligent people.
All people who solve robberies are detectives.
Thus, all people who solve robberies are intelligent people.

	Categorical Syllogisms	Form	Terms
b.	No servants at the mansion are robbers. Some servants at the mansion are butlers. So, some butlers are not robbers.	No M are P. Some M are S. Some S are not P.	S: butlers P: robbers M: servants

Argument of the same form as argument b:
No people over 90 years old are detectives.
Some people over 90 years old are butlers.
So, some butlers are not detectives.

4.6 Exercise Read each argument and then circle its form. Writing the form of the argument is often helpful, but it is not required. Remember, *S* is the subject term of the conclusion; *P* is the predicate term of the conclusion; and *M* is the term that is in the premises, but not in the conclusion.

1. **Example:**
   All suspects in the case are people living in the Clarke Mansion.
   Some police officers are not people living in the Clarke Mansion.
   _____
   Therefore, some police officers are not suspects in the case.

   Terms:
   S = police officers
   P = suspects in the case
   M = people living in the Clarke Mansion

   Form:

   All *P* are *M*.
   Some *S* are not *M*.
   _____
   Some *S* are not *P*.

   (a.) All *P* are *M*.
   Some *S* are not *M*.
   _____
   Some *S* are not *P*.

   b. All *P* are *M*.
   Some *M* are not *S*.
   _____
   Some *S* are not *P*.

   c. All *M* are *P*.
   Some *S* are not *M*.
   _____
   Some *S* are not *P*.

   d. All *M* are *P*.
   Some *M* are not *S*.
   _____
   Some *S* are not *P*.

2. All people living in the Clarke Mansion are robbery suspects.
   No police officers are robbery suspects.
   _____
   So, no police officers are people living in the Clarke Mansion.

   Terms:
   S = police officers
   P = people living in Clarke Mansion
   M = robbery suspects

   Form:

   a. All *P* are *M*.
   No *S* are *M*.
   _____
   No *S* are *P*.

   b. All *P* are *M*.
   No *M* are *S*.
   _____
   No *S* are *P*.

   c. All *M* are *P*.
   No *S* are *M*.
   _____
   No *S* are *P*.

   d. All *M* are *P*.
   No *M* are *S*.
   _____
   No *S* are *P*.

(Continued)

3. No suspects are victims of foul play.
   Some victims of foul play are people who have been robbed.
   ───
   So, some people who have been robbed are not suspects.

Terms: **Form:**

S = people who have been robbed
P = suspects
M = victims of foul play

a. No P are M.
   Some S are M.
   ───────────────
   Some S are not P.

b. No P are M.
   Some M are S.
   ───────────────
   Some S are not P.

c. No M are P.
   Some S are M.
   ───────────────
   Some S are not P.

d. No M are P.
   Some M are S.
   ───────────────
   Some S are not P.

4. Some detectives in the case are members of the LAPD.
   All detectives in the case are puzzled people.
   ───
   Thus, some puzzled people are members of the LAPD.

Terms: **Form:**

S = puzzled people
P = member of the LAPD
M = detectives in the case

a. Some P are M.
   All S are M.
   ───────────────
   Some S are P.

b. Some P are M.
   All M are S.
   ───────────────
   Some S are P.

c. Some M are P.
   All S are M.
   ───────────────
   Some S are P.

d. Some M are P.
   All M are S.
   ───────────────
   Some S are P.

5. Some guests at last night's party are not police detectives.
    All guests at last night's party are robbery suspects.
    _____
    Therefore, some robbery suspects are not police detectives.

Terms: **Form:**
S = robbery suspects
P = police detectives
M = guests at last night's party

a. Some P are not M.   b. Some P are not M.
    All S are M.   All M are S.
    _____   _____
    Some S are not P.   Some S are not P.

c. Some M are not P.   d. Some M are not P.
    All S are M.   All M are S.
    _____   _____
    Some S are not P.   Some S are not P.

6. Some people who slept in a locked room are robbery victims.
    All robbery victims are victims of foul play.
    _____
    So, some victims of foul play are people who slept in a locked room.

Terms: **Form:**
S = victims of foul play
P = people who slept in a locked room
M = robbery victims

a. Some P are M.   b. Some P are M.
    All S are M.   All M are S.
    _____   _____
    Some S are P.   Some S are P.

c. Some M are P.   d. Some M are P.
    All S are M.   All M are S.
    _____   _____
    Some S are P.   Some S are P.

(Continued)

7. No victims of foul play were detectives.
    Some victims of foul play were people who slept in a locked room.
    So, some people who slept in a locked room were not detectives.

    Terms:

    S = people who slept in a locked room
    P = detectives
    M = victims of foul play

    Form:

    a. No *P* are *M*.
       Some *S* are *M*.
       Some *S* are not *P*.

    b. No *P* are *M*.
       Some *M* are *S*.
       Some *S* are not *P*.

    c. No *M* are *P*.
       Some *S* are *M*.
       Some *S* are not *P*

    d. No *M* are *P*.
       Some *M* are *S*.
       Some *S* are not *P*.

8. Some person who robbed Emily Dorn is a person who stayed in Clarke Mansion last night.
    All persons who stayed in Clarke Mansion last night are robbery suspects.
    Thus, some robbery suspect is a person who robbed Emily Dorn.

    Terms:

    S = robbery suspect
    P = person who robbed Emily Dorn
    M = person who stayed in Clarke Mansion last night

    Form:

    a. Some *P* are *M*.
       All *S* are *M*.
       Some *S* are *P*.

    b. Some *P* are *M*.
       All *M* are *S*.
       Some *S* are *P*.

    c. Some *M* are *P*.
       All *S* are *M*.
       Some *S* are *P*.

    d. Some *M* are *P*.
       All *M* are *S*.
       Some *S* are *P*.

9. All robbery suspects are people who stayed in Clarke Mansion last night.
No people who stayed in Clarke Mansion last night are members of the LAPD.
Therefore, no members of the LAPD are robbery suspects.

Terms:
S = members of the LAPD
P = robbery suspects
M = people who stayed in Clarke Mansion last night

Form:

a. All P are M.
   No S are M.
   No S are P.

b. All P are M.
   No M are S.
   No S are P.

c. All M are P.
   No S are M.
   No S are P.

d. All M are P.
   No M are S.
   No S are P.

10. Some people who attended the party are robbers.
All people who attended the party are suspects.
So, some suspects are not robbers.

Terms:
S = suspects
P = robbers
M = people who attended the party

Form:

a. Some P are M.
   All S are M.
   Some S are not P.

b. Some P are M.
   All M are S.
   Some are not P.

c. Some M are P.
   All S are M.
   Some S are not P.

d. Some M are P.
   All M are S.
   Some S are not P.

Remember:

1	2	3
Validity is a property of an argument's form. If one argument of a form is valid, all arguments of that form are valid.	If one argument of a form is invalid, all arguments of that form are invalid. If an argument form is valid, it is impossible for all of its premises to be true and its conclusion to be false.	So, if there is an argument which has true premises and a false conclusion, *any argument of that form is invalid*.

Method of Deductive Counterexamples

One method to prove an argument is invalid is to produce a deductive counterexample. A deductive counterexample is an argument of the same form with true premises and a false conclusion.

	Deductive Counterexample	Form	Terms or Claims
a.	Some robbers are not evil people No evil people are generous people. ——————————————— So, some generous people are not robbers.	Some *P* are not *M*. No *M* are *S*. —————— Some *S* are not *P*.	*S* = generous people *P* = robbers *M* = evil people
	Deductive Counterexample Some people who spent the night in Clarke Mansion are not robbery suspects. No robbery suspects are people found tied to their chairs late in the day. ————————————————————————————————————— So, some people found tied to their chairs late in the day are not people who spent the night in Clarke Mansion.		
b.	If Detective Wise is the robber, then she lives a secret life. Detective Wise is not the robber. ——————————————— Therefore, Detective Wise does not live a secret life.	If *p*, then *q*. Not *p*. —————— Not *q*.	*p* = Detective Wise is the robber *q* = Detective Wise lives a secret life
	Deductive Counterexample If Bill Gates has all the money in the U.S. Treasury, then he is wealthy. Bill Gates does not have all the money in the U.S. Treasury. ————————————————————————————————————— Therefore, Bill Gates is not wealthy.		

4.7   Exercise Write the form of the argument and then circle its deductive counterexample.

1. **Example:**
Some people who attended the party are suspects.
No servants at Clarke Mansion are suspects.

Therefore, some servants at Clarke Mansion are not people who attended the party.

Terms:
S = servants at Clarke Mansion
P = people who attended the party
M = suspects

Form:

$$\text{Some } P \text{ are } M.$$
$$\text{No } S \text{ are } M.$$
$$\overline{\text{Some } S \text{ are not } P.}$$

a. Some Republicans are Democrats.
No senators are Democrats.
Therefore, some senators are not Republicans.

b. Some students are intelligent people.
No politicians are intelligent people.
Therefore, no politicians are students.

c. **Some Chevrolets are trucks.**
No Corvettes are trucks.
Therefore, some Corvettes are not Chevrolets.

d. Some Chevrolets are not trucks.
No Corvettes are trucks.
Therefore, some Corvettes are Chevrolets.

(Continued)

2. If John Clarke committed the robbery, then he was at the party.
    John Clarke was at the party.
    So, John Clarke committed the robbery.

    Claims:
    p = John Clarke committed the robbery
    q = he was at the party

    Form:

    a. If George Washington was president, then the Constitution was in effect by 1790.
        The Constitution was in effect by 1790.
        So, George Washington was president.

    b. If Detective Wise works for the Chicago Police Department, then a robbery occurred at the Clarke Mansion in Los Angeles.
        A robbery occurred at the Clarke Mansion in Los Angeles.
        So, Detective Wise works for the Chicago Police Department.

    c. If John Clarke owns a mansion, then Detective Wise works for the Chicago Police Department.
        Detective Wise works for the Chicago Police Department.
        So, John Clarke owns a mansion.

    d. If Detective Wise works for the LAPD, then there was a robbery at Clarke Mansion.
        Detective Wise works for the LAPD.
        So, there was a robbery at Clarke Mansion.

3. All robbery suspects were party guests.
    No robbery suspects are servants at Clarke Mansion.
    So, no servants at Clarke Mansion were party guests.

Terms: **Form:**

S = servants at Clarke Mansion
P = party guests
M = robbery suspects

a. All Chevrolets are cars made by   b. No dogs are cats.
    General Motors.   Some longhairs are not dogs.
    No Chevrolets are cars made by Ford   So, no longhairs are cats.
    Motor Company.
    So, no cars made by Ford Motor
    Company are cars made by General
    Motors.

c. All maple trees are trees with needles.   d. All maple trees are trees with broad
    No pine trees are trees with needles.   leaves.
    So, no pine trees are maple trees.   No maple trees are oak trees.
                                                  So, no oak trees are trees with
                                                  broad leaves.

(Continued)

4. Either Clarke was the robber or Giles was the robber.
    Clarke was the robber.
    _____
    Thus, Giles was not the robber.

Claims: **Form:**
p = Clarke was the robber
q = Giles was the robber

a. Either the president of the United   b. Either John Wilkes Booth shot
    States lives in the White House, or   President Lincoln, or Henry Ford was
    the president of the United States is a   president of the United States.
    U.S. citizen.   John Wilkes Booth shot
    The president of the United States   President Lincoln.
    lives in the White House.   _____
    _____   Thus, Henry Ford was not president of
    Thus, the president of the United   the United States.
    States is not a U.S. citizen.

c. Either John Wilkes Booth shot   d. Either Fords are made by General
    President Lincoln, or Henry Ford was   Motors or Fords are made by Toyota.
    president of the United States.   Fords are made by General Motors.
    Henry Ford was not president of the   _____
    United States.   Thus, Fords are not made by Toyota.
    _____
    Thus, John Wilkes Booth shot
    President Lincoln.

5. If the dresser hides a secret staircase, then there was a way someone could have gotten into the locked room.
If there was a way someone could have gotten into the locked room, then John Clarke is a suspect.
_____
Therefore, if the dresser hides a secret staircase, then John Clarke is not a suspect.

Claims:

p = the dresser hides a secret staircase
q = there was a way someone could have gotten into a locked room
r = John Clarke is a suspect

Form:

a. If Detective Wise works for the LAPD, then she's investigating the robbery at Clarke Mansion.
If Detective Wise works for the LAPD, then one of the guests at Clarke Mansion was robbed.
_____
Therefore, if Detective Wise is investigating the robbery at Clarke Mansion, then one of the guests at Clarke Mansion was robbed.

b. If Detective Wise works for the LAPD, then she's investigating the robbery at Clarke Mansion.
If Detective Wise works for the LAPD, then one of the guests at Clarke Mansion was robbed.
_____
Therefore, if Detective Wise is investigating the robbery at Clarke Mansion, then one of the guests at Clarke Mansion was not robbed.

c. If Detective Wise works for the LAPD, then she's investigating the robbery at Clarke Mansion.
If Detective Wise is investigating the robbery at Clarke Mansion, then one of the guests at Clarke Mansion was robbed.
_____
Therefore, if Detective Wise works for the LAPD, one of the guests at Clarke Mansion was not robbed.

d. If Detective Wise is investigating the robbery at Clarke Mansion, then one of the guests at Clarke Mansion was robbed.
If Detective Wise works for the LAPD, then she's investigating a robbery at Clarke Mansion.
_____
Therefore, if one of the guests at Clarke Mansion was robbed, Detective Wise does not work for the LAPD.

(Continued)

6. No servants are suspects.
   No party guests are suspects.
   So, no party guests are servants.

Terms:
S = party guests
P = servants
M = suspects

Form:

a. No Fords are Chevrolets.
   No Fords are Corvettes.
   So, no Corvettes are Chevrolets.

b. No Thunderbirds are Fords.
   No Model-Ts are Fords.
   So, no Model-Ts are Thunderbirds.

c. No Corvettes are Fords.
   No Chevrolets are Fords.
   So, no Chevrolets are Corvettes.

d. No Fords are Chevrolets.
   All Corvettes are Chevrolets.
   So, all Corvettes are Fords.

7. Some suspects are residents of Clarke Mansion.
   Some residents of Clarke Mansion are not servants.
   So, some servants are not suspects.

Terms:
S = servants
P = suspects
M = residents of Clarke Mansion

Form:

a. Some butterflies are insects.
   Some insects are not houseflies.
   So, some houseflies are not butterflies.

b. Some butterflies are insects.
   Some termites are not butterflies.
   So, some termites are not insects.

c. Some butterflies are not termites.
   Some termites are insects.
   So, some insects are not butterflies.

d. Some insects are butterflies.
   Some butterflies are not monarch butterflies.
   So, some monarch butterflies are not insects.

8. If John Clarke is the robber, then the engagement was troublesome; and if Giles is the robber, then the servants did not like Emily.
The engagement was troublesome and the servants did not like Emily.
Thus, either John Clarke was the robber or Giles was the robber.

Claims:

p = John Clarke is the robber
q = the engagement was troublesome
r = Giles is the robber
s = the servants did not like Emily

Form:

a. If dogs are vertebrates, then butterflies are mammals; and if tarantulas are spiders, then lizards are not birds. Butterflies are mammals and lizards are not birds.
Thus, either dogs are vertebrates or tarantulas are spiders.

b. If dogs are vertebrates, then tarantulas are spiders. If tarantulas are spiders, then lizards are reptiles.
Thus, if lizards are reptiles, then dogs are not vertebrates

c. If butterflies are mammals, then dogs are vertebrates; and if lizards are spiders, then tarantulas are not birds. Dogs are vertebrates and tarantulas are not birds.
Thus, either butterflies are mammals or lizards are spiders.

d. If butterflies are mammals, then dogs are vertebrates; and if lizards are spiders, then tarantulas are not birds. Either dogs are vertebrates or tarantulas are not birds.
Thus, butterflies are mammals and lizards are spiders.

9. Some suspects are people who attended the party.
All people who live in Clarke Mansion are suspects.
So, some people who live in Clarke Mansion are people who attended the party.

Terms:

S = people who live in Clarke Mansion
P = people who attended the party
M = suspects

Form:

a. Some insects are butterflies.
All termites are insects.
So, some termites are butterflies.

b. Some butterflies are insects.
All insects are termites.
So, some butterflies are termites.

c. Some insects are not butterflies.
All termites are insects.
So, some butterflies are not termites.

d. Some butterflies are not insects.
All termites are insects.
So, some termites are not insects.

(Continued)

10. All people who live in Clarke Mansion are suspects.
Some party guests are suspects.
_____
So, some party guests are people who live in Clarke Mansion.

Terms: **Form:**
S = party guests
P = people who live in Clark Mansion
M = suspects

a. Some insects are termites.
All termites are things that like to chomp on wood.
_____
So, some things that like to chomp on wood are insects.

b. All termites are things that like to chomp on wood.
Some termites are insects.
_____
So, some insects are things that like to chomp on wood.

c. All termites are things that like to chomp on wood.
Some beavers are things that like to chomp on wood.
_____
So, some beavers are termites.

d. All termites are things that like to chomp on wood.
Some beavers are things that like to chomp on wood.
_____
So, some termites are beavers.

CASE 15

City of Los Angeles Police Department

[1]At 1:30 a.m., six people were arrested while attempting to plant explosives under the I-110 overpass at South Hoover Street. [2]The police had been on high alert, since at 3:00 a.m. Eastern Time, there had been explosions under overpasses in New York and Atlanta and at 3:00 a.m. Central Time, there had been similar explosions in Chicago and Dallas. [3]Before the night was over, Denver, Santa Fe, and Seattle were added to the roster, each having an overpass assaulted at precisely 3:00 a.m. local time. [4]Fortunately, no one was injured in any of the attacks. [5]Further, the overpasses were damaged but not destroyed.

[6]A band of terrorists took credit the next morning. [7]The following message was delivered to the police in the seven affected cities:

[8]We're old, we're bald, and we're bitter! [9]We've been stereotyped as fat and dumb! [10]We've been denied jobs because we're not considered beautiful! [11]Hair-replacement programs suggest we're undesirable! [12]This has to stop! [13]Until you stop passing us over, your overpasses will be in jeopardy!

[14]The Old Bald Guys

[15]By midmorning, the whole country was in a state of panic.

[16]Detective Wise was called in to work on the case at 4:00 a.m. [17]The six people arrested had immediately hired lawyers and stopped talking to the police.

[18]As news of the bombings came in from across the country, Detective Wise wondered whether L.A. had been the site of an intended attack. [19]There had been two attacks in each of the other three time zones. [20]She knew that all six of the people arrested were bald men over the age of sixty. [21]She also knew that each person arrested had been wearing a "Bald is Beautiful!" T-shirt. [22]"Perhaps the terrorists can be traced through the explosives," she mused. [23]"Aren't all explosives manufacturers required to chemically tag their products?" she asked herself. [24]"And aren't they required to keep strict records of their sales? [25]Maybe we'll get a break!"

4.8 Induction: How much evidence does a particular invalid argument provide for the truth of its conclusion?

Any argument that is not a valid argument provides only some evidence for the truth of its conclusion even if all its premises are true. These are inductive arguments. Inductive arguments conclude probability and not certainty. We will take a closer look at inductive arguments in Chapter 7.

Inductive Generalizations

Some inductive arguments reach general conclusions on the basis of properties of individuals. These arguments are called **inductive generalizations**. The conclusion might be universal (concerning all things of a kind) or less than universal. The general form of an inductive generalization is as follows:

A is a thing of kind x, and it has property p.
B is a thing of kind x, and it has property p.
C is a thing of kind x, and it has property p.
N is a thing of kind x, and it has property p.
So, all (most, many) things of kind x have property p.

Examples of inductive generalizations in Case 15:

	Inductive Generalizations	Evidence	Conclusion
a.	John McCann was arrested and he was bald. José Sanchez was arrested and he was bald. Gerhard Holtz was arrested and he was bald. So, all the men arrested were bald.	John McCann was arrested and he was bald. José Sanchez was arrested and he was bald. Gerhard Holtz was arrested and he was bald.	All the men arrested were bald.
b.	All the members of The Old Bald Guys who were arrested were over sixty years old. So, all members of the Old Bald Guys are over sixty years old.	All the members of The Old Bald Guys who were arrested were over sixty years old.	All the members of The Old Bald Guys are over sixty years old.
c.	"It is my experience," Detective Wise remarked, "that we catch about sixty percent of terrorists. So, overall about sixty percent of terrorists are caught." (There is a generalization from one person's experience to a general factual claim.)	It is my experience that we catch about sixty percent of terrorists.	About sixty percent of terrorists are caught.

4.9   Exercise What kind of argument is each of the following? Circle the correct answer.

1. **Example:**
   The attempts to blow up overpasses in New York, Atlanta, Chicago, Dallas, Denver, Santa Fe, and Seattle were made by The Old Bald Guys. So, all attempts to blow up overpasses are made by The Old Bald Guys.
   a. **This is an inductive generalization.**
   b. This is an inductive argument, but it is not an inductive generalization.
   c. This is a valid argument.
   d. This is not an argument.

2. All overpasses attacked by The Old Bald Guys were attacked with dynamite. So, the overpass attacked by The Old Bald Guys in Denver was attacked with dynamite.
   a. This is an inductive generalization.
   b. This is an inductive argument, but it is not an inductive generalization.
   c. This is a valid argument.
   d. This is not an argument.

3. According to his driver's license, one of the men arrested is Henry DeWitt, a tall man of sixty-two with short gray hair. The man from whom the license was taken, however, is completely bald.
   a. This is an inductive generalization.
   b. This is an inductive argument, but it is not an inductive generalization.
   c. This is a valid argument.
   d. This is not an argument.

4. Henry DeWitt was arrested under the overpass in L.A., and he is sixty-two. Keith Liebowitz was arrested under the overpass in L.A., and he is seventy. Mark Schwartz was arrested under the overpass in L.A., and he is sixty-eight. So, everyone arrested under the overpass in L.A. was over sixty years old.
   a. This is an inductive generalization.
   b. This is an inductive argument, but it is not an inductive generalization.
   c. This is a valid argument.
   d. This is not an argument.

5. Henry DeWitt, Keith Liebowitz, and Mark Schwartz were arrested under an overpass in L.A. while packing dynamite into holes. Hector Hernandez was arrested under an overpass in L.A. So, Hector Hernnandez was arrested while packing dynamite into holes.
   a. This is an inductive generalization.
   b. This is an inductive argument, but it is not an inductive generalization.
   c. This is a valid argument.
   d. This is not an argument.

(Continued)

6. Detective Wise found the bombing case frustrating. Sergeant O'Tool found the bombing case frustrating. Lieutenant Brazilton found the bombing case frustrating. So, it is likely that all the police working on the bombing case found it frustrating.
    a. This is an inductive generalization.
    b. This is an inductive argument, but it is not an inductive generalization.
    c. This is a valid argument.
    d. This is not an argument.

7. The bombing case in Los Angeles is like the bombing cases in New York, Atlanta, Chicago, Dallas, Denver, Santa Fe, and Seattle. So, it is likely that the criminals in Los Angeles are part of the The Old Bald Guys gang that was responsible for the other bombings.
    a. This is an inductive generalization.
    b. This is an inductive argument, but it is not an inductive generalization.
    c. This is a valid argument.
    d. This is not an argument.

8. If Detective Wise cracks the bombing case, then her next case will be a murder case. But her next case will not be a murder case. So, she does not crack the bombing case.
    a. This is an inductive generalization.
    b. This is an inductive argument, but it is not an inductive generalization.
    c. This is a valid argument.
    d. This is not an argument.

9. All the police who worked on the bombing case in New York were puzzled. All the police who worked on the bombing case in Atlanta were puzzled. All the police who worked on the bombing cases in Chicago, Dallas, Denver, Santa Fe, and Seattle were puzzled. So, all the police who worked on the bombing cases were puzzled.
    a. This is an inductive generalization.
    b. This is an inductive argument, but it is not an inductive generalization.
    c. This is a valid argument.
    d. This is not an argument.

10. Most of the members of The Old Bald Guys are explosives experts. All explosives experts are people who know the difference between dynamite and plastic explosives. So, it's likely that most members The Old Bald Guys are people who know the difference between dynamite and plastic explosives.
    a. This makes an inductive generalization followed by a valid argument.
    b. This is an inductive argument, but it is not an inductive generalization.
    c. This is a valid argument.
    d. This is not an argument.

Argument by Analogy

Another common type of inductive argument is an **argument by analogy**. Analogies are comparisons that state a similarity between two or more things. Some analogies are arguments and some are not. An argument by analogy compares the properties of two or more things are concludes that because they are similar in a number of ways, they are similar in yet another way. The general form of the argument is:

A has property w, x, y, z.
B has property w, x, y, z.
C has property w, x, y, z.
D has property w, x, y.
_____
Therefore, it is likely D has property z.

An argument by analogy compares at least two or more things and compares at least two or more properties.   There is also no generalization made about a class in an argument by analogy as there is in an inductive generalization.

Examples of arguments by analogy in Case 15:

a.	Detective Wise and Officer Smart have both worked for the LAPD for ten years. Officer Smart has reached the rank of lieutenant. Therefore, Detective Wise has reached the rank of lieutenant.
b.	The bombing attempt in Los Angeles was like the other bombings across the country insofar as it was an attack on an overpass at 3:00 a.m. and dynamite was the explosive used. The other bombings were perpetrated by The Old Bald Guys. So, it's likely that the attempted bombing in LA was also perpetrated by The Old Bald Guys.
c.	New York, Atlanta, Chicago, Dallas, Denver, Santa Fe, Seattle, and Los Angles are alike insofar as they are relatively large cities. In New York, Atlanta, Chicago, Dallas, Denver, Santa Fe, and Seattle, the traffic is lighter at 3:00 a.m. than most other times of the day. So, we may conclude that in Los Angeles the traffic is lighter at 3:00 a.m. than most other times of the day.

4.10 Exercise What kind of argument is each of the following? Circle the correct answer. Writing the form of the argument is often helpful, but it is not required.

1. **Example:**
   Detective Wise learned that all of the dynamite planted by the Old Bald Guys contained a chemical tag unique to the N-Dynamite Company. The dynamite planted in L.A. also contained the same chemical tag. So, Detective Wise thought that the dynamite planted in L.A. was propbably planted by the Old Bald Guys.
   a. **This is an argument by analogy.**
   b. This is a generalization.
   c. This is a valid argument.
   d. This is not an argument.

   OBGD has properties POBG and N.
   LAD has property N.
   _____
   LAD probably has the property POBG.

2. All six men who were arrested were bald, over sixty years old, and had served in the U. S. Army during the Vietnam War. Four of the six men received demolitions training in the Army. So, it is likely that the other two men also received demolitions training in the Army.
   a. This is an argument by analogy.
   b. This is an inductive generalization.
   c. This is a valid argument.
   d. This is not an argument.

3. Harvey Rosenberg is one of the six men arrested. He is 5 feet, 6 inches tall and weighs 210 pounds. His head is very shiny: "I buff it with paste wax three times every week," he said. He also claims to have designed the "Bald Is Beautiful" T-shirts.
   a. This is an argument by analogy.
   b. This is an inductive generalization.
   c. This is a valid argument.
   d. This is not an argument.

4. Dynamite is like heart medicine insofar as they both contain nitroglycerine. Dynamite is highly explosive. So, heart medicine is highly explosive.
   a. This is an argument by analogy.
   b. This is an inductive generalization.
   c. This is a valid argument.
   d. This is not an argument.

5. Detective Wise said she became a police officer to carry on a family tradition: Both of her parents and one of her grandfathers had been police officers.
   a. This is an argument by analogy.
   b. This is an inductive generalization.
   c. This is a valid argument.
   d. This is not an argument.

6. Explosives experts are like SWAT (Special Weapons and Tactics) team members insofar as they are specially trained. Explosive experts know how to position dynamite to have a maximal effect. So, SWAT team members know how to position dynamite to have a maximal effect.
   a. This is an argument by analogy.
   b. This is an inductive generalization.
   c. This is a valid argument.
   d. This is not an argument.

7. Henry DeWitt, Keith Liebowitz, Mark Schwartz, and Harvey Rosenberg were arrested while placing dynamite under the I-110 at South Hoover Street overpass. They were all trained as explosives specialists in the army. So, all the men who were arrested while placing dynamite under the I-110 at South Hoover Street overpass were trained as explosives specialists in the army.
   a. This is an argument by analogy.
   b. This is an inductive generalization.
   c. This is a valid argument.
   d. This is not an argument.

8. Detective Wise lives in Los Angeles. Officer Baker lives in Los Angeles. Henry DeWitt, Keith Liebowitz, Mark Schwartz, and Harvey Rosenberg live in Los Angeles. So, most of the people associated with the case live in Los Angeles.
   a. This is an argument by analogy.
   b. This is an inductive generalization.
   c. This is a valid argument.
   d. This is not an argument.

(Continued)

9. Either the six men arrested in Los Angeles were part of a national conspiracy or they weren't. If they were part of a national conspiracy, then The Old Bald Guys pose a serious threat to our roadways; if they weren't part of a national conspiracy, then strange things continue to happen in Los Angeles. So, either The Old Bald Guys pose a serious threat to our roadways or strange things continue to happen in Los Angeles.
    a. This is an argument by analogy.
    b. This is an inductive generalization.
    c. This is a valid argument.
    d. This is not an argument.

10. A terrorist operation is like honest work insofar as it requires commitment, planning, and execution. Success in honest work often requires some luck. So, a successful terrorist operation often requires some luck.
    a. This is an argument by analogy.
    b. This is an inductive generalization.
    c. This is a valid argument.
    d. This is not an argument.

Argument to the Best Explanation

Arguments claim to prove something, but explanations tell us why or how something happened. In an argument to the best explanation, however, we have both an argument and an explanation. The argument to the best explanation argues that the "best" explanation for a set of facts is probably true. The general form of the argument to the best explanation is:

F1 . . . Fn are facts that need an explanation.
Hypothesis H is the best explanation of facts.
Therefore, H is probably true.

A hypothesis is an educated guess which attempts to explain why or how something happened. Hypothesis are usually better if they allow us to explain more facts or events. They are also better if they are closely related to widely-accepted explanations; for example, scientific explanations are better than superstitious explanations. In Chapter 7 we will examine the criteria for evaluating hypothesis and figuring out which one is the best hypothesis. This is important because how probable our conclusion is and thus the strength of our argument will depend upon our evaluation of the hypothesis.

Examples of arguments to the best explanation in Case 15:

	Arguments to an Explanation	Evidence	Conclusion
a.	The chances of causing few injuries would explain both why the bombers chose 3:00 a.m. to explode the dynamite and why the charges were not large enough to destroy the overpass. So, it's likely that the bombers didn't want to cause many injuries.	The chances of causing few injuries would explain both why the bombers chose 3:00 a.m. to explode the dynamite and why the charges were not large enough to destroy the overpass.	It's likely that the bombers didn't want to cause many injuries.
b.	E-mail correspondence discussing explosives was found between two of the men arrested in LA and other men from across the country. If The Old Bald Guys were involved in a nationwide conspiracy, this would explain why e-mails concerning explosive had been exchanged. So, it's likely that The Old Bald Guys were involved in a nationwide conspiracy.	E-mail correspondence discussing explosives was found between two of the men arrested in LA and other men from across the country. If The Old Bald Guys were involved in a nationwide conspiracy, this would explain why e-mails concerning explosive had been exchanged.	It's likely that The Old Bald Guys were involved in a nationwide conspiracy.
c.	If the six men arrested in LA are associated with The Old Bald Guys, that would explain why each man was wearing a "Bald is Beautiful" T-shirt. So, it's likely that the six men arrested in LA were associated with The Old Bald Guys.	If the six men arrested in LA are associated with The Old Bald Guys, that would explain why each man was wearing a "Bald is Beautiful" T-shirt.	It's likely that the six men arrested in LA were associated with The Old Bald Guys.

4.11 Exercise What kind of argument is each of the following? Circle the correct answer.
Writing the form of the argument is often helpful, but it is not required.

1. **Example:**
    Sherman LaRuse came from a poor neighborhood. His
    father deserted the family when he was four and his
    mother had a serious drinking problem. He ran away from
    home at twelve. That's why he entered a life of crime.

    No argument form

    a.) **This is an argument to an explanation.**
    b. This is an argument by analogy.
    c. This is an inductive generalization.
    d. This is a valid deductive argument.

2. Blowing up an overpass with explosives is like blowing
    up a building with explosives. It takes talent to blow up
    a building and not hurt anyone. So, it probably takes
    talent to blow up an overpass and not hurt anyone.
    a. This is an argument to an explanation.
    b. This is an argument by analogy.
    c. This is an inductive generalization.
    d. This is a valid deductive argument.

3. The explosives the gang used all had the same
    chemical tag marks from the same batch of explosives.
    That's why the gang was a well-planned conspiracy to
    act together.
    a. This is an argument to an explanation.
    b. This is an argument by analogy.
    c. This is an inductive generalization.
    d. This is a valid deductive argument.

4. If the group of six men arrested all wore a similar
    T-shirt, then they must have been acting in a concerted
    plan together.   If they were acting in a concerted plan
    together, then they were acting in a conspiracy. So, if
    the group of six men arrested all wore a similar T-shirt,
    then they were acting in a conspiracy.
    a. This is an argument to an explanation.
    b. This is an argument by analogy.
    c. This is an inductive generalization.
    d. This is a valid deductive argument.

5. Detective Wise probably decided to become a police officer to keep up a family tradition, for both her parents and one of her grandfathers were police officers.
   a. This is an argument to an explanation.
   b. This is an argument by analogy.
   c. This is an inductive generalization.
   d. This is a valid deductive argument.

6. Detective Wise is a dedicated public servant. Sergeant Sanchez is a dedicated public servant. Officer Baker is a dedicated public servant. So, most police officers are dedicated public servants.
   a. This is an argument to an explanation.
   b. This is an argument by analogy.
   c. This is an inductive generalization.
   d. This is a valid deductive argument

7. The Old Bald Guys probably picked 3 a.m. as the time to blow up overpasses because they did not really wish to harm any people during a busy time of driving.
   a. This is an argument to an explanation.
   b. This is an argument by analogy.
   c. This is an inductive generalization.
   d. This is a valid deductive argument.

8. The first bald man did not have a criminal record, and neither did the second, third, fourth, nor fifth bald man have a previous criminal record. So, it is likely that the sixth bald man also did not have a criminal record.
   a. This is an argument to an explanation.
   b. This is an argument by analogy.
   c. This is an inductive generalization.
   d. This is a valid deductive argument.

9. The gang probably chose to use explosives because several members of the gang were in the army demolition corps and they learned quite a bit about explosives during their time in the army.
   a. This is an argument to an explanation.
   b. This is an argument by analogy.
   c. This is an inductive generalization.
   d. This is a valid deductive argument.

(Continued)

10. The gang probably chose to concentrate its activities in large cities because they wanted to get publicity in all the major newspapers and television broadcasting stations.
    a. This is an argument to an explanation.
    b. This is an argument by analogy.
    c. This is an inductive generalization.
    d. This is a valid deductive argument.

CASE 16	City of Los Angeles Police Department

[1]It was the fourth letter demanding money for silence. [2]Dani Drugas was running for city council. [3]Her campaign called for a return to high moral standards in government. [4]The twenty-year-old picture the blackmailer threatened to give the press showed her riding with the Silver Shadows motorcycle gang. [5]The demands had risen from $1,000 with the first letter to $10,000 with this one. [6]Dani had paid the first three times. [7]Now she called the police.

[8]She met Detective Wise at Julio's Italian Restaurant on Sunset Boulevard.   [9]While eating a large plate of spaghetti, Dani described her problem. [10]"I don't deny that I rode with a motorcycle gang as a kid. [11]It wasn't a hard-core gang. [12]We made a lot of noise. [13]We painted some graffiti. [14]We weren't into murder and theft. [15]Those with whom I've stayed in contact have gone straight. [16]Big Steve is now an investment banker. [17]Wee Willie runs a construction company. [18]Little Lilly teaches kindergarten. [19]But the picture would ruin my campaign. [20]If my supporters find my history isn't squeaky-clean, they'll jump like rats from a sinking ship."

[21]Detective Wise thought about the case. [22]"Who could have taken the picture?" she asked.

"[23]We got around. [24]We could have been in the background in a newspaper photo. [25]Wild Wanda Greene was always shooting pictures. [26]She was a jealous sort. [27]I don't know what happened to her.   [28]When the gang broke up, I believe she hooked up with the Red Riders gang."

"[29]It couldn't have been from a newspaper photo," remarked Detective Wise. [30]"If it had been from a newspaper photo, your opponents would have found it. [31]If they'd have found it, they'd have published it. [32]It hasn't been published. [33]They wouldn't have resorted to blackmail."

4.12 Review Exercise Circle the form that best represents each argument. Writing the form of the argument is often helpful, but it is not required.

1. **Example:**
   If it had been a newspaper photo, your opponents would have found it. If your opponents would have found it, they'd have published it. So, if it had been a newspaper photo, your opponents would have published it.

$$\text{If } p, \text{ then } q.$$
$$\text{If } q, \text{ then } r.$$
$$\overline{\text{If } p, \text{ then } r.}$$

   (a.) **If p, then q.**
   If q, then r.
   If p, then r.

   b. If p, then q.
   If r, then q.
   If p, then r.

   c. If p, then q.
   Not q.
   Not p.

   d. If p, then q.
   p.
   q.

2. If it had been a newspaper photo, your opponents would have published it. They didn't publish it. So, it wasn't a newspaper photo.

   a. If p, then q.
   If q, then r.
   If p, then r.

   b. If p, then q.
   If r, then q.
   If p, then r.

   c. If p, then q.
   Not q.
   Not p.

   d. If p, then q.
   p.
   q.

3. Either the photo was in a newspaper or it was taken by a private party. The photo was not in a newspaper. So, it was taken by a private party.

   a. Either p or q.
   p.
   q.

   b. Either p or q.
   Not p.
   Not q.

   c. Either p or q.
   Not p.
   q.

   d. Either p or q.
   p.
   Not q.

4.	Either Wild Wanda is a blackmailer or Big Steve is a blackmailer, but they are not both blackmailers. So, Big Steve is not a blackmailer, for Wild Wanda is a blackmailer.

a.	Either *p* or *q*, but
not both *p* and *q*.
p.
q.

b.	Either *p* or *q*, but
not both *p* and *q*.
Not *p*.
Not *q*.

c.	Either *p* or *q*, but
not both *p* and *q*.
Not *p*.
q.

d.	Either *p* or *q*, but
not both *p* and *q*.
p.
Not *q*.

5.	Dani Drugas is a candidate for city council. So, either Dani Drugas is a candidate for city council or Wild Wanda is serving time at Valley State Prison for Women.

a.	*p*.
Either not *p* or *q*.

b.	*p*.
Either *p* or *q*.

c.	*p*.
If *p*, then *q*.

c.	*p*.
If *p*, then *q*.

6.	Both Dani and Wanda were members of the Silver Shadows gang. So, Dani was a member of the Silver Shadows gang.

a.	*p* and *q*.
q.

b.	*p* and *q*.
p.

c.	Either *p* or *q*.
Not *q*.

d.	Either *p* or *q*.
p.

(Continued)

7. If Detective Wise is a blackmailer, then there is
    corruption in the police department; and if Dani Drugas
    is being blackmailed, then someone knows Dani's
    secrets. Either Detective Wise is a blackmailer or
    Dani Drugas is being blackmailed. Therefore, there is
    corruption in the police department or someone knows
    Dani's secrets.

    a. If p, then q; and if r, then s.
        Either p or r.
        _____
        Either q or s.

    b. If p, then q; and if r, then s.
        Either not q or not r.
        _____
        Either not p or not s.

    c. If p, then q; and if r, then s.
        Not p and not r.
        _____
        Not q and not s.

    d. If p, then q; and if r, then s.
        Not q and not s.
        _____
        Not p and not r.

8. If Dani Drugas wins the race for city council, then
    Mayor O'Hare is in trouble; and if Wanda Greene
    wins the race for city council, then everyone will be
    shocked. It is neither the case that Mayor O'Hare is
    in trouble, nor will everyone be shocked. So, neither
    Dani Drugas nor Wanda Greene wins the race for city
    council.

    a. If p, then q; and if r, then s.
        Either p or r.
        _____
        Either q or s.

    b. If p, then q; and if r, then s.
        Either not q or not r.
        _____
        Either not p or not s.

    c. If p, then q; and if r, then s.
        Not p and not r.
        _____
        Not q and not s.

    d. If p, then q; and if r, then s.
        Not q and not s.
        _____
        Not p and not r.

9. If Wanda is the blackmailer, then Wee Willie had a
    hand in the crime; and if Big Steve is the blackmailer,
    then Dani will be surprised. Either Wee Willie did not
    have a hand in the crime or Dani is not surprised. So,
    either Wanda is not the blackmailer or Big Steve is not
    the blackmailer.

    a. If p, then q; and if r, then s.
        Either p or r.
        _____
        Either q or s.

    b. If p, then q; and if r, then s.
        Either not q or not s.
        _____
        Either not p or not r.

    c. If p, then q; and if r, then s.
        Not p and not r.
        _____
        Not q and not s.

    d. If p, then q; and if r, then s.
        Not q and not s.
        _____
        Not p and not r.

10. If both Dani and Wanda were members of Red Riders, then Big Steve's investment bank should be examined. Wanda was a member of Red Riders, but Big Steve's investment bank should not be examined. So, Dani was not a member of Red Riders.

a. If p and q, then r.
p and q.
r.

b. If p and q, then r.
p and not r.
q.

c. If p and q, then r.
q and not r.
p.

d. If p and q, then r.
q and not r.
Not p.

4.13 Review Exercise Circle the argument that best matches the argument form.

1. **Example:**
If p, then q.
p.
q.

a. If Dani was in the Silver Shadows, then Wanda was in the Silver Shadows. Wanda was not in the Silver Shadows. So, Dani was not in the Silver Shadows.
b. Dani was in the Silver Shadows, for Wanda was in the Silver Shadows, and if Dani was in the Silver Shadows, then Wanda was in the Silver Shadows.
c. If Dani was in the Silver Shadows, then Wanda was in the Silver Shadows. Dani was not in the Silver Shadows. So, Wanda was not in the Silver Shadows.
d. **Wanda was in the Silver Shadows, for Dani was in the Silver Shadows, and if Dani was in the Silver Shadows, then Wanda was in the Silver Shadows.**

2. If p, then q.
Not q.
Not p.

a. If Dani was in the Silver Shadows, then Wanda was in the Silver Shadows. Wanda was not in the Silver Shadows. So, Dani was not in the Silver Shadows.
b. Dani was in the Silver Shadows, for Wanda was in the Silver Shadows, and if Dani was in the Silver Shadows, then Wanda was in the Silver Shadows.
c. If Dani was in the Silver Shadows, then Wanda was in the Silver Shadows. Dani was not in the Silver Shadows. So, Wanda was not in the Silver Shadows.
d. Wanda was in the Silver Shadows, for Dani was in the Silver Shadows, and if Dani was in the Silver Shadows, then Wanda was in the Silver Shadows.

(Continued)

3. If *p*, then *q*.
    If *q*, then *r*.
    ‾‾‾‾‾‾‾‾‾‾‾
    If *p*, then *r*.

    a. If Big Steve is an investment banker, then he has gone straight. If Big Steve has gone straight, then Dani can expect no trouble from him. So, if Dani can expect no trouble from Big Steve, then Big Steve is an investment banker.
    b. If Big Steve is an investment banker, then he has gone straight. So, if Dani can expect no trouble from Big Steve, then Dani can expect no trouble from him, for if Big Steve is an investment banker, then Dani can expect no trouble from him.
    c. If Big Steve is an investment banker, then he has gone straight. So, if Big Steve is an investment banker, Dani can expect no trouble from him, for if Big Steve has gone straight, then Dani can expect no trouble from him.
    d. If Big Steve has gone straight, then he is an investment banker. So, if Big Steve is an investment banker, Dani can expect no trouble from him, for if Big Steve has gone straight, then Dani can expect no trouble from him.

4. *p* or *q*.
    Not *q*.
    ‾‾‾‾‾
    p.

    a. Either Dani or Wanda has gone straight. Dani has not gone straight. So, Wanda has gone straight.
    b. Either Dani or Wanda has gone straight. Wanda has not gone straight. So, Dani has gone straight.
    c. Dani has gone straight or Wanda has gone straight. Dani has gone straight. So, Wanda has not gone straight.
    d. Dani has gone straight or Wanda has gone straight. Wanda has gone straight. So, Dani has not gone straight.

5.   If *p*, then *q*; and if *r*, then *s*.
     Either *p* or *r*.
     _____
     Either *q* or *s*.

   a. Either Dani has given up her relationship with the gang or she has not. If Dani has given up her relationship with the gang, then Big Steve is honest as the day is long; and if Dani has not given up her relationship with the gang, then Wild Wanda is serving time in the big house. So, either Big Steve is honest as the day is long or Wild Wanda is serving time in the big house.

   b. If Dani has given up her relationship with the gang, then Big Steve is honest as the day is long; and if Wee Willie's construction company is a front for the mob, then Wild Wanda is serving time in the big house. Either Dani has given up her relationship with the gang or Wee Willie's construction company is a front for the mob. So, either Big Steve is as honest as the day is long or Wild Wanda is serving time in the big house.

   c. Either Big Steve is not as honest as the day is long or Wild Wanda is not in the big house. If Dani has given up her relationship with the gang, then Big Steve is honest as the day is long; and if Wee Willie's construction company is a front for the mob, then Wild Wanda is serving time in the big house. So, either Dani has not given up her relationship with the gang or Wee Willie's construction company is not a front for the mob.

   d. If Wanda Greene has a home in Beverly Hills, then she is a successful businesswoman; and if Big Steve Watts runs an investment bank on North Broadway, then he is a successful businessman. Either Wanda Greene does not have a home in Beverly Hills or Big Steve Watts does not run an investment bank on North Broadway. So, neither is Wanda Greene a successful businesswoman, nor is Big Steve Watts a successful businessman.

(Continued)

6. If *p*, then *q*; and if *r*, then *s*.
   Not *q* or not *s*.
   _____
   Not *p* or not *r*.

   a. Either Dani has given up her relationship with the gang or she has not. If Dani has given up her relationship with the gang, then Big Steve is honest as the day is long; and if Dani has not given up her relationship with the gang, then Wild Wanda is serving time in the big house. So, either Big Steve is honest as the day is long or Wild Wanda is serving time in the big house.
   b. If Dani has given up her relationship with the gang, then Big Steve is honest as the day is long; and if Wee Willie's construction company is a front for the mob, then Wild Wanda is serving time in the big house. Either Big Steve is as honest as the day is long or Wild Wanda is serving time in the big house. So, either Dani has given up her relationship with the gang or Wee Willie's construction company is a front for the mob.
   c. If Dani has given up her relationship with the gang, then Big Steve is honest as the day is long; and if Wee Willie's construction company is a front for the mob, then Wild Wanda is serving time in the big house. Either Big Steve is not as honest as the day is long or Wild Wanda is not in the big house. So, either Dani has not given up her relationship with the gang or Wee Willie's construction company is not a front for the mob.
   d. If Wanda Greene has a home in Beverly Hills, then she is a successful businesswoman; and if Big Steve Watts runs an investment bank on North Broadway, then he is a successful businessman. Either Wanda Greene does not have a home in Beverly Hills or Big Steve Watts does not run an investment bank on North Broadway. So, neither is Wanda Greene a successful businesswoman nor is Big Steve Watts a successful businessman.

7. *p* and *q*.
   _____
   q.

   a. Big Steve runs an investment bank even though Wild Wanda is serving time in the big house. So, Wild Wanda is serving time in the big house.
   b. If Wanda Greene has a home in Beverly Hills, then she is a successful businesswoman; on the condition that if Big Steve Watts runs an investment bank on North Broadway, then he is a successful businessman. So, if Big Steve Watts runs an investment bank on North Broadway, then he is a successful businessman.
   c. If Wanda Greene has a home in Beverly Hills, then she is a successful businesswoman; and if Big Steve Watts runs an investment bank on North Broadway, then he is a successful businessman. So, if Big Steve Watts runs an investment bank on North Broadway, then he is a successful businessman.
   d. Big Steve runs an investment bank unless Wild Wanda is serving time in the big house. So, Big Steve runs investment bank.

8. Either *p* or *q*, but not both *p* and *q*.
   $$\frac{q.}{\text{Not } p.}$$

   a. Either Dani or Wanda served time, but they didn't both serve time. So, Dani didn't serve time, since Wanda did.
   b. Either Dani or Wanda served time, but they didn't both serve time. So, Dani served time, since Wanda didn't.
   c. Wanda served time or Dani ran for city council. Dani ran for city council. So, Wanda did not serve time.
   d. Both Wanda and Dani served time. So, it is not the case that either Wanda or Dani ran for city council.

9. $$\frac{p.}{p \text{ or } q.}$$

   a. Wee Willie builds buildings. So, Wee Willie builds buildings and Big Steve runs a bank, or Dani is running for city council.
   b. Wee Willie builds buildings. So, Wee Willie builds buildings or Big Steve runs a bank.
   c. Wee Willie builds buildings. So, if Wee Willie builds buildings and Big Steve runs a bank, then Dani is running for city council.
   d. Wee Willie builds buildings. So, Wee Willie builds buildings, and if Big Steve runs a bank, then Dani is running for city council.

10. If either *p* or *q*, then *r*.
    $$\frac{p.}{r.}$$

    a. Little Lilly teaches kindergarten. So, Dani is running for city council. For if either Little Lilly teaches kindergarten or Big Steve runs a bank, then Dani is running for city council.
    b. If either Little Lilly teaches kindergarten or Big Steve runs a bank, then Dani is running for city council. So, Dani is running for city council, since Big Steve runs a bank.
    c. If Little Lilly teaches kindergarten, then either Big Steve runs a bank or Dani is running for city council. Little Lilly teaches kindergarten. So, Dani is running for city council.
    d. If Little Lilly teaches kindergarten and Big Steve runs a bank, then Dani is running for city council. Big Steve runs a bank. So, if Little Lilly teaches kindergarten, then Dani is running for city council.

4.14 Review Exercise Circle the form that best represents each argument. Remember, *S* is the subject term of the conclusion; *P* is the predicate term of the conclusion; and *M* is the term that is in the premise, but not in the conclusion.

1. **Example:**
   Some people running for city council are not former motorcycle gang members.
   All people running for city council are Los Angles residents.

   So, some Los Angeles residents are not former motorcycle gang members.

   Terms: **Form:**
   S = Los Angeles residents
   P = former motorcycle gang members
   M = people running for city council

   $$\frac{\begin{array}{l}\text{Some } M \text{ are not } P.\\ \text{All } M \text{ are } S.\end{array}}{\text{Some } S \text{ are not } P.}$$

   a. Some *M* are not *P*.   b. Some *P* are not *M*.
      All *S* are *M*.   All *S* are *M*.
      ‾‾‾‾‾‾‾‾‾‾‾‾‾‾   ‾‾‾‾‾‾‾‾‾‾‾‾‾
      Some *S* are not *P*.   Some *S* are not *P*.

   ⓒ **Some *M* are not *P*.**   d. Some *P* are not *M*.
      All *M* are *S*.   All *M* are *S*.
      ‾‾‾‾‾‾‾‾‾‾‾‾   ‾‾‾‾‾‾‾‾‾‾‾‾
      Some *S* are not *P*.   Some *S* are not *P*.

2. Some former motorcycle gang members are people being blackmailed.
   Some candidates for city council are people being blackmailed.

   So, some candidates for city council are not former motorcycle gang members.

   Terms: **Form:**
   S = candidates for city council
   P = former motorcycle gang members
   M = people being blackmailes

   a. Some *M* are *P*.   b. Some *P* are *M*.
      Some *S* are *M*.   Some *S* are *M*.
      ‾‾‾‾‾‾‾‾‾‾‾‾   ‾‾‾‾‾‾‾‾‾‾‾‾
      Some *S* are not *P*.   Some *S* are not *P*.

   c. Some *M* are *P*.   d. Some *P* are *M*.
      Some *M* are *S*.   Some *M* are *S*.
      ‾‾‾‾‾‾‾‾‾‾‾‾   ‾‾‾‾‾‾‾‾‾‾‾‾
      Some *S* are not *P*.   Some *S* are not *P*.

3. No police officers are candidates for city council.
    No candidates for city council are famous Americans.
    _____
    So, some famous Americans are not police officers.

Terms: **Form:**

S = famous Americans
P = police officers
M = candidates for city council

a. No *M* are *P.*   b. No *P* are *M.*
   No *S* are *M.*   No *S* are *M.*
   _____   _____
   Some *S* are not *P.*   Some *S* are not *P.*

c. No *M* are *P.*   d. No *P* are *M.*
   No *M* are *S.*   No *M* are *S.*
   _____   _____
   Some *S* are not *P.*   Some *S* are not *P.*

4. No police officers are victims of blackmail.
    Some city council candidates are victims of blackmail.
    _____
    So, some city council candidates are not police officers.

Terms: **Form:**

S = city council candidates
P = police officers
M = victims of blackmail

a. No *M* are *P.*   b. No *P* are *M.*
   Some *S* are *M.*   Some *S* are *M.*
   _____   _____
   Some *S* are not *P.*   Some *S* are not *P.*

c. No *M* are *P.*   d. No *P* are *M.*
   Some *M* are *S.*   Some *M* are *S.*
   _____   _____
   Some *S* are not *P.*   Some *S* are not *P.*

(Continued)

5. All blackmailers are people seeking power.
    No blackmailers are law-abiding citizens.
    So, no law-abiding citizens are people seeking power.

    Terms: **Form:**
    S = law-abiding citizens
    P = people seeking power
    M = blackmailers

    a. All *M* are *P*.   b. All *P* are *M*.
       No *S* are *M*.   No *S* are *M*.
       No *S* are *P*.   No *S* are *P*.

    c. All *M* are *P*.   d. All *P* are *M*.
       No *M* are *S*.   No *M* are *S*.
       No *S* are *P*.   No *S* are *P*.

6. No honest people are blackmailers, so some people who know Dani Drugas are not
    honest people, since some people who know Dani Drugas are blackmailers.

    Terms: **Form:**
    S = people who know Dani Drugas
    P = honest people
    M = blackmailers

    a. No *M* are *P*.   b. No *P* are *M*.
       Some *S* are *M*.   Some *S* are *M*.
       Some *S* are not *P*.   Some *S* are not *P*.

    c. No *M* are *P*.   d. No *P* are *M*.
       All *M* are *S*.   Some *M* are *S*.
       Some *S* are not *P*.   Some *S* are not *P*.

7. Since some blackmailers are people seeking revenge, and no blackmailers are members of the LAPD, it follows that some members of the LAPD are not people seeking revenge.

Terms:
S = members of the LAPD
P = people seeking revenge
M = blackmailers

Form:

a. Some M are P.
   No S are M.
   ——————————
   Some S are not P.

b. Some P are M.
   No S are M.
   ——————————
   Some S are not P.

c. Some M are P.
   No M are S.
   ——————————
   Some S are not P.

d. Some M are P.
   No M are S.
   ——————————
   Some S are P.

8. No motorcycle gang members are people who hate to drive, so no members of the Silver Shadows are people who hate to drive, for all members of the Silver Shadows are motorcycle gang members.

Terms:
S = members of the Silver Shadows
P = people who hate to drive
M = motorcycle gang members

Form:

a. No M are P.
   All S are M.
   ——————————
   No S are P.

b. No P are M.
   All S are M.
   ——————————
   No S are P.

c. No M are P.
   All M are S.
   ——————————
   No S are P.

d. No P are M.
   All M are S.
   ——————————
   No S are P.

(Continued)

9. Some people being blackmailed are former motorcycle gang members, and some former motorcycle gang members are people running for city council. So, some people running for city council are people being blackmailed.

Terms: **Form:**
S = people running for city council
P = people being blackmailed
M = former motorcycle gang members

   a. Some *M* are *P*.   b. Some *P* are *M*.
      Some *S* are *M*.   Some *S* are *M*.
      Some *S* are *P*.   Some *S* are *P*.

   c. Some *M* are *P*.   d. Some *P* are *M*.
      Some *M* are *S*.   Some *M* are *S*.
      Some *S* are *P*.   Some *S* are *P*.

10. Some members of the LAPD are not members of the Silver Shadows, for some members of the LAPD are not people running for mayor, and some people running for mayor are not members of the Silver Shadows.

Terms: **Form:**
S = members of the LAPD
P = members of the Silver Shadows
M = people running for mayor

   a. Some *M* are not *P*.   b. Some *P* are not *M*.
      Some *S* are not *M*.   Some *S* are not *M*.
      Some *S* are not *P*.   Some *S* are not *P*.

   c. Some *M* are not *P*.   d. Some *P* are not *M*.
      Some *M* are not *S*.   Some *M* are not *S*.
      Some *S* are not *P*.   Some *S* are not *P*.

4.15 Review Exercise Which argument is a deductive counterexample of the given argument? Circle the correct answer.

1. **Example:**
If Dani is elected to city council, then either her past remains unknown or Detective Wise rigs the election. Detective Wise does not rig the election.
So, Dani is not elected to the city council.

If p, then q or r.
Not r.
_____
Not p.

a. **If Cincinnati is in Ohio, then either Omaha is in Nebraska or New York City is in Colorado.**
New York City is not is Colorado
_____
So, Cincinnati is not in Ohio.

b. If Cincinnati is in Ohio, then either Omaha is in New Hampshire or New York City is in Colorado.
New York City is not in Colorado.
_____
So, Cincinnati is not in Ohio.

c. If Cincinnati is in Pennsylvania, then either Omaha is in New Hampshire or New York City is in Colorado.
New York City is not in Colorado.
_____
So, Cincinnati is not in Pennsylvania.

d. If Cincinnati is in Pennsylvania, then either Omaha is in Nebraska or New York City is in New York.
New York City is in New York.
_____
So, Cincinnati is not in Pennsylvania.

2. Some former motorcycle gang members are people who go on to live productive lives.
Some people who serve prison terms are people who go on to live productive lives.
_____
So, some people who serve prison terms are former motorcycle gang members.

a. Some politicians are liars.
Some liars are generally dishonest people.
_____
So, some generally dishonest people are politicians.

b. Some reptiles are mammals.
Some lizards are mammals.
_____
So, some lizards are reptiles.

c. Some dogs are mammals.
Some cows are mammals.
_____
So, some cows are dogs.

d. Some dogs are not mammals.
Some lizards are dogs.
_____
So, some lizards are not dogs.

(Continued)

3. If both Big Steve and Wild Wanda were members of the Red Riders, then the current mayor of Los Angles was a member of the Red Riders.
    The current mayor of Los Angeles was not a member of the Red Riders.
    So, Big Steve was not a member of the Red Riders.

    a. If both dogs and cats are mammals, then humans are mammals.
        Humans are mammals.
        So, dogs are not mammals.

    b. If both frogs and lizards are amphibians, then dogs are amphibians.
        Dogs are not amphibians.
        So, frogs are not amphibians.

    c. If both cows and horses are reptiles, then lizards are reptiles.
        Lizards are reptiles.
        So, horses are reptiles.

    d. If both frogs and toads are amphibians, then lizards are amphibians.
        Lizards are not amphibians.
        So, frogs are not amphibians.

4. Some residents of the city are not former motorcycle gang members.
    Some former motorcycle gang members are not candidates for city council.
    So, all candidates for city council are residents of the city.

    a. Some cats are not dogs.
        Some cats are not horses.
        So, all horses are dogs.

    b. Some dogs are not cats.
        Some cats are not horses.
        So, all horses are dogs.

    c. Some cats are not dogs.
        No horses are dogs.
        So, all horses are not cats.

    d. Some cats are not horses.
        Some cats are dogs.
        So, some horses are not dogs.

5. If both Big Steve and Little Lilly were members of the
    Silver Shadows, then Detective Wise works for the
    LAPD and Dani Drugas is running for city council.
    Either Big Steve or Little Lilly was a member of the
    Silver Shadows.
    So, Dani Drugas is running for city council.

a. If both George W. Bush and George
    Washington were twenty-first century
    American presidents, then frogs are
    mammals and cows are mammals.
    Either George W. Bush or George
    Washington was a twenty-first century
    American president.
    So, frogs are mammals.

b. If either George W. Bush or George
    Washington was a twenty-first century
    American president, then cows are
    mammals and frogs are mammals.
    Both George W. Bush and George
    Washington were twenty-first century
    American presidents.
    So, frogs are mammals.

c. If either George W. Bush or George
    Washington was a twenty-first century
    American president, then cows are
    mammals and frogs are mammals.
    Both George W. Bush and George
    Washington were twenty-first century
    American presidents.
    So, cows are mammals.

d. If both George W. Bush and George
    Washington were twenty-first century
    American presidents, then cows are
    mammals and frogs are mammals.
    Either George W. Bush or George
    Washington was a twenty-first century
    American president.
    So, frogs are mammals.

6. Given that all blackmailers are greedy people and
    that all blackmailers are criminals, it follows that all
    criminals are greedy people.

a. All cats are meat-eaters.
    All cats are mammals.
    So, all mammals are meat-eaters.

b. All meat-eaters are cats.
    All cats are mammals.
    So, all mammals are meat-eaters.

c. All mammals are meat-eaters.
    All cats are meat-eaters.
    So, all cats are mammals.

d. All mammals are meat-eaters.
    All mammals are cats.
    So, all cats are meat-eaters.

(Continued)

7. If Big Steve belonged to the Silver Shadows, then Little Lilly belonged to the Silver Shadows and Dani belonged to the Silver Shadows. So, Little Lilly belonged to the Silver Shadows. For either Dani belonged to the Silver Shadows or Big Steve belonged to the Silver Shadows.

a. If cows eat meat, then both mice always drink wine with dinner and cats eat meat.
   Either cats eat meat or cows eat meat.
   So, mice always drink wine with dinner.

c. If cats eat meat, then both mice always drink wine with dinner and cows eat meat.
   Either cats eat meat or mice always drink wine with dinner.
   So, cows eat meat.

b. If cats eat meat, then both mice always drink wine with dinner and cows eat meat.
   Either cats eat meat or cows eat meat.
   So, mice always drink wine with dinner.

d. If cows eat meat, the both mice always drink wine with dinner and cats eat meat.
   Either cows eat meat or mice always drink wine with dinner.

8. Some corporate executives are people who have secret information, for no corporate executives are blackmailers, and all blackmailers are people who have secret information.

a. No reptiles are mammals.
   All lizards are reptiles.
   So, some lizards are mammals.

b. All rubies are valuable stones.
   No pennies are rubies.
   So, some pennies are not valuable stones.

c. All rubies are valuable stones.
   No pennies are rubies.
   So, some pennies are valuable stones.

d. All lizards are reptiles.
   No mammals are lizards.
   So, no mammals are reptiles.

9. Some blackmailers are former gang members. So, some outstanding citizens are former gang members, for some blackmailers are not outstanding citizens.

a. All poppies are flowers.
    Some flowers are not roses.
    _____
    So, some roses are not poppies.

b. Some flowers are poppies.
    Some flowers are roses.
    _____
    So, some roses are not poppies.

c. Some flowers are not poppies.
    Some flowers are not roses.
    _____
    So, some poppies are not roses.

d. Some flowers are poppies.
    Some flowers are not roses.
    _____
    So, some roses are poppies.

10. Some terrorists are not suicide bombers, for all terrorists are criminals, and some criminals are not suicide bombers.

a. Some people are not politicians.
    All presidents are people.
    _____
    So, some presidents are not politicians.

b. All people are politicians.
    All presidents are people.
    _____
    So, some presidents are politicians.

b. Some people are politicians.
    All presidents are people.
    _____
    So, some presidents are not politicians.

d. Some people are not politicians.
    All presidents are people.
    _____
    So, some presidents are politicians.

4.16 Review Exercise What kind of argument is each of the following? Circle the correct answer.

1. **Example:**
    Dani Drugas was a member of the Silver Shadows and became a productive member of society. Big Steve was a member of the Silver Shadows and became a productive member of society. Little Lilly was a member of the Silver Shadows and became a productive member of society. Wee Willie was a member of the Silver Shadows and became a productive member of society. So, most members of the Silver Shadows became productive members of society.
    a. This is an argument to an explanation.
    b. This is an argument by analogy.
    c. **This is an inductive generalization.**
    d. This is a valid argument.

(Continued)

2. Wild Wanda Greene was released from Valley State Prison for Woman two months ago. Wild Wanda had taken pictures when she and Dani were members of the Silver Shadows. She had been jealous of Dani. Dani had been campaigning for city council for three months, but the blackmail letters started just under two months ago. So, it is reasonable to conclude that Wild Wanda is the blackmailer.
   a. This is an argument to an explanation.
   b. This is an argument by analogy.
   c. This is an inductive generalization.
   d. This is a valid argument.

3. Dani Drugas is like the current mayor insofar as both were members of motorcycle gangs in their youth. The mayor managed to hide the fact that he'd been a member of a motorcycle gang. So, it's reasonable to conclude that Dani also can hide the fact that she was a member of the motorcycle gang.
   a. This is an argument to an explanation.
   b. This is an argument by analogy.
   c. This is an inductive generalization.
   d. This is a valid argument.

4. If Wee Willie has a hand in the blackmail, then Wild Wanda is playing a role in the blackmail. If Wild Wanda is playing a role in the blackmail, then Wee Willie and Wild Wanda have remained in contact over the years. So, if Wee Willie has a hand in the blackmail, then Wee Willie and Wild Wanda have remained in contact over the years.
   a. This is an argument to an explanation.
   b. This is an argument by analogy.
   c. This is an inductive generalization.
   d. This is a valid argument.

5. Detective Wise has worked on seven previous blackmail cases. She solved all of them. Dani Drugas' case is a blackmail case. So, it's likely that Detective Wise will solve it.
   a. This is an argument to an explanation.
   b. This is an argument by analogy.
   c. This is an inductive generalization.
   d. This is a valid argument.

6. Dani is running for city council on a strong anti-crime platform. If she is elected, it is likely that organized crime will be dealt a serious blow. So, it is likely that she is being blackmailed to prevent a crackdown on organized crime.
   a. This is an argument to an explanation.
   b. This is an argument by analogy.
   c. This is an inductive generalization.
   d. This is a valid argument.

7. Detective Wise works for the LAPD, and she is not a blackmailer. Sergeant McCoy works for the LAPD, and he is not a blackmailer. Officer Baker works for the LAPD and he is not a blackmailer. Captain Schwartz works for the LAPD, and she is not a blackmailer. So, it's likely that no one who works for the LAPD is a blackmailer.
   a. This is an argument to an explanation.
   b. This is an argument by analogy.
   c. This is an inductive generalization.
   d. This is a valid argument.

8. If Captain Schwartz is on the case, then she'll be puzzled; and if Detective Wise is on the case, then she'll solve it. Either Captain Schwartz is on the case or Detective Wise is on the case. So, either Captain Schwartz will be puzzled or Detective Wise will solve the case.
   a. This is an argument to an explanation.
   b. This is an argument by analogy.
   c. This is an inductive generalization.
   d. This is a valid argument.

9. Camilla Greene is Wanda's sister. Camilla kept all her sister's things while Wanda was in jail. Camilla found the pictures of Dani Drugas and the Silver Shadows. Camilla talked with Wanda about the pictures shortly before Wanda was released from jail. So, it's likely that Camilla played a role in the blackmail scheme.
   a. This is an argument to an explanation.
   b. This is an argument by analogy.
   c. This is an inductive generalization.
   d. This is a valid argument.

10. Wild Wanda Greene was released from the Valley State Prison for Woman on June 4. She was arrested for shoplifting on June 8. The blackmail letters began on June 15. Any blackmail letters Wanda had tried to send from jail would have been detected by the police. So, Wanda couldn't have been the only person having a hand in the blackmail.
    a. This is an argument to an explanation.
    b. This is an argument by analogy.
    c. This is an inductive generalization.
    d. This is a valid argument.

11. Dani Drugas' case is like a case four years go in which Jorge Gonzalez ran for city council, but he had been a member of a motorcycle gang in his youth and someone had tried to blackmail him. Detective Wise was able to solve Jorge's case. So, it's likely she will solve Dani's case, too.
    a. This is an argument to an explanation.
    b. This is an argument by analogy.
    c. This is an inductive generalization.
    d. This is a valid argument.

(Continued)

12. Either Wanda was running the blackmail by herself or she had help. Wanda wasn't running the blackmail by herself. So, she had help.
   a. This is an argument to an explanation.
   b. This is an argument by analogy.
   c. This is an inductive generalization.
   d. This is a valid argument.

13. When Sergeant McCoy broke a big case, he was promoted. When Captain Schwartz broke a big case, she was promoted. When Officer Baker broke a big case, he was promoted. The Drugas case is a big case, and Detective Wise will break it. So, we can expect her to be promoted, too.
   a. This is an argument to an explanation.
   b. This is an argument by analogy.
   c. This is an inductive generalization.
   d. This is a valid argument.

14. When Sergeant McCoy broke a big case, he was promoted. When Captain Schwartz broke a big case, she was promoted. When Officer Baker broke a big case, he was promoted. So, whenever a police officer breaks a big case, he or she is promoted.
   a. This is an argument to an explanation.
   b. This is an argument by analogy.
   c. This is an inductive generalization.
   d. This is a valid argument.

15. Big Steve Watts has kept in contact with Wild Wanda. Big Steve's bank is connected with organized crime in the city. Electing Dani Drugas would threaten organized crime in the city. So, there is reason to believe that Big Steve had a hand in the blackmailing.
   a. This is an argument to an explanation.
   b. This is an argument by analogy.
   c. This is an inductive generalization.
   d. This is a valid argument.

Chapter 4 Quiz

Choose the best answer for each of the following questions.

1. The strongest evidence for the truth of an argument's conclusion is provided by:
    a. an argument to an explanation.
    b. a sound argument.
    c. a valid argument.
    d. an argument by analogy.

2. Invalid arguments with true premises:
    a. provide conclusive evidence for the truth of their conclusions.
    b. provide no evidence for the truth of their conclusions.
    c. can provide only some evidence for the truth of their conclusions.
    d. usually have false premises and a true conclusion.

3. If a valid argument has all true premises, then:
    a. its conclusion must also be true.
    b. it shows that the conclusion is only probably true.
    c. it is an argument by analogy.
    d. its premises are inconsistent.

4. If two arguments have the same form (structure), then:
    a. all premises of both arguments are true.
    b. both arguments are inductive.
    c. both arguments are valid or both arguments are invalid.
    d. both arguments provide strong inductive evidence for their conclusions.

5. A deductive counterexample shows that:
    a. a deductive argument is valid.
    b. an inductive argument if valid.
    c. an argument form is invalid.
    d. an argument form is only sometimes valid.

6. Arguments by analogy:
    a. proceed from many individual cases to a general conclusion.
    b. reach general conclusions and apply those conclusions to a particular case.
    c. are valid arguments.
    d. compare the properties of two or more things and conclude that because they are similar in a number of ways, they are similar in yet another way.

7. An inductive generalization:
    a. always reaches a conclusion about all things of a certain kind.
    b. reaches a conclusion about all, most, or many things of a kind.
    c. is the only kind of inductive argument.
    d. is a valid argument.

(Continued)

8. An argument to the best explanation:
    a. concludes that because a certain account will explain a number of facts, it is probably the correct explanation.
    b. reaches a universal conclusion.
    c. is a valid inductive argument.
    d. both a and c

9. A sound deductive argument:
    a. is a valid argument.
    b. is a strong inductive argument.
    c. is an argument that has only true premises.
    d. fulfills both conditions a and c.

10. Inductive arguments:
    a. are all valid arguments.
    b. are all invalid arguments.
    c. are sometimes valid arguments.
    d. always proceed from particular premises to a general conclusion.

CHAPTER 5

- Arguments Based on Claims
- Review

Overview

Most of the valid arguments found in ordinary life are based on the relations among the truth and falsehood of claims. Different kinds of claims are true or false under different conditions. When these claims are put together to form arguments, some of those arguments are valid. This chapter examines:

1. the conditions under which some kinds of claims are true.

2. the most common argument forms based on claims, and how to determine whether they are valid.

3. complex arguments based on those common forms.

| CASE 17 | City of Los Angeles Police Department |

[1]Here are the facts: [2]Juan Sanchez was robbed at gunpoint. [3]He had been on the ninth hole of the Griffith Park Golf Course at the time of the robbery. [4]The robber was wearing jeans, a Hollywood Bowl T-shirt, and a gorilla mask. [5]The robber got away with sixty dollars in cash and a number of golf balls.

[6]Detective Wise wondered how some of these claims fit together.

[7]Since Juan Sanchez was robbed at gunpoint, it is false that Juan Sanchez was not robbed at gunpoint.

[8]Either Sanchez had been on the ninth hole of the Griffith Park Golf course at the time of the robbery or the robber was wearing jeans, a Hollywood Bowl T-shirt, and a gorilla mask.

[9]The robber was wearing jeans, a Hollywood Bowl T-shirt, and a gorilla mask and the robber got away with sixty dollars in cash and a number of golf balls.

[10]If Juan Sanchez was robbed at gunpoint, then the robber got away with sixty dollars in cash and a number of golf balls.

[11]"Hmm," thought Detective Wise. [12]"By itself, knowing how to put claims together will not help us solve the crime."

5.1 Simple and Compound Claims

Most of the arguments we find in everyday life concern relations among claims. Claims assert facts; for example, "Joe went to the store." Simple claims are claims that do not have another claim as a proper part. Compound claims do have another claim as a proper part; for example, "Joe went to the store and Mary went to a movie."

We shall be concerned with those compound claims in which the truth or falsehood—its truth-value—of the whole claim depends upon the truth-value of its parts. These are called truth-functional compound claims.

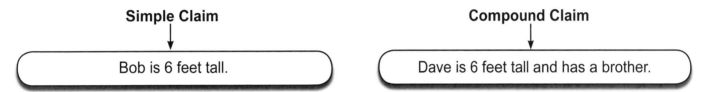

Simple Claim
Bob is 6 feet tall.

Compound Claim
Dave is 6 feet tall and has a brother.

Examples of claims and their denials in Case 17:

Note: If a claim is true, its denial is false. If a claim is false, its denial is true.

	Claim	Truth Value	Denial of Claim	Denial's Truth Value
a.	"Juan Sanchez was robbed at gunpoint."	True	"Juan Sanchez was not robbed at gunpoint."	False
b.	"The robber was wearing a tuxedo."	False *The robber was wearing jeans and a T-shirt.*	"The robber was not wearing a tuxedo."	True
c.	"The robber got away with $1,000 in cash."	False *The robber only got $60.*	"The robber did not get away with $1,000" in cash."	True
d.	"Sanchez was robbed and the robber got away."	True	"It is not the case that both Sanchez was robbed and the robber got away."	False

The primary purpose of this book is to teach claims and arguments in ordinary language. However, we will also introduce a few symbols (see below). Symbols make it easier for some people to see the structure of a claim or arguments. Truth tables (see below) show all the conditions in which a claim can be true or false. Every claim is true or false. If a claim is true, its denial is false. If a claim is false, its denial is true. Where *p* is any claim, and T stands for true, F stands for false:

Claim:
p: The light is on.

Claim	Claim's Denial
p	Not *p.*
T	F
F	T

> Some people like symbols. They say symbols allow one to clearly see the relations among claims. The symbol for denial is the tilde (~). "Not *p*" is represented as "~*p*".

A **conjunction** is composed of two claims. A conjunction is true if and only if both its component claims—the **conjuncts**—are true. The most common word used for conjunction is *and*. Other words showing conjunction include but, yet, even though, although, and however.

Conjunction	Form	Claims (conjuncts)
Rover is a dog and Rover has black fur.	*p* and *q*.	*p:* Rover is a dog. *q:* Rover has black fur.

p	*q*	*p* and *q*.
T	T	T
T	F	F
F	T	F
F	F	F

Conjunction ("and") can be represented by an ampersand (&). "*p* and *q*" can be represented by "*p* & *q*".

Examples of conjunctions in Case 17:

Note: *And* is commonly used to show conjunction. Other words that show a conjunction are *but, yet, although*, and *nevertheless*.

	Conjunction	Form	Claims	Truth Value
a.	"Sanchez was robbed and the robber got away with $60."	*p* and *q*.	*p:* Sanchez was robbed. *q:* The robber got away with $60.	Both claims are true. So, the conjunction is true.
b.	"Sanchez was robbed and the robber got away with $1,000."	*p* and *q*.	*p:* Sanchez was robbed. *q:* The robber got away with $1,000.	The first conjunct is true. The second conjunct is false. So, the conjunction is false.
c.	"The robber was wearing a tuxedo and the robber got away with $60."	*p* and *q*.	*p:* The robber was wearing a tuxedo. *q:* The robber got away with $60.	The first conjunct is false. The second conjunct is true. So, the conjunction is false.
d.	"The robber was wearing a tuxedo and the robber got away with $1,000."	*p* and *q*.	*p:* The robber was wearing a tuxedo. *q:* The robber got away with $1,000.	The first conjunct is false. The second conjunct is false. So, the conjunction is false.

A disjunction[1] is composed of two claims. A disjunction is true except when both its component claims—the **disjuncts**—are false.

Disjunction	Form	Claims
John went to the store or Mary went to a movie.	p or q.	p: John went to the store. q: Mary went to a movie.

p	q	p or q.
T	T	T
T	F	T
F	T	T
F	F	F

Disjunction ("or") can be represented by a wedge ($\vee$). "Either p or q" can be represented by "$p \vee q$".

Examples of disjunctions in Case 17:

Note: *Or* is the most common word used in a disjunction. *Unless* can also be used to show disjunction.

	Disjunction	Form	Claims	Truth Value
a.	"Either Sanchez was robbed or the robber was wearing jeans."	p or q.	p: Sanchez was robbed. q: The robber was wearing jeans.	The first disjunct is true. The second disjunct is true. So, the disjunction is true.
b.	"Either Sanchez was robbed or the robber was wearing a tuxedo."	p or q.	p: Sanchez was robbed. q: The robber was wearing a tuxedo.	The first disjunct is true. The second disjunct is false. So, the disjunction is true.
c.	"The robber was wearing a tuxedo unless the robber got away with $60."	p or q.	p: The robber was wearing a tuxedo. q: The robber got away with $60.	The first disjunct is false. The second disjunct is true. So, the disjunction is true.
d.	"The robber was wearing a tuxedo unless the robber got away with $1,000."	p or q.	p: The robber was wearing a tuxedo. q: The robber got away with $1,000.	The first disjunct is false. The second disjunct is false. So, the disjunction is false.

---

1 This disjunction is known as an *inclusive* disjunction. Sometimes the sense of *or* is *exclusive*. When the menu in the restaurant says, "soup or salad is included with the meal," the "or" is exclusive. It means soup or salad is included, but not both. Inclusive disjunction is assumed by all the argument forms in 5.2

A **conditional claim** is composed of two claims. The *if*-clause is called the **antecedent**. The *then*-clause is called the **consequent**. It is true except when the antecedent is true and the consequent is false.

Conditional	Form	Claims
If I get hungry I will walk to the store.	If *p*, then *q*.	*p:* I get hungry. *q:* I will walk to the store.

p	*q*	If *p*, then *q*.
T	*T*	*T*
T	*F*	*F*
F	*T*	*T*
F	*F*	*T*

The conditional can be represented by an arrow ($\rightarrow$). "If *p*, then *q*" can be represented by "$p \rightarrow q$".

Examples of conditional claims in Case 17:

	Conditional	Form	Claims	Truth Value
a.	"If Sanchez was robbed, then the robber wore a gorilla mask."	If *p*, then *q*.	*p:* Sanchez was robbed. *q:* The robber wore a gorilla mask.	The antecedent is true. The consequent is true. So, the conditional claim is true.
b.	"If Sanchez was robbed, then the robber wore a tuxedo."	If *p*, then *q*.	*p:* Sanchez was robbed. *q:* The robber wore a tuxedo.	The antecedent is true. The consequent is false. So, the conditional claim is false.
c.	"The robber wore a tuxedo only if the robber wore a gorilla mask."	If *p*, then *q*.	*p:* The robber wore a tuxedo. *q:* The robber wore a gorilla mask.	The antecedent—"The robber wore a tuxedo"—is false. The consequent—"The robber wore a gorilla mask"—is true. So, the conditional claim is true.
d.	"The robber wore a tuxedo provided that the robber was running naked across the golf course."	If *p*, then *q*.	*p:* The robber was running naked across the golf course. *q:* The robber wore a tuxedo.	The antecedent—"The robber was running naked across the golf course"—is false. The consequent—"The robber was wearing a tuxedo"—is false. So, the conditional claim is true.

The antecedent commonly introduced by "if" and the consequent commonly introduced by "then" can be introduced by other words. For example, the antecedent can also be introduced by the antededent: "provided that," "on condition that," "implies that." The consequent can also be introduced by "only if."

5.2   Exercise Circle the type of claim. Writing the form of the claim is often helpful, but it is not required. *Optional compound claims reference sheet available on page 293.

1. **Example:**
    If Juan was robbed, then Detective Wise is puzzled.
    a. Denial
    b. Conjunction
    c. Disjunction
    d.) **Conditional***

    If p, then q.

    *Leave the connecting words (and, or, if ... then ..., not) and abbreviate the simple claims to a letter. "Juan was robbed" might be abbreviated J. "Detective Wise is puzzled" might be abbreviated D. If you have "If J, then D," its form is the same as "If *p*, then *q*." It's a conditional claim.

2. Either the robber was wearing a gorilla mask or the robber was wearing a tuxedo.
    a. Denial
    b. Conjunction
    c. Disjunction
    d. Conditional

3. Juan was robbed and the robber stole some golf balls.
    a. Denial
    b. Conjunction
    c. Disjunction
    d. Conditional

4. The robber was not robbed.
    a. Denial
    b. Conjunction
    c. Disjunction
    d. Conditional

5. Detective Wise is puzzled provided that the robber got away.
    a. Denial
    b. Conjunction
    c. Disjunction
    d. Conditional

6. Juan Sanchez was playing golf unless the robbery took place in the clubhouse.
    a. Denial
    b. Conjunction
    c. Disjunction
    d. Conditional

(Continued)

7. The robber did not wear a tuxedo during the robbery.
   a. Denial
   b. Conjunction
   c. Disjunction
   d. Conditional

8. Even though Juan Sanchez was robbed, he finished his game of golf.
   a. Denial
   b. Conjunction
   c. Disjunction
   d. Conditional

9. The robber stole $60 only if Juan Sanchez carried $60 on the golf course.
   a. Denial
   b. Conjunction
   c. Disjunction
   d. Conditional

10. Juan was robbed, but the robber got away.
    a. Denial
    b. Conjunction
    c. Disjunction
    d. Conditional

Sometimes a compound claim is itself composed of **compound claims**.

Examples of compound claims that are composed of compound claims in Case 17:

	Compound Claim	Form	Claim Name(s)
a.	"If Sanchez was robbed but the robber got away, Detective Wise is puzzled."	If *p* and *q*, then *r*.	The main claim is a conditional. Its antecedent is a conjunction.
b.	"Juan was not hurt, although he was robbed."	Not *p* and *q*.	The main claim is a conjunction. Its first conjunct is a denial.
c.	"Either Juan was robbed and the robber got away, or Detective Wise caught the robber on the golf course."	Either *p* and *q*, or *r*.	The main claim is a disjunction. The first disjunct is a conjunction.
d.	"If the robber did not wear a tuxedo, then either the robber wore jeans or the robber wore a gorilla mask."	If not *p*, then either *q* or *r*.	The main claim is a conditional. The antecedent is a denial. The consequent is a disjunction.

5.3 **Exercise** Identify all the types of claims found in each compound claim. Circle the best answers. Writing the form of the claim is often helpful, but it is not required. *Optional claims form reference sheet available on page 293.

1. **Example:**
   Either Sanchez and the robber were playing golf, or the robber was trespassing on the golf course.
   a. Denial
   (b.) **Conjunction**
   (c.) **Disjunction**
   d. Conditional

   p and q, or r.

2. If Sanchez didn't chase the robber, then Sanchez continued playing golf.
   a. Denial
   b. Conjunction
   c. Disjunction
   d. Conditional

3. Either both Sanchez and Detective Wise are puzzled, or there has been a break in the case.
   a. Denial
   b. Conjunction
   c. Disjunction
   d. Conditional

4. It is not the case that both Sanchez was robbed and the robber got away only if there has been a break in the case.
   a. Denial
   b. Conjunction
   c. Disjunction
   d. Conditional

5. Juan Sanchez was robbed but the robber dropped her gun.
   a. Denial
   b. Conjunction
   c. Disjunction
   d. Conditional

6. If Juan was robbed but the robber didn't get away, then either Detective Wise was on the ball or Sanchez attacked the robber.
   a. Denial
   b. Conjunction
   c. Disjuncton
   d. Conditional

7. Juan Sanchez was robbed, yet the robber either wore jeans or a gorilla mask.
    a. Denial
    b. Conjunction
    c. Disjunction
    d. Conditional

8. Juan Sanchez was robbed only if either the robber stole $60 or Detective Wise has close ties to a criminal gang.
    a. Denial
    b. Conjunction
    c. Disjunction
    d. Conditional

9. Juan Sanchez was playing golf provided that Griffith Park Golf Course was open and it was not raining.
    a. Denial
    b. Conjunction
    c. Disjunction
    d. Conditional

10. Juan Sanchez was playing golf but he was not robbed, on the condition that security at Griffith Park Golf Club was increased or Juan hit the robber with a three iron.
    a. Denial
    b. Conjunction
    c. Disjunction
    d. Conditional

CASE 18 | City of Los Angeles Police Department

[1]There was a robbery at the Gold Exchange. [2]More than fifty thousand dollars in gems and jewelry was stolen. [3]Detective Wise was trying to figure out how the crime was committed. [4]Her reasoning was as follows:

[5]If they broke into the Exchange, then there should be evidence of a break-in. [6]They did break into the Exchange. [7]Therefore, there should be evidence of a break-in.

[8]If they came in through one of the doors, then the alarm would have sounded. [9]But the alarm didn't sound. [10]So they didn't come in through one of the doors.

[11]If the robbers broke in through the air vents, then they could have replaced the vent when they left. [12]If they replaced the vent when they left, there would have been no evidence of a break-in. [13]So, if the robbers broke in through the air vents, there would have been no evidence of a break-in. [14]There was no evidence of a break-in. [15]But nothing follows from that.

[16]Either it was an inside job or there was evidence of a break-in. [17]There was no evidence of a break-in. [18]So, it was an inside job.

[19]If there was no evidence of a break-in, then it was an inside job; but if there was evidence of a break-in but we didn't find it yet, then we're up against a clever robber. [20]Either there was no evidence of a break-in or there was evidence of a break-in but we didn't find it yet. [21]So, either it was an inside job or we're up against a clever robber.

[22]There was a robbery at the Gold Exchange. [23]So, either there was a robbery at the Gold Exchange or "hot" gems are for sale on the black market.

[24]There was a robbery at the Gold Exchange. [25]More than fifty thousand dollars in gems and jewelry was stolen. [26]So, there was a robbery at the Gold Exchange and more than fifty thousand dollars in gems and jewelry was stolen.

[27]There was a robbery at the Gold Exchange and we have no suspects. [28]So, we have no suspects.

[29]If it was an inside job, then some employees lied about where they were this weekend; if we're up against a clever robber, then the case will go unsolved. [30]Either all the employees were truthful (that is, not lying) about their whereabouts this weekend or we will solve the case (that is, it will not go unsolved). [31]So, either it wasn't an inside job or we're not up against a clever robber.

5.4 Common Argument Forms

Affirming the Antecedent* (*modus ponens*)
*The name of this argument tells what the second (nonconditional) premise does relative to the conditional premise.

Example	Form	Claims
If John went to the store, then Sally went to a movie. John went to the store. So, Sally went to a movie.	If p, then q. $\dfrac{p.}{q.}$	p: John went to the store. q: Sally went to a movie.

The truth table shows that there is no case in which all the premises are true and the conclusion is false. It shows that the argument is valid. Whenever the premises are true in a valid argument, the conclusion is also true.

p q	If p, then q.	p.	q.
T T	T	T	T
T F	F	T	F ✓
F T	T	F	T
F F	T	F	F ✓

Let three dots in a triangular shape ($\therefore$) mean "therefore." Affirming the Antecedent may be represented as:
$$p \rightarrow q$$
$$p$$
$$\therefore q$$

Examples of affirming the antecedent in Case 18:

	Affirming the Antecedent	Form	Claims
a.	If they broke into the Exchange, then there should be evidence of a break-in. They broke into the Exchange. Therefore, there should be evidence of a break-in (sentences 5–7).	If p, then q. $\dfrac{p.}{q.}$	p: They broke into the Exchange. q: There should be evidence of a break-in.
b.	If Detective Wise is perplexed, then the crime might not be solved. Detective Wise is perplexed. Therefore, the crime might not be solved.	If p, then not q. $\dfrac{q.}{\text{Not } q.}$	p: Detective Wise is perplexed. q: The crime might be solved.

Denying the Consequent* (modus tollens)

*The name of the argument tells what the second (nonconditional) premise does relative to the conditional premise.

Example	Form	Claims
If John went to the store, then Sally went to a movie Sally did not go to a movie. Therefore, John did not go to the store.	If *p*, then *q*. Not *q*. _____ Not *p*.	*p:* John went to the store. *q:* Sally went to a movie.

p *q*	If *p*, then *q*.	Not *q*.	Not *p*.	Denying the Consequent
T T	T	F	F✓	$p \rightarrow q$
T F	F	T	F✓	$\sim q$
F T	T	F	T	$\therefore \sim p$
F F	T	T	T	

Examples of denying the consequent in Case 18:

	Denying the Consequent	Form	Claims
a.	If they came in through one of the doors, then the alarm would have sounded. But the alarm didn't sound. Therefore, they didn't come in through one of the doors (sentences 8–10).	If *p*, then *q*. *Not q.* _____ Not *p*.	*p:* They came in through one of the doors. *q:* The alarm would have sounded.
b.	If Detective Wise is perplexed, then the crime might not be solved. It is not the case that the crime might not be solved. Therefore, Detective Wise is not perplexed.	If *p*, then *q*. Not *q*. _____ Not *p*.	*p:* Detective Wise is perplexed. *q:* The case might not be solved.

Disjunctive Syllogism

Example	Form	Claims
Either John went to the store or Sally went to a movie. John did not go to the store. Therefore, Sally went to a movie.	Either p or q. Not p. q.	p: John went to the store. q: Sally went to a movie.

Example	Form 2	Claims
Either John went to the store or Sally went to a movie. Sally did not go to a movie. Therefore, John went to the store.	Either p or q. Not q. p.	p: John went to the store. q: Sally went to a movie.

	p q	Either p or q.	Not p.	q.
Form 1	T T	T	F	T
	T F	T	F	F✓
	F T	T	T	T
	F F	F	T	F✓

	p q	Either p or q.	Not q.	p.
Form 2	T T	T	F	T
	T F	T	T	T
	F T	T	F	F✓
	F F	F	T	F✓

Disjunctive Syllogism

Form 1:
$$p \lor q$$
$$\sim p$$
$$\therefore q$$

Form 2:
$$p \lor q$$
$$\sim q$$
$$\therefore p$$

Examples of disjunctive syllogism in Case 18:

	Disjunctive Syllogism	Form	Claims
a.	Either it was an inside job or there was evidence of a break-in. There was no evidence of a break-in. Therefore, it was an inside job (sentences 16–18).	p or q. Not q. p.	p: It was an inside job. q: There was evidence of a break-in.
b.	Either Detective Wise is puzzled or the crime will be solved. Detective Wise is not puzzled. Therefore, the crime will be solved.	p or q. Not p. q.	p: Detective Wise is puzzled. q: The crime will be solved.

Hypothetical Syllogism

Example	Form	Claims
If John goes to the store, then Sally goes to a movie. If Sally goes to a movie, then Juanita goes dancing. Therefore, if John goes to the store, then Juanita goes dancing.	If p, then q. If q, then r. $\overline{\text{If } p, \text{ then } r.}$	p: John went to the store. q: Sally went to a movie. r: Juanita goes dancing.

			1st Premise	2nd Premise	Conclusion
p	q	r	$p \rightarrow q$	$q \rightarrow r$	$p \rightarrow r$
T	T	T	T	T	T
T	T	F	T	F	F✓
T	F	T	F	T	T
T	F	F	F	T	F✓
F	T	T	T	T	T
F	T	F	T	F	T
F	F	T	T	T	T
F	F	F	T	T	T

Hypothetical Syllogism

$p \rightarrow q$
$q \rightarrow r$
$\therefore p \rightarrow r$

Examples of hypothetical syllogism in Case 18:

	Hypothetical Syllogism	Form	Claims
a.	If the robbers broke in through the air vents, then they could have replaced the vent when they left. If they replaced the vent when they left, there would have been no evidence of a break-in. Therefore, if the robbers broke in through the air vents, there would have been no evidence of a break-in (sentences 11–13).	If p, then q. If q, then r. $\overline{\text{If } p, \text{ then } r.}$	p: The robbers broke in through the air vents. q: They could have replaced the vent when they left. r: There would have been no evidence of a break-in.*
b.	If the Gold Exchange is on North Figueroa, then it was in the heart of the city. If the Gold Exchange was in the heart of the city, then the robbers could have hidden in a neighboring building. Therefore, if the Gold Exchange is on North Figueroa, then the robbers could have hidden in a neighboring building.	If p, then q. If q, then r. $\overline{\text{If } p, \text{ then } r.}$	p: The Gold Exchange is on North Figueroa. q: The Gold Exchange was in the heart of the city. r: The robbers could have hidden in a neighboring building.

*Variables can be negated claims. See page 217 for more information.

Important: Please remember the following:

Variables, *p*, *q*, *r*, *s* can represent simple claims or compound claims. They can also represent negated claims or non-negated claims.

In categorical syllogisms, the major premise comes first, followed by the minor premise, and finally the conclusion.

In argument forms other than the categorical syllogism, the order of the premises does not affect the form of the argument; however, you might need to rearrange the premises in order to recognize the form.

The easiest way to identify an argument form is to:

1. Symbolize the argument using capital letters for simple claims. If it is a negated claim, then do not forgtet to write 'not' or put ~ before the letter.
2. Then look at the form. Does it fit any patterns you have learned? If so, it will be easy to figure out what the variables *p*, *q*, *r*, or *s* stand for. If you do not recognize the form, then it could be that the premises are in a different order than the pattern.

Example:

If Detective Wise can figure out the case, then the robbers will not escape. It is not the case that the robbers will not escape. So, Detective Wise did not figure out the case.

Step 1: Rough out the form using capital letters for simple claims.

If D, then not E.
Not, not E.
———————
Not D

Step 2: Identify what the variables represent.

p = D
q = Not E or ~E

Step 3: Plug the variables into the roughed-out form.

If *p*, then *q*.
Not *q*.
————
Not *p*.

The form is denying the consequent.

5.5   Exercise Circle the argument form of each of the following arguments. Writing the form of the argument is often helpful, but it is not required. *Optional argument reference sheet is available on page 293.

1. **Example:**
   Either the robbers will escape or Detective Wise will solve another case. The robbers will not escape. So, Detective Wise will solve another case.
   a. Affirming the antecedent
   b. Denying the consequent
   (c.) **Disjunctive syllogism**
   d. Hypothetical syllogism

   Either p or q.
   $\sim p$.
   $\overline{q.}$

2. If Detective Wise will solve the case, then she'll be promoted. Detective Wise will solve the case. Therefore, she'll be promoted.
   a. Affirming the antecedent
   b. Denying the consequent
   c. Disjunctive syllogism
   d. Hypothetical syllogism

3. If Detective Wise solves another case, then she'll be promoted. If Detective Wise is promoted, she'll be able to choose the cases she investigates. Thus, if Detective Wise solves another case, she'll be able to choose the cases she investigates.
   a. Affirming the antecedent
   b. Denying the consequent
   c. Disjunctive syllogism
   d. Hypothetical syllogism

4. If the robbers pulled off the perfect crime, then the police will find no clues. It is not the case that the police will find no clues. So, the robbers did not pull off the perfect crime.
   a. Affirming the antecedent
   b. Denying the consequent
   c. Disjunctive syllogism
   d. Hypothetical syllogism

5. If It was an inside job, then the alarms were not set. If the alarms were not set, then the alarms didn't sound. So, if it was an inside job, the alarms didn't sound.
   a. Affirming the antecedent
   b. Denying the consequent
   c. Disjunctive syllogism
   d. Hypothetical syllogism

6. Either it was an inside job or the robbers were very clever. It was not an inside job. So, the robbers were very clever.
   a. Affirming the antecedent
   b. Denying the consequent
   c. Disjunctive syllogism
   d. Hypothetical syllogism

7. If the robbers escaped to Mexico, then they will not be caught. It is not the case that the robbers will not be caught. So, the robbers did not escape to Mexico.
   a. Affirming the antecedent
   b. Denying the consequent
   c. Disjunctive syllogism
   d. Hypothetical syllogism

8. If Detective Wise will solve the case, then she will receive credit in the newspapers. Detective Wise will solve the case. So, Detective Wise will receive credit in the newspapers.
   a. Affirming the antecedent
   b. Denying the consequent
   c. Disjunctive syllogism
   d. Hypothetical syllogism

9. If the Gold Exchange was robbed on Saturday night, then the robbers had more than a day to get away. If the robbers had more than a day to get away, then the crime will be hard to solve. So, if the Gold Exchange was robbed on Saturday night, then the crime will be hard to solve.
   a. Affirming the antecedent
   b. Denying the consequent
   c. Disjunctive syllogism
   d. Hypothetical syllogism

10. If Detective Wise will solve the case, then Officer Baker will get a promotion. Detective Wise will solve the case. So, Officer Baker will get a promotion.
    a. Affirming the antecedent
    b. Denying the consequent
    c. Disjunctive syllogism
    d. Hypothetical syllogism

(Continued)

11. If the Gold Exchange is a family business, then Mrs. Hunt has a key to the store. If Mr. Hunt owns the Gold Exchange, then the Gold Exchange is a family business. So, if Mr. Hunt owns the Gold Exchange, Mrs. Hunt has a key to the store.
    a. Affirming the antecedent
    b. Denying the consequent
    c. Disjunctive syllogism
    d. Hypothetical syllogism

12. Mrs. Hunt does not have a key to the store. If Mr. Hunt owns the Gold Exchange, then Mrs. Hunt has a key to the store. So, Mr. Hunt does not own the Gold Exchange.
    a. Affirming the antecedent
    b. Denying the consequent
    c. Disjunctive syllogism
    d. Hypothetical syllogism

13. Mrs. Hunt does not have a key to the store. Mrs. Hunt has a key to the store or Mr. Hunt does not own the business. Therefore, Mr. Hunt does not own the business.
    a. Affirming the antecedent
    b. Denying the consequent
    c. Disjunctive syllogism
    d. Hypothetical syllogism

14. Mrs. Hunt is not a suspect, for if Mrs. Hunt were a suspect, then she would have a key to the store, but she does not have key to the store.
    a. Affirming the antecedent
    b. Denying the consequent
    c. Disjunctive syllogism
    d. Hypothetical syllogism

15. The Gold Exchange was robbed provided that the alarm was not set when the store closed. If Mr. Hunt was involved in the crime, then the alarm was not set when the store closed. So, Mr. Hunt was involved in the crime only if the Gold Exchange was robbed.
    a. Affirming the antecedent
    b. Denying the consequent
    c. Disjunctive syllogism
    d. Hypothetical syllogism

16. Mr. Hunt was not involved in the crime because it was not an inside job; for if Mr. Hunt was involved in the crime, it was an inside job.
    a. Affirming the antecedent
    b. Denying the consequent
    c. Disjunctive syllogism
    d. Hypothetical syllogism

17. Mr. Hunt runs the Gold Exchange provided that he inherited the business from his family. Mr. Hunt inherited the business from his family. So, Mr. Hunt runs the Gold Exchange.
    a. Affirming the antecedent
    b. Denying the consequent
    c. Disjunctive syllogism
    d. Hypothetical syllogism

18. Mr. Hunt runs the Gold Exchange unless it is a front for organized crime. The Gold Exchange is not a front for organized crime. So, Mr. Hunt runs the Gold Exchange.
    a. Affirming the antecedent
    b. Denying the consequent
    c. Disjunctive syllogism
    d. Hypothetical syllogism

19. If Detective Wise is perplexed and it was an inside job, then the robbers will get away. The robbers will not get away. So, it is not the case that both Detective Wise is perplexed and it was an inside job.
    a. Affirming the antecedent
    b. Denying the consequent
    c. Disjunctive syllogism
    d. Hypothetical syllogism

20. It was an inside job provided that Detective Wise is perplexed. Mr. Hunt had a hand in the crime on condition that it was an inside job. So, Detective Wise is perplexed only if Mr. Hunt had a hand in the crime.
    a. Affirming the antecedent
    b. Denying the consequent
    c. Disjunctive syllogism
    d. Hypothetical syllogism

5.6 Common Arguments

If a disjunction is true, then at least one of its disjuncts is true. So, if you know that a claim *p* is true, you can infer that either the claim *p* or some other claim *q* is true.
This is an argument form known as **addition**.

Addition		
Example a.	**Form**	**Claims**
John went to the store. Therefore, either John went to the store or Sally went to a movie.	*p.* ――― *p* or *q.*	*p:* John went to the store. *q:* Sally went to a movie.
Example b.	**Form**	**Claims**
John went to the store and Sally went to a movie. Therefore, either John went to the store and Sally went to a movie or Sally did not go to a movie.	*p.* ――― *p* or *q.*	*p:* John went to the store and Sally went to a movie.* *q:* Sally did not go to a movie.*

*Variables can represent simple claims or compound claims. They can also represent negated claims.

p q	*p.*	*p* or *q.*	Addition
T T	T	T	*p*
T F	T	T	$\therefore p \vee q$
F T	F	T	
F F	F	F✓	

Examples of addition in Case 18:

	Addition	**Form**	**Claims**
a.	There was a robbery at the Gold Exchange. Therefore, either there was a robbery at the Gold Exchange or "hot" gems are for sale on the black market. (sentences 22–23).	*p.* ――― *p* or *q.*	*p:* There was a robbery at the Gold Exchange. *q:* "Hot" gems are for sale on the black market.
b.	Detective Wise will solve the crime. Therefore, Detective Wise will solve the crime or the criminals will escape to Mexico.	*p.* ――― *p* or *q.*	*p:* Detective Wise will solve the crime. *q:* The criminals will escape to Mexico.

A conjunction is true if and only if both of its conjuncts are true. So, if a conjunction is true, you know its conjuncts are true. This is a pair of argument forms known as **simplification**.

Simplification

Example	Form 1	Claims
John went to the store and Sally went to a movie. Therefore, John went to the store.	p and q. $\overline{p.}$	p: John went to the store. q: Sally went to a movie.
Example	**Form 2**	**Claims**
John went to the store and Sally went to a movie, but Carol went neither to the store nor to a movie. Therefore, Carol neither went to the store nor to a movie.	p and q. $\overline{q.}$	p: John went to the store and Sally went to a movie.* q: Carol neither went to the store nor to a movie.*

*Variables can represent simple claims or compound claims. They can also represent negated claims.

	p q	p and q.	p.
Form 1	T T T F F T F F	T F F F	T T F✓ F✓

	p q	p and q.	q.
Form 2	T T T F F T F F	T F F F	T F✓ T F✓

Simplification

Form 1

p & q
$\therefore p$

Form 2

p & q
$\therefore q$

Examples of simplification in Case 18:

	Simplification	Form	Claims
a.	There was a robbery at the Gold Exchange and Detective Wise was assigned to the case. Therefore, there was a robbery at the Gold Exchange.	p and q. $\overline{p.}$	p: There was a robbery at the Gold Exchange. q: Detective Wise was assigned to the case.
b.	There was a robbery at the Gold Exchange and we have no suspects. Therefore, we have no suspects (sentences 27–28).	p and q. $\overline{q.}$	p: There was a robbery at the Gold Exchange. q: We have no suspects.

A conjunction is true if and only if both of its conjuncts are true. So, if two claims are each true, then it follows that the conjunction of those two claims is true. This is the argument form known as **conjunction.**

Conjunction			
Example a.	**Form**	**Claims**	
John went to the store. Sally went to a movie. Therefore, John went to the store and Sally went to a movie.	*p.* *q.* ――― *p* and *q.*	*p:* John went to the store. *q:* Sally went to a movie.	
Example b.	**Form**	**Claims**	
John went to the store and Sally went to a movie. Carol neigher went to the store nor to a movie. Therefore, John went to the store and Sally went to a movie, but Carol neither went to the store nor to a movie.	*p.* *q.* ――― *p* and *q.*	*q:* John went to the store and Sally went to a movie.* *p:* Carol neither went to the store nor to a movie.*	

*Variables can represent simple claims or compound claims. They can also represent negated claims.

p q	*p.*	*q.*	*p* and *q.*
T T	T	T	T
T F	T	F	F✓
F T	F	T	F✓
F F	F	F	F✓

Conjunction

p
q
∴ *p* & *q*

Examples of conjunction in Case 18:

	Conjunction	**Form**	**Claims**
a.	There was a robbery at the Gold Exchange. More than fifty thousand dollars in gems and jewelry was stolen. Therefore, there was a robbery at the Gold Exchange and more than fifty thousand dollars in gems and jewelry was stolen (sentences 24–26).	*p.* *q.* ――― *p* and *q.*	*p:* There was a robbery at the Gold Exchange. *q:* More than fifty thousand dollars in gems and jewelry was stolen.
b.	Mr. Hunt runs the Gold Exchange. Detective Wise is on the case. Therefore, Mr. Hunt runs the Gold Exchange and Detective Wise is on the case.	*p.* *q.* ――― *p* and *q.*	*p:* Mr. Hunt runs the Gold Exchange. *q:* Detective Wise is on the case.

If a conjunction of two conditional claims is true and either the antecedent of the first or the antecedent of the second conditional claim is true, then it follows that either the consequent of the first conditional or the consequent of the second conditional is true. This is known as a **constructive dilemma.**

Constructive Dilemma

Example	Form	Claims
If John goes to the store, then Sally goes to a movie; and if Juanita goes dancing, then Gustav attends a concert. Either John goes to the store or Juanita goes dancing. Therefore, either Sally goes to a movie or Gustav attends a concert.	If *p*, then *q*; and if *r*, then *s*. Either *p* or *r*. ⎯⎯⎯⎯⎯⎯⎯ Either *q* or *s*.	*p:* John goes to the store. *q:* Sally goes to a movie. *r:* Juanita goes dancing. *s:* Gustav attends a concert.

Note: Since the first premise is composed of two compound statements, we need a column for each of those which are used only to determine the truth values of the conditional statements. Only the columns for the premises and conclusion are used to determine whether the argument form is valid.

p *q* *r* *s*	If *p*, then *q*; and if *r*, then *s*.			Either *p* or *r*.	Either *q* or *s*.
T T T T	T	T	T	T	T
T T T F	T	F	F	T	T
T T F T	T	T	T	T	T
T T F F	T	T	T	T	T
T F T T	F	F	T	T	T
T F T F	F	F	F	T	F✓
T F F T	F	F	T	T	T
T F F F	F	F	T	T	F✓
F T T T	T	T	T	T	T
F T T F	T	F	F	T	T
F T F T	T	T	T	F	T
F T F F	T	T	T	F	T
F F T T	T	T	T	T	T
F F T F	T	F	F	T	F✓
F F F T	T	T	T	F	T
F F F F	T	T	T	F	F✓
		↑		↑	↑

Constructive Dilemma

Parentheses are used as punctuation marks.

They group compound claims in more complex claims.

$(p \rightarrow q)$ & $(r \rightarrow s)$
$p \vee r$
$\therefore q \vee s$

The columns for the premises and conclusion are marked at the bottom with an arrow (↑).
Examples of constructive dilemma in Case 18:

	Constructive Dilemma	Form	Claims
a.	If Mr. Hunt was involved in the break-in, then Detective Wise is puzzled; and if Mrs. Hunt had a hand in the crime, then the police will find an important clue. Either Mr. Hunt was involved in the break-in or Mrs. Hunt had a hand in the crime. Therefore, either Detective Wise is puzzled or the police will find an important clue.	If p, then q; and if r, then s. Either p or r. ——— Either q or s.	p: Mr. Hunt was involved in the break-in. q: Detective Wise is puzzled. r: Mrs. Hunt had a hand in the crime. s: The police will find an important clue.
b.	If there was no evidence of a break-in, then it was an inside job; but if there was evidence of a break-in but we didn't find it yet, then we're up against a clever robber. Either there was no evidence of a break-in or there was evidence of a break-in but we didn't find it yet. Therefore, either it was an inside job or we're up against a clever robber (sentences 19–21).	If p, then q; and if r, then s. Either p or r. ——— Either q or s.	p: There was no evidence of a break-in. q: It was an inside job. r: There was evidence of a break-in and we didn't find it yet. s: We're up against a clever robber.

If a conjunction of two conditional claims is true and either the consequent of the first or the consequent of the second conditional claim is false, then either the antecedent of the first conditional or the antecedent of the second conditional is false. So, if you know that the consequent of at least one of those conditionals is false, then either the antecedent of the first conditional or the antecedent of the second conditional is false. This is known as a **destructive dilemma**.

Destructive Dilemma		
Example	**Form**	**Claims**
If John goes to the store, then Sally goes to a movie; and if Juanita goes dancing, then Gustav attends a concert. Either Sally does not go to a movie or Gustav does not attend a concert. Therefore, either John does not go to the store or Juanita does not go dancing.	If p, then q; and if r, then s. Either not q or not s. ——— Either not p or not r.	p: John goes to the store. q: Sally goes to a movie. r: Juanita goes dancing. s: Gustav attends a concert.

Note: Destructive dilemma is similar to denying the consequent. It is a case in which you know that two conditionals are true and the consequent of at least one of those conditionals is false.

p q r s	If p, then q; and if r, then s.			Not q or not s.			Not p or not r.			Destructive Dilemma
T T T T	T	T	T	F	F	F	F	F✓	F	$(p \rightarrow q) \mathrel{\&} (r \rightarrow s)$
T T T F	T	F	F	F	T	T	F	F✓	F	$\sim q \vee \sim s$
T T F T	T	T	T	F	F	F	F	T	T	$\therefore \sim p \vee \sim r$
T T F F	T	T	T	F	T	T	F	T	T	
T F T T	F	F	T	T	T	F	F	F✓	F	
T F T F	F	F	F	T	T	T	F	F✓	F	
T F F T	F	F	T	T	T	F	F	T	T	
T F F F	F	F	T	T	T	T	F	T	T	
F T T T	T	T	T	F	F	F	T	T	F	
F T T F	T	F	F	F	T	T	T	T	F	
F T F T	T	T	T	F	F	F	T	T	T	
F T F F	T	T	T	F	T	T	T	T	T	
F F T T	T	T	T	T	T	F	T	T	F	
F F T F	T	F	F	T	T	T	T	T	F	
F F F T	T	T	T	T	T	F	T	T	T	
F F F F	T	T	T	T	T	T	T	T	F	
			↑			↑			↑	

Examples of destructive dilemma in Case 18:

	Destructive Dilemma	Form	Claims
a.	If Mr. Hunt was involved in the break-in, then Detective Wise is puzzled; and if Mrs. Hunt had a hand in the crime, then the police will find an important clue. Either Detective Wise is not puzzled or the police will not find an important clue. Therefore, either Mr. Hunt was not involved in the break-in or Mrs. Hunt did not have a hand in the case.	If p, then q; and if r, then s. Either not q or not s. ――――――――― Either not p or not r.	p: Mr. Hunt was involved in the break-in. q: Detective Wise is puzzled. r: Mrs. Hunt had a hand in the crime. s: The police will find an important clue.
b.	If it was an inside job, then we don't know where all the employees were over the weekend; if we're up against a clever robber, then the case will go unsolved. Either it is not the case that we don't know where all the employees were over the weekend or the case will not go unsolved. Therefore, either it wasn't an inside job or we're not up against a clever robber (sentences 29–31).	If p, then q; and if r, then s. Either not q or not s. ――――――――― Either not p or not r.	p: It was an inside job. q: We don't know where all the employees were over the weekend. r: We're up against a clever robber. s: The case will go unsolved.

5.7 **Exercise** Circle the argument form of each of the following arguments. Writing the form of the argument is often helpful, but it is not required. *Optional argument forms reference sheet is available on pages 293-294.

1. **Example:**
   Either Mrs. Hunt had a hand in the crime or Mr. Hunt runs the Gold Exchange, for Mrs. Hunt had a hand in the crime.

   $$\frac{p.}{\text{Either } p \text{ or } q.}$$

   (a.) Addition
   b. Simplification
   c. Conjunction
   d. Constructive dilemma
   e. Destructive dilemma

2. If it was an inside job, then the robbers will get away; and if Detective Wise finds a significant clue, then the robbers will be captured. Either it was an inside job or Detective Wise finds a significant clue. So, either the robbers will get away or the robbers will be captured.
   a. Addition
   b. Simplification
   c. Conjunction
   d. Constructive dilemma
   e. Destructive dilemma

3. Detective Wise is a lieutenant. So, Detective Wise is a lieutenant and Officer Baker is a sergeant, for Officer Baker is a sergeant.
   a. Addition
   b. Simplification
   c. Conjunction
   d. Constructive dilemma
   e. Destructive dilemma

4. If Detective Wise will solve the crime, then she will find some important clues; and if the owners were involved in the crime, then the crime was an inside job. Either Detective Wise will not find some important clues or the crime was not an inside job. So, either Detective Wise will not solve the crime or the owners were not involved in the crime.
   a. Addition
   b. Simplification
   c. Conjunction
   d. Constructive dilemma
   e. Destructive dilemma

(Continued)

5. Detective Wise works for the LAPD and Mr. Hunt owns the Gold Exchange. So, Mr. Hunt owns the Gold Exchange.
    a. Addition
    b. Simplification
    c. Conjunction
    d. Constructive dilemma
    e. Destructive dilemma

6. If Mrs. Hunt is involved in the crime, then the crime will not be solved; and if Mr. Hunt was involved in the crime, then Detective Wise will be puzzled. Either Mrs. Hunt was involved in the crime or Mr. Hunt was involved in the crime. Therefore, either the crime will not be solved or Detective Wise will be puzzled.
    a. Addition
    b. Simplification
    c. Conjunction
    d. Constructive dilemma
    e. Destructive dilemma

7. Detective Wise works for the LAPD. So, either Detective Wise or Mr. Hunt works for the LAPD.
    a. Addition
    b. Simplification
    c. Conjunction
    d. Constructive dilemma
    e. Destructive dilemma

8. If there was a robbery at the Gold Exchange, then Detective Wise is puzzled; and if the robbery was an inside job, Officer Baker will be puzzled. So, if the robbery was an inside job, Officer Baker will be puzzled.
    a. Addition
    b. Simplification
    c. Conjunction
    d. Constructive dilemma
    e. Destructive dilemma

9. Security Consultants, Inc. played a role in the robbery if the security system was disabled; although Henry "the Mole" Smith was involved provided that entry was gained through the air ducts. So, either Security Consultants, Inc. played a role in the robbery or Henry "the Mole" Smith was involved, for the security system was disabled, unless entry was gained through the air ducts.
    a. Addition
    b. Simplification
    c. Conjunction
    d. Constructive dilemma
    e. Destructive dilemma

10. Henry "the Mole" Smith had a hand in the crime. Security Consultants, Inc. played a role in the robbery. So, Henry "the Mole" Smith had a hand in the crime and Security Consultants, Inc. played a role in the robbery.
    a. Addition
    b. Simplification
    c. Conjunction
    d. Constructive dilemma
    e. Destructive dilemma

11. If the robbery was not an inside job, then Henry "the Mole" Smith had a hand in the affair; and Gold Exchange is on Sunset Boulevard provided the robbery occurred two years ago. So, either it is not the case that the robbery was not an inside job, or the robbery did not occur two years ago. For Henry "the Mole" Smith did not have a hand in the affair, unless the Gold Exchange is not on Sunset Boulevard.
    a. Addition
    b. Simplification
    c. Conjunction
    d. Constructive dilemma
    e. Destructive dilemma

(Continued)

12. If Detective Wise is puzzled, then the robbery was an inside job. So, either Detective Wise was puzzled only if the robbery was an inside job, or Henry "the Mole" Smith is Mr. Hunt's cousin.
    a. Addition
    b. Simplification
    c. Conjunction
    d. Constructive dilemma
    e. Destructive dilemma

13. Detective Wise is puzzled only if there is a lack of clues; and Mrs. Hunt is missing if she played a role in the break-in. There is not a lack of clues or Mrs. Hunt is not missing. So, Detective Wise is not puzzled, unless Mrs. Hunt did not play a role in the break-in.
    a. Addition
    b. Simplification
    c. Conjunction
    d. Constructive dilemma
    e. Destructive dilemma

14. If Detective Wise is puzzled, then there is a lack of clues; and if Mrs. Hunt played a role in the break-in, then we can explain why the alarm didn't sound. So, if Mrs. Hunt played a role in the break-in, we can explain why the alarm didn't sound.
    a. Addition
    b. Simplification
    c. Conjunction
    d. Constructive dilemma
    e. Destructive dilemma

15. If the crime will be solved, then the robbers did not escape to Mexico; and if Detective Wise will be promoted, then the crime will be solved. Either it is not the case that the robbers did not escape to Mexico, or the crime will not be solved. So, either the crime will not be solved or Detective Wise will not be promoted.
    a. Addition
    b. Simplification
    c. Conjunction
    d. Constructive dilemma
    e. Destructive dilemma

5.8 Fallacies

A fallacy is a defective argument. There are many different types of fallacies, though fallacies are generally divided into two basic groups, formal and informal. Formal fallacies are committed due to a defect in the argument's form and are found when we examine the form of the argument. Informal fallacies, however, are not concerned with the form or pattern of the argument. They are concerned with errors in reasoning, weak premises, or shifts in the meaning of words. We will explore informal fallacies in Chapter 8. Two common formal fallacies are affirming the consequent and denying the antecedent. Both are invalid arguments.

Fallacy of Affirming the Consequent*		
*The name of the argument tells what the second (nonconditional) premise does relative to the conditional premise.		
Example	**Form**	**Claims**
If Harry Potter defeated Darth Vadar, then Harry Potter is a great wizard. Harry Potter is a great wizard. _____ Therefore, Harry Potter defeated Darth Vadar.	If p, then q. $\dfrac{q.}{p.}$	p: Harry Potter defeated Darth Vadar. q: Harry Potter is a great wizard.

This argument is invalid because the premises are true, but the conclusion is false. This shows that this argument form is not logically reliable.

p q	If p, then q.	q.	p.
T T	T	F	T
T F	F	T	T
F T	T	F	F✓
F F	T	T	F✓

Fallacy of Affirming the Consequent

$$p \rightarrow q$$
$$q$$
$$\therefore p$$

The fourth row of the truth table shows that the argument form is invalid, since it shows that it is possible for all the premises to be true and the conclusion false.

Examples of the fallacy of affirming the consequent in Case 18:

	Fallacy of Affirming the Consequent	**Form**	**Claims**
a.	If the robbers broke in through the air vents, there would have been no evidence of a break-in. There was no evidence of a break-in. Therefore, the robbers broke in through the air vents (sentences 13–14). Note: the conclusion was not drawn in the case.	If p, then q. $\dfrac{q.}{p.}$	p: The robbers broke in through the air vents. q: There was (would have been) no evidence of a break-in.
b.	If Mr. Hunt had a hand in the crime, then the robbery was an inside job. The robbery was an inside job. Therefore, Mr. Hunt had a hand in the crime.	If p, then q. $\dfrac{q.}{p.}$	p: Mr. Hunt had a hand in the crime. q: The robbery was an inside job.

Fallacy of Denying the Antecedent*

*The name of the fallacy tells what the second (nonconditional) premise does relative to the conditional premise.

Example	Form	Claims
If Harry Potter defeated Darth Vadar, then Harry Potter is a great wizard. Harry Potter did not defeat Darth Vadar. ___ Therefore, Harry Potter is not a great wizard.	If p, then q. Not p. ___ Not q.	p: Harry Potter defeated Darth Vadar. q: Harry Potter is a great wizard.

This argument is invalid because the premises are true, but the conclusion is false. This shows that this argument form is not logically reliable.

p q	If p, then q.	Not p.	Not q.	Fallacy of Denying the Antecedent
T T	T	F	F ✓	
T F	F	F	T	$p \rightarrow q$
F T	T	T	F ✓	$\sim p$
F F	T	T	T	$\therefore \sim q$

The third row of the truth table shows that the argument form is invalid, since it shows that it is possible for all the premises to be true and the conclusion false.

Examples of the fallacy of denying the antecedent in Case 18:

	Fallacy of Denying the Antecedent	Form	Claims
a.	If Detective Wise works for the Chicago Police Department, then there was not a robbery at the Gold Exchange. Detective Wise does not work for the Chicago Police Department. Therefore, it is not the case that there was not a robbery at the Gold Exchange.	If p, then q. Not p. ___ Not q.	p: Detective Wise works for the Chicago Police Department. q: There was not a robbery at the Gold Exchange.
b.	If Mrs. Sanchez owns the Gold Exchange, then it was not an inside job. Mrs. Sanchez does not own the Gold Exchange. Therefore, it is not the case that it was not an inside job.	If p, then q. Not p. ___ Not q.	p: Mrs. Sanches owns the Gold Exchange. q: It was not an inside job.

5.9 Exercise
Circle the argument form of each of the following arguments. Writing the form of the argument is often helpful, but it is not required.

1. **Example:**
   If there was a break-in at the Gold Exchange, then the police are puzzled. The police are puzzled. So, there was a break-in at the Gold Exchange.
   a. Affirming the antecedent
   b. **Fallacy of affirming the consequent**
   c. Denying the consequent
   d. Fallacy of denying the antecedent

   If p, then q.
   q.
   —
   p.

2. If Detective Wise works for the LAPD, then she's certain to crack the case. Detective Wise works for the LAPD. So, Detective Wise is certain to crack the case.
   a. Affirming the antecedent
   b. Fallacy of affirming the consequent
   c. Denying the consequent
   d. Fallacy of denying the antecedent

3. If Mrs. Hunt had a hand in the crime, then Henry "the Mole" Smith actually pulled off the job. Mrs. Hunt did not have a hand in the crime. So, Henry "the Mole" Smith did not actually pull off the job.
   a. Affirming the antecedent
   b. Fallacy of affirming the consequent
   c. Denying the consequent
   d. Fallacy of denying the antecedent

4. If the air vents were used to break into the store, then Henry "the Mole" Smith was the mastermind behind the robbery. Henry "the Mole" Smith was not the mastermind behind the robbery. So, the air vents were not used to break into the store.
   a. Affirming the antecedent
   b. Fallacy of affirming the consequent
   c. Denying the consequent
   d. Fallacy of denying the antecedent

5. Detective Wise is puzzled only if the Hartshorne Diamond was stolen. Detective Wise is not puzzled. So the Hartshorne Diamond was not stolen.
   a. Affirming the antecedent
   b. Fallacy of affirming the consequent
   c. Denying the consequent
   d. Fallacy of denying the antecedent

(Continued)

6. Detective Wise is puzzled if the Hartshorne Diamond was not stolen. The Hartshorne Diamond was not stolen. Therefore, Detective Wise is puzzled.
   a. Affirming the antecedent
   b. Fallacy of affirming the consequent
   c. Denying the consequent
   d. Fallacy of denying the antecedent

7. Mrs. Hunt is a suspect. Mrs. Hunt is a suspect if she cannot be found in the city. Therefore Mrs. Hunt cannot be found in the city.
   a. Affirming the antecedent
   b. Fallacy of affirming the consequent
   c. Denying the consequent
   d. Fallacy of denying the antecedent

8. Henry "the Mole" Smith is not a suspect only if he is in prison. Henry "the Mole" Smith is not in prison. Therefore, it is not the case that Henry "the Mole" Smith is not a suspect.
   a. Affirming the antecedent
   b. Fallacy of affirming the consequent
   c. Denying the consequent
   d. Fallacy of denying the antecedent

9. Freddy "Bang-Bang" Connor is a suspect. Freddy "Bang-Bang" Connor is a suspect if an explosion blew a hole in the floor of the Gold Exchange. Hence, an explosion blew a hole in the floor of the Gold Exchange.
   a. Affirming the antecedent
   b. Fallacy of affirming the consequent
   c. Denying the consequent
   d. Fallacy of denying the antecedent

10. Freddy "Bang-Bang" Connor is a suspect only if an explosion blew a hole in the floor of the Gold Exchange. Freddy "Bang-Bang" Connor is not a suspect. So, an explosion did not blow a hole in the floor of the Gold Exchange.
    a. Affirming the antecedent
    b. Fallacy of affirming the consequent
    c. Denying the consequent
    d. Fallacy of denying the antecedent

5.10 Exercise Circle the argument form in each of the following arguments. Writing the form of the argument is often helpful, but it is not required.

1. **Example:**
   If the case is not solved in seven days, then the case will not be solved. The case will not be solved. So, the case will not be solved in seven days.
   a. Affirming the antecedent
   b. Denying the consequent
   c. Destructive dilemma
   (d.) **Fallacy of affirming the consequent**
   e. Fallacy of denying the antecedent

   If p, then q.
   q.
   ___
   p.

2. If the case is solved in seven days, then Detective Wise will have a much-needed vacation; and if the case grinds on for more than two weeks, then Detective Wise will take a day of sick-leave. Either the case will be solved in seven days or it will grind on for more than two weeks. So, either Detective Wise will have a much-needed vacation or she will take a day of sick-leave.
   a. Disjunctive syllogism
   b. Hypothetical syllogism
   c. Constructive dilemma
   d. Destructive dilemma
   e. Fallacy of affirming the consequent

3. Unless Henry "the Mole" Smith has come up with a new idea, the police will solve the case. Henry "the Mole" Smith has not come up with a new idea. So, the police will solve the case.
   a. Disjunctive syllogism
   b. Hypothetical syllogism
   c. Addition
   d. Constructive dilemma
   e. Destructive dilemma

4. Constance Cruz breezed into town. There was a robbery at the Gold Exchange. So, Constance Cruz breezed into town and there was a robbery at the Gold Exchange.
   a. Affirming the antecedent
   b. Denying the consequent
   c. Disjunctive syllogism
   d. Simplification
   e. Conjunction

(Continued)

5. Constance Cruz breezed into town only if she had a hand in the robbery. Constance Cruz breezed into town. Hence, she had a hand in the robbery.
   a. Affirming the antecedent
   b. Denying the consequent
   c. Hypothetical syllogism
   d. Fallacy of affirming the consequent
   e. Fallacy of denying the antecedent

6. Constance Cruz breezed into town if she had a hand in the robbery. Constance did not have a hand in the robbery. So, Constance Cruz did not breeze into town.
   a. Affirming the antecedent
   b. Denying the consequent
   c. Disjunctive syllogism
   d. Fallacy of affirming the consequent
   e. Fallacy of denying the antecedent

7. If Freddy "Bang-Bang" Connor had a hand in the robbery, then a large hole was blown in the floor of the store. Fire alarms would have sounded if a large hole was blown in the floor of the store. So, Freddy "Bang-Bang" Connor had a hand in the robbery only if fire alarms would have sounded.
   a. Affirming the antecedent
   b. Denying the consequent
   c. Disjunctive syllogism
   d. Hypothetical syllogism
   e. Addition

8. Freddy "Bang-Bang" Connor had a hand in the robbery only if fire alarms would have sounded. The fire alarms didn't sound. So Freddy "Bang-Bang" Connor did not have a hand in the robbery.
   a. Affirming the antecedent
   b. Denying the consequent
   c. Constructive dilemma
   d. Destructive dilemma
   e. Fallacy of denying the antecedent

9. Henry "the Mole" Smith played a role in the robbery. So, Henry "the Mole" Smith played a role in the robbery unless Freddy "Bang-Bang" Connor was playing with dynamite.
   a. Addition
   b. Simplification
   c. Conjunction
   d. Constructive dilemma
   e. Destructive dilemma

10. If Constance Cruz had a hand in the crime, then everything went smoothly; and if Freddy "Bang-Bang" Connor played a role, then the robbery went off with a bang. So, if Constance Cruz had a hand in the crime, then everything went smoothly.
   a. Hypothetical syllogism
   b. Addition
   c. Simplification
   d. Constructive dilemma
   e. Destructive dilemma

11. Constance Cruz played a role in the robbery unless Mrs. Hunt masterminded the break-in. Mrs. Hunt did not mastermind the break-in. So, Constance Cruz played a role in the robbery.
   a. Affirming the antecedent
   b. Denying the consequent
   c. Disjunctive syllogism
   d. Constructive dilemma
   e. Fallacy of denying the antecedent

12. If Constance Cruz had a hand in the crime, then everything went smoothly; and if Freddy "Bang-Bang" Connor played a role, then the robbery went off with a bang. Either not everything went smoothly or the robbery did not go off with a bang. Hence, either Constance Cruz did not have a hand in the crime or Freddy "Bang-Bang" Connor did not play a role.
   a. Hypothetical syllogism
   b. Constructive dilemma
   c. Destructive dilemma
   d. Fallacy of affirming the consequent
   e. Fallacy of denying the antecedent

(Continued)

13. Mrs. Hunt was not the mastermind behind the robbery. If Mrs. Hunt was the mastermind behind the robbery, then it was an inside job. So, it was not an inside job.
    a. Affirming the antecedent
    b. Denying the consequent
    c. Disjunctive syllogism
    d. Fallacy of affirming the consequent
    e. Fallacy of denying the antecedent

14. Mrs. Hunt was the mastermind behind the robbery only if it was an inside job. So, it was an inside job, for Mrs. Hunt was the mastermind behind the robbery.
    a. Affirming the antecedent
    b. Denying the consequent
    c. Disjunctive syllogism
    d. Hypothetical syllogism
    e. Fallacy of affirming the consequent

15. Constance Cruz had a hand in the operation only if Detective Wise described it as a slick crime. Detective Wise described it as a slick crime. So, Constance Cruz had a hand in the operation.
    a. Affirming the antecedent
    b. Constructive dilemma
    c. Destructive dilemma
    d. Fallacy of affirming the consequent
    e. Fallacy of denying the antecedent

16. The robbery was not planned in San Diego. The robbery was planned in San Diego provided that Mr. Hunt played a role in planning the robbery. So, Mr. Hunt did not play a role in planning the robbery.
    a. Affirming the antecedent
    b. Denying the consequent
    c. Disjunctive syllogism
    d. Hypothetical syllogism
    e. Addition

17. The robbery was not planned in San Diego. The robbery was planned in San Diego only if Mr. Hunt played a role in planning the robbery. So, Mr. Hunt did not play a role in planning the robbery.
    a. Denying the consequent
    b. Disjunctive syllogism
    c. Destructive dilemma
    d. Fallacy of affirming the consequent
    e. Fallacy of denying the antecedent

18. If the robbery was planned in Guadalajara, then the robbers escaped to Mexico; and if the robbery was planned in San Diego, then the robbers are likely to be arrested. The robbery was planned in Guadalajara unless it was planned in San Diego. Hence, either the robbers escaped to Mexico or they are likely to be arrested.
    a. Disjunctive syllogism
    b. Simplification
    c. Constructive dilemma
    d. Destructive dilemma
    e. Fallacy of denying the antecedent

19. Henry "the Mole" Smith ran the operation only if the crime was planned in San Diego; but Constance Cruz ran the operation if it had been planned in Guadalajara. The crime was not planned in San Diego unless Constance Cruz did not run the operation. Thus, either Henry "the Mole" Smith did not run the operation or the operation was not planned in Guadalajara.
    a. Conjunction
    b. Constructive dilemma
    c. Destructive dilemma
    d. Fallacy of affirming the consequent
    e. Fallacy of denying the antecedent

20. Constance Cruz and Henry "the Mole" Smith worked together unless each independently planned a break-ins at the Gold Exchange. Constance Cruze and Henry "the Mole" Smith did not work together. Hence, each independently planned a break-in at the Gold Exchange.
    a. Denying the consequent
    b. Disjunctive syllogism
    c. Simplification
    d. Destructive dilemma
    e. Fallacy of denying the antecedent

CASE 19	City of Los Angeles Police Department

[1]Molly Malone disappeared. [2]She is president of Clams and Mussels From the Sea, a commercial seafood company. [3]She might have left town, or it could have been a kidnapping or worse. [4]Detective Wise's job was to figure out what happened to her.

[5]Malone was last seen in her office at 11:30 on the evening of January 31. [6]She didn't make it home. [7]If she had made it home, then she would have checked through the security gate in her subdivision. [8]If she had checked through the security gate, then the security system computer would have had a record that she swiped her electronic key at the gate. [9]But the computer had no record that she swiped her electronic key at the gate.

[10]Her car was found in an alley off Sunset Boulevard. [11]It had been wiped clean of fingerprints. [12]If there were no fingerprints, Malone was probably a victim of a crime.

[13]If she was the victim of a kidnapping, then we should receive a call for a ransom; and if she was murdered, then the body should turn up eventually. [14]So, either we should receive a call for a ransom or the body should turn up eventually.

[15]Either she left town or she didn't. [16]If she left town, then there should be a record that she bought a plane, train, or bus ticket; and if she didn't leave town, she was probably kidnapped.

[17]So, either there should be a record that she bought a plane, train, or bus ticket or she was probably kidnapped. [18]There is no record that she bought a plane, train, or bus ticket. [19]So, she was probably kidnapped. [20]If she was kidnapped, there should have been a ransom demand. [21]There was no ransom demand. [22]If she was not kidnapped, then she was probably the victim of foul play. [23]If she was a victim of foul play, then the police must act quickly. [24]If the police must act quickly, police action could save Malone's life. [25]So, police action could save Malone's life.

[26]The Clams and Mussels From the Sea jet is missing. [27]If the corporate jet is missing, then either Malone staged an elaborate disappearing act or a crime was committed by one of the company's executives.

[28]If the crime was committed by another company executive, then Malone is not the only company executive who is missing. [29]It is not the case that Malone is not the only company executive who is missing. [30]So, Malone must have staged an elaborate disappearing act.

[31]If Malone staged an elaborate disappearing act, then she flew to Dublin, Ireland. [32]If Malone flew to Dublin, Ireland, then she is wandering the streets of Dublin. [33]So, if Malone staged an elaborate disappearing act, then she is wandering the streets of Dublin.

[34]If Malone is wandering the streets of Dublin, then Molly is looking for Trinity College. [35]So, if Malone staged an elaborate disappearing act, Molly is looking for Trinity College. [36]Malone staged an elaborate disappearing act. [37]So, Molly is looking for Trinity College.

5.11 Enthymemes and Argument Chains

An **enthymeme** is an argument with an unstated premise or conclusion. By paying attention to the argument forms, it is usually easy to figure out what the missing premise or conclusion has to be.

Examples of enthymemes in Case 19:

	Enthymemes	Form	Claims	Reasoning/Conclusion
a.	Malone's car had been wiped clean of fingerprints. If Malone's car was wiped clean of fingerprints, Malone was probably a victim of a crime (sentences 11-12).	If p, then q. p. —— q.	p: Malone's car had been wiped clean of fingerprints. q: Malone was probably a victim of a crime. *Therefore, Malone was probably a victim of crime.	There are two claims. One is a conditional claim. The other is the antecedent of the conditional. So, these are the premises of an argument of the form affirming the antecedent. The missing conclusion is: "Malone was probably a victim of a crime."
b.	If Molly Malone flew to Dublin, then she was a fan of the old song, "Clams and Mussels." Molly was not a fan of the old song, "Clams and Mussels."	If p, then q. Not q. —— Not p.	p: Molly Malone flew to Dublin. q: Molly was a fan of the old song, "Clams and Mussels." *Therefore, Molly Malone did not fly to Dublin.	There are two claims. One is a conditional claim. The other is the denial of the consequent of the conditional claim. So, these are the premises of an argument of the form denying the consequent. So, the missing conclusion must be: "Molly Malone did not fly to Dublin."
c.	If she was the victim of a kidnapping, then we should receive a call for a ransom; and if she was murdered, then the body should turn up eventually. So, either we should receive a call for a ransom or the body should turn up eventually (sentences 13-14).	If p, then q; and if r, then s. Either p or r. —— Either q or s.	p: She was the victim of a kidnapping. q: We should receive a call for ransom. r: She was murdered. s: The body should turn up eventually. *Either p or r: Either she was a victim of a kidnapping or she was murdered.	There are two claims. One is a conjunction of conditional claims. The other is a disjunction. The disjunction is marked as the conclusion by the word *so*. So, we have an argument whose premise is a conjunction of conditional claims and whose conclusion is a disjunction of the consequents of the conditionals in the premise. So, the argument has to be a constructive dilemma with the missing premise: "Either she was a victim of a kidnapping or she was murdered."

*Unstated premise or conclusion

5.12 Exercise Circle the best answer for each of the following arguments. Writing the form of the argument is often helpful, but it is not required.

1. **Example:**
   If Molly Malone staged an elaborate disappearing act, then she had been "borrowing" company funds. So, she had been "borrowing" company funds.

   a. **It is an affirming the antecedent with the missing premise, "Molly Malone staged an elaborate disappearing act."**

   b. It is a disjunctive syllogism with the missing premise, "Molly Malone did not stage an elaborate disappearing act."

   c. It is a destructive dilemma with the missing conclusion, "Either Molly Malone staged an elaborate disappearing act or she had been 'borrowing' company funds."

   d. It is a hypothetical syllogism with the missing premise, "If Molly had been 'borrowing' company funds, then she was facing criminal charges."

   If p, then q.
   p. (assumed premise)
   —
   q.

2. Either Molly was "borrowing" company funds or she's running away from her lover. So, Molly was "borrowing" company funds.

   a. It is an affirming the antecedent with the missing premise, "Molly was running away from her lover."

   b. It is a disjunctive syllogism with the missing premise, "Molly was not running away from her lover."

   c. It is denying the consequent with the missing conclusion, "Molly was not 'borrowing' company funds."

   d. It is a constructive dilemma with the missing conclusion, "Either Molly was 'borrowing' company funds or Molly's lover is in Dublin."

3. If Molly "borrowed" funds from the company, then the company accountant discovered problems with the books. But the company accountant did not discover problems with the books.

   a. It is a conjunction with the missing premise, "Molly flew to Dublin."

   b. It is a denying the consequent with the missing premise, "Molly did not 'borrow' funds from the company."

   c. It is a disjunctive syllogism with the missing conclusion, "Molly 'borrowed' funds from the company."

   d. It is a denying the consequent with the missing conclusion, "Molly did not 'borrow' funds from the company."

4. If Molly's car was abandoned near Sunset Boulevard, then foul play is suspected; and if Molly "borrowed" funds from the company, then she had good reasons to disappear. So, either Molly's car was not abandoned near Sunset Boulevard or Molly did not "borrow" funds from the company.

    a. It is a denying the consequent with the missing premise, "Foul play is not suspected even though Molly did not 'borrow' funds from the company."

    b. It is a destructive dilemma with the missing premise, "Either foul play is not suspected or Molly did not have good reasons to disappear."

    c. It is a disjunctive syllogism with the missing conclusion, "Foul play is suspected."

    d. It is a constructive dilemma with the missing conclusion, "Either foul play is suspected or Molly had good reasons to disappear."

5. Molly's car was abandoned near Sunset Boulevard. So, Molly's car was abandoned near Sunset Boulevard and she staged her own disappearance.

    a. This is a conjunction with the missing premise, "Molly staged her own disappearance."

    b. This is a constructive dilemma with the missing premise, "If all the fingerprints had been wiped from Molly's car, then her car was abandoned near Sunset Boulevard; and if Molly few to Dublin, then she staged her own disappearance."

    c. This is simplification with the missing conclusion, "Molly staged her own disappearance."

    d. This is a disjunctive syllogism with the missing conclusion, "Molly staged her own disappearance."

6. If Molly few to Dublin, then she staged her own disappearance; and if Molly's car was found near Sunset Boulevard, then Molly was probably a victim of a crime. Molly flew to Dublin unless her car was found near Sunset Boulevard.

    a. This is a fallacy of affirming the consequent with the missing premise, "Molly staged her own disappearance."

    b. This is a destructive dilemma with the missing premise, "Either Molly did not stage her own disappearance or Molly was probably not a victim of a crime."

    c. This is a disjunctive syllogism with the missing conclusion, "Molly was probably a victim of a crime."

    d. This is a constructive dilemma with the missing conclusion, "Either Molly staged her own disappearance or she was probably a victim of a crime."

(Continued)

7. If Molly flew to Dublin, then she had good reasons to leave the country. So, if Molly few to Dublin, then Detective Wise will be surprised.
   a. This is a fallacy of denying the antecedent with the missing premise, "Molly did not fly to Dublin."
   b. This is a hypothetical syllogism with the missing premise, "If Molly had good reasons to leave the country, then Detective Wise will be surprised."
   c. This is a hypothetical syllogism with the missing conclusion, "If Detective Wise will be puzzled, then Molly flew to Dublin."
   d. This is a constructive dilemma with the missing conclusion, "Either Molly had good reasons to leave the country or Detective Wise will be puzzled."

8. If Molly few to Dublin, then she had good reasons to leave the country. If Molly had good reasons to leave the country, then Interpol (the international police organization) will be on the lookout for her.
   a. This is constructive dilemma with the missing premise, "Either Molly flew to Dublin or Molly had good reasons to leave the country."
   b. This is a denying the consequent with the missing premise, "Interpol (the international police organization) will not be on the lookout for Molly."
   c. This is a destructive dilemma with the missing conclusion, "Either Molly did not fly to Dublin or Molly did not have good reasons to leave the country."
   d. This is a hypothetical syllogism with the missing conclusion, "If Molly flew to Dublin, then Interpol (the international police organization) will be on the lookout for her."

9. If Molly disappeared, then Clams and Mussels From
the Sea will need to find a new president; and if Molly
"borrowed" money from the company, then Clams and
Mussels From the Sea will hire a private detective to
find her. So, either Clams and Mussels From the Sea
will need to find a new president or Clams and Mussels
From the Sea will hire a private detective to find Molly.
   a. This is an affirming the antecedent with the missing
      premise, "Molly disappeared."
   b. This is a constructive dilemma with the missing
      premise, "Either Molly disappeared or Molly
      'borrowed' money from the company."
   c. This is an addition with the missing conclusion,
      "Either Molly 'borrowed' money from the company or
      Detective Wise will crack another case."
   d. This is a destructive dilemma with the missing
      conclusion, "Either Molly did not disappear or Molly
      did not 'borrow' money from the company."

10. If Molly flew to Dublin, Ireland, then she had to have her
passport checked when she arrived. So Molly didn't fly
to Dublin, Ireland.
   a. This is an affirming the antecedent with the missing
      premise, "Molly did not have to have her passport
      checked when she arrived."
   b. This is a denying the consequent with the missing
      premise, "Molly did not have to have her passport
      checked when she arrived."
   c. This is an affirming the antecedent with the missing
      conclusion, "Molly had to have her passport checked
      with she arrived."
   d. This is a fallacy of denying the antecedent with the
      missing conclusion, "Molly did not have to have her
      passport checked when she arrived."

Simple arguments often are put together to form complex arguments or **argument chains**. In such chains the conclusion of one argument is the premise of the next.

Examples of argument chains in Case 19:

	Argument Chains	**Form**	**Claims**	**Reasoning/Conclusion**
a.	Either Molly flew to Dublin or she flew to Mexico City. She did not fly to Mexico City. So, Molly flew to Dublin. If Molly flew to Dublin, then she's going trace her family tree. Therefore, Molly is going to trace her family tree.	Either p or q. Not q. $\overline{\text{So, } p.}$ If p, then r. $\overline{r.}$	p: Molly flew to Dublin. q: Molly flew to Mexico City. r: Molly is going to trace her family tree.	The first argument is a disjunctive syllogism with the conclusion, "Molly few to Dublin." That conclusion is used as a premise in an affirming the antecedent with the conclusion, "Molly is going to trace her family tree."
b.	If Molly flew to Dublin, then her company is in trouble. Molly flew to Dublin. Therefore, her company is in trouble. If Molly's company is in trouble, then either she has been "borrowing" company funds or the company vice president, Sean Gilley, has been selling fish for personal profits. So, either Molly has been "borrowing" company funds or the company vice president, Sean Gilley, has been selling fish for personal profits. Molly has not been "borrowing" company funds. Therefore, the company vice president, Sean Gilley, has been selling fish for personal profits.	If p, then q. $\underline{p.}$ $q.$ If q, then either r or s. $\overline{\text{Either } r \text{ or } s.}$ Not s. $\overline{r.}$	p: Molly flew to Dublin. q: Molly's company is in trouble. r: Molly has been "borrowing" company funds. s: The company vice president, Sean Gilley, has been selling fish for personal profits.	The first argument is an affirming the antecedent with the conclusion, "Her company is in trouble." The second argument is also affirming the antecedent with the conclusion of the first argument as a premise. The conclusion of the second argument is, "Either Molly has been 'borrowing' company funds or the company vice president, Sean Gilley, has been selling fish for personal profits." That conclusion becomes the disjunctive premise for a disjunctive syllogism with the conclusion, "The company vice president, Sean Gilley, has been selling fish for personal profits."

	Argument Chains	Form	Claims	Reasoning/Conclusion
c.	Either she left town or she didn't. If she left town, then there should be records that she bought a plane, train, or bus ticket; and if she didn't leave town, she was probably kidnapped. Therefore, either there should be a record that she bought a plane, train, or bus ticket or she was probably kidnapped. There is no record that she bought a plane, train, or bus ticket. Therefore, she was probably kidnapped (sentences 15-19).	Either p or not p. If p, then q; and if not p, then r. $\overline{\text{Either } q \text{ or } r.}$ Not q. $\overline{r.}$	p: Molly left town. q: There should be records that Molly bought a plane, train, or bus ticket. r: Molly was probably kidnapped.	"Either there should be a record that she bought a plane, train, or bus ticket or she was probably kidnapped," follows from the first two claims by constructive dilemma. Given that conclusion, and "There is no record that she bought a plane, train, or bus ticket," supports the conclusion, "She was probably kidnapped" by disjunctive syllogism.
d.	If Malone staged an elaborate disappearing act, then she flew to Dublin, Ireland. If Malone flew to Dublin, Ireland, then she is wandering the streets of Dublin. Therefore, if Malone staged an elaborate disappearing act, then Molly is wandering the streets of Dublin. If Malone is wandering the streets of Dublin, then Molly is looking for Trinity College. So, if Malone staged an elaborate disappearing act, then Molly is looking for Trinity College. Malone staged an elaborate disappearing act. Therefore, Molly is looking for Trinity College (sentences 31-38).	If p, then q. If q, then r. $\overline{\text{If } p, \text{ then } r.}$ If r, then s. $\overline{\text{If } p, \text{ then } s.}$ p. $\overline{s.}$	p: Malone staged an elaborate disappearing act. q: Malone flew to Dublin, Ireland. r: Malone is wandering the streets of Dublin. s: Molly is looking for Trinity College	The first argument is a hypothetical syllogism with the conclusion, "If Malone staged an elaborate disappearing act, then she is wandering the streets of Dublin." This conclusion is the first premise of a hypothetical syllogism with the conclusion, "If Malone staged an elaborate disappearing act, then Molly is looking for Trinity College." This conclusion together with the premise, "Malone staged an elaborate disappearing act," are the premises for an affirming antecedent with the conclusion, "Molly is looking for Trinity College."

A chain is only as strong as its weakest link. So, if a fallacy is committed in the course of a chain of arguments, that breaks the chain. One cannot go further in the chain.

Examples of argument chains with a fallacious component argument in Case 19:

	Argument Chains With a Fallacious Component Argument	Form	Claims	Reasoning/Conclusion
a.	If Molly was kidnapped, then Sean Gilley had a hand in the affair. Sean Gilley had a hand in the affair. Therefore, Molly was kidnapped. If Molly was kidnapped, then both Detective Wise and Sergeant Baker will be puzzled. Therefore, both Detective Wise and Sergeant Baker will be puzzled. So, Sergeant Baker will be puzzled.	If p, then q. $\underline{q.}$ $p.$ If p, then both r $\underline{\text{and } s.}$ r and $s.$ $s.$	p: Molly was kidnapped. q: Sean Gilley had a hand in the affair. r: Detective Wise will be puzzled. s: Sergeant Baker will be puzzled.	The first argument, "If Molly was kidnapped, then Sean Gilley had a hand in the affair. Sean Gilley had a hand in the affair. So Molly was kidnapped," is an instance of the fallacy of affirming the consequent. So, the conclusion, "Molly was kidnapped," *does not follow* with validity. Since this first argument is fallacious, one cannot know that the conclusion of the first argument is true. Hence, one cannot know that any conclusions based upon the conclusion of the first argument are true. Because the first argument is invalid, the entire chain is unsound.
b.	If Molly was kidnapped, then Detective Wise is on the case. If Detective Wise is on the case, then the LAPD is on full alert. Therefore, if Molly was kidnapped, then the LAPD is on full alert. But Molly was not kidnapped. Therefore, the LAPD is not on full alert.	If p, then q. $\underline{\text{If } q, \text{ then } r.}$ If p, then r. $\underline{\text{Not } p.}$ Not r.	p: Molly was kidnapped. q: Detective Wise is on the case. r: The LAPD is on full alert.	The first three sentences form a hypothetical syllogism. So, the conclusion, "If Molly was kidnapped, then the LAPD is on full alert," follows. But the argument, "If Molly was kidnapped, then the LAPD is on full alert. Molly was not kidnapped. So, the LAPD is not on full alert," commits the fallacy of denying the antecedent. Since the argument is invalid, one cannot know that its conclusion is true. The chain is unsound.

5.13 Exercise What conclusion is reached in each of the following argument chains? Circle the best answer. Writing the form of the argument is often helpful, but it is not required.

1. **Example:**
   Either Molly flew to Dublin or Sean Gilley is stealing company funds. Molly did not fly to Dublin. So, Sean Gilley is stealing company funds. If Sean Gilley is stealing company funds, then the case will take an interesting turn. So, the case will take an interesting turn.
   a. Molly did not fly to Dublin.
   b. Sean Gilley is stealing company funds.
   c. If Sean Gilley is stealing company funds, then the case will take an interesting turn.
   d. The case will take an interesting turn.

   Either p or q.
   $\sim p$.
   q.
   If q, then r.
   r.

2. If Molly flew to Dublin, then Detective Wise will be puzzled; and if Sean is stealing company funds, then Clams and Mussels From the Sea is in trouble. Either Molly flew to Dublin or Sean is stealing company funds. So, either Detective Wise will be puzzled, or Clams and Mussels From the Sea is in trouble. Detective Wise will not be puzzled. So, Clams and Mussels From the Sea is in trouble.
   a. Clams and Mussels From the Sea is in trouble.
   b. Detective Wise will not be puzzled.
   c. Either Molly flew to Dublin or Sean is stealing company funds.
   d. Either Detective Wise will be puzzled, or Clams and Mussels From the Sea is in trouble.

3. If Molly Malone disappeared, it was either a kidnapping or an attempt to avoid the authorities. Molly Malone disappeared. So, it was either a kidnapping or an attempt to avoid the authorities. If it was a kidnapping, then Clams and Mussels From the Sea will pay a ransom; and if it was an attempt to avoid the authorities, then Molly skipped the country. So, either Clams and Mussels From the Sea will pay a ransom or Molly skipped the country. So, Clams and Mussels From the Sea will pay a ransom, for Molly did not skip the country.
   a. It was either a kidnapping or an attempt to avoid the authorities.
   b. Either Clams and Mussels From the Sea will pay a ransom or Molly skipped the country.
   c. Clams and Mussels From the Sea will pay a ransom.
   d. Molly did not skip the country.

(Continued)

4. If Molly flew to Dublin, then she is tracing her family tree; and if Sean is stealing company funds, then he'll disappear to Mexico. Either Molly is not tracing her family tree or Sean will not disappear to Mexico. So, either Molly did not fly to Dublin or Sean is not stealing company funds. It is not the case that Molly did not fly to Dublin. So, Sean is not stealing company funds. If Sean is not stealing company funds, then Clams and Mussels From the Sea is a thriving business. So, Clams and Mussels From the Sea is a thriving business.
    a. Either Molly is not tracing her family tree or Sean will not disappear to Mexico.
    b. Clams and Mussels From the Sea is a thriving business.
    c. Sean is not stealing company funds.
    d. Either Molly did not fly to Dublin or Sean is not stealing company funds.

5. If Molly is missing, then the company is in trouble. If Detective Wise is puzzled, then the case will go unsolved. So, if Molly is missing, then the company is in trouble; and if Detective Wise is puzzled, then the case will go unsolved. Either Molly is missing or the Detective Wise is puzzled. So, either the company is in trouble or the case will go unsolved. The case will not go unsolved. So, the company is in trouble. If the company is in trouble, then Sean Gilley will head the company and seafood sales are going along splashingly. So, Sean Gilley will head the company and seafood sales are going along splashingly. So, Sean Gilley will head the company.
    a. Sean Gilley will head the company.
    b. Molly is missing.
    c. Either the company is in trouble or the case will go unsolved.
    d. If Molly is missing, then the company is in trouble; and if Detective Wise is puzzled, then the case will go unsolved.

6. If Molly left the country on the corporate jet, then she flew to Australia. Molly did not fly to Australia. So, Molly did not leave the country on the corporate jet. If Molly is in trouble, then she left the country on the corporate jet. So, Molly is not in trouble. If Molly was "borrowing" company funds, then she is in trouble. So, Molly was not "borrowing" company funds. If Molly went into hiding, then she was "borrowing" company funds. So, Molly didn't go into hiding. Either Molly went into hiding or she was kidnapped. So, she was kidnapped.
   a. Molly did not leave the country on the corporate jet.
   b. Molly is not in trouble.
   c. Molly was kidnapped.
   d. Molly was not "borrowing" company funds.

7. If Molly was kidnapped, then there will be a ransom demand. If there is a ransom demand, then the ransom will be paid. So, if Molly was kidnapped, then the ransom will be paid. If the ransom is paid, then the kidnappers will get away with more than a million dollars. So, if Molly was kidnapped, then the kidnappers will get away with more than a million dollars. If Detective Wise is on the case, then Molly will be found. If Molly is found, then the mystery will be solved. So, if Detective Wise is on the case, then the mystery will be solved. So, if Molly was kidnapped, then the kidnappers will get away with more than a million dollars; and if Detective Wise is on the case, then the mystery will be solved. Either Molly was kidnapped or Detective Wise is on the case. So, either the kidnappers will get away with more than a million dollars or the mystery will be solved.
   a. If Molly was kidnapped, then the kidnappers will get away with more than a million dollars.
   b. Either the kidnappers will get away with more than a million dollars or the mystery will be solved.
   c. If Detective Wise is on the case, then the mystery will be solved.
   d. Either Molly was kidnapped or Detective Wise is on the case.

(Continued)

8. Either Molly was kidnapped or Sean Gilley is engaged
    in fishy activities. Molly was not kidnapped. So, Sean
    Gilley is engaged in fishy activities. If Sean Gilley is
    engaged in fishy activities, then Clams and Mussels
    From the Sea is in trouble. So, Clams and Mussels
    From the Sea is in trouble. If Clams and Mussels From
    the Sea is in trouble, then Molly's disappearance is not
    the only problem. So, Molly's disappearance is not the
    only problem. Either Molly's disappearance is the only
    problem or Detective Wise will have a difficult day. So,
    Detective Wise will have a difficult day.
    a. Detective Wise will have a difficult day.
    b. Sean Gilley is engaged in fishy activities.
    c. Clams and Mussels From the Sea is in trouble.
    d. Molly's disappearance is not the only problem.

9. If Sean is engaged in fishy activities, then Clams and Mussels From the Sea is in trouble. Clams and Mussels From the Sea is in trouble. So, Sean is engaged in fishy activities. If Sergeant Baker found a secret compartment in Molly's desk, then Detective Wise has a hot clue. Sergeant Baker found a secret compartment in Molly's desk. So, Detective Wise has a hot clue. So, Sean is engaged in fishy activities and Detective Wise has a hot clue. If Sean is engaged in fishy activities and Detective Wise has a hot clue, then ransom money will not be paid. So, ransom money will not be paid.

   a. Sean is engaged in fishy activities.
   b. Detective Wise has a hot clue.
   c. Ransom money will not be paid.
   d. Sean is engaged in fishy activities and Detective Wise has a hot clue.

(Continued)

10. Molly was kidnapped or Sergeant Baker will rewrite the story
    as a novel. If Molly was kidnapped, then Sean Gilley had
    a hand in the affair. If Sean Gilley had a hand in the affair,
    then the future of Clams and Mussels From the Sea is up
    in the air. So, if Molly was kidnapped, the future of Clams
    and Mussels From the Sea is up in the air. If Sergeant
    Baker will rewrite the story as a novel, then Detective Wise
    will be a fictitious hero. If Detective Wise will be a fictitious
    hero, then Detective Wise's Uncle Sherlock will be pleased.
    So, if Sergeant Baker will rewrite the story as a novel, then
    Detective Wise's Uncle Sherlock will be pleased. So, if
    Molly was kidnapped, the future of Clams and Mussels From
    the Sea is up in the air; and if Sergeant Baker will rewrite
    the story as a novel, then Detective Wise's Uncle Sherlock
    will be pleased. The future of Clams and Mussels From the
    Sea is not up in the air. So, either the future of Clams and
    Mussels From the Sea is up in the air or Detective Wise's
    Uncle Sherlock will be pleased. So, Detective Wise's Uncle
    Sherlock will be pleased.
    a. Detective Wise's Uncle Sherlock will be pleased.
    b. Either the future of Clams and Mussels From the Sea
       is up in the air or Detective Wise's Uncle Sherlock will
       be pleased.
    c. If Molly was kidnapped, the future of Clams and
       Mussels From the Sea is up in the air; and if
       Sergeant Baker will rewrite the story as a novel, then
       Detective Wise's Uncle Sherlock will be pleased.
    d. The intended conclusion was probably, "Detective
       Wise's Uncle Sherlock will be pleased," but the
       argument, "If Molly was kidnapped, the future of
       Clams and Mussels From the Sea is up in the air.
       The future of Clams and Mussels From the Sea is
       not up in the air. So, Molly was not kidnapped," is
       an instance of the fallacy of denying the antecedent.
       So, the only conclusion that follows with validity is, "If
       Sergeant Baker will rewrite the story as a novel, then
       Detective Wise's Uncle Sherlock will be pleased."

In the previous arguments, the intermediate conclusions were stated. Often intermediate conclusions—conclusions of arguments early in the chain—are not stated. The arguments are **enthymematic**. In those cases you need to work out the intermediate conclusions and use them as premises in other arguments. Sometimes, even the final conclusion is unstated.

Examples of argument chains containing enthymematic arguments in Case 19:

	Argument Chains Containing Enthymematic Arguments	Form	Reasoning/Conclusion
a.	She didn't make it home. If she had made it home, then she would have checked through the security gate in her subdivision. If she had checked through the security gate, then the security system computer would have had a record that she swiped her electronic key at the gate. But the computer had no record that she swiped her electronic key at the gate (sentences 6-9).	Not p. (While given first, this is the conclusion of the argument.) If p, then q. If q, then r. ‾‾‾‾‾‾‾‾‾‾‾ If p, then r. (assumed conclusion) Not r. ‾‾‾‾‾‾‾‾‾‾‾ Not p.	From, "If she had made it home, then she would have checked through the security gate in her subdivision" and, "If she had checked through the security gate, then the security system computer would have had a record that she swiped electronic key at the gate," it follows by hypothetical syllogism that, "If she had made it home, then the security system computer would have had a record that she swiped her electronic key at the gate." Given this and the premise, "The computer had no record that she swiped her electronic key at the gate," it follows that, "She didn't make it home." (If you prefer, the conclusion follows by two instances of denying the consequent.)
b.	(1) If Molly was kidnapped, then Detective Wise is on the case; and if Sean Gilley had a hand in the affair, Sergeant Baker will find an important clue. (2) Either Molly was kidnapped or Sean Gilly had a hand in the affair. (3) Sergeant Baker will not find an important clue. (4) If Detective Wise is on the case, the kidnappers took Molly to San Diego. (5) If the kidnappers took Molly to San Diego, then she'll be smuggled onto a navy ship. (6) Therefore, Molly will be smuggled onto a navy ship.* *It is often helpful to number claims in an argument in order to follow the reasoning of the argument.	If p, then q; and if r, then s. Either p or r. ‾‾‾‾‾‾‾‾‾‾‾ Either q or s. (assumed conclusion) Not s. ‾‾‾‾‾‾‾‾‾‾‾ q. (assumed conclusion) If q, then t. ‾‾‾‾‾‾‾‾‾‾‾ t. (assumed conclusion) If t, then u. ‾‾‾‾‾‾‾‾‾‾‾ u.	From the first two sentences, it follows that either Detective Wise is on the case or Sergeant Baker will find an important clue. From that conclusion and sentence (3), it follows that Detective Wise is on the case. Given that Detective Wise is on the case and sentence (4), it follows by affirming the antecedent that the kidnappers took Molly to San Diego. Given that the kidnappers took Molly to San Diego and sentence (5), sentence (6) follows by affirming the antecedent.

It is often helpful to number the claims in an argument and to give each additional conclusion (our assumed conclusion) a new number. Numbered claims help us in symbolizing and diagraming arguments as well as following the reasoning of the arguments.

	Argument Chains Containing Enthymematic Arguments	Form	Reasoning/Conclusion
c.	(1) If Molly skipped the country, then she's involved in a crime. (2) If Molly is involved in a crime, then Clams and Mussels From the Sea is a front for a criminal gang. (3) If Clams and Mussels From the Sea is the front for a criminal gang, then Sean Gilley is not the gentleperson he appears to be. (4) If Sean Gilley is not the gentleperson he seems to be, then Sean's involved in a kidnapping. (5) Sean is not involved in a kidnapping, even though Detective Wise is puzzled. (6) If Detective Wise is puzzled, then Sergeant Baker is looking for clues. (7) Therefore, Molly did not skip the country and Sergeant Baker is looking for clues.	(1) If M, then I. (2) If I, then C. (8) If M, then C. (assumed conclusion) (3) If C, then ~G. (9) If M, then ~G. (assumed conclusion) (4) If ~G, then S. (10) If M, then S. (assumed conclusion) (11) ~S (assumed conclusion from the simplication of (5) ~S and D.) (12) ~M (assumed conclusion) (13) D. (assumed conclusion from the simplication of (5) ~S and D.) (6) If D, then B. (14) B (assumed conclusion) (12) ~M. (see 12 above) (7) ~M and B.	(8) "If Molly skipped the country, then Clams and Mussels From the Sea is a front for a criminal gang" is from (1) and (2) by hypothetical syllogism. (9) "If Molly skipped the country, then Sean Gilley is not the gentleperson he seems to be" is from (8) and (3) by hyppothetical sylogism. (10) "If Molly skipped the country, then Sean's involved in a kidnapping" is from (9) and (4) by hypothetical syllogism. (11) "Sean is not involved in a kidnapping" is from the simplification of (5). (12) "Molly did not skip from the country" is from (10) and (11) by denying the consequent. (13) "Detective Wise is puzzled" is from the simplication of (5). (14) "Sergeant Baker is looking for clues" is from (13) and (6) by affirming the antecedent. (7) is from (12) and (14) by conjunction.

5.14 Exercise What conclusion is reached in each of the following argument chains? Circle the correct answer. You will need to work out intermediate conclusions to determine the conclusion at the end of the chain. You should use each premise at least once. No fallacies are committed in the following arguments. The conclusion will be either a simple claim or the denial of a simple claim.

1. **Example:**
   1. If Molly disappeared, then Clams and Mussels From the Sea is in trouble.
   2. If Clams and Mussels From the Sea is in trouble, Sean Gilley skipped the country.
   3. Molly disappeared.

   So, ...
   a. Molly disappeared.
   b. Clams and Mussels From the Sea is in trouble.
   c. **Sean Gilley skipped the country.*** ⟵ (circled)
   d. Molly did not disappear.

   Reasoning:
   (4) If Molly disappeared, then Sean Gilley skipped the country. From 1 and 2 hypothetical syllogism.
   (5) Sean Gilley skipped the country.
   From 4 and 3 affirming the antecedent.

   1. If p, then q.
   2. If q, then r.
   _____
   4. If p, then r.
   (assumed conclusion)

   3. p.
   _____
   5. r.
   (assumed conclusion)

2.
   1. Either Molly disappeared or Sean disappeared.
   2. If Molly disappeared, then company funds were missing; and if Sean disappeared, members of the Internal Revenue Service were planning a visit.
   3. Members of the Internal Revenue Service were not planning a visit.

   So, ...
   a. Molly disappeared.
   b. Members of the Internal Revenue Service were planning a visit.
   c. Company funds were missing.
   d. Either company funds were missing or members of the Internal Revenue Service were planning a visit.

(Continued)

3.   1. If Molly is missing, then Sean skipped the country; and if Detective Wise is puzzled, then Sergeant Baker is clueless.
      2. It is not the case that Detective Wise is not puzzled.
      3. Either Sean did not skip the country or Sergeant Baker is not clueless.

So, …
a. Molly is not missing.
b. Sergeant Baker is clueless.
c. Sean did not skip the country.
d. If Molly is missing, then Sean skipped the country.

4.   1. If either Molly or Sean is missing, then Clams and Mussels From the Sea is in trouble.
      2. Molly is missing.
      3. If Clams and Mussels From the Sea is in trouble, then Detective Wise is not puzzled.
      4. Either Detective Wise is puzzled, or Sergeant Baker has found an important clue.

So, …
a. Sean is missing.
b. Clams and Mussels From the Sea is in trouble.
c. Detective Wise is not puzzled.
d. Sergeant Baker has found an important clue.

5.   1. If Molly is missing, then Sean has skipped the country.
      2. If Detective Wise is puzzled, then Sergeant Baker is clueless.
      3. Either Sean has not skipped the country or Sergeant Baker is not clueless.
      4. If either Molly is not missing or Detective Wise is not puzzled, then the FBI will join the investigation.

So , …
a. The FBI will join the investigation.
b. Molly is not missing.
c. Either Molly is not missing or Detective Wise is not puzzled.
d. Either Sergeant Baker is clueless or the FBI will join the investigation.

6.   1. Detective Wise is puzzled and Sergeant Baker found a key clue.
      2. If Detective Wise is puzzled, then Sergeant Baker found a key clue; and if Sean Gilley skipped the country, then Clams and Mussels From the Sea is in trouble.
      3. Sergeant Baker did not find a key clue or Clams and Mussles From the Sea is not in trouble.
      4. If Sergeant Baker found a key clue and Sean Gilley did not skip the country, then the LAPD will solve another case.

So, …
a. Detective Wise is puzzled.
b. Sergeant Baker found a key clue.
c. The LAPD will solve another case.
d. Sean Gilley did not skip the country.

7.   1. Molly left in the company jet and Sean Gilley took over the company.
      2. If Molly left in the company jet, then she's Dublin-bound.
      3. If Sean Gilley took over the company, then there is certain to be a scandal.
      4. If Molly is Dublin-bound and there is certain to be a scandal, then Clams and Mussels From the Sea is not going to have a rosy future.
      5. Either Clams and Mussels From the Sea is going to have a rosy future or the IRS is launching an investigation.

So, …
a. Sean Gilley took over the company.
b. There is certain to be a scandal.
c. Clams and Mussels From the Sea is going to have a rosy future.
d. The IRS is launching an investigation.

(Continued)

8.
1. If Molly went to Dublin, then she's researching squid at Trinity College.
2. If Molly is researching squid at Trinity College, then Clams and Mussels From the Sea is producing a new commercial.
3. Either Molly went to Dublin or Sean is stealing company funds.
4. If Sean is stealing company funds, then Detective Wise will solve the case.
5. Clams and Mussels From the Sea is not producing a new commercial.

So, …
a. Detective Wise will solve the case.
b. Molly did not go to Dublin.
c. Sean stealing company funds.
d. Molly is researching squid at Trinity College.

9.
1. If Detective Wise solves the case, then Molly flew to Dublin.
2. If Molly flew to Dublin, then Clams and Mussels From the Sea is an Irish company.
3. If Clams and Mussels From the Sea is an Irish company, then Molly speaks Irish.
4. Either Molly does not speak Irish or Sean does not speak Spanish.
5. It is not the case that Detective Wise does not solve the case.
6. If Sean steals company funds, then he is heading for Mexico.
7. If Sean is heading for Mexico, then he planning to settle in Peru.
8. If Sean is planning to settle in Peru, then he speaks Spanish.

So, …
a. Detective Wise solves the case.
b. Sean doesn't steal company funds.
c. Molly speaks Irish.
d. Sean does not speak Spanish.

10.   1.   Sean is heading for Mexico.
         2.   If either Sean is heading for Mexico or Molly is
              heading for Dublin, then Detective Wise has
              uncovered a big clue.
         3.   If Detective Wise has uncovered a big clue,
              then the case is solved.
         4.   Company funds are missing if the case is
              solved.
         5.   The fact that company funds are missing
              implies that Molly was not the crook.
         6.   Either Molly was the crook or Sean is the
              crook.

So, ...
a. Molly is heading for Dublin.
b. The case is solved.
c. Molly is not the crook.
d. Sean is the crook.

CASE 20	City of Los Angeles Police Department

[1]The books at Moorhead Marine, a private business owned by Mr. Moorhead, were "well-cooked." [2]More than thirty million dollars was missing. [3]Some of the company's officers were also missing. [4]Detective Wise was called in to see if there was a connection between the missing money and the missing officers.

[5]Moorhead Marine builds boats. [6]Several million dollars in checks had been written to PUR Plastics. [7]Each check was signed by Melissa Shipley, the accountant of Moorhead Marine. [8]PUR Plastics went out of business in 1955. [9]"Either Shipley didn't know that PUR Plastics was a fake or she was stealing from Moorhead Marine," reasoned Detective Wise. [10]"If she was stealing from the company, then we can explain Shipley's disappearance. [11]So, if Shipley knew PUR Plastics was a fake, we can explain her disappearance."

[12]Company Vice President Seymour Fish was in charge of marketing glass-bottomed boats. [13]The boats were not selling. [14]He sold all their glass-bottomed boats to Shark Views of New Zealand at a loss of more than three million dollars. [15]Shark Views is owned by Ima Scam, who is also known as Mrs. Seymour Fish. [16]Fish delivered the boats himself and stayed in New Zealand. [17]Detective Wise reasoned, if Fish were responsible for the missing funds, then he was in the company bookkeeping department and his disappearance was not obvious. [18]But his disappearance was obvious. [19]So, Fish is not responsible for the missing funds.

[20]Then there was Sydney Sneed, the treasurer. [21]On Friday, July 30, he wired $20 million in company funds to a real estate company in Buenos Aires. [22]He flew to Argentina that night. [23]He now owns a huge cattle ranch. [24]His misuse of company funds was not discovered until Monday, August 2. [25]"Sneed is a crook, but he's not responsible for the missing funds," Detective Wise concluded. [26]If Sneed was responsible for the missing funds, either his criminal acts were not easily detected or he tried to cover his tracks. [27]But his acts were easily detected and he did not try to cover his tracks. [28]So, he's not responsible.

[29]Detective Wise was puzzled. [30]Melissa Shipley might be at her husband's estate in Spain. [31]If her husband were not independently wealthy, Melissa would have been a suspect. [32]Could it be someone else?

[33]Detective Wise discovered that Adel Rich, of Housekeeping, recently purchased a *nice* house is Beverly Hills. [34]It was a cash deal. [35]She had also served time for computer hacking and accounting irregularities. [36]Could those facts be important?

5.15 Logically Equivalent Claims

Two claims are logically equivalent if they are true under the same circumstances. When one claim is true, the other is true. When one claim is false, the other is false. We use the tribar (≡) to represent logical equivalence.

A claim is logically equivalent to its **double negation.** Let "p" equal "It is true that John went to the store." Let "not, not p" equal "It is not true that John did not go to the store."

p is logically equivalent to not, not p.

Detective Wise is a good detective.	≡	It is false that she is not a good detective.
p.	≡	Not, not p.

Truth tables can also be used to show that two statements are logically equivalent. Two statements are logically equivalent if they always have the same truth-values. So, for example, truth tables show that any statement p is logically equivalent to not, not-p (double negation).	p	Not p.	Not, not p.
	T	F	T
	F	T	F
	↑		↑

Notice that each row of the columns marked with an upward pointing arrow ↑ have the same truth-values. The two statements are, therefore, logically equivalent.

Examples of double negation in Case 20:

	Double Negation	Form
a.	"It is not so that Sydney Sneed was not good as a treasurer" is logically equuivalent to "Sydney Sneed was good as a treasurer"	Not, not S ≡ S.
b.	"It is not the case that Adel Rich was not involved in the crime," is logically equivalent to "Adel Rich was involved in the crime."	~~A ≡ A.
c.	"Detective Wise was not unconcerned about the missing funds" is logically equivalent to, "Detective Wise was concerned about the missing funds."	~~p ≡ p.

These equivalences are known as **De Morgan's Theorems.**

"Not (p or q) is logically equivalent to "Not p and not q."

It is not the case that either John will go or that Mary will go.	≡	John will not go and Mary will not go.
Not either p or q.	≡	Not p and not q.
~($p \lor q$)	≡	(~p & ~q)

"Not (*p* and *q*) is logically equivalent to "Not *p* or not *q*."

It is not the case that both John and Mary will go.	≡	Either John will not go or Mary will not go.
Not both *p* and *q*.	≡	Either not *p* or not *q*.
~(*p* & *q*)	≡	(~*p* ∨ ~*q*)

Truth tables for De Morgan's Theorems show that, "Not either *p* or *q*" is logically equivalent to "Not *p* and not *q*," and "Not both *p* and *q*" is logically equivalent to "Not *p* or not *q*." The relevant columns are marked with up arrows.

p	*q*	Not either *p* or *q*.		Not *p* and not *q*.		
T	T	F	T	F	F	F
T	F	F	T	F	F	T
F	T	F	T	T	F	F
F	F	T	F	T	T	T
		(↑)			(↑)	

p	*q*	Not both *p* and *q*.		Not *p* or not *q*.		
T	T	F	T	F	F	F
T	F	T	F	F	T	T
F	T	T	F	T	T	F
F	F	T	F	T	T	T
		(↑)			(↑)	

Examples of De Morgan's Theorems in Case 20:

	De Morgan's Theorems	Form
a.	"Not both Melissa Moorhead and Sydney Sneed stole money from the company," is logically equivalent to, "Either Melissa Moorhead did not steal money from the company or Sydney Sneed did not steal money from the company."	Not (M and S) ≡ Not (M or S).
b.	"Not either Sydney Sneed or Adel Rich is an honest person," is logically equivalent to, "Sydney Sneed is not an honest person and Adel Rich is not an honest person."	~(S or A) ≡ (~S and ~A).
c.	"Either he was not in the company bookkeeping department or it is not the case that his disappearance was not obvious," is logically equivalent to "It is not the case that he was in the company bookkeeping department and his disappearance was not obvious."	(~C or ~~D) ≡ ~(C or ~D).
d.	"His acts were easily detected and he did not try to cover his tracks," (sentence 27) is logically equivalent to, "It is not the case that either his criminal acts were not easily detected or he would have tried to cover his tracks." Note: This recognizes that "His acts were easily detected," is logically equivalent to, "It is not the case the his acts were not easily detected," due to double negation.	(*p* and ~*q*) ≡ ~(~*p* or *q*).

When the positions of the antecedent and the consequent of a conditional are switched, both statements are denied. This is known as **transposition**.

"If *p,* then *q*" is logically equivalent to "If not *q*, then not *p*."

If John goes, then Mary goes.	≡	If Mary does not go, then John does not go.
If *p,* then *q*.	≡	If not *q*, then not *p*.
(*p* → *q*)	≡	(~*q* → ~*p*)

A truth table shows that a conditional statement is logically equivalent to its transposition.

p	*q*	If *p,* then *q*.	If not *q*, then not *p*.		
T	T	T	F	T	F
T	F	F	T	F	F
F	T	T	F	T	T
F	F	T	T	T	T

Examples of transposition in Case 20:

	Transposition	Form
a.	"If Melissa is in Spain, then her husband owns an estate," is logically equivalent to, "If Melissa's husband does not own an estate, then Melissa is not in Spain."	If M, then H. ≡ If ~H, then ~M.
b.	"If Sydney Sneed is a crook, then he owns a ranch in Argentina," is logically equivalent to, "If Sydney Sneed does not own a ranch in Argentina, then he is not a crook."	If C, then A. ≡ If ~A, then ~C.
c.	"If Adel Rich had a hand in the affair, then she's putting her old skills to work," is logically equivalent to, "If Adel Rich is not putting her old skills to work, then she did not have a hand in the affair."	If A, then S. ≡ If ~S, then ~A.
d.	"Seymour Fish sold the boats for less than cost provided that he was planning to move to New Zealand," is logically equivalent to, "If Seymour Fish did not sell the boats for less than cost, then he was not planning to move to New Zealand."	If *p,* then *q*. ≡ If ~*q*, then ~*p*.

A conditional claim is logically equivalent to the denial of the antecedent disjoined to the consequent. This is known as **material implication**.

"If *p,* then *q*" is logically equivalent to "Either not *p* or *q*."

If the sun has risen, then it is day.	≡	Either the sun has not risen or it is day.
If *p,* then *q*.	≡	Either not *p* or *q*.
(*p* → *q*)	≡	(~*p* ∨ *q*)

		p	q	If p, then q.	Not p, or q.
A truth table shows that a statement of the form "If p, then q" is logically equivalent to, "Either not p, or q (material implication)."		T	T	T	F T T
		T	F	F	F F F
		F	T	T	T T T
		F	F	T	T T F
				↑	↑

Examples of material implication in Case 20:

	Material Implication	Form	Reasoning/Conclusion
a.	"Either Moorhead didn't know that PUR Plastics was a fake or she was stealing from her company," (sentence 9) is logically equivalent to, "If Moorhead knew that PUR Plastics was a fake, then she was stealing from her company."	Either ~K or S. ≡ If K, then S.	Simple equivalance
b.	"If Sneed was stealing from the company, then we know why he's in Argentina," is logically equivalent to, "Either Sneed was not stealing from the company or we know why he's in Argentina."	If S, then K. ≡ Either ~S or K.	Simple equivalance
c.	"If Seymour Fish is missing, then something smells fishy," is logically equivalent to, "Either something smells fishy or Seymour Fish is not missing."	If M, then S. ≡ If ~S, then ~M. ≡ Either S or ~M.	"If Seymour Fish is missing, then something smells fishy," is logically equivalent to, "If something does not smell fishy, then Seymour Fish is not missing," by transposition. "If something does not smell fishy, then Seymour Fish is not missing," is logically equivalent to, "Either something smells fishy or Seymour Fish is not missing," by material implication.

	Material Implication	Form	Reasoning/Conclusion
d.	"If Adel Rich had a hand in the affair, then she's up to her old tricks," is logically equivalent to, "It is not the case that Adel Rich had a hand in the affair and she's not up to her old tricks."	If A, then O. $\equiv$ Either ~A or O. $\equiv$ Either ~A or ~~O. $\equiv$ ~(A and ~O).	The conditional is logically equivalent to, "Either Adel Rich did not have a hand in the affair or she's up to her old tricks." Double negating the second disjunct gives one, "Either Adel Rich did not have a hand in the affair or it is not the case that she's not up to her old tricks." Using De Morgan's Theorem on the statement gives one, "It is not the case that Adel Rich had a hand in the affair and she's not up to her old tricks."

5.16 Exercise Are claims 1 and 2 logically equivalent? Circle the best answer. Writing the form of the claim is often helpful, but it is not required.

1. **Example:**
    1. If Adel Rich is suddenly wealthy, then she doesn't earn all her money by cleaning.
    2. Either Adel Rich is not suddenly wealthy or she doesn't earn all her money by cleaning.

    If p, then ~q.
    Either ~p or ~q.

    (a.) **Logically equivalent:**
    (If *p*, then *q*) ≡ (Not *p* or *q*)
    b. Logically equivalent:
    (If *p*, then *q*) ≡ (If not *q*, then not *p*)
    c. Logically equivalent:
    (If p, then q) ≡ (Not p and q)
    d. Not logically equivalent

2.
    1. If Sydney Sneed is in Argentina, then Sydney is a crook.
    2. If Sydney is a crook, then Sydney Sneed is in Argentina.

    a. Logically equivalent:
    (If *p*, then *q*) ≡ (Not *p* or *q*)
    b. Logically equivalent:
    (If *p*, then *q*) ≡ (If not *q*, then not *p*)
    c. Logically equivalent:
    (If *p*, then *q*) ≡ (Not *p* and *q*)
    d. Not logically equivalent

3.
    1. It is not the case that both Melissa and Sydney are crooks.
    2. Either Melissa is not a crook or Sydney is not a crook.

    a. Logically equivalent:
    Not (*p* and *q*) ≡ (Not *p* or not *q*)
    b. Logically equivalent:
    (If *p*, then *q*) ≡ (If not *q*, then not *p*)
    c. Logically equivalent:
    (If *p*, then *q*) ≡ (Not *p* and *q*)
    d. Not logically equivalent:
    (If *p*, then *q*) ≡ (Not *p* and *q*)

4.   1. If Detective Wise is puzzled, then Adel will not be detected.
       2. If Adel will be detected, then Detective Wise is not puzzled.

  a. Logically equivalent:
     (If p, then not q) ≡ (Not p or q)
  b. Logically equivalent:
     (If p, then not q) ≡ (Not p and q)
  c. Logically equivalent:
     (If p, then not q) ≡ (If q, then not p)
  d. Not logically equivalent

5.   1. It is not the case that either Adel or Melissa stole money from the company.
       2. Either Adel did not steal money from the company or Melissa did not steal money from the company.

  a. Logically equivalent:
     (If p, then q) ≡ (If not q, then not p)
  b. Logically equivalent:
     Not (p and q) ≡ (Not p or not q)
  c. Logically equivalent:
     Not (p or q) ≡ (Not p and not q)
  d. Not logically equivalent

6.   1. It is not the case that both Adel and Melissa stole money from the company.
       2. Adel did not steal money from the company and Melissa did not steal money from the company.

  a. Logically equivalent:
     (If p, then q) ≡ (If not q, then not p)
  b. Logically equivalent:
     Not (p and q) ≡ (Not p or not q)
  c. Logically equivalent:
     Not (p or q) ≡ (Not p and not q)
  d. Not logically equivalent

(Continued)

7. 1. It is not the case that there is not something
       fishy about Seymour Fish.
    2. There is something fishy about Seymour Fish.
    a. Logically equivalent:
       (Not, not p) ≡ (p)
    b. Logically equivalent:
       (If p, then q) ≡ (If not q, then not p)
    c. Logically equivalent:
       (Not p or not q) ≡ Not (p and q)
    d. Not logically equivalent

8. 1. Melissa is not a crook and Adel is not a crook.
    2. It is not the case that either Melissa or Adel is
       a crook.
    a. Logically equivalent: (Not, not p) ≡ (p)
    b. Logically equivalent:
       (If p, then q) ≡ (If not q, then not p)
    c. Logically equivalent:
       (Not p and not q) ≡ Not (p or q)
    d. Not logically equivalent

9. 1. Either Melissa is honest or Adel is a crook.
    2. It is not the case that both Melissa is
       dishonest and Adel is not a crook.
    a. Logically equivalent:
       (p or q) ≡ Not (not p and not q)
    b. Logically equivalent:
       (If p, then q) ≡ (If not q, then not p)
    c. Logically equivalent:
       (Not p or not q) ≡ Not (p and q)
    d. Not logically equivalent

10. 1. If Melissa is dishonest, then Adel is not a
       crook.
    2. If Melissa is honest, then Adel is a crook.
    a. Logically equivalent:
       (If not p, then not q) ≡ (If q, then not p)
    b. Logically equivalent:
       (If p, then q) ≡ (If not q, then not p)
    c. Logically equivalent:
       (Not p or not q) ≡ Not (p and q)
    d. Not logically equivalent

11.
    1. Either Sydney is a crook or Adel is a crook.
    2. Sydney is not a crook and Adel is a crook.
a. Logically equivalent:
   $p \equiv$ (Not, not p)
b. Logically equivalent:
   (If p, then q) $\equiv$ (If not q, then not p)
c. Logically equivalent:
   (p or q) $\equiv$ Not (not p and not q)
d. Not logically equivalent

12.
    1. It is not the case that both Adel is a crook and Seymour went to New Zealand.
    2. If Seymour went to New Zealand, then Adel is a crook.
a. Logically equivalent:
   (If p, then not q) $\equiv$ (Not p or q)
b. Logically equivalent:
   [Not (p and q)] $\equiv$ (If p then, not q)
c. Logically equivalent:
   (If p, then q) $\equiv$ (If q, then not p)
d. Not logically equivalent

13.
    1. Neither Adel nor Melissa stole money from the company.
    2. Melissa did not steal money from the company but Adel did.
a. Logically equivalent:
   (p and q) $\equiv$ Not (not p or not q)
b. Logically equivalent:
   (Not p and not q) $\equiv$ Not (p or q)
c. Logically equivalent:
   (If p, then q) $\equiv$ (If q, then not p)
d. Not logically equivalent

(Continued)

14.   1.   If Adel stole money from the company,
               then Melissa did not steal money from the
               company.
          2.   It is not the case that both Adel and Melissa
               stole money from the company.
     a. Logically equivalent:
        (If p, then not q) ≡ (Not p or not q)
     b. Logically equivalent:
        (If p, then not q) ≡ Not (p and q)
     c. Logically equivalent:
        (If p, then q) ≡ (If not q, then not p)
     d. Not logically equivalent

15.   1.   If both Adel and Melissa are crooks, then
               Sydney will not be put on trial.
          2.   Sydney will not be put on trial unless either
               Adel is not a crook or Melissa is not a crook.
     a. Logically equivalent:
        [If (p and q), then not r] ≡ [Not p or not q) or not r]
     b. Logically equivalent:
        [If (p and q), then not r] ≡ [Not (p or q) or not r]
     c. Logically equivalent:
        [If (p and q), then not r] ≡ [not r or (either not p or
        not q]
     d. Not logically equivalent

CASE 21	City of Los Angeles Police Department

[1]There was a series of armed robberies at the We Are Nuts shops. [2]In each case, two people wearing ski masks and carrying automatic weapons demanded cash—and two pounds of candied pecans. [3]Company President I. M. Nuts said, "The robberies are discouraging, but the robbers have good taste." [4]Detective Wise tried to figure out who did it.

[5]There are five branches of We Are Nuts, each run by a different member of the Nuts family. [6]The robbers at each were about 5 feet, 6 inches tall and 6 feet, 4 inches tall. [7]"The short one," remarked Penelope P. Nuts, "was wearing old-fashioned women's shoes like my grandmother used to wear." [8]At the 12th Street store, they were seen leaving in a late-model Honda. [9]At the store on Wilshire, they left on a motorcycle. [10]At the store on Sunset, they left in a Honda, and R. U. Nuts was able to get a partial license plate number.

[11]The car was traced to I. B. Squirrel. [12]Mr. Squirrel is eighty-five and confined to a wheelchair. [13]"I haven't seen the car since my wife left me a couple months ago," said Mr. Squirrel. [14]"She's eighty-three but built like a seventy-two-year-old. [15]She's about five-six in her platform shoes. [16]If she did it, it was just for the adventure—and the nuts." [17]A two-pound bag of We Are Nuts candied pecans was on his table.

[18]Detective Wise considered the facts. [19]If Ms. Squirrel was one of the robbers, then she had a partner. [20]If she had a partner, her partner is about six-four. [21]So, if Ms. Squirrel was one of the robbers, her partner is about six-four. [22]If Mr. Squirrel is telling the truth, then he was not involved; and if Ms. Squirrel was involved in the crime, then I. B. has a source for candied pecans. [23]Either Mr. Squirrel is telling the truth, or Ms. Squirrel was involved in the crime. [24]So, either Mr. Squirrel was not involved or I. B. has a source for candied pecans. [25]If I. B. has a source for candied pecans—which he does—then he's probably involved.

"[26]This squirrelly case is driving me nuts!" thought Detective Wise.

5.17 Review Exercise Circle all the compound claims in each of the following arguments.

1. **Example:**
   Either I. M. Nuts or R. U. Nuts is involved in the robbery provided that I. B. Squirrel is telling the truth.
   a. Denial
   b. Conjunction
   (c.) **Disjunction**
   (d.) **Conditional**

   If p, then either q or r.

2. If Bill and Dan pointed squirt guns at the clerk, then they are not serious robbers.
   a. Denial
   b. Conjunction
   c. Disjunction
   d. Conditional

3. Both Wally Nuts and R. U. Nuts are innocent, on the condition that they were in the stores when the stores were robbed.
   a. Denial
   b. Conjunction
   c. Disjunction
   d. Conditional

4. I. B. Squirrel does not like Detective Wise.
   a. Denial
   b. Conjunction
   c. Disjunction
   d. Conditional

5. If Ms. Squirrel was involved in the crime, then so were both I. B. and their son, Rocky.
   a. Denial
   b. Conjunction
   c. Disjunction
   d. Conditional

6. Unless one of the Nuts had a hand in the crime, Ms. Squirrel helped pull the jobs.
   a. Denial
   b. Conjunction
   c. Disjunction
   d. Conditional

7. Wally Nuts is running short of cash, even though he was involved in the crime only if he is a friend of Rocky Squirrel.
   a. Denial
   b. Conjunction
   c. Disjunction
   d. Conditional

8. Detective Wise is puzzled, unless either I. B. Squirrel was involved in the crime or it was an inside job.
   a. Denial
   b. Conjunction
   c. Disjunction
   d. Conditional

9. If I. M. Nuts is stealing from his own company, then there is not a single Squirrel involved in the crime.
   a. Denial
   b. Conjunction
   c. Disjunction
   d. Conditional

10. Candied pecans are a tasty treat, yet R. U. Nuts had a hand in the robbery only if Penelope P. Nuts was not vacationing in Jamaica.
    a. Denial
    b. Conjunction
    c. Disjunction
    d. Conditional

5.18 Review Exercise Circle the argument forms of each of the following arguments.

1. **Example:**
   If Ms. Squirrel was one of the robbers, then she had a partner. If she had a partner, her partner is about six-four. So, if Ms. Squirrel was one of the robbers, her partner is about six-four.
   a. Affirming the antecedent
   b. Denying the consequent
   c. Disjunctive syllogism
   (d.) **Hypothetical syllogism**
   e. Addition

If p, then q.
If q, then r.
___
If p, then r.

(Continued)

2. If Mr. Squirrel is telling the truth, then he was not involved; and if Ms. Squirrel was involved in the crime, then I. B. has a source for candied pecans. Either Mr. Squirrel is telling the truth, or Ms. Squirrel was involved in the crime. So, either Mr. Squirrel was not involved or I. B. has a source for candied pecans.
   a. Addition
   b. Simplification
   c. Conjunction
   d. Constructive dilemma
   e. Destructive dilemma

3. Either R. U. Nuts had a hand in the crime or I. B. Squirrel had a hand in the crime. R. U. Nuts did not have a hand in the crime. So, I. B. Squirrel had a hand in the crime.
   a. Affirming the antecedent
   b. Denying the consequent
   c. Disjunctive syllogism
   d. Conjunction
   e. Fallacy of denying the antecedent

4. I. M. Nuts is president of the company. R. U. Nuts works at the store on Sunset Boulevard. So, I. M. Nuts is president of the company and R. U. Nuts works at the store on Sunset Boulevard.
   a. Addition
   b. Simplification
   c. Conjunction
   d. Fallacy of affirming the consequent
   e. Fallacy of denying the antecedent

5. If I. M. Nuts had a hand in the crime, then it was an inside job. I. M. Nuts did not have a hand in the crime. So, it was not an inside job.
   a. Affirming the antecedent
   b. Denying the consequent
   c. Hypothetical syllogism
   d. Fallacy of affirming the consequent
   e. Fallacy of denying the antecedent

6. If Penelope P. Nuts had a hand in the affair, then she has heavy gambling debts. Penelope P. Nuts does not have heavy gambling debts. So Penelope P. Nuts did not have a hand in the affair.
   a. Affirming the antecedent
   b. Denying the consequent
   c. Hypothetical syllogism
   d. Fallacy of affirming the consequent
   e. Fallacy of denying the antecedent

7. If I. B. Squirrel is faking his handicap, then he is the tall robber; and if Cash U. Nuts is deep in debt, then he had a hand in the robbery. Either I. B. Squirrel is not the tall robber or Cash U. Nuts did not have a hand in the robbery. Hence, either I. B. Squirrel is not faking his handicap or Cash U. Nuts is not deep in debt.
   a. Affirming the antecedent
   b. Denying the consequent
   c. Addition
   d. Constructive dilemma
   e. Destructive dilemma

8. If the Internal Revenue Service is investigating We Are Nuts, then I. M. Nuts is in trouble. So, if the Internal Revenue Service is investigating We Are Nuts, then I. M. Nuts is in trouble; unless Ms. Squirrel had a hand in the crime.
   a. Disjunctive syllogism
   b. Hypothetical syllogism
   c. Addition
   d. Simplification
   e. Fallacy of affirming the consequent

9. R. U. Nuts was present at the robbery unless he called in sick. So, R. U. Nuts was present at the robbery, for he did not call in sick.
   a. Denying the consequent
   b. Disjunctive syllogism
   c. Destructive dilemma
   d. Fallacy of affirming the consequent
   e. Fallacy of denying the antecedent

(Continued)

10. If I. M. Nuts has tax problems, then he is president of
    We Are Nuts. I. M. Nuts is president of We Are Nuts.
    Therefore, I. M. Nuts has tax problems.
    a. Affirming the antecedent
    b. Denying the consequent
    c. Simplification
    d. Fallacy of affirming the consequent
    e. Fallacy of denying the antecedent

11. R. U. Nuts is president of We are Nuts, if he has tax
    problems. R. U. Nuts does not have tax problems.
    Hence, R.U. Nuts is not president of We are Nuts.
    a. Affirming the antecedent
    b. Denying the consequent
    c. Addition
    d. Fallacy of affirming the consequent
    e. Fallacy of denying the antecedent

12. I. B. Squirrel has a criminal record only if he pulled a
    bank job twenty years ago. If I. B. Squirrel pulled a bank
    job twenty years ago, then he's the mastermind behind
    the robberies. Thus, I. B. Squirrel is the mastermind
    behind the robberies on the condition that he has a
    criminal record.
    a. Disjunctive syllogism
    b. Hypothetical syllogism
    c. Addition
    d. Constructive dilemma
    e. Destructive dilemma

13. If Detective Wise is puzzled, then the crime might go
    unsolved; and if I. M. Rich had a hand in the affair, then
    I. B. Squirrel is in his employ. Thus, if I. M. Rich had a
    hand in the affair, then I. B. Squirrel is in his employ.
    a. Affirming the antecedent
    b. Disjunctive syllogism
    c. Simplification
    d. Conjunction
    e. Constructive dilemma

14. Either Rocky Squirrel was the tall robber or none of
    the suspects committed the crime. If Rocky Squirrel
    is the tall robber, then Ms. Squirrel is the short robber;
    and if none of the suspects committed the crime, then
    Detective Wise is puzzled. So, Ms. Squirrel is the short
    robber unless Detective Wise is puzzled.
    a. Disjunctive syllogism
    b. Constructive dilemma
    c. Destructive dilemma
    d. Fallacy of affirming the consequent
    e. Fallacy of denying the antecedent

15. Penelope P. Nuts hates candied pecans provided that
    she is not involved in the crime. Penelope P. Nuts is
    not involved in the crime. So, Penelope P. Nuts hates
    candied pecans.
    a. Affirming the antecedent
    b. Denying the consequent
    c. Hypothetical syllogism
    d. Fallacy of affirming the consequent
    e. Fallacy of denying the antecedent

16. I. M. Nuts was out of town when the robbery occurred
    on Sunset. So, Rocky Squirrel might get away with the
    robbery, even though I. M. Nuts was out of town when
    the robbery occurred on Sunset, for Rocky Squirrel might
    get away with the robbery.
    a. Hypothetical syllogism
    b. Addition
    c. Simplification
    d. Conjunction
    e. Destructive dilemma

17. If Rocky Squirrel had a hand in the crime, then Ms.
    Squirrel was the short robber. So, Ms. Squirrel was
    the short robber, since Rocky Squirrel had a hand in
    the crime.
    a. Affirming the antecedent
    b. Disjunctive syllogism
    c. Hypothetical syllogism
    d. Constructive dilemma
    e. Fallacy of affirming the consequent

(Continued)

18. If Rocky Squirrel had a hand in the crime, then Ms. Squirrel was the short robber. So, Rocky Squirrel had a hand in the crime, since Ms. Squirrel was the short robber.
    a. Affirming the antecedent
    b. Disjunctive syllogism
    c. Hypothetical syllogism
    d. Constructive dilemma
    e. Fallacy of affirming the consequent

19. Rocky Squirrel had a hand in the crime provided that Ms. Squirrel was the short robber; and I. M. Squirrel was the mastermind, provided he cannot get out of his wheelchair. So, Rocky Squirrel had a hand in the crime unless I. M. Squirrel was the mastermind, for either Ms. Squirrel was the short robber or I. M. Squirrel cannot get out of his wheelchair.
    a. Constructive dilemma
    b. Affirming the antecedent.
    c. Destructive dilemma
    d. Addition
    e. Conjunction

20. If the Nuts had no hand in the crime, then the Squirrels are serious suspects. The Squirrels are serious suspects. Hence, the Nuts had no hand in the crime.
    a. Fallacy of affirming the consequent
    b. Hypothetical syllogism
    c. Disjunctive syllogism
    d. Affirming the antecedent
    e. Destructive dilemma

5.19 Review Exercise What conclusion is reached in each of the following argument chains? Circle the best answer

1. **Example:**
   If it was an inside job, then the Nuts are involved. If the Nuts are involved, then the Squirrels are being falsely accused. The Squirrels are not being falsely accused.
   So, …
   a. The Nuts are involved.
   b. **It was not an inside job.**
   c. The Squirrels are being falsely accused.
   d. The Nuts are not involved.

   1. If p, then q.
   2. If q, then r.
   4. $\overline{\text{If } p, \text{ then } r.}$
   3. $\sim r$.
   5. $\overline{\sim p}$.

2. If I. B. Squirrel has a source for candied pecans—
    which he does—then he's probably involved.
    So,...
    a. I. B. Squirrel has a source for candied pecans.
    b. I. B. Squirrel does not have a source for candied
       pecans.
    c. I. B. Squirrel is probably involved.
    d. I. B. Squirrel is probably not involved.

3. If I. B. Squirrel has a source for candied pecans, then
    he's probably involved; and if Ms. Squirrel is involved,
    then she prefers automatics to revolvers. Either I.
    B. Squirrel has a source for candied pecans or Ms.
    Squirrel is involved. Ms. Squirrel does not prefer
    automatics to revolvers. If I. B. Squirrel is involved,
    then Rocky is the tall robber.
    So, ...
    a. Rocky is the tall robber.
    b. I. B. Squirrel has a source for candied pecans.
    c. Ms. Squirrel is involved.
    d. Ms. Squirrel is not involved.

4. If I. M. Nuts is robbing his own stores, then the
    nut business is not healthy. If the nut business is
    not healthy, then R. U. Nuts is looking for a job in
    construction. If Detective Wise is puzzled, then the
    case is certain to take an interesting turn. Either
    I. M. Nuts is robbing his own stores or Detective
    Wise is puzzled. R. U. Nuts is not looking for a job
    in construction. If the case is certain to take an
    interesting turn, then Ms. Squirrel will be cleared
    of suspicion.
    So, ...
    a. The nut business is not healthy.
    b. The case is certain to take an interesting turn.
    c. Ms. Squirrel will be cleared of suspicion.
    d. I. M. Nuts is robbing his own stores.

(Continued)

5. If either Ms. Squirrel or Rocky is involved in the crime, then I. B. Squirrel is the mastermind. If I. B. Squirrel is the mastermind, then it was not an inside job. Either it was an inside job or Rocky drives a Harley-Davidson. Ms. Squirrel is involved in the crime. If Rocky drives a Harley-Davidson, then he needs money to make his monthly payments.
    So, ...
    a. Rocky drives a Harley-Davidson.
    b. It was not an inside job.
    c. I. B. Squirrel is the mastermind.
    d. Rocky needs money to make his monthly payments.

6. Either Wally Nuts acted behind the scenes or Ms. Squirrel is after more than nuts. If I. M. Nuts is involved in the crime, then it's an inside job; and if I. B. Squirrel has an unreported source of income, then he's the mastermind. It is not the case that I. B. Squirrel does not have an unreported source of income. Either it's not an inside job or I. B. Squirrel is not the mastermind. If I. M. Nuts is not involved in the crime, then Wally Nuts did not act behind the scenes.
    So, ...
    a. I. M. Nuts is not involved in the crime.
    b. Ms. Squirrel is after more than nuts.
    c. It's an inside job.
    d. Wally Nuts did not act behind the scenes.

7. If both I. M. Nuts and R. U. Nuts are innocent, then Ms. Squirrel had a hand in the affair. If Rocky Squirrel was the tall robber, then I. M. Nuts is innocent; and Rocky Squirrel was the tall robber. Either Penelope P. Nuts steals money from the cash register or R. U. Nuts is innocent. If Ms. Squirrel had a hand in the affair, then Ms. Squirrel did not leave her husband. Penelope P. Nuts does not steal money from the cash register.
    So, ...
    a. Ms. Squirrel had a hand in the affair.
    b. Rocky Squirrel is the tall robber.
    c. R. U. Nuts is innocent.
    d. Ms. Squirrel did not leave her husband.

8. If Detective Wise will solve the case, then the case will make headlines in the *Los Angeles Tribune*. Ms. Squirrel did not leave her husband and I. B. Squirrel is the mastermind behind the scheme. If I. B. Squirrel is the mastermind behind the scheme, then Detective Wise will solve the case; and if Cash U. Nuts has heavy gambling debts, then the case will go unsolved. So, …
   a. the case will make headlines in the Los Angeles *Tribune*.
   b. Detective Wise will solve the case.
   c. Ms. Squirrel did not leave her husband.
   d. I. B. Squirrel is the mastermind behind the scheme.

9. If Detective Wise solves the crime, then there will be headlines in the *Tribune*; and if I. B. Squirrel is the mastermind behind the scheme, then Rocky Squirrel drives a Harley. If either there will be headlines in the *Tribune* or Rocky Squirrel drives a Harley, then We Are Nuts will recover its losses. Detective Wise solves the crime.
   So, …
   a. There will be headlines in the *Tribune*.
   b. Rocky Squirrel drives a Harley.
   c. We Are Nuts will recover its losses.
   d. I. B. Squirrel is the mastermind behind the scheme.

10. Either Ms. Squirrel is the only 5 foot, 6 inch suspect, or Penelope P. Nuts is 5 feet, 6 inches tall. I. M. Nuts will not be charged with the crime and R. U. Nuts will not be above suspicion. If Wally Nuts was in the store during the robbery, then R. U. Nuts will be above suspicion. If Wally Nuts was not in the store during the robbery, then Ms. Squirrel is not the only 5 foot, 6 inch suspect.
   So, …
   a. Penelope P. Nuts is 5 feet, 6 inches tall.
   b. Wally Nuts was in the store during the robbery.
   c. I. M. Nuts will not be changed with the crime.
   d. Ms. Squirrel is not the only 5 foot, 6 inch suspect.

(Continued)

11. Rocky Squirrel drives a Harley. If both I. M. Nuts and I. B. Squirrel are suspects, then it was an inside job. Cash U. Nuts was out of town at the time of the robbery on Sunset. If Cash U. Nuts was out of town at the time of the robbery on Sunset, then I. M. Nuts is a suspect. If either Rocky Squirrel or Ms. Squirrel drives a Harley, then I. B. Squirrel is a suspect.
So, ...
a. I. M. Nuts is a suspect.
b. It was an inside job.
c. Ms. Squirrel drives a Harley.
d. Cash U. Nuts was not out of town at the time of the robbery on Sunset.

12. If R. U. Nuts was involved in the crime, then both Penelope P. Nuts and Rocky Squirrel played a part in the crime. If Rocky Squirrel played a part in the crime, then if either I. M. Nuts or I. B. Squirrel was the mastermind behind the crime, then We Are Nuts is in trouble with the government. R. U. Nuts was involved in the crime and I. M. Nuts was the mastermind behind the crime.
So, ...
a. Penelope P. Nuts played a part in the crime.
b. I. M. Nuts was the mastermind behind the crime.
c. I. B. Squirrel was not the mastermind behind the crime.
d. We Are Nuts is in trouble with the government.

13. If Rocky Squirrel drives a Harley and Penelope P. Nuts drives a BMW motorcycle, they met at a motorcycle rally. If Rocky and Penelope met at a motorcycle rally, then Rocky is not a robber. Rocky drives a Harley. If I. M. Nuts drives a Mercedes-Benz, then either R. U. Nuts drives a Lexus or Penelope P. Nuts drives a BMW motorcycle. Either Rocky is a robber or Detective Wise is investigating a very puzzling case. I. M. Nuts drives a Mercedes-Benz, but R. U. Nuts does not drive a Lexus.
So, ...
a. Detective Wise is investigating a very puzzling case.
b. Rocky and Penelope met at a motorcycle rally.
c. Penelope P. Nuts drives a BMW motorcycle.
d. I. M. Nuts drives a Mercedes-Benz.

14. If Penelope is a suspect, then Rocky is not a suspect; and if R. U. is a suspect, then Wally is not a suspect. If I. M. Nuts is innocent, then Rocky is a suspect; and if I. B. Squirrel is innocent, then Wally is a suspect. Either Penelope is a suspect or R. U. is a suspect. It is not the case that I. M. Nuts is not innocent. So, …
   a. Rocky is a suspect.
   b. Wally is not a suspect.
   c. Penelope is a suspect.
   d. I. B. Squirrel is not innocent.

5.20 Review Exercise Write ≡ (logically equivalent) or ≢ (not logically equivalent).

1. **Example:**

If I. M. Nuts is a crook, then I. B Squirrel is not a crook.		Either I. M. Nuts is a crook or I. B. Squirrel is a crook.
If p, then not q.	≢	*Either p or q.*

2.

I. B. Squirrel is the mastermind behind the robberies.		It is not the case that I. B. Squirrel is not the mastermind behind the robberies.

3.

If Penelope P. Nuts is involved, then Rocky Squirrel is involved.		If Rocky Squirrel is not involved, then Penelope P. Nuts is not involved.

(Continued)

4.

It is not the case that both I. B. Squirrel was involved in the robbery and R. U. Nuts was involved in the robbery.		I. B. Squirrel was not involved in the robbery and R. U. Nuts was not involved in the robbery.

5.

Rocky Squirrel is not a crook and Cash U. Nuts is not a crook.		It is not the case that either Rocky Squirrel is a crook or Cash U. Nuts is a crook.

6.

Rocky Squirrel is not a crook or Penelope P. Nuts is a crook.		It is not the case that both Rocky Squirrel is a crook and Penelope P. Nuts is not a crook.

7.

If R. U. Nuts played a role in the robberies, then Ms. Squirrel was not the short robber.		Either R. U. Nuts played role in the robberies or Ms. Squirrel was not the short robber.

8.

Either I. B. Squirrel is a crook or I. M. Nuts is a crook.		It is not that case that both I. B. Squirrel is not a crook and I. M. Nuts is not a crook.

9.

If Wally Nuts is a crook, then Cash U. Nuts is a crook.		It is not the case that both Wally Nuts is not a crook and Cash U. Nuts is a crook.

10.

Either I. B. Squirrel is a crook or I. M. Nuts is a crook.		It is not the case that either I. B. Squirrel is not a crook or I. M. Nuts is not a crook.

11.

Cash U. Nuts and Wally Nuts are both store managers.		It is not the case that either Cash U. Nuts is not a store manager or Wally Nuts is not a store manager.

(Continued)

12.

| If Rocky owns a Harley, then either Penelope owns a BMW motorcycle or R. U. Nuts drives a Kawasaki. | | Either Rocky does not own a Harley or if Penelope owns a BMW motorcycle then R.U. Nuts does not drive a Kawasaki. |

13.

| If Rocky owns a Harley, then either Penelope owns a BMW motorcycle or R. U. Nuts drives a Kawasaki. | | Rocky does not own a Harley, and if Penelope does not a BMW motorcycle then R. U. Nuts drives a Kawasaki. |

14.

| If Rocky owns a Harley, then either Penelope owns a BMW motorcycle or R. U. Nuts drives a Kawasaki. | | Either Rocky does not own a Harley or it is not the case that both Penelope does not own a BMW motorcycle and R. U. Nuts does not own a Kawasaki. |

15.

| Either I. M. Rich is not a crook or it is not the case that both Ms. Squirrel is the short robber and Rocky Squirrel is the tall robber. | | If I. M. Rich is a crook, then if Ms. Squirrel is the short robber then Rocky Squirrel is not the tall robber. |

Chapter 5 Quiz

Choose the best answer for each of the following questions.

1. Compound claims are:
    a. claims that involve the words if, and, or, or not.
    b. claims that have another claim as a proper part.
    c. claims whose truth-value depends upon the truth-values of their parts.
    d. claims that everyone accepts as true.

2. Truth-functional compound claims are:
    a. claims that tell us about states of our minds.
    b. claims whose truth or falsehood depends upon facts in the world.
    c. claims that cannot be false.
    d. claims whose truth-value depends upon the truth-values of their parts.

3. The most common word used for conjunction is *and*. Other words showing conjunction include:
    a. *but, yet, although, however.*
    b. *unless, or.*
    c. *only if, given that, provided that.*
    d. none of the above.

4. The inclusive sense of "or" means:
    a. a disjunction is true if either of its disjuncts is true, but not if both disjuncts are true.
    b. a disjunction is true if either or both of its disjuncts are true.
    c. a disjunction is false if either of its disjuncts are false.
    d. a disjunction is the denial of a conjunction containing the same claims.

5. Affirming the antecedent:
    a. concludes that the antecedent of a conditional is true.
    b. asserts that both a conditional and its antecedent are true, and therefore its consequent is true, as well.
    c. is sometimes known as *modus ponens*.
    d. both b and c.

6. Where *p* and *q* are claims, a disjunctive syllogism is an argument of the form:
    a. If *p*, then *q*.
       Not *q*.
       $\overline{\text{Not } p.}$
    b. Either *p* or *q*.
       $\underline{p.}$
       Not *p*.
    c. *p* and *q*.
       Not *p*.
       $\overline{q.}$
    d. Either *p* or *q*.
       Not *p*.
       $\overline{q.}$

(Continued)

7. If both a claim and its denial follow from a set of premises:
    a. the argument is invalid.
    b. no other claims follow from the premises.
    c. any claim follows from the premises.
    d. both a and b.

8. An enthymeme is:
    a. an argument with a missing premise or a missing conclusion.
    b. an invalid argument.
    c. a special case of denying the consequent.
    d. an argument that depends on an exclusive sense of or.

9. A claim p is logically equivalent to:
    a. Morgan Stanley's theorems.
    b. not (p or q).
    c. its double negation: not, not p.
    d. the denial of the antecedent.

10. Transposition occurs when:
    a. the positions of the antecedent and the consequent of a conditional are switched and both negated.
    b. the positions of the antecedent and the consequent of a conditional are switched but never negated.
    c. p = not, not p.
    d. there is a hypothetical syllogism.

Compound Claim and Argument Reference Sheet

ARGUMENT	FORM	EXAMPLE
Conjunction Claim	*p* and *q*.	Rover is a dog and Rover has black fur.
Disjunction Claim	*p* or *q*.	The light is on or the light is off.
Conditional Claim	If *p,* then *q*.	If I get hungry then I will walk to the store.
Affirming the Antecedent	If *p,* then *q*. *p.* <hr> *q.*	If the sun is shinning, it is day. The sun is shining. <hr> It is day.
Denying the Consequent	If *p,* then *q*. Not *q.* <hr> Not *p.*	If the sun is shining, it is day. It is not day. <hr> The sun is not shining.
Disjunctive Syllogism (Form 1)	*p* or *q*. Not *p.* <hr> *p.*	Either Susan will go or Mary will go. Susan will not go. <hr> Mary will go.
Disjunctive Syllogism (Form 2)	*p* or *q*. Not *q.* <hr> *p.*	Either Susan will go or Mary will go. Mary will not go. <hr> Susan will go.
Hypothetical Syllogism	If *p,* then *q*. If *q,* then *r*. <hr> If *p,* then *r*.	If Susan goes, then Mary goes. If Mary goes, then Barbara goes. <hr> If Susan goes, then Barbara goes.
Addition	*p.* <hr> *p* or *q*.	The prince is coming. <hr> The prince is coming or anybody else is coming.
Simplification (Form 1)	*p* and *q*. <hr> *p.*	The prince is coming and the king, too. <hr> The prince is coming.
Simplification (Form 2)	*p* and *q*. <hr> *q.*	The prince is coming and the king, too. <hr> The king is coming.
Constructive Dilemma	If *p,* then *q*; and if *r,* then *s*. Either *p* or *r*. <hr> Either *q* or *s*.	If the prince is coming, then the queen is, also; and if a royal person is coming, then a sword will be there. Either the prince is coming or a royal person is coming. <hr> Therefore, either the queen is coming or a sword will be there.

(Continued)

Destructive Dilemma	If p, then q; and if r, then s. Either not q or not s. Either not p or not r.	If the prince is coming, then the queen is, also; and if a royal person is coming, then a sword will be there. Either the queen is not coming or a sword will not be there. Therefore, either the prince is not coming or a royal person is not coming.
Fallacy of Affirming the Consequent	If p, then q. q. p.	If it rains, then my car gets wet. My car is getting wet. Therefore, it is raining.
Fallacy of Denying the Antecedent	If p, then q. Not p. Not q.	If it rains, then my car gets wet. It is not raining. Therefore, my car is not getting wet.

CHAPTER 6

- Categorical Syllogisms
- Review

Overview

Categorical syllogisms show the relations among three sets of things.

CASE 22	City of Los Angeles Police Department

[1]There is a strike at the McGoo Candy Company. [2]All the workers are workers out on strike. [3]No candy is being produced. [4]Some workers are people who want to go back to work. [5]Some workers are not people who want to go back to work. [6]Mona McGoo, the company president, was afraid things were going to get sticky. [7]She called her friend, Stephanie Wise, for advice.

[8]Munching on McGoo's Great Gooey Gobs, Mona laid out her problem. "[9]All workers of mine are workers on strike. [10]No workers on strike are people who produce candy. [11]So, no workers of mine are people who produce candy. [12]But some workers of mine are people who need money. [13]All people who need money are people who are willing to go back to work. [14]So, some workers of mine are people who are willing to go back to work. [15]No union members are people who are willing to go back to work. [16]Some people who are willing to go back to work are Great Gooey Gobs makers. [17]So, some Great Gooey Gobs makers are not union members. [18]But all Great Gooey Gobs makers are people who must work if we are going to make Gooey Gobs. [19]Some Great Gooey Gobs makers are not people who are willing to return to work. [20]So, some people who must work if we are going to make Gooey Gobs are not people who are willing to return to work. [21]What should I do?"

[22]Matching Mona's slightly stilted style, Detective Wise replied, "No actions that have occurred at McGoo Candy are actions that violate laws. [23]All actions in which the police can be involved are actions that violate laws. [24]Therefore, no actions in which the police can be involved are actions that have occurred at McGoo Candy. [25]Sorry!"

[26]Three days later, the Great Gooey Gobs machine was riddled with bullets. [27]Detective Wise returned and talked with union chief Candy Kane. [28]Ms. Kane said, "No union members are people who have a grudge against the company. [29]Some person who shot the candy machine is a person who has a grudge against the company. [30]Hence, some person who shot the candy machine is not a union member."

[31]Mona replied, "Some person who shot the machine is either a person who has a grudge against the company or a person who has a grudge against candy."

"[32]Could it be a dentist?" asked Detective Wise.

6.1 Categorical Claims

Categorical claims are claims about *all* or *some* set or class of objects.
A universal claim is a claim about all members of a group.

Universal Affirmative	Form	Terms
All beagles are dogs.	All *S* are *P*.*	*S:* beagles *P:* dogs

Examples of universal affirmative claims in Case 22:

a.	All the workers are workers out on strike (sentence 2).
b.	All my workers are workers on strike (sentence 9).
c.	All people who need money are people who are willing to go back to work (sentence 13).
d.	All Gooey Gobs makers are people who must work if we are going to make Gooey Gobs (sentence 18).

Universal negative claims are claims that *no* members of one set are members of another.

Universal Negative	Form	Terms
No dogs are cats.	No *S* are *P*.*	*S:* dogs *P:* cats

Examples of universal negative claims in Case 22:

a.	No candy is being produced (sentence 3).
b.	No workers on strike are people who produce candy (sentence 10).
c.	No union members are people who are willing to go back to work (sentence 15).
d.	No actions that have occurred at McGoo Candy are actions that violate laws (sentence 22).

*Other forms of the verb *to be* may occur; for example:
"All Fruity Fudge *is* a Great Gooey Gob."
"No company president *is* a person who likes strikes."
"All robberies at the Frank 'n' Stein stands *were* inside jobs."

Claiming one or more members of one set are members of another set, is a **particular affirmative** claim.

Particular Affirmative	Form	Terms
Some dogs are beagles.	Some *S* are *P.**	*S:* dogs *P:* beagles

Examples of particular affirmative claims in Case 22:

a.	Some workers are people who want to go back to work (sentence 4).
b.	Some workers of mine are people who need money (sentence 12).
c.	Some people who are willing to go back to work are people who produce Great Gooey Gobs (sentence 16).
d.	Some person who shot the candy machine is a person who has a grudge against the company (sentence 29).

Particular negative claims claim one or more members of one set are *not* members of another set.

Particular Negative	Form	Terms
Some dogs are not beagles.	Some *S* are not *P.**	*S:* dogs *P:* beagles

Examples of particular negative claims in Case 22:

a.	Some workers are not people who want to go back to work (sentence 5).
b.	Some Great Gooey Gobs makers are not union members (sentence 17).
c.	Some people who must work if we are going to make Gooey Gobs are not people who would are willing to return to work (sentence 20).
d.	Some person who shot the candy machine is not a union member (sentence 30).

*Other forms of the verb *to be* may occur such as seen in both of the **d.** examples above.

6.2   Exercise Circle the answer that correctly identifies each categorical claim. Writing the form of the claim is often helpful, but it is not required.

1. **Example:**
   Some cases are stranger than other cases.
   a. Universal affirmative
   b. Universal negative
   c. **Particular affirmative**
   d. Particular negative

   Some S are P.

2. All strange cases are interesting cases.
   a. Universal affirmative
   b. Universal negative
   c. Particular affirmative
   d. Particular negative

3. No candy fans are people who like strikes at candy factories.
   a. Universal affirmative
   b. Universal negative
   c. Particular affirmative
   d. Particular negative

4. Some people are not fans of McGoo's Great Gooey Gobs.
   a. Universal affirmative
   b. Universal negative
   c. Particular affirmative
   d. Particular negative

5. Some detectives are people who are smarter than other detectives.
   a. Universal affirmative
   b. Universal negative
   c. Particular affirmative
   d. Particular negative

6. No candy fans are people who dislike sugar.
   a. Universal affirmative
   b. Universal negative
   c. Particular affirmative
   d. Particular negative

(Continued)

7. Some union bosses are people with a sweet tooth.
   a. Universal affirmative
   b. Universal negative
   c. Particular affirmative
   d. Particular negative

8. All candymakers are jolly people.
   a. Universal affirmative
   b. Universal negative
   c. Particular affirmative
   d. Particular negative

9. Some jolly people are not candy fans.
   a. Universal affirmative
   b. Universal negative
   c. Particular affirmative
   d. Particular negative

10. Some people who work for McGoo Candies are people who eat sweets.
    a. Universal affirmative
    b. Universal negative
    c. Particular affirmative
    d. Particular negative

Every categorical claim has
exactly 4 parts.

Quantifier	Subject	Verb	Predicate
All	chocolates	are	cocoa products.
No	candy makers	are	sad people.
Some	people who eat chocolate bars	are	people who love McGoo's Great Gooey Gobs.
Some	companies that make many kinds of candy	are not	companies that make sugar whistles in many colors.

6.3   Exercise Circle the answer that correctly identifies the subject and the predicate in each categorical claim. Writing the form of the claim is often helpful, but it is not required.

1. **Example:**
   No candy unions that go out on strike are groups of people who have a sweet tooth.
   a. Subject: go out on strike
      Predicate: have a sweet tooth
   (b.) Subject: candy unions that go out on strike
       Predicate: groups of people who have a
                    sweet tooth
   c. Subject: groups of people who have a sweet tooth
      Predicate: candy unions that go out on strike
   d. Subject: candy unions
      Predicate: people who have a sweet tooth

   No S are P.

2. All candymakers are happy people.
   a. Subject: makers
      Predicate: people
   b. Subject: candy
      Predicate: are
   c. Subject: candymakers
      Predicate: happy people
   d. Subject: happy people
      Predicate: candymakers

3. Some people who call Detective Wise are people who know her outside her role as a police officer.
   a. Subject: Detective Wise
      Predicate: police officer
   b. Subject: police officer
      Predicate: Detective Wise
   c. Subject: people who call Detective Wise
      Predicate: people who know her outside her role as a police officer
   d. Subject: people
      Predicate: people

4. Some detectives who work for the LAPD are people who enjoy helping their friends.
   a. Subject: detectives who work for the LAPD
      Predicate: people who enjoy helping their friends
   b. Subject: detectives
      Predicate: people
   c. Subject: some detectives who work for the LAPD
      Predicate: are people who enjoy helping their friends
   d. Subject: people
      Predicate: detectives

5. All candymakers who are company officers are people who become nervous during a strike.
    a. Subject: candymakers
        Predicate: people
    b. Subject: company officers
        Predicate: people who become nervous
    c. Subject: people who become nervous during a strike
        Predicate: candymakers who are company officers
    d. Subject: candymakers who are company officers
        Predicate: people who become nervous during
                         a strike

6. No detectives are people who eat excessive numbers of McGoo's Great Gooey Gobs.
    a. Subject: detectives
        Predicate: people who eat excessive numbers of
                         McGoo's Great Gooey Gobs
    b. Subject: people who eat excessive numbers of
                         McGoo's Great Gooey Gobs
        Predicate: detectives
    c. Subject: people
        Predicate: McGoo's Great Gooey Gobs
    d. Subject: detectives are people who eat
        Predicate: excessive numbers of McGoo's Great
                         Gooey Gobs

7. Some candy company officers are not people who eat excessive amounts of chocolate.
    a. Subject: officers
        Predicate: not people who eat excessive amounts
                         of chocolate
    b. Subject: people
        Predicate: candy company officers
    c. Subject: candy company officers
        Predicate: people who eat excessive amounts
                         of chocolate
    d. Subject: candy company
        Predicate: people who eat

(Continued)

8. Some candy company officers are not LAPD detectives.
    a. Subject: LAPD detectives
       Predicate: candy company officers
    b. Subject: officers
       Predicate: detectives
    c. Subject: candy company officers
       Predicate: LAPD detectives
    d. Subject: candy
       Predicate: officers

9. All people who are candymakers are people who have
    an acute sense of taste.
    a. Subject: people
       Predicate: candymakers are people who have an
                   acute sense of taste
    b. Subject: people who are candymakers are people
       Predicate: who have an acute sense of taste
    c. Subject: people
       Predicate: people
    d. Subject: people who are candymakers
       Predicate: people who have an acute sense of taste

10. Some people who are doing this problem are people
    who would rather be eating McGoo's Great Gooey Gobs.
    a. Subject: people who
       Predicate: doing this problem
    b. Subject: people who are doing this problem
       Predicate: people who would rather be eating
                   McGoo's Great Gooey Gobs
    c. Subject: people who would rather be eating
                 McGoo's Great Gooey Gobs
       Predicate: people who are doing this problem
    d. Subject: people
       Predicate: people

6.4 Categorical Syllogisms

A **categorical syllogism** is an argument composed of 3 categorical claims: the Major Premise, the Minor Premise, and the Conclusion.

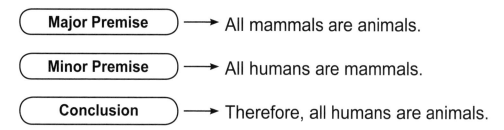

(**Major Premise**) ⟶ All mammals are animals.

(**Minor Premise**) ⟶ All humans are mammals.

(**Conclusion**) ⟶ Therefore, all humans are animals.

All categorical syllogisms have 3 terms:

Major (P) Term	Minor (S) Term	Middle (M) Term
Predicate term of the conclusion and found in the major premise.	Subject term of the conclusion and found in the minor premise.	Term found in the premises, but not the conclusion
		Symbolized **M**
Symbolized **P**	Symbolized **S**	

Example

All (mammals) are animals.
All humans are (mammals).
Therefore, all humans are animals.

All mammals are animals.   All M are P.
All humans are mammals.   All S are M.
Therefore, all humans are animals.   All S are P.

Reminder: When written in standard form, the claims of the categorical syllogism are listed in a specific order. The major premise, which contains the Major (P) Term, is listed first. The minor premise, which contains the Minor (S) Term, is listed second. And finally, the conclusion is listed.

Examples of identifying the terms in a syllogism.

	Categorical Syllogism	Form	Terms
a.	All dogs are animals. All beagles are dogs. So, all beagles are animals.	All *M* are *P*. All *S* are *M*. All *S* are *P*.	*S*: beagles *M*: dogs *P*: animals
b.	No workers on strike are people who produce candy. All workers of mine are workers on strike. So, no workers of mine are people who produce candy.	No *M* are *P*. All *S* are *M*. No *S* are *P*.	*S*: workers of mine *M*: workers on strike *P*: people who produce candy
c.	No union members are people who are willing to go back to work. Some people who are willing to go back to work are Great Gooey Gobs makers. So, some Great Gooey Gobs makers are not union members.	No *P* are *M*. Some *M* are *S*. Some *S* are not *P*.	*S*: Great Gooey Gobs makers *M*: people who are willing to go back to work *P*: union members
d.	Some Great Gooey Gobs makers are not people who are willing to return to work. All Great Gooey Gobs makers are people who must work if we are going to make Gooey Gobs. So, some people who must work if we are going to make Gooey Gobs are not people who are willing to return to work.	Some *M* are not *P*. All *M* are *S*. Some *S* are *P*.	*S*: people who must work if we are going to make Great Gooey Gobs *M*: Great Gooey Gobs makers *P*: people who are willing to return to work

6.5   Exercise Identify the Major Term (*P*), the Minor Term (*S*), and the Middle Term (*M*) in each of the following categorical syllogisms. It is often helpful to write the form and terms of the syllogism as you read each exercise, but it is not required. Circle the correct answers.

1. **Example:**
   All chocolates are candies.
   All truffles are chocolates.
   So, all truffles are candies.
   a. Major (*P*) Term: chocolates
      Minor (*S*) Term: truffles
      Middle (*M*) Term: candies

   b. Major (*P*) Term: truffles
      Minor (*S*) Term: candies
      Middle (*M*) Term: chocolates

   (c.) **Major (*P*) Term: candies**
      Minor (*S*) Term: truffles
      Middle (*M*) Term: chocolates

   d. Major (*P*) Term: truffles
      Minor (*S*) Term: chocolates
      Middle (*M*) Term: candies

Form:

All *M* are *P*.
All *S* are *M*.
_____
All *S* are *P*.

Terms:

P: candies

S: truffles

M: chocolates

2. Some Great Gooey Gobs are things made of peanuts.
   All Great Gooey Gobs are things made of chocolate.
   So, some things made of chocolate are things made of peanuts.
   a. Major (*P*) Term: Great Gooey Gobs
      Minor (*S*) Term: things made of chocolate
      Middle (*M*) Term: things made of peanuts

   b. Major (*P*) Term: things made of chocolate
      Minor (*S*) Term: Great Gooey Gobs
      Middle (*M*) Term: things made of peanuts

   c. Major (*P*) Term: things made of peanuts
      Minor (*S*) Term: things made of chocolate
      Middle (*M*) Term: Great Gooey Gobs

   d. Major (*P*) Term: Great Gooey Gobs
      Minor (*S*) Term: things made of peanuts
      Middle (*M*) Term: things made of chocolate

Form:

Terms:
P:

S:

M:

(Continued)

3. All Great Gooey Gobs are things made from caramel. Some things made with pecans are not Great Gooey Gobs.

   Some things made with pecans are not things made with caramel.

   a. Major (P) Term: Great Gooey Gobs
      Minor (S) Term: things made from caramel
      Middle (M) Term: things made with pecans

   b. Major (P) Term: things made from caramel
      Minor (S) Term: Great Gooey Gobs
      Middle (M) Term: things made with pecans

   c. Major (P) Term: things made with pecans
      Minor (S) Term: things made from caramel
      Middle (M) Term: Great Gooey Gobs

   d. Major (P) Term: things made from caramel
      Minor (S) Term: things made with pecans
      Middle (M) Term: Great Gooey Gobs

Form:

Terms:
P:
S:
M:

4. No actions that have occurred at McGoo Candy are actions that violate laws.
   All actions in which the police can be involved are actions that violate laws.

   Ergo, no actions in which the police can be involved are actions that have occurred at McGoo Candy.

   a. Major (P) Term: actions in which the police can be involved
      Minor (S) Term: actions that have occurred at McGoo Candy
      Middle (M) Term: actions that violate laws

   b. Major (P) Term: actions that have occurred at McGoo Candy
      Minor (S) Term: actions in which the police can be involved
      Middle (M) Term: actions that violate laws

   c. Major (P) Term: actions that have occurred at McGoo Candy
      Minor (S) Term: actions that violate laws
      Middle (M) Term: actions in which the police can be involved

   d. Major (P) Term: actions in which the police can be involved
      Minor (S) Term: actions that have occurred at McGoo Candy
      Middle (M) Term: actions that violate laws

Form:

Terms:
P:
S:
M:

5. No Fruity Fudge is a Great Gooey Gob, for all Great Gooey Gobs are products of caramel, chocolate, and peanuts, while some Fruity Fudge is not a product of caramel, chocolate, and peanuts.

   a. Major (*P*) Term: Fruity Fudge
      Minor (*S*) Term: Great Gooey Gobs
      Middle (*M*) Term: products of caramel, chocolate, and peanuts

   b. Major (*P*) Term: Great Gooey Gobs
      Minor (*S*) Term: Fruity Fudge
      Middle (*M*) Term: products of caramel, chocolate, and peanuts

   c. Major (*P*) Term: Fruity Fudge
      Minor (*S*) Term: products of caramel, chocolate, and peanuts
      Middle (*M*) Term: Great Gooey Gobs

   d. Major (*P*) Term: Great Gooey Gobs
      Minor (*S*) Term: products of caramel, chocolate, and peanuts
      Middle (*M*) Term: Fruity Fudge

Form:

Terms:
P:

S:

M:

6. Some employees are people who want to go back to work, and some employees are Great Gooey Gobs fans. Hence, some Great Gooey Gobs fans are people who want to go back to work.

   a. Major (*P*) Term: people who want to go back to work
      Minor (*S*) Term: Great Gooey Gobs fans
      Middle (*M*) Term: employees

   b. Major (*P*) Term: employees
      Minor (*S*) Term: people who want to go back to work
      Middle (*M*) Term: Great Gooey Gobs fans

   c. Major (*P*) Term: Great Gooey Gobs fans
      Minor (*S*) Term: employees
      Middle (*M*) Term: people who want to go back to work

   d. Major (*P*) Term: people who want to go back to work
      Minor (*S*) Term: employees
      Middle (*M*) Term: Great Gooey Gobs fans

Form:

Terms:
P:

S:

M:

(Continued)

7. All employees are Fruity Fudge fans,
    for some Fruity Fudge fans are Caramel Clumps fans,
    and all employees are Caramel Clumps fans.
    a. Major (*P*) Term: employees
        Minor (*S*) Term: Fruity Fudge fans
        Middle (*M*) Term: Caramel Clumps fans

    b. Major (*P*) Term: Caramel Clumps fans
        Minor (*S*) Term: employees
        Middle (*M*) Term: Fruity Fudge fans

    c. Major (*P*) Term: Fruity Fudge fans
        Minor (*S*) Term: Caramel Clumps fans
        Middle (*M*) Term: employees

    d. Major (*P*) Term: Fruity Fudge fans
        Minor (*S*) Term: employees
        Middle (*M*) Term: Caramel Clumps fans

Form:

Terms:
P:

S:

M:

8. No pieces of Fruity Fudge are Great Gooey Gobs, so
    no Great Gooey Gobs are Caramel Clumps, for no
    Caramel Clumps are pieces of Fruity Fudge.
    a. Major (*P*) Term: Great Gooey Gobs
        Minor (*S*) Term: pieces of Fruity Fudge
        Middle (*M*) Term: Caramel Clumps

    b. Major (*P*) Term: pieces of Fruity Fudge
        Minor (*S*) Term: Great Gooey Gobs
        Middle (*M*) Term: Caramel Clumps

    c. Major (*P*) Term: Caramel Clumps
        Minor (*S*) Term: Great Gooey Gobs
        Middle (*M*) Term: pieces of Fruity Fudge

    d. Major (*P*) Term: Caramel Clumps
        Minor (*S*) Term: pieces of Fruity Fudge
        Middle (*M*) Term: Great Gooey Gobs

Form:

Terms:
P:

S:

M:

9. Some employees are Fruity Fudge makers, for some employees are Caramel Clumps makers, and no Caramel Clumps makers are Fruity Fudge makers.

   a. Major (*P*) Term: Fruity Fudge makers
      Minor (*S*) term: employees
      Middle (*M*) Term: Caramel Clump makers

   b. Major (*P*) Term: employees
      Minor (*S*) Term: Fruity Fudge makers
      Middle (*M*) Term: Caramel Clumps makers

   c. Major (*P*) Term: Caramel Clumps makers
      Minor (*S*) Term: employees
      Middle (*M*) Term: Fruity Fudge makers

   d. Major (*P*) Term: Fruity Fudge makers
      Minor (*S*) Term: Caramel Clumps makers
      Middle (*M*) Term: employees

Form:

Terms:

P:

S:

M:

6.6 Rules for Evaluating Categorical Syllogisms

Some categorical syllogisms are valid. Some categorical syllogisms are invalid. One way to determine which categorical syllogisms are valid is a set of six rules.

> **Rule 1:** Every valid categorical syllogism must contain three terms (Major Term, Minor Term, and Middle Term). The meaning of each term must be consistent throughout the argument.

Examples of syllogisms that violate Rule 1:

	Syllogisms That Violate Rule 1	Form	Terms
a.	All cats are small, furry animals. All products of the Caterpillar Corporation are Cats. <hr> All products of the Caterpillar Corporation are small, furry animals.	All M are P. All S are M.* <hr> All S are P. *Notice the meaning of the middle term changes from the Major to the Minor Premise.	S: products of the Caterpillar Corporation P: small, furry animals M: cats M*: cats
b.	All rats are contemptible people. Some small rodents are rats. <hr> Some small rodents are contemptible people.	All M are P. Some S are M*. <hr> Some S are P.	S: small rodents P: contemptible people M: rats M*: rats
c.	No alligators are lions. All people who play football for Detroit are Lions. <hr> No people who play football for Detroit are alligators.	No P are M. All S are M*. <hr> No S are P.	S: people who play football for Detroit P: alligators M: lions M*: Lions
d.	Some pieces of chocolate are sweet hearts. All sweethearts are people who are loved by someone. <hr> So, some people who are loved by someone are pieces of chocolate. In the Major Premise, *sweet heart* means a heart-shaped thing that is sweet to the taste. In the Minor Premise, *sweetheart* means someone who is loved.	Some P are M. All M* are S. <hr> Some S are P.	S: people who are loved by someone P: pieces of chocolate M: sweet hearts M*: sweethearts

> **Rule 2:** Every valid Categorical Syllogism's middle term must be distributed (refer to an entire set of objects) exactly once.

A term is **distributed** if it refers to an entire class of objects. The following chart shows the distribution of categorical claims. Let *S* and *P* stand for the subject and predicate terms of categorical claims.

Claim Type	Claim's Form	*S* Term	*P* Term
Universal Affirmative	All *S* are *P*.	Distributed	Undistributed
Universal Negative	No *S* are *P*.	Distributed	Distributed
Particular Affirmative	Some *S* are *P*.	Undistributed	Undistributed
Particular Negative	Some *S* are not *P*.	Undistributed	Distributed

Examples of syllogisms that violate Rule 2:

	Syllogisms That Violate Rule 2	Form	Terms
a.	Some animals are dogs. Some animals are cats. So, some cats are dogs. The Middle Term, *animals*, is undistributed in both premises. It violates Rule 2.	Some *M* are *P*. Some *M* are *S*. ― Some *S* are *P*.	*S*: cats *P*: dogs *M*: animals
b.	All mammals are vertebrates. All mammals are furry animals. So, some furry animals are vertebrates. The Middle Term, *mammals*, is distributed twice. It violates Rule 2.	All *M* are *P*. All *M* are *S*. ― Some *S* are *P*.	*S*: furry animals *P*: vertebrates *M*: mammals
c.	All Great Gooey Gobs are candies containing caramel. All Caramel Clumps are candies containing caramel. So, all Caramel Clumps are Great Gooey Gobs. The Middle Term, *candies containing caramel*, is undistributed. So, the syllogism breaks Rule 2. The syllogism is invalid.	All *P* are *M*. All *S* are *M*. ― All *S* are *P*.	*S*: Caramel Clumps *P*: Great Gooey Gobs *M*: candies containing caramel
d.	No Great Gooey Gobs are Caramel Clumps. Some things made of chocolate are not Great Gooey Gobs. Some things made of chocolate are not Caramel Clumps. The Middle Term, *Great Gooey Gobs*, is distributed twice. So, the syllogism breaks Rule 2. The syllogism is invalid.	No *M* are *P*. Some *S* are not *M*. ― Some *S* are not *P*.	*S*: things made of chocolate *P*: Caramel Clumps *M*: Great Gooey Gobs

> **Rule 3:** Every valid categorical syllogism's Major Term must be distributed in both the Major Premise and the conclusion, or it must be undistributed in both the Major Premise and the conclusion.

> **Rule 4:** Every valid categorical syllogism's Minor Term must be distributed in both the Minor Premise and the conclusion, or it must be undistributed in both the Minor Premise and the conclusion.

Examples of syllogisms that violate Rules 3 and 4:

	Syllogisms That Violate Rules 3 and 4	Form	Terms
a.	All beagles are dogs. All dogs are mammals. _____ All mammals are beagles. The Major Term, *beagles*, is distributed in the Major Premise, but not in the conclusion. This violates Rule 3. The Minor Term, *mammals*, is distributed in the conclusion but not in the Minor Premise. This violates Rule 4. The syllogism is therefore invalid.	All *P* are *M*. All *M* are *S*. _____ All *S* are *P*.	S: mammals P: beagles M: dogs
b.	Some cats are tabbies. No dogs are cats. _____ So, some dogs are not tabbies. The Major Term, *tabbies*, is distributed in the conclusion, but not distributed in the Major Premise. This violates Rule 3. The Minor Term, *dogs*, is distributed in the Minor Premise, but not in the conclusion. This violates Rule 4. The syllogism is therefore invalid.	Some *M* are *P*. No *S* are *M*. _____ Some *S* are not *P*.	S: dogs P: tabbies M: cats
c.	All employees who want to go back to work are employees who eat candies from the production line. No employees Mona wants back at work are employees who eat candies from the production line. _____ So, some employees Mona wants back at work are employees who want to go back to work. Both the Major and Minor Terms, *employees who want to go back to work* and *employees Mona wants back at work*, are distributed in the premises but not in the conclusion. This breaks Rules 3 and 4. The syllogism is therefore invalid.	All *P* are *M*. No *S* are *M*. _____ Some *S* are *P*.	S: employees Mona wants back at work P: employees who want to go back to work M: employees who eat candies from the production line

	Syllogisms That Violate Rules 3 and 4	Form	Terms
d.	All employees who want to go back to work are employees who eat candies from the production line. Some employees Mona wants back at work are employees who eat candies from the production line. _____ So, some employees Mona wants back at work are employees who want to go back to work. The Major Term, *employees who want to go back to work*, is distributed in the Major Premise, but it is not distributed in the conclusion. This breaks Rule 3. However, the Minor Term, *employees Mona wants back at work*, is distributed in *neither* the minor premise *nor* in the conclusion; so, the syllogism *does not* violate Rule 4. Also notice, however, that the Middle Term, *employees who eat candies from the production line*, is distributed in neither premise, so it violates Rule 2. The syllogism is therefore invalid.	All *P* are *M*. Some *S* are *M*. _____ Some *S* are *P*.	*S*: employees Mona wants back at work *P*: employees who want to go back to work *M*: employees who eat candies from the production line

6.7 **Exercise** What rules are broken in the following arguments? Circle all the rules that are broken. Writing the form of the argument is often helpful, but it is not required.

1. **Example:**
   Some candies are things made of caramel.
   No Tangy Treats are things made of caramel.
   ───────────────────────────────
   So, some Tangy Treats are not candies.
   a. The argument breaks Rule 1.
   b. The argument breaks Rule 2.
   (c.) **The argument breaks Rule 3.**
   (d.) **The argument breaks Rule 4.**
   e. The argument does not break any rules.

   Some P are M.
   No S are M.
   ──────────────
   Some S are not P.

2. All chocolate candies are sweet things to eat.
   All Great Gooey Gobs are chocolate candies.
   ───────────────────────────────
   So, all Great Gooey Gobs are sweet things to eat.
   a. The argument breaks Rule 1.
   b. The argument breaks Rule 2.
   c. The argument breaks Rule 3.
   d. The argument breaks Rule 4.
   e. The argument does not break any rules.

3. No Caramel Clumps are Great Gooey Gobs.
   All Great Gooey Gobs are combinations of chocolate, caramel, and peanuts.
   ───────────────────────────────
   So, no combinations of chocolate, caramel, and peanuts are Caramel Clumps.
   a. The argument breaks Rule 1.
   b. The argument breaks Rule 2.
   c. The argument breaks Rule 3.
   d. The argument breaks Rule 4.
   e. The argument does not break any rules.

4. All employees who want to return to work are employees who make Great Gooey Gobs.
   No employees who make Sweetie Pies are employees who want to return to work.
   ───────────────────────────────
   So, no employees who make Sweetie Pies are employees who make Great Gooey Gobs.
   a. The argument breaks Rule 1.
   b. The argument breaks Rule 2.
   c. The argument breaks Rule 3.
   d. The argument breaks Rule 4.
   e. The argument does not break any rules.

5. All employees who want to return to work are employees who make Great Gooey Gobs.
All employees who want to return to work are employees who are short on cash.
So, all employees who are short on cash are employees who make Great Gooey Gobs.
    a. The argument breaks Rule 1.
    b. The argument breaks Rule 2.
    c. The argument breaks Rule 3.
    d. The argument breaks Rule 4.
    e. The argument does not break any rules.

6. All Tangy Treats are candies made with lemon and lime.
Some candies made with lemon and lime are sour candies.
So, some sour candies are Tangy Treats.
    a. The argument breaks Rule 1.
    b. The argument breaks Rule 2.
    c. The argument breaks Rule 3.
    d. The argument breaks Rule 4.
    e. The argument does not break any rules.

7. Some Tangy Treats are Chocolate Chilies.
All Tangy Treats are candies made with lemon and lime..
So, some candies made with lemon and lime are Chocolate Chilies.
    a. The argument breaks Rule 1.
    b. The argument breaks Rule 2.
    c. The argument breaks Rule 3.
    d. The argument breaks Rule 4.
    e. The argument does not break any rules.

8. Some employees are good workers.
All employees are people who like sweets.
So, some people who like sweets are good workers.
    a. The argument breaks Rule 1.
    b. The argument breaks Rule 2.
    c. The argument breaks Rule 3.
    d. The argument breaks Rule 4.
    e. The argument does not break any rules.

(Continued)

9. Some employees are people who would like to work ten hours every day.
No people who would like to work ten hours every day are people who are on strike.

So, some people who are on strike are not employees.
a. The argument breaks Rule 1.
b. The argument breaks Rule 2.
c. The argument breaks Rule 3.
d. The argument breaks Rule 4.
e. The argument does not break any rules.

10. Some people who make Great Gooey Gobs are not people who make Tangy Treats.
All people who make Tangy Treats are people who like citrus fruits.

So, no people who like citrus fruits are people who make Great Gooey Gobs.
a. The argument breaks Rule 1.
b. The argument breaks Rule 2.
c. The argument breaks Rule 3.
d. The argument breaks Rule 4.
e. The argument does not break any rules.

+

> **Rule 5**: Every valid categorical syllogism must have either exactly one negative premise and a negative conclusion or neither a negative premise nor a negative conclusion.

Examples of categorical syllogisms that violate Rule 5 in Case 22:

	Syllogisms That Violate Rule 5	Form	Terms
a.	No Great Gooey Gobs makers are Tangy Treats makers. No Chocolate Chilies makers are Tangy Treats makers. So, no Chocolate Chilies makers are Great Gooey Gobs makers. Both premises are negative, but there is only one negative conclusion. So, the argument breaks Rule 5. It also breaks Rule 2.	No *P* are *M*. No *S* are *M*. No *S* are *P*.	*S*: Chocolate Chilies makers *P*: Great Gooey Gobs makers *M*: Tangy Treats makers
b.	No Great Gooey Gobs makers are Chocolate Chilies makers. Some Chocolate Chilies makers are not Tangy Treats makers. So, some Tangy Treats makers are not Great Gooey Gobs makers. Both premises are negative, but there is only one negative conclusion. So, the argument breaks Rule 5. It also breaks Rule 4.	No *P* are *M*. Some *M* are not *S*. Some *S* are not *P*.	*S*: Tangy Treats makers *P*: Great Gooey Gobs makers *M*: Chocolate Chilies makers
c.	All employees of McGoo Candies are people out on strike. All Caramel Clumps makers are employees of McGoo Candies. So, no Caramel Clumps makers are people out on strike. There are two affirmative premises, but there is a negative conclusion. So, the argument breaks Rule 5. It also breaks Rule 3.	All *M* are *P*. All *S* are *M*. No *S* are *P*.	*S*: Caramel Clumps makers *P*: people out on strike *M*: employees of McGoo Candies
d.	All employees of McGoo Candies are people out on strike. Some people out on strike are diet cola drinkers. So, some diet cola drinkers are not employees of McGoo Candies. There are two affirmative premises, but there is a negative conclusion. So, the argument breaks Rule 5. It also breaks Rule 2.	All *P* are *M*. Some *M* are *S*. Some *S* are not *P*.	*S*: diet cola drinkers *P*: employees of McGoo Candies *M*: people out on strike

> **Rule 6:** Every valid categorical syllogism must have either exactly one particular premise and a particular conclusion or neither a particular premise nor a particular conclusion.

Examples of categorical syllogisms that break Rule 6 in Case 22:

	Syllogisms That Violate Rule 6	Form	Terms
a.	Some employees on strike are union members. All union members are people who will honor the strike. _____ So, all people who will honor the strike are employees. There is one particular premise, but the conclusion is universal. So, the argument breaks Rule 6. It also breaks Rule 4.	Some *P* are *M*. All *M* are *S*. _____ All *S* are *P*.	*S*: people who will honor the strike *P*: employees *M*: union members
b.	No employees on strike are people who will cross the picket line. All members of the candy workers union are employees on strike. _____ So, some members of the candy workers union are not people who will cross the picket line. The conclusion is particular, but both premises are universal. So, the argument breaks Rule 6. It also breaks Rule 4.	No *M* are *P*. All *S* are *M*. _____ Some *S* are not *P*.	*S*: members of the candy workers union *P*: people who will cross the picket line *M*: employees on strike
c.	Some Great Gooey Gobs makers are Tangy Treats makers. Some Tangy Treats makers are Chocolate Chilies makers. _____ So, some Chocolate Chilies makers are Great Gooey Gobs makers. There are two particular premises, but there is one particular conclusion. So, the argument breaks Rule 6. It also breaks Rule 2.	Some *P* are *M*. Some *M* are *S*. _____ Some *S* are *P*.	*S*: Chocolate Chilies makers *P*: Great Gooey Gobs makers *M*: Tangy Treats makers
d.	No Great Gooey Gobs makers are Tangy Treats makers. No Sweetie Pie makers are Tangy Treats makers. _____ So, some Sweetie Pie Makers are Great Gooey Gobs makers. There are two universal premises, but there is a particular conclusion. So, the argument breaks Rule 6. It also breaks Rules 2, 3, 4, and 5.	No *P* are *M*. No *S* are *M*. _____ Some *S* are *P*.	*S*: Sweetie Pie makers *P*: Great Gooey Gobs makers *M*: Tangy Treats makers

If an argument breaks *any* of the rules, it is **invalid.** If an argument breaks *none* of the rules, it is a **valid categorical syllogism.** Remember, if an argument breaks Rule 1, it is *not* a categorical syllogism. Since it is *not* a categorical syllogism, it can break *none* of Rules 2-6. If a categorical syllogism breaks any one of Rules 2-6, it will break *at least* one other rule.

Rules Reference Sheet

Rule 1: Every valid categorical syllogism must contain three terms. The meaning of each term must be consistent throughout the argument.	All fruity things are things that contain fruit. All Fruity Fudge makers are fruity things. So, all Fruity Fudge makers are things that contain fruit.

In the Major Premise, *fruity* means containing fruit. In the Minor Premise, *fruity* means odd.

Rule 2: Every valid categorical syllogism's Middle Term must be distributed (refer to an entire class of objects) exactly once.	Some candies are sweet things. Some candies are chocolates. Some chocolates are sweet things.

The Middle Term, *candies*, is undistributed. The syllogism breaks Rules 2. It also breaks Rule 6. The syllogism is invalid.

Rule 3: Every valid categorical syllogism's Major Term must be distributed in both the Major Premise and the conclusion, or it must be undistributed in both the Major Premise and the conclusion.	All Caramel Clumps are things made of caramel. All things made of caramel are sweet things. So, all sweet things are Caramel Clumps.

The Major Term, *Caramel Clumps*, is distributed in the Major Premise but not in the conclusion. So, the syllogism breaks Rule 3. It also breaks Rule 2. The syllogism is invalid.

Rule 4: Every valid categorical syllogism's Minor Term must be distributed in both its Minor Premise and the conclusion, or it must be undistributed in both its Minor Premise and the conclusion.	Some Sweetie Pies are candies containing raisins. No Caramel Clumps are Sweetie Pies. So, some Caramel Clumps are not candies containing raisins.

The Minor Term, *Caramel Clumps*, is distributed in the Minor Premise but not distributed in the conclusion. So, the syllogism breaks Rule 4. It also breaks Rule 3. The syllogism is invalid.

Rule 5: Every valid categorical syllogism must have either exactly one negative premise and a negative conclusion or neither a negative premise nor a negative conclusion.	No Great Gooey Gobs makers are Chocolate Chilies makers. No Chocolate Chilies makers are Tangy Treats makers. So, no Tangy Treat makers are Great Gooey Gobs makers.

Both claims are negative, but there is only one negative term in the conclusion. So, the argument breaks Rule 5. It also breaks Rule 2. The syllogism is invalid.

Rule 6: Every valid categorical syllogism must have either exactly one particular premise and a particular conclusion or neither a particular premise nor a particular conclusion.	Some employees on strike are union members. All union members are people who will honor the strike. So, all people who will honor the strike are employees.

There is one particular premise, but the conclusion is universal. So, the argument breaks Rule 6. It also breaks Rule 4. The syllogism is invalid.

6.8   Exercise Which of the following arguments break the rules for determining the validity of categorical syllogisms? Circle all the rules broken. Writing the form of the argument is often helpful, but it is not required.

1. **Example:**
    Some Great Gooey Gobs makers are Sweetie Pie makers.
    Some Caramel Clumps makers are Sweetie Pie makers.
    _____
    So, no Caramel Clumps makers are Great Gooey Gobs makers.

    Some P are M.
    Some S are M.
    _____
    No S are P.

    a. The argument breaks Rule 1.
    b. **The syllogism breaks Rule 2.**
    c. **The syllogism breaks Rule 3.**
    d. **The syllogism breaks Rule 4.**
    e. **The syllogism breaks Rule 5.**
    f. **The syllogism breaks Rule 6**.
    g. The syllogism is valid.

2. Some employees who make Great Gooey Gobs are people who think Mona is their friend.
    All employees who make Great Gooey Gobs are people who are out on strike.
    _____
    So, all people who are out on strike are people who think Mona is their friend.

    a. The argument breaks Rule 1.
    b. The syllogism breaks Rule 2.
    c. The syllogism breaks Rule 3.
    d. The syllogism breaks Rule 4.
    e. The syllogism breaks Rule 5.
    f. The syllogism breaks Rule 6.
    g. The syllogism is valid.

3. All employees of McGoo Candies are people who are out on strike.
    All employees of McGoo Candies are people on a sugar high.
    _____
    So, no people on a sugar high are people out on strike.

    a. The argument breaks Rule 1.
    b. The syllogism breaks Rule 2.
    c. The syllogism breaks Rule 3.
    d. The syllogism breaks Rule 4.
    e. The syllogism breaks Rule 5.
    f. The syllogism breaks Rule 6.
    g. The syllogism is valid.

4. Some Caramel Clumps makers are people who are out on strike.
Some people who are out on strike are people who are short of cash.

So, some people who are short of cash are not Caramel Clumps makers.
a. The argument breaks Rule 1.
b. The syllogism breaks Rule 2.
c. The syllogism breaks Rule 3.
d. The syllogism breaks Rule 4.
e. The syllogism breaks Rule 5.
f. The syllogism breaks Rule 6.
g. The syllogism is valid.

5. No company president is a person who likes strikes.
No union chief is a company president.

So, no union chief is a person who likes strikes.
a. The argument breaks Rule 1.
b. The syllogism breaks Rule 2.
c. The syllogism breaks Rule 3.
d. The syllogism breaks Rule 4.
e. The syllogism breaks Rule 5.
f. The syllogism breaks Rule 6.
g. The syllogism is valid.

6. Some company employees are not people who like strikes.
No company presidents are people who like strikes.

So, no company presidents are company employees.
a. The argument breaks Rule 1.
b. The syllogism breaks Rule 2.
c. The syllogism breaks Rule 3.
d. The syllogism breaks Rule 4.
e. The syllogism breaks Rule 5.
f. The syllogism breaks Rule 6.
g. The syllogism is valid.

7. Some company employees are people who like strikes.
No union chiefs are people who like strikes.

So, some union chiefs are not company employees.
a. The argument breaks Rule 1.
b. The syllogism breaks Rule 2.
c. The syllogism breaks Rule 3.
d. The syllogism breaks Rule 4.
e. The syllogism breaks Rule 5.
f. The syllogism breaks Rule 6.
g. The syllogism is valid.

(Continued)

8. No union chief is a person who likes to go on strike.
   Some people who like to go on strike are not people
   who like to work.
   _____
   So, some people who like to work are not union chiefs.
   a. The argument breaks Rule 1.
   b. The syllogism breaks Rule 2.
   c. The syllogism breaks Rule 3.
   d. The syllogism breaks Rule 4.
   e. The syllogism breaks Rule 5.
   f. The syllogism breaks Rule 6.
   g. The syllogism is valid.

9. Some union members are chiefs.
   All chiefs are Native Americans.
   _____
   So, some Native Americans are union members.
   a. The argument breaks Rule 1.
   b. The syllogism breaks Rule 2.
   c. The syllogism breaks Rule 3.
   d. The syllogism breaks Rule 4.
   e. The syllogism breaks Rule 5.
   f. The syllogism breaks Rule 6.
   g. The syllogism is valid.

10. Some union members are happy people.
    Some union members are candymakers.
    _____
    So, some candymakers are happy people.
    a. The argument breaks Rule 1.
    b. The syllogism breaks Rule 2.
    c. The syllogism breaks Rule 3.
    d. The syllogism breaks Rule 4.
    e. The syllogism breaks Rule 5.
    f. The syllogism breaks Rule 6.
    g. The syllogism is valid.

11. All candymakers are happy people.
    Some company officers are candymakers.
    _____
    So, some company officers are happy people.
    a. The argument breaks Rule 1.
    b. The syllogism breaks Rule 2.
    c. The syllogism breaks Rule 3.
    d. The syllogism breaks Rule 4.
    e. The syllogism breaks Rule 5.
    f. The syllogism breaks Rule 6.
    g. The syllogism is valid.

12. Some candymakers are not happy people.
    All people who eat Great Gooey Gobs are
    happy people.
    _____
    So, no people who eat Great Gooey Gobs are
    candymakers.
    a. The argument breaks Rule 1.
    b. The syllogism breaks Rule 2.
    c. The syllogism breaks Rule 3.
    d. The syllogism breaks Rule 4.
    e. The syllogism breaks Rule 5.
    f. The syllogism breaks Rule 6.
    g. The syllogism is valid.

13. No union chiefs are company officers.
    No company officers are people on the production lines.
    _____
    So, all people on the production lines are union chiefs.
    a. The argument breaks Rule 1.
    b. The syllogism breaks Rule 2.
    c. The syllogism breaks Rule 3.
    d. The syllogism breaks Rule 4.
    e. The syllogism breaks Rule 5.
    f. The syllogism breaks Rule 6.
    g. The syllogism is valid.

14. Some candymakers are union members.
    Some candymakers are not people who eat lots
    of sweets.
    _____
    So, some people who eat lots of sweets are not union
    members.
    a. The argument breaks Rule 1.
    b. The syllogism breaks Rule 2.
    c. The syllogism breaks Rule 3.
    d. The syllogism breaks Rule 4.
    e. The syllogism breaks Rule 5.
    f. The syllogism breaks Rule 6.
    g. The syllogism is valid.

15. All union members are people who support the strike.
    No company officers are people who support the strike.
    _____
    So, some company officers are not union members.
    a. The argument breaks Rule 1.
    b. The syllogism breaks Rule 2.
    c. The syllogism breaks Rule 3.
    d. The syllogism breaks Rule 4.
    e. The syllogism breaks Rule 5.
    f. The syllogism breaks Rule 6.
    g. The syllogism is valid.

(Continued)

16. Some Great Gooey Gobs machines are things riddled with bullets.
All things riddled with bullets are things deserving a proper funeral.
———
So, some things deserving a proper funeral are not Great Gooey Gobs machines.
a. The argument breaks Rule 1.
b. The syllogism breaks Rule 2.
c. The syllogism breaks Rule 3.
d. The syllogism breaks Rule 4.
e. The syllogism breaks Rule 5.
f. The syllogism breaks Rule 6.
g. The syllogism is valid.

17. No Great Gooey Gobs machines are things deserving a proper funeral.
Some Great Gooey Gobs machines are things filled with chocolate and caramel.
———
So, some things filled with chocolate and caramel are things deserving a proper funeral.
a. The argument breaks Rule 1.
b. The syllogism breaks Rule 2.
c. The syllogism breaks Rule 3.
d. The syllogism breaks Rule 4.
e. The syllogism breaks Rule 5.
f. The syllogism breaks Rule 6.
g. The syllogism is valid.

18. All candymakers are happy people.
All happy people are people who eat chocolate.
———
So, all people who eat chocolate are candymakers.
a. The argument breaks Rule 1.
b. The syllogism breaks Rule 2.
c. The syllogism breaks Rule 3.
d. The syllogism breaks Rule 4.
e. The syllogism breaks Rule 5.
f. The syllogism breaks Rule 6.
g. The syllogism is valid.

19. Some candymakers are not union members.
    Some candymakers are not people with a sweet tooth.
    So, some people with a sweet tooth are union members.
    a. The argument breaks Rule 1.
    b. The syllogism breaks Rule 2.
    c. The syllogism breaks Rule 3.
    d. The syllogism breaks Rule 4.
    e. The syllogism breaks Rule 5.
    f. The syllogism breaks Rule 6.
    g. The syllogism is valid.

6.9 Venn Diagrams for Categorical Claims

The British mathematician John Venn (1834-1923) developed a way to represent categorical claims using circles. These are known as **Venn diagrams**.

A Venn diagram represents a categorical claim using two interlocked circles. There are four areas where *S* is the subject term and *P* is the predicate term.

These areas are as follows:

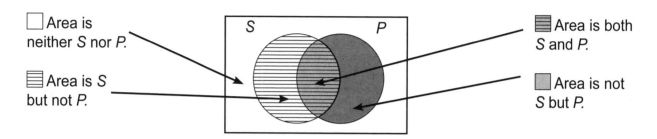

☐ Area is neither *S* nor *P*.

☰ Area is *S* but not *P*.

▓ Area is both *S* and *P*.

▒ Area is not *S* but *P*.

Venn diagrams represent universal claims by showing which empty area is shaded.

Universal Affirmative	Form	Venn Diagram
All candymakers are people with a sweet tooth.	All *S* are *P*.	
All people with a sweet tooth are candymakers.	All *P* are *S*.	

Universal Negative	Form	Venn Diagram
No candymakers are racecar drivers.	No *S* are *P*.	
No racecar drivers are candymakers.	No *P* are *S*.	

Particular claims are represented in a Venn diagram by placing the *X* in an area where the members of that class are found.

Particular Affirmative	Form	Venn Diagram
Some candymakers are people who like sweets.	Some *S* are *P*.	
Some people who like sweets are candymakers.	Some *P* are *S*.	

Particular Negative	Form	Venn Diagram
Some candymakers are not racecar drivers.	Some *S* are not *P*.	
Some racecar drivers are not candymakers.	Some *P* are not *S*.	

6.10   Exercise Which Venn diagram best represents the following categorical claims? Circle the correct answer.

1. **Example:**
    All Great Gooey Gobs (*S*) are mixtures of caramel, chocolate, and nuts (*P*).

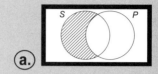 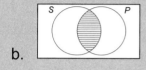 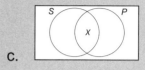 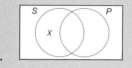

a.   b.   c.   d.

2. Some Great Gooey Gobs (*S*) are not Caramel Clumps (*P*).

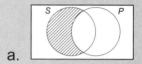 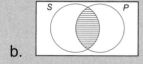 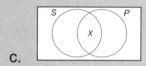 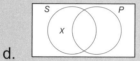

a.   b.   c.   d.

3. No piece of Fruity Fudge (*S*) is a Great Gooey Gob (*P*).

 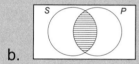 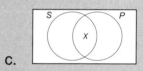 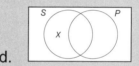

a.   b.   c.   d.

4. Some candymakers (*S*) are company officers (*P*).

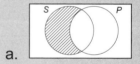 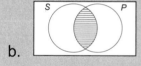 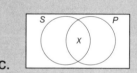 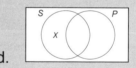

a.   b.   c.   d.

5. All Fruity Fudge (*S*) is stuff containing fruit and nuts (*P*).

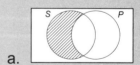 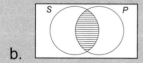 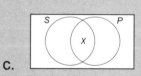 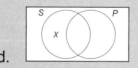

a.   b.   c.   d.

6. Some Sweetie Pies (S) are things eaten by people over sixty (*P*).

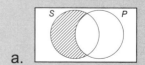 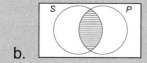 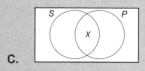 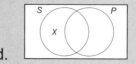

a.   b.   c.   d.

7. No people who eat Great Gooey Gobs (*S*) are people who have dentists as close personal friends (*P*).

a.    b.    c. 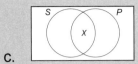   d.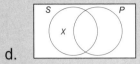

8. Some people who eat Sweetie Pies (*S*) are people who like raisin pie (*P*).

a.    b. 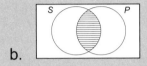   c. 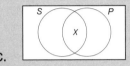   d.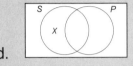

9. Some Great Gooey Gobs fans (*S*) are not Fruity Fudge fans (*P*).

a. 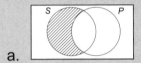   b.    c. 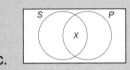   d.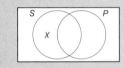

10. No person who eats Chocolate Chilies to excess (*S*) is an employee of McGoo Candy Company (*P*).

a. 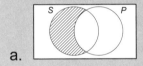   b. 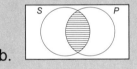   c. 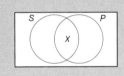   d.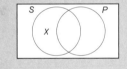

6.11 Venn Diagrams for Categorical Syllogisms

Representing categorical syllogisms with Venn diagrams requires three circles: one for the Major Term, one for the Minor Term, and one for the Middle Term. If you can produce the conclusion of the syllogism by diagramming the premises of the syllogism, the syllogism is valid. If you cannot produce the conclusion by diagramming the premises, the syllogism is invalid.

Example 1

All mammals are animals.	All M are P.
All humans are mammals.	All S are M.
So, all humans are animals.	All S are P.

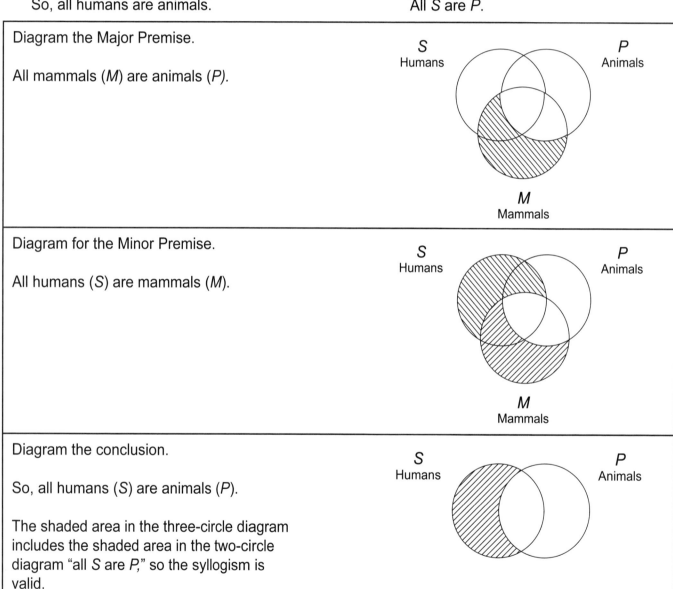

Diagram the Major Premise. All mammals (M) are animals (P).	
Diagram for the Minor Premise. All humans (S) are mammals (M).	
Diagram the conclusion. So, all humans (S) are animals (P). The shaded area in the three-circle diagram includes the shaded area in the two-circle diagram "all S are P," so the syllogism is valid.	

Example 2

No union members (*P*) are company administrators (*M*).   No *P* are *M*.
All officers of the company (*S*) are company administrators (*M*).   All *S* are *M*.
So, no officers of the company (*S*) are union members (*P*).   No *S* are *P*.

Diagram the Major Premise. No union members (*P*) are company administrators (*M*).	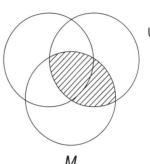
Diagram for the Minor Premise. All officers of the company (*S*) are company administrators (*M*).	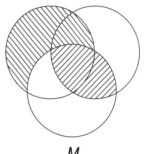
Diagram the conclusion. No officers of the company (*S*) are union members (*P*). "No company officers (*S*) are union members (*P*)." The shaded area in the 3-circle diagram includes the shaded area in the 2-circle diagram, so the syllogism is valid.	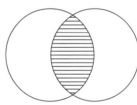

Example 3

All Great Gooey Gobs (*P*) are chocolate candies (*M*).   All *P* are *M*.
All Sweetie Pies (*S*) are chocolate candies (*M*).   All *S* are *M*.
So, all Sweetie Pies (*S*) are Great Gooey Gobs (*P*).   All *S* are *P*.

All Great Gooey Gobs (*P*) are chocolate candies (*M*).	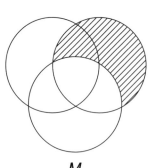
All Sweetie Pies (*S*) are chocolate candies (*M*).	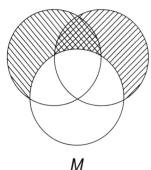
So, all Sweetie Pies (*S*) are Great Gooey Gobs (*P*). The shaded area in the 3-circle diagram does not include the entire conclusion in the 2-circle diagram, so the syllogism is *invalid*.	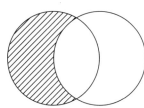

Example 4

No Great Gooey Gobs are Caramel Clusters.   No *M* are *P*.
No Great Gooey Gobs are Sweetie Pies.   No *M* are *S*.
So, no Sweetie Pies are Caramel Clusters.   No *S* are *P*.

No Great Gooey Gobs (*M*) are Caramel Clusters (*P*). No *M* are *P*.	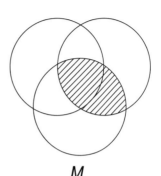
No Great Gooey Gobs (*M*) are Sweetie Pies (*S*) No *M* are *S*.	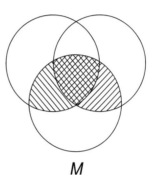
So, no Sweetie Pies (S) are Caramel Clusters (P). No *S* are *P*. The shaded area "No *S* are *P*" in the 3-circle diagram does not include the entire shaded area in the conclusion. So, the argument is *invalid*.	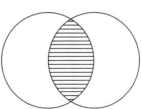

6.12 Exercise Circle the correct Venn diagram for each of the following syllogisms and then label the argument valid or invalid. Writing the form of the syllogism is often helpful, but it is not required.

1. **Example:**
All Sweeties Pies (*P*) are Great Gooey Gobs (*M*).
All Great Gooey Gobs (*M*) are candies made from caramel (*S*).

So, no candies made from caramel (*S*) are Sweetie Pies (*P*).

All *P* are *M*.
All *M* are *S*.
―――――――――
No *S* are *P*.

a. 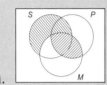   b.

c.   d.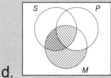

e. Valid
f. **Invalid**

Premises

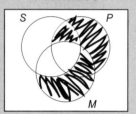

Conclusion

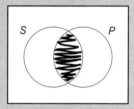

2. All Great Gooey Gobs (*P*) are candies made from caramel (*M*).
No pieces of Fruity Fudge (*S*) are candies made from caramel (*M*).

Therefore, no pieces of Fruity Fudge (*S*) are Great Gooey Gobs (*P*).

a.   b.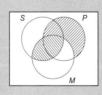

c.   d.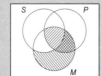

e. Valid
f. Invalid

Premises

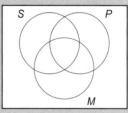

Conclusion

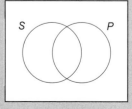

3. No Sweetie Pies (*M*) are Great Gooey Gobs (*P*).
    No Sweety Pies (*M*) are Caramel Clumps (*S*).
    _____
    So, all Caramel Clumps (*S*) are Great Gooey Gobs (*P*).

a.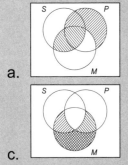

b.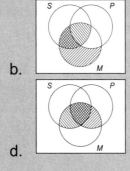

c.

d.

e. Valid
f. Invalid

Premises

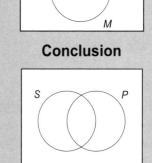

Conclusion

4. All Great Goody Gobs (*P*) are caramel candies (*M*).
    No caramel candies (*M*) are pieces of Fruity Fudge (*S*).
    _____
    So, no pieces of Fruity Fudge (*S*) are Great Gooey Gobs (*P*).

a.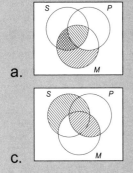

b.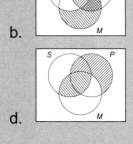

c.

d.

e. Valid
f. Invalid

Premises

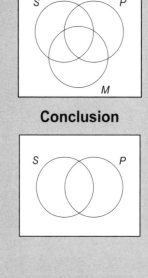

Conclusion

(Continued)

5. No union members (P) are people presently working (M).
    All people presently working (M) are company officers (S).
    So, all company officers (S) are union members (P).

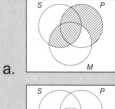
a.

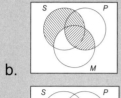
b.

c.   d.

e. Valid
f. Invalid

Premises

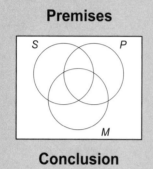

Conclusion

6. All Great Gooey Gobs fans (M) are union members (P).
    All Great Gooey Gobs fans (M) are company officers (S).
    So, no company officers (S) are union members (P).

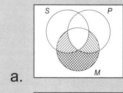
a.

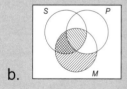
b.

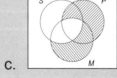
c.

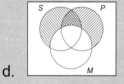
d.

e. Valid
f. Invalid

Premises

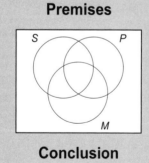

Conclusion

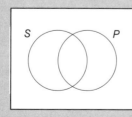

7. All members of Candy Workers Local 275 (*M*) are people out on strike (*P*).
    No officers of McGoo Candy (*S*) are members of Candy Workers Local 275 (*M*).
    So, all officers of Mc Goo Candy (*S*) are people out on strike (*P*).

a. 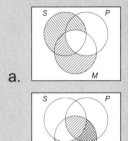   b.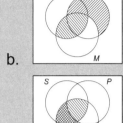

c.   d.

e. Valid
f. Invalid

Premises

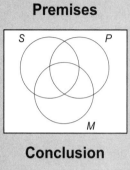

Conclusion

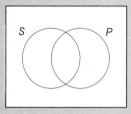

8. No union members (*P*) are Fruity Fudge fans (*M*).
    No company officers (*S*) are Fruity Fudge fans (*M*).
    Thus, no company officers (*S*) are union members (*P*).

a. 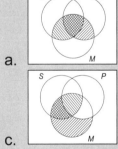   b.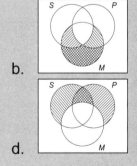

c.   d.

e. Valid
f. Invalid

Premises

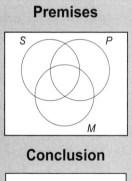

Conclusion

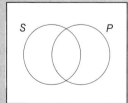

(Continued)

9. No members of Candy Workers Local 275 (*M*) are officers of McGoo Candy (*P*).
    All production-line workers (S) are members of Candy Workers Local 275 (*M*).
    _____
    All production-line workers (*S*) are officers of McGoo Candy (*P*).

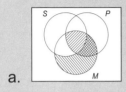
a.

b.

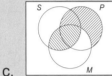
c.

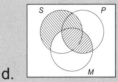
d.

e. Valid
f. Invalid

Premises

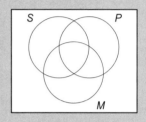

Conclusion

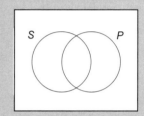

10. No people who eat Fruity Fudge (*P*) are members of Candy Workers Local 275 (*M*).
    No members of Candy Workers Local 275 (*M*) are officers of McGoo Candy (*S*).
    _____
    Hence, all officers of McGoo Candy (*S*) are people who eat Fruity Fudge (*P*).

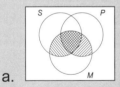
a.

b.

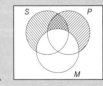
c.

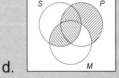
d.

e. Valid
f. Invalid

Premises

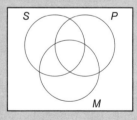

Conclusion

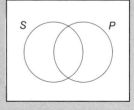

When diagramming particular claims on a two circle Venn diagram, mark the relevant area with an *X* to show that at least one thing is there.

Some dogs are brown.
(Some *S* are *P*.)

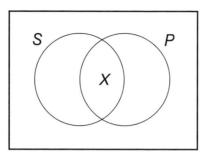

When diagramming particular claims on a three circle diagram, we don't know if the members identified by particular claim (*X*) are also members of the unmentioned class so we place the *X* in the correct area, but on the line of the unmentioned class.

Example 1

Some dogs are brown.
(Some *S* are *P*.)

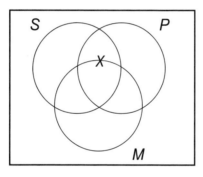

Example 2

Some dogs are not brown.
(Some *S* are not *P*.)

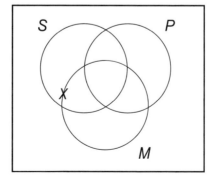

Syllogisms With at Least One Particular Premise			
All candymakers are candy lovers. Some union members are candymakers. _____ So, some union members are candy lovers.	S: union members P: candy lovers M: candymakers	All M are P. Some S are M. ‾‾‾‾‾‾‾‾‾ Some S are P.
All candymakers are candy lovers.	All M are P.	
Some union members are candymakers. *Without the universal claim above "pushing" the X off the line, the X would be where the small X is located, but since the universal claim tells us that nothing is both X and M, the X is "pushed" off the line and to the area where the large X is located.	Some S are M.	
So, some union members are candy lovers.	Some S are P.	
Since the X in the 3-circle diagram is in the area where the S-circle and the P-circle overlap, it shows that the syllogism is **valid**.		

If a syllogism is valid, there is never an X on a line. All valid syllogisms with a particular premise also have a universal premise (Rule 6, Section 6.6). If the syllogism is valid, the shading of the universal premise "pushes" the X off the line since shading shows nothing is in that area. For this reason, it is helpful to diagram a universal premise before a particular premise.

Syllogisms With at Least One Particular Premise

No union members (*P*) are company officers (*M*). Some company officers (M) are candy lovers (*S*). <hr>So, some candy lovers (*S*) are not union members (*P*).	*S*: candy lovers *P*: union members *M*: company officers	No *P* are *M*. Some *M* are *S*. <hr>Some *S* are not *P*.
No union members are company officers. Note: Since this syllogism contains a particular claim, we diagram the universal claim first.	No *P* are *M*.	
Some company officers are candy lovers.	Some *M* are *S*.	
So, some candy lovers (*S*) are not union members (*P*).	Some *S* are not *P*.	

The *X* is in the area that is *S* and not *P*. So, the diagram shows that the argument is **valid**.

Syllogisms With at Least One Particular Premise

Some candymakers (P) are not union members (M). All union members (M) are people on strike (S). So, some people on strike (S) are not candymakers (P).	S: people on strike P: candy-makers M: union members	Some P are not M. All M are S. Some S are not P.
All union members are people on strike.* *Since the argument has a particular and universal claim, we diagram the universal claim first to see if it pushes the particular claim off the line.	All M are S.	
Some candymakers are not union members. Note: Since we do not know if the candy-makers (P) are or are not people on strike (S), we put the X on the line that separates those two groups.	Some P are not M.	
So, some people on strike are not candymakers.	Some S are not P.	

If the conclusion were diagrammed, there would need to be an X in the area that is S but not P. The X is not in that area. The X is "on the line." So, the diagram shows that the argument is **invalid**.

Syllogisms With at Least One Particular Premise		
Some candymakers (*M*) are union members (*P*). Some candymakers (*M*) are not auto makers (*S*). <hr> So, some automakers (*S*) are not union members (*P*).	*S*: auto-makers *P*: union members *M*: candy-makers	Some *M* are *P*. Some *M* are not *S*. <hr> Some *S* are not *P*.
Some candymakers are union members.	Some *M* are *P*.	
Some candymakers are not auto-makers.	Some *M* are not *S*.	
So, some automakers are not union members.	Some *S* are not *P*.	
If the conclusion were diagrammed, there would need to be an *X* in the area that is *S* but not *P*. Neither *X* is in that area. Both are "on the line." So, the diagram shows that the argument is **invalid**.		

Note: Venn diagrams can be used to determine whether any *categorical syllogism* is valid. They *cannot* tell one whether an argument is a categorical syllogism. One can do that *only* by asking whether there are three terms given the same meaning throughout the argument. So, even if one uses Venn diagrams to determine whether syllogisms are valid, one must still pay attention to Rule 1 in Section 6.6.

6.13 Exercise Circle the correct Venn diagram for each of the following syllogisms and then label the argument valid or invalid. Writing the form of the argument is often helpful, but it is not required.

1. **Example:**
   All Great Gooey Gobs (*M*) are candies made from caramel (*P*).
   Some Sweetie Pies (*S*) are not Great Gooey Gobs (*M*).
   _____
   Some Sweetie Pies (*S*) are not candies made from caramel (*P*).

   All *M* are *P*.
   Some *S* are not *M*.
   _____
   Some *S* are not *P*.

   a. This argument violates Rule 1. It is not a categorical syllogism.

   Premises

   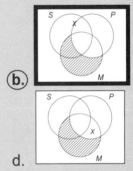
   b.

   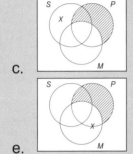
   c.

   d.

   e.

   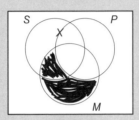

   Conclusion

   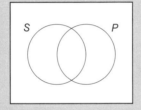

   f. Valid
   g. **Invalid**

2. No caramel candies (*M*) are candies your dentist likes (*P*).
    Some caramel candies (*M*) are Caramel Clumps (*S*).
    So, some Caramel Clumps (*S*) are candies your dentist likes (*P*).

    a. This argument violates Rule 1. It is not a categorical syllogism.

    Premises

    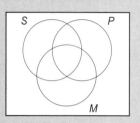

    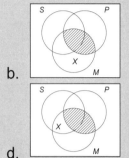

    b.

    c.

    Conclusion

    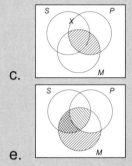

    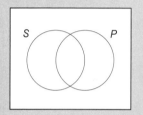

    d.

    e.

    f. Valid
    g. Invalid

3. Some people who work at McGoo Candies (*M*) are union members (*P*).
    Some members of Candy Workers Local 275 (*S*) are not people who work at McGoo Candies (*M*).
    So, some members of Candy Workers Local 275 (*S*) are union members (*P*).

    a. This argument violates Rule 1. It is not a categorical syllogism.

    Premises

    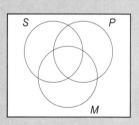

    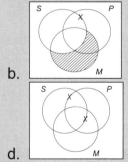

    b.

    c.

    Conclusion

    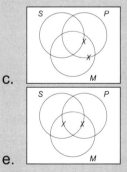

    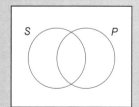

    d.

    e.

    f. Valid
    g. Invalid

(Continued)

4. Some Great Gooey Gobs (*M*) are not Caramel
    Clumps (*P*).
    All Great Gooey Gobs (*M*) are things made of chocolate
    and peanuts (*S*).
    _____
    So, some things made of chocolate and peanuts (*S*) are
    not Caramel Clumps (*P*).

    a. This argument violates Rule 1. It is not a
        categorical syllogism.

    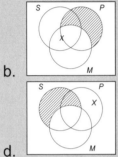   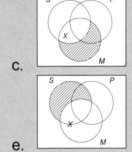

    b.   c.

    d.   e.

    f. Valid
    g. Invalid

Premises

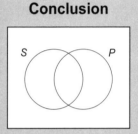

Conclusion

5. Some union members (*P*) are candy lovers (*M*).
    No candy lovers (*M*) are people who have dentists as
    close friends (*S*).
    _____
    So, some people who have dentists as close friends (*S*)
    are not union members (*P*).

    a. This argument violates Rule 1. It is not a
        categorical syllogism.

    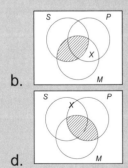   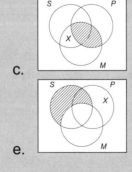

    b.   c.

    d.   e.

    f. Valid
    g. Invalid

Premises

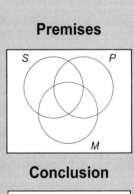

Conclusion

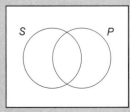

6. All Sweetie Pies are things made with raisins.
    Some happy people are sweetie pies.
    So, some happy people are things made with raisins.

    a. This argument violates Rule 1. It is not a
        categorical syllogism.

    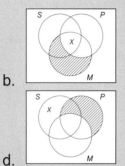

    b.

    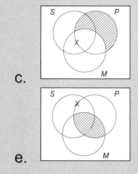

    c.

    d.

    e.

    f. Valid
    g. Invalid

Premises

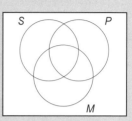

Conclusion

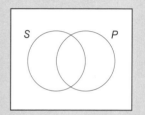

7. All candymakers are people who like sweets.
    Some candymakers are people who eat Great
    Gooey Gobs.
    So, some people who eat Great Gooey Gobs are people
    who like sweets.

    a. This argument violates Rule 1. It is not a categorical
        syllogism.

    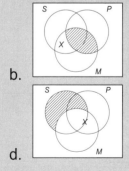

    b.

    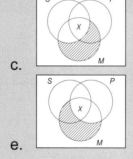

    c.

    d.

    e.

    f. Valid
    g. Invalid

Premises

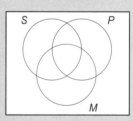

Conclusion

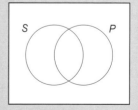

(Continued)

8. All things made with sugar are sweet things.
    All Great Gooey Gobs are things made with sugar.
    So, all Great Gooey Gobs are sweet things.

    a. This argument violates Rule 1. It is not a
        categorical syllogism.

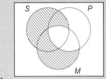

b.

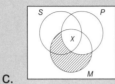

c.

d.

e.

    f. Valid
    g. Invalid

Premises

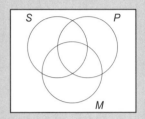

Conclusion

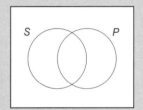

9. Some Great Gooey Gobs are not Caramel Clumps.
    Some Caramel Clumps are things made from butter
    and sugar.
    So, some things made from butter and sugar are Great
    Gooey Gobs.

    a. This argument violates Rule 1. It is not a
        categorical syllogism.

b.

c.

d.

e.

    f. Valid
    g. Invalid

Premises

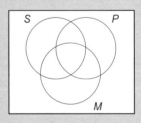

Conclusion

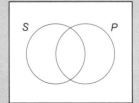

10. Some Sweetie Pies are not Great Gooey Gobs.
    No Caramel Clumps are Great Gooey Gobs.
    So, some Caramel Clumps are not Sweetie Pies.

    a. This argument violates Rule 1. It is not a
       categorical syllogism.

    b. 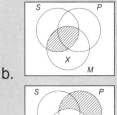   c.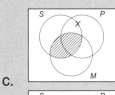

    d.   e.

    f. Valid
    g. Invalid

Premises

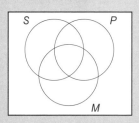

Conclusion

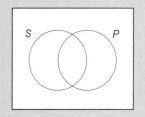

11. No Caramel Clumps are Great Gooey Gobs, for some
    Caramel Clumps are not Sweetie Pies, and some
    Sweetie Pies are not Great Gooey Gobs.

    a. This argument violates Rule 1. It is not a
       categorical syllogism.

    b. 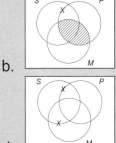   c.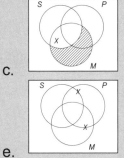

    d.    e.

    f. Valid
    g. Invalid

Premises

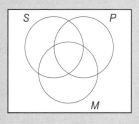

Conclusion

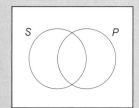

(Continued)

12. No candies made from caramel are pieces of Fruity Fudge, so some Great Gooey Gobs are not pieces of Fruity Fudge, for some candies made with caramel are Great Gooey Gobs.

a. This argument violates Rule 1. It is not a categorical syllogism.

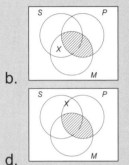

b.

c.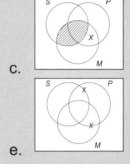

d.

e.

f. Valid
g. Invalid

Premises

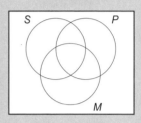

Conclusion

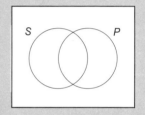

13. Some Caramel Clumps are candies made from butter and sugar, for some pieces of Fruity Fudge are not candies made from butter and sugar, and no Caramel Clumps are pieces of Fruity Fudge.

a. This argument violates Rule 1. It is not a categorical syllogism.

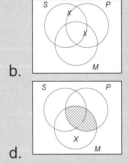

b.

c.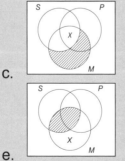

d.

e.

f. Valid
g. Invalid

Premises

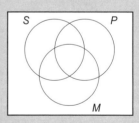

Conclusion

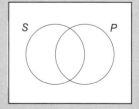

14. Some union members are happy strikers, so some production line workers are not union members, for all production line workers are happy strikers.

a. This argument violates Rule 1. It is not a categorical syllogism.

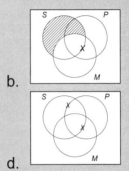

b.

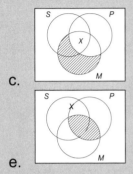

c.

d.

e.

f. Valid
g. Invalid

Premises

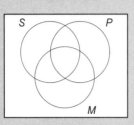

Conclusion

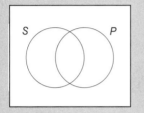

15. Some secret candy lovers are not dentists, for all secret candy lovers are people who sneak a piece of candy when no one is looking, and some dentists are people who sneak a piece of candy when no one is looking.

a. This argument violates Rule 1. It is not a categorical syllogism.

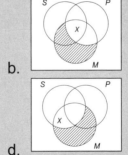

b.

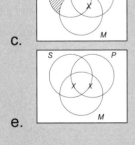

c.

d.

e.

f. Valid
g. Invalid

Premises

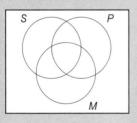

Conclusion

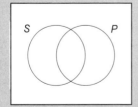

(Continued)

16. Since no Caramel Clumps are Sweetie Pies, and all
    Caramel Clumps are candies made from butter and
    sugar, we may conclude that some Sweetie Pies are not
    candies made from butter and sugar.

    a. This argument violates Rule 1. It is not a
       categorical syllogism.

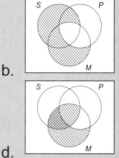

    b.

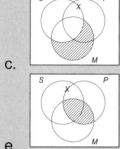

    c.

    d.

    e.

    f. Valid
    g. Invalid

Premises

Conclusion

17. No Great Gooey Gobs are Caramel Clumps, so some
    Caramel Clumps are candies made from butter and
    sugar, for some candies made from butter and sugar are
    Great Gooey Gobs.

    a. This argument violates Rule 1. It is not a
       categorical syllogism.

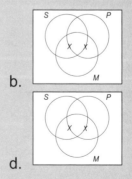

    b.

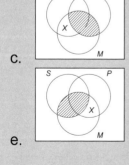

    c.

    d.

    e.

    f. Valid
    g. Invalid

Premises

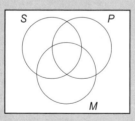

Conclusion

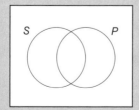

18. Since some Great Gooey Gobs are chocolaty treats, and some Sweetie Pies are chocolaty treats, we may conclude that some Great Gooey Gobs are Sweetie Pies.

a. This argument violates Rule 1. It is not a categorical syllogism.

b.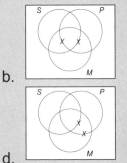

c.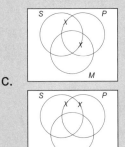

d.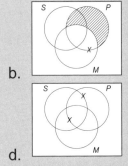

e.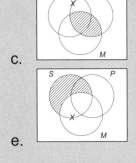

f. Valid
g. Invalid

Premises

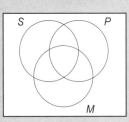

Conclusion

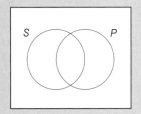

19. Some union members are not people favoring the strike, so some members of Candy Workers Local 275 are people favoring the strike, for all members of Candy Workers Local 275 are union members.

a. This argument violates Rule 1. It is not a categorical syllogism.

b.

c.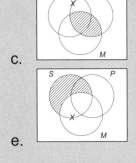

d.

e.

f. Valid
g. Invalid

Premises

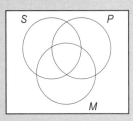

Conclusion

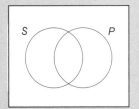

(Continued)

20. Since no Great Gooey Gobs are Caramel Clumps, and all Caramel Clumps are candies made from butter and sugar, it follows that some Great Gooey Gobs are candies made from butter and sugar.

a. This argument violates Rule 1. It is not a categorical syllogism.

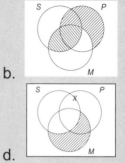
b.

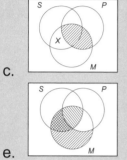
c.

d.

e.

f. Valid
g. Invalid

Premises

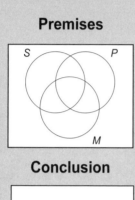

Conclusion

CASE 23	City of Los Angeles Police Department

¹There was a series of robberies at the Frank 'n' Stein hot dog and root beer stands throughout the city. ²Dr. Acula, the company president, said, "In every case, two people entered the stand. ³The tall one was dressed like the Frankenstein monster, and the short one was dressed like Count Dracula. ⁴No one thought much of the outfits, since that's how all our employees dress. ⁵Sometimes they'd come shortly before the change of shift. ⁶They'd relieve the workers, take the money, and leave before the real employees appeared. ⁷Sometimes they posed as employees sent to pick up part of the day's receipts. ⁸It was only in the last few robberies that they pulled guns and demanded cash, a gallon of root beer, and two of our monster dogs."

⁹Detective Wise interviewed I. M. D. Count, manager of the shop on Wilshire. ¹⁰"All our robberies were events that occurred at night. ¹¹So, all cases in which money, root beer, and hot dogs were taken were events that occurred at night."

¹²Mary Shelley, who worked at the shop on Sunset, said, "No robberies were events that occurred during the lunch or supper shifts. ¹³But some events that occurred during the lunch and supper shifts were events in which Frankenstein and Dracula characters were present. ¹⁴So, I'll let you draw your own conclusions."

¹⁵Bram Stoker, manager of the shop at Union Station, remarked, "Every robbery was carefully planned. ¹⁶No robbery could be carefully planned unless it was an inside job. ¹⁷So, each and every robbery must have been an inside job."

¹⁸Detective Wise pondered the facts. ¹⁹All the employees dress like Frankenstein or Dracula. ²⁰So, some of the employees dress like Frankenstein or Dracula. ²¹No employees work in three-piece suits. ²²So, it is not the case that some employees work in three-piece suits. ²³If we know that some of the employees were not robbers, does it follow that no employees were robbers?

6.14 Toward Ordinary Language Syllogisms: Enthymemes

All the syllogisms we have considered up to this point are **standard form categorical syllogisms.** Standard form categorical syllogisms are composed of **standard form categorical claims** and are arranged Major Premise, Minor Premise, conclusion. A standard form categorical claim contains the quantifiers *All*, *No*, or *Some*, it contains a **subject term**, a **predicate term**, and a form of the verb *to be*.

Few categorical syllogisms in ordinary English are given in standard form. In this and the next few sections we consider ways to restate categorical syllogisms in ordinary English as standard form categorical syllogisms. This is called **translating** or **reducing a categorical syllogism to standard form**.

An **enthymeme** is a deductive argument that is not fully stated. There are ways to determine what the missing conclusion or the missing premise *must be* if the syllogism is valid.

If you encounter an argument, with a missing or implied conclusion, you can construct a Venn diagram to determine what follows from the premises.

Example 1

Argument
No dinosaurs are animals alive today. Some animals alive today are hunters. So, ???

Since the conclusion is missing, we don't know which term is the Minor Term or the Major Term of the conclusion. However, we can identify the Middle Term. The next step is to randomly assign the Minor and Major terms and then create a Venn diagram to identify the likely conclusion.
If we assign *S: hunters* and *P: dinosaurs*, then we have:

Terms	Form	Venn Diagram
S: hunters *P:* dinosaurs *M:* animals alive today	*No P are M.* *Some M are S.* —————————— —————————— ——————————	
Since no "*S are P*" is only partially covered, it cannot be the conclusion. The only other *S* and *P* relationship shown in the diagram is "Some *S* are not *P*." So, the conclusion that follows must be "Some *S* are not *P*."		

Example 2

Argument
All robberies are crimes.
No crimes are honest activities.
So, ???

We can identify the Middle Term as *crimes*, so the next step is to assign the other two terms to the Minor and Major terms and then make a Venn diagram of the premises to try to identify the missing conclusion.

If we make *S: honest activities* and *P: robberies*, we have:

Terms	Form	Venn Diagram
S: honest activities P: robberies M: crimes	All *P* are *M*. No *M* are *S*. _____ _____ _____	

The areas that represent both honest activites and robberies are shaded, so the conclusion must be No *S* are *P*: "No honest activities are robberies."

Example 3

Argument
No robberies are honest activities.   No kidnappings are robberies.   So, ???

We can identify the Middle Term as *robberies*, so the next step is to assign the other two terms to the Minor and Major terms, so we can make a Venn diagram of the syllogism.

If we make *S: kidnappings* and *P: honest activities*, we have:

Terms	Form	Venn Diagram
S: kidnappings *P:* honest activities *M:* robberies	No *M* are *P*. No *S* are *M*. ——————— ——————— ———————	
The shading in the *S* and *P* circles represents no determinate relationships between the Minor Term and the Major Term. The syllogism is invalid.		

Example 4

Argument
All robbers are crooks. Some crooks are not nasty people. So, ???

We can identify the Middle Term as *crooks*, since it appears in both premises. Next, we need to identify the remaining claims, ("*robbers*" and "*nasty people*"), so we can create a Venn diagram to try to identify a valid conclusion.

Terms	Form	Venn Diagram
S: nasty people *P:* robbers *M:* crooks	All *P* are *M*. Some *M* are not *S*. ——————— ———————	
No categorical claim is represented by the shading and *X* in the *P* and *S* circles. The syllogism is invalid.		

6.15 Exercise What conclusion, if any, follows from each of the following pairs of premises? Circle the best answer. Using the Venn diagram and writing the form of the argument often helps, but it is not required.

1. **Example:**
   All robbers are crooks.
   Some blackmailers are robbers.
   So, ...
   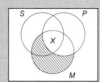
   All M are P.
   Some S are M.
   - (a.) **some blackmailers are crooks.**
   - b. some blackmailers are not crooks.
   - c. no crooks are blackmailers.
   - d. nothing follows.

2. Some robbers are people who wear costumes.
   Some people who wear costumes are not actors.
   So, ...
   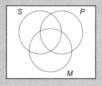
   - a. some actors are not robbers.
   - b. some robbers are not actors.
   - c. some robbers are actors.
   - d. nothing follows.

3. No robbers are Supreme Court justices.
   All Supreme Court justices are people over fifty.
   So, ...
   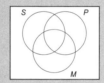
   - a. no robbers are people over fifty.
   - b. all people over fifty are robbers.
   - c. some robbers are not people over fifty.
   - d. nothing follows.

4. Some robbers are not people in jail.
   All robbers are criminals.
   So, ...

   - a. no criminals are people in jail.
   - b. some people in jail are not criminals.
   - c. some criminals are not people in jail.
   - d. nothing follows.

5. Some people in jail are not criminals.
No people in jail are people wearing Dracula costumes.

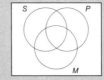

So, ...
   a. some people wearing Dracula costumes are not criminals.
   b. some people wearing Dracula costumes are criminals.
   c. all people wearing Dracula costumes are people in jail.
   d. nothing follows.

6. Some hot dog fans are people in Dracula costumes.
All hotdog fans are people who like french fries.

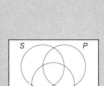

So, ...
   a. all people who like french fries are people in Dracula costumes.
   b. some people in Dracula costumes are not people who like french fries.
   c. some people who like french fries are people in Dracula costumes.
   d. nothing follows.

7. Some people who like french fries are not hot dog fans.
All people who like french fries are people who like fatty foods.

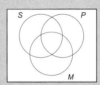

So, ...
   a. some people who like fatty foods are not hot dog fans.
   b. some hot dog fans are not people who like fatty foods.
   c. some people who like fatty foods are hot dog fans.
   d. nothing follows.

8. No gourmets are people who like hot
    dogs.
    Some people who like pastries are people
    who like hot dogs.

    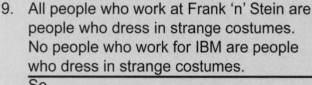

    So, ...
    a. some people who like pastries are
       gourmets.
    b. some people who like pastries are not
       gourmets.
    c. some gourmets are not people who like
       hot dogs.
    d. nothing follows.

9. All people who work at Frank 'n' Stein are
    people who dress in strange costumes.
    No people who work for IBM are people
    who dress in strange costumes.

    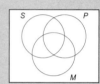

    So, ...
    a. no people who work for IBM are people
       who work at Frank 'n' Stein.
    b. all people who work at Frank 'n' Stein
       are people who work for IBM.
    c. some people who work for IBM are not
       people who work at Frank 'n' Stein.
    d. nothing follows.

10. All people who dress in strange costumes
    are people who work at Frank 'n' Stein.
    Some people who work for IBM are not
    people who dress in strange costumes.

    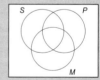

    So, ...
    a. some people who work for IBM are not
       people who work at Frank 'n' Stein.
    b. some people who work at Frank 'n'
       Stein are not people who work for IBM.
    c. no people who work for IBM are people
       who work at Frank 'n' Stein.
    d. nothing follows.

Sometimes a premise is not stated in an argument. When this happens, you can use the rules to determine what premise, if any, will yield a valid syllogism. Here is the procedure:

1. Check to see whether each of the terms is used with the same meanings (consistently) throughout. If one or more terms shifts meaning, the argument violates Rule 1. It is invalid.

2. Make sure the term common to the given premise and the conclusion (the Major Term or Minor Term) has the same distribution. If it does not, it violates Rule 3 or Rule 4. It is invalid.

3. Make sure there is not a particular premise and a universal conclusion. If there is, it violates Rule 6. It is invalid.

4. Make sure there is not a negative premise and an affirmative conclusion. If there is, it violates Rule 5. It is invalid.

   If one finds none of these, there is a premise that will yield a valid syllogism.

5. If the conclusion is universal (All …, No …), the missing premise is universal.

6. If the conclusion is particular (Some …) and there is a universal premise, the missing premise is particular. If there is particular premise, the missing premise is universal.

7. If the conclusion is affirmative (All … are …, or Some … are …), the missing premise will be affirmative.

8. If the conclusion is negative (No … are …, or Some … are not …) and there is an affirmative premise, the missing premise is negative. If there is a negative premise, the missing premise is affirmative.

9. Distribute the Major Term or Minor Term in the premise so it is the same distribution as it has in the conclusion.

10. Distribute the Middle Term exactly once. (If it is distributed in the given premise, it is undistributed in the missing premise. If it is undistributed in the given premise, it is distributed in the missing premise. If you have done everything correctly up to this point, the distribution of the middle term should "automatically" turn out correctly.)

11. Double-check to make sure all the terms retain the same meaning throughout the syllogism. If the meaning of one of the terms must shift for the missing premise to be true, it violates Rule 1.

Finding a Missing Premise

Example 1

Argument
All mammals are animals. So, all humans are animals.

The Major Term (*P*) is *animals*. The Minor Term (*S*) is *humans*. The Middle Term (*M*) is *mammals*. The given premise is the Major Premise. The terms appear to be used consistently throughout (1). The Major Term is undistributed in both the premise and the conclusion (2). We have neither a universal conclusion from a particular premise nor an affirmative conclusion from a negative premise (3 and 4). So, there *is* a premise that will yield a valid syllogism. Both the given premise and the conclusion are universal affirmative claims. So, the missing premise must be a universal affirmative (5 and 7). The Minor Term, *humans*, is distributed in the conclusion, so it must be distributed in the premise. So the premise must begin, "All humans …" (9). The middle term is distributed in the given premise. So, it must be *undistributed* in the missing premise (10). So, the missing premise must be, "All humans are mammals." The meaning of the three terms is the same throughout (11).

Categorical Claims	Terms	Form
Major Premise: All mammals are animals. Minor Premise: Conclusion: _____ So, all humans are animals.	*S*: humans *P*: animals *M*: mammals	All *M* are *P*. _____ _____ All *S* are *P*.

Example 2

Argument
No robberies are accidents.
So, some events at the Frank 'n' Stein stands were not accidents.

The Major Term is *accidents*. The Minor Term is *events at the Frank 'n' Stein stands*. The Middle Term is *robberies*. The terms appear to be used consistently throughout (1). The Major Term is distributed in both the premise and the conclusion (2). The premise is universal and the conclusion is particular (3). Both the premise and the conclusion are negative claims (4). So, there is a premise that will yield a valid categorical syllogism. The conclusion is particular and the given premise is universal. So, the missing premise must be particular (6). Both the given premise and the conclusion are negative. So, the missing premise must be affirmative (8). So, the missing premise will take the form, "Some ... are ... ." The Minor Term is *undistributed* in the conclusion. So, it must be *undistributed* in the premise (9). The Middle Term is *distributed* in the given premise. So, it must be *undistributed* in the missing premise (10). So, the missing premise must be "Some events at the *Frank 'n' Stein* stands were robberies" *or* "Some robberies were events at the Frank 'n' Stein stands." The three terms seem to be have the same meaning throughout the syllogism (11).

Categorical Claims	Terms	Form
Major Premise: No robberies are accidents. Minor Premise: Conclusion: So, some events at the Frank 'n' Stein stands were not accidents.	*S*: events at Frank'n' Stein stands *P*: accidents *M*: robberies	No *M* are *P*. ————————— ————————— Some *S* are not *P*.

Example 3

Argument
Some people who work at Frank 'n' Stein are not robbers.
So, some people who wear strange costumes are not robbers.

The Major Term is *robbers*. The Minor Term is *people who wear strange costumes*. The Middle Term is *people who work at Frank 'n' Stein*. The terms seem to be assigned the same meaning throughout (1). The Major Term is distributed in both the given premise and the conclusion (2). The given premise and the conclusion are both particular negatives (3 and 4). So, there is a premise that will yield a valid categorical syllogism. Both the given premise and the conclusion are particular claims. So, the missing premise must be universal (6). The given premise and the conclusion are both negative. So, the missing premise must be affirmative (8). So, the form of the conclusion will be "All ... are ... ." The Minor Term is *undistributed* in the conclusion. So, it must be *undistributed* in the missing premise (9). The Middle Term is *undistributed* in the given premise. So, it must be *distributed* in the missing premise (10). So, the missing premise must be "All people who work at Frank 'n' Stein are people who wear strange costumes." The three terms seem to be assigned the same meanings throughout (11).

Categorical Claims	Terms	Form
Major Premise: Some people who work at Frank 'n' Stein are not robbers.	S: people who wear strange costumes	Some *M* are not *P*.
Minor Premise:	P: robbers	
So, some people who wear strange costumes are not robbers.	M: people who work at Frank 'n' Stein	Some *S* are not *P*.

Example 4

Argument
No robbers are nice people.
So, all nice people are people who follow the laws.

The Major Term is *people who follow the laws*. The Minor Term is *nice people*. The Middle Term is *robbers*. The terms seem to be used consistently throughout (1). The Minor Term has the same distribution throughout (2). Both the given premise and the conclusion are universal (3). The premise is negative and the conclusion is affirmative (4). So, the argument violates Rule 5. It is invalid. *No premise will yield a valid categorical syllogism.*

Categorical Claims	Terms	Form
Major Premise: Minor Premise: No robbers are nice people. So, all nice people are people who follow the laws.	*S*: nice people *P*: people who follow the laws. *M*: robbers	_____ No *M* are *S*. All *S* are *P*.

Example 5

Argument
Some people who work at Frank 'n' Stein are crazy people.
So, some people who work for McGoo Candies are not people who work at Frank 'n' Stein.

The Major Term is *people who work at Frank 'n' Stein*. The Minor Term is *people who work for McGoo Candies*. The Middle Term is *crazy people*. The terms appear to be used consistently throughout (1). The Major Term is distributed in the conclusion but not in the premise (2). So, the argument violates Rule 3. It is invalid. No premise will yield a valid syllogism.

Categorical Claims	Terms	Form
Major Premise: Some people who work at Frank 'n' Stein are crazy people. Minor Premise: ——————————— So, some people who work for McGoo Candies are not people who work at Frank 'n' Stein.	*S*: people who work for McGoo Candies *P*: people who work at Frank 'n' Stein *M*: crazy people	Some *P* are *M*. ——————————— ——————————— Some *S* are not *P*.

Example 6

Argument
All cats are small domestic animals.
So, all lions are small domestic animals.

The Major Term is *small domestic animals*. The Minor Term is *lions*. The Middle Term is *cats*. The terms appear to be used consistently throughout (1), although the fact that the conclusion is false, *suggests* that there might be a problem. The Major Term is undistributed in both the given premise and the conclusion (2). Both the premise and the conclusion are universal affirmatives (3 and 4). So, there should be a premise that yields a valid categorical syllogism. The missing premise must be universal and affirmative (5 and 7). The Minor Term, *lions*, must be distributed in the premise (9), and the Middle Term, *cats*, must be undistributed in the missing premise (10). So, the missing premise must be "All lions are cats." But the Middle Term, *cats*, does not have the same meaning in both premises: the Major Premise concerns house cats, while the Minor Premise concerns a family of animals that includes domestic cats and much larger cats (11). So, the argument violates Rule 1. It is invalid.

Categorical Claims	Terms	Form
Major Premise: All cats are small domestic animals.	S: lions	All M are P.
Minor Premise:	P: small domestic animals	_____
So, all lions are small domestic animals.	M: cats	All S are P.

6.16 Exercise What premise, if any, will yield a valid categorical syllogism? Circle the correct answer. Writing the form of the argument is often helpful, but it is not required.

1. **Example:**
   All employees at Frank 'n' Stein are odd people. _____
   So, some odd people are not people who like root beer.
   a. Some people who like root beet are not employees at Frank 'n' Stein.
   b.) **Some employees at Frank 'n' Stein are not people who like root beer.**
   c. No employees at Frank 'n' Stein are people who like root beer.
   d. No premise will yield a valid syllogism.

   All M are S.
   Some M are not P.
   Some S are not P.

2. No person who wears a Dracula costume is a person who is easily embarrassed. _____
   So, some employee at Frank 'n' Stein is not a person who is easily embarrassed.
   a. Some person who wears a Dracula costume is an employee at Frank 'n' Stein.
   b. No person who wears a Dracula costume is an employee at Frank 'n' Stein.
   c. Some employee at Frank 'n' Stein is not a person who wears a Dracula costume.
   d. No premise will yield a valid syllogism.

3. All employees at Frank 'n' Stein are suspects in the robberies. _____
   So, some employees at Frank 'n' Stein are people looking at jail terms.
   a. Some people looking at jail terms are suspects in the robberies.
   b. Some suspects in the robberies are not people looking at jail terms.
   c. All suspects in the robberies are people looking at jail terms.
   d. No premise will yield a valid syllogism.

4. Some Transylvanian count is an ancestor of Dr. Acula.

So, no ancestor of Dr. Acula is a person from Philadelphia.
   a. No person from Philadelphia is a Transylvanian count.
   b. Some person from Philadelphia is not a Transylvanian count.
   c. All Transylvanian counts are persons from Philadelphia.
   d. No premise will yield a valid syllogism.

5. Some people who dress in Frankenstein suits are people who guzzle root beer by the jug.

So, some people who guzzle root beer by the jug are Frank 'n' Stein robbers.
   a. All Frank 'n' Stein robbers are people who dress in Frankenstein suits.
   b. All people who dress in Frankenstein suits are Frank 'n' Stein robbers.
   c. Some people who dress in Frankenstein suits are Frank 'n' Stein robbers.
   d. No premise will yield a valid syllogism.

6. No Frank 'n' Stein employees are people who would eat hamburgers with root beer.

So, no Burgers Are We employees are Frank 'n' Stein employees.
   a. Some Burgers Are We employees are not people who would eat hamburgers with root beer.
   b. All people who would eat hamburgers with root beer are Burgers Are We employees.
   c. All Burgers Are We employees are people who would eat hamburgers with root beer.
   d. No premise will yield a valid syllogism.

7. No people who are fond of Count Dracula are people who prefer hot dogs to hamburgers.

So, some people who prefer hot dogs to hamburgers are not Frank 'n' Stein employees.
   a. All people who are fond of Count Dracula are Frank 'n' Stein employees.
   b. Some people who are Frank 'n' Stein employees are people who are fond of Count Dracula.
   c. Some people who are Frank 'n' Stein employees are not people who are fond of Count Dracula.
   d. No premise will yield a valid syllogism.

(Continued)

8. Some Frank 'n' Stein employees are not robbers.

So, some Frank 'n' Stein employees are not people who'd rather munch on a Biggie Burger.
   a. All people who would rather munch on a Biggie Burger are robbers.
   b. All robbers are people who would rather munch on a Biggie Burger.
   c. No people who would rather munch on a Biggie Burger are robbers.
   d. No premise will yield a valid syllogism.

9. No officers of Frank 'n' Stein are robbers.

So, no officers of McGoo Candies are robbers.
   a. Some officers of McGoo Candies are officers of Frank 'n' Stein.
   b. All officers of Frank 'n' Stein are officers of McGoo Candies.
   c. All officers of McGoo Candies are officers of Frank 'n' Stein.
   d. No premise will yield a valid syllogism.

10. All employees of Frank 'n' Stein are people who wear strange outfits.

So, all people who rob Frank 'n' Stein stands are employees of Frank 'n' Stein.
   a. All people who rob Frank 'n' Stein stands are people who wear strange outfits.
   b. All people who wear strange outfits are people who rob Frank 'n' Stein stands.
   c. Some people who rob Frank 'n' Stein stands are not people who wear strange outfits.
   d. No premise will yield a valid syllogism.

6.17 Toward Ordinary Language Syllogisms: Immediate Inferences and Squares of Opposition

An **immediate inference** is a conclusion that can be drawn from one premise. From the truth or falsehood of one claim, one can infer the truth or falsehood of another claim. These are inferences based on the form of a claim. For example, if the claim "All humans are mortals" is true, it immediately follows that "Some humans are not mortals" is false.

Two claims are **contradictories** if the truth of one entails the falsehood of the other, and the falsehood of one entails the truth of the other.

	Examples of Contradictories	**Truth Value**	**Form**
Claim	"Some robbers are not nice people."	False	Some *S* are not *P.*
Claim's Contradictory	"All robbers are nice people."	True	All *S* are *P.*
Claim	"All robberies at the Frank 'n' Stein stands were inside jobs."	True	All *S* are *P.*
Claim's Contradictory	"Some robberies at the Frank 'n' Stein stands were not inside jobs."	False	Some *S* are not *P.*
Claim	"No officer of Frank 'n' Stein is a crook."	True	No *S* are *P.*
Claim's Contradictory	"Some officer of Frank 'n' Stein is a crook."	False	Some *S* are *P.*
Claim	"Some employees of Frank 'n' Stein are robbers."	False	Some *S* are *P.*
Claim's Contradictory	"No employees of Frank 'n' Stein are robbers."	True	No *S* are *P.*

Boolean Square of Opposition

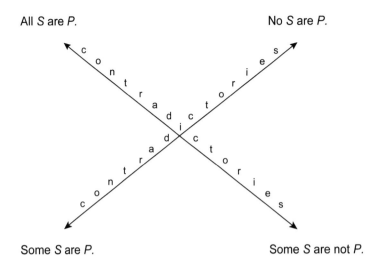

All *S* are *P*.   No *S* are *P*.

Some *S* are *P*.   Some *S* are not *P*.

The relationship of contradictoriness between universal affirmatives and particular negatives, and between universal negatives and particular affirmatives, is represented in a chart called the **Boolean Square of Opposition**.

The only immediate inferences allowed are shown by the arrows.

6.18 Exercise Given the Boolean Square of Opposition and given the truth-value of Claim 1, what can one infer regarding the truth-value of claim 2? Circle the correct answer. Writing the form of the claim is often helpful, but it is not required.

1. **Example:**
    1. "Some Frank 'n' Stein employees are people who wear Dracula costumes" is true.
    2. "All Frank 'n' Stein employees are people who wear Dracula costumes."
  a. Claim 2 is true.
  b. Claim 2 is false.
  (c.) **One can make no inference regarding the truth-value of Claim 2.**

Some S are P.
All S are P.

2.
    1. "Some Frank 'n' Stein employees are not people who like hot dogs" is true.
    2. "All Frank 'n' Stein employees are people who like hot dogs."
  a. Claim 2 is true.
  b. Claim 2 is false.
  c. One can make no inference regarding the truth-value of Claim 2.

3.
    1. "No Frank 'n' Stein employees are people who work for McGoo Candies" is true.
    2. "Some Frank 'n' Stein employees are people who work for McGoo Candies."
  a. Claim 2 is true.
  b. Claim 2 is false.
  c. One can make no inference regarding the truth-value of Claim 2.

4.
    1. "All people who rob Frank 'n' Stein stands are people who like hot dogs" is true.
    2. "No people who rob Frank 'n' Stein stands are people who like hot dogs."
  a. Claim 2 is true.
  b. Claim 2 is false.
  c. One can make no inference regarding the truth-value of Claim 2.

(Continued)

5. 1. "All people who rob Frank 'n' Stein stands are people who drink root beer" is false.
    2. "Some people who rob Frank 'n' Stein stands are not people who drink root beer."
    a. Claim 2 is true.
    b. Claim 2 is false.
    c. One can make no inference regarding the truth-value of Claim 2.

6. 1. "Some LAPD detectives are not people who find this case amusing" is false.
    2. "All LAPD detectives are people who find this case amusing."
    a. Claim 2 is true.
    b. Claim 2 is false.
    c. One can make no inference regarding the truth-value of Claim 2.

7. 1. "Some LAPD detectives are not people who find this case amusing" is false.
    2. "Some LAPD detectives are people who find this case amusing."
    a. Claim 2 is true.
    b. Claim 2 is false.
    c. One can make no inference regarding the truth-value of Claim 2.

8. 1. "No police officers are Frank 'n' Stein employees" is true.
    2. "Some police officers are not Frank 'n' Stein employees."
    a. Claim 2 is true.
    b. Claim 2 is false.
    c. One can make no inference regarding the truth-value of Claim 2.

9. 1. "All LAPD detectives are root beer fans" is true.
    2. "Some LAPD detectives are root beer fans."
    a. Claim 2 is true.
    b. Claim 2 is false.
    c. One can make no inference regarding the truth-value of Claim 2.

10.
1. "No people who operate hot dog stands are people who worry about fat" is false.
2. "Some people who operate hot dog stands are people who worry about fat."

a. Claim 2 is true.
b. Claim 2 is false.
c. One can make no inference regarding the truth-value of Claim 2.

There are two interpretations of categorical claims: the **Boolean interpretation** and the **Aristotelian interpretation.** The difference between the two interpretations centers around **existential import.** Existential import is concerned with the existence of things. The existential import of a claim is the assumtion that the subject term (the thing being talked about in the claim) actually exists and identifies at least one thing. Each interpretation has its own basic ground rules. This book primarily uses the Boolean interpretation though it is important to be aware of the Aristotelian interpretation.

The **Boolean interpretation**[1] is neutral abut whether or not the subject term of a universal claim really exists. This means that the truth of a universal claim *does not* require that there be any members of the subject set.

For example, "All unicorns are one-horned horses" is true by definition because "unicorn" means one-horned horse, but the claim does not imply that unicorns actually exist.

The claim, "No frogs are vehicles" is true, but the claim does not imply the existence of frogs.

The contradictories of these two universal claims—"Some unicorns are not one-horned horses" and "Some frogs are vehicles" —are both false since the Boolean Square of Opposition aplies regardless of whether or not the claims refer to things that actually exist.

The Boolean interpretation follows the rules in Section 6.6 and Venn diagrams as well as in 6.20 and the sections thereafter.

Aristotelian interpretation[2] assumes that universal claims about *existing things* do have existential import. However, universal claims about things that do not actually exist do not have existential import. This means that the claim "All unicorns are one-horned horses" does not imply that unicorns exist, while the claim "No frogs are vehicles" does imply that frogs do exist. This is important because the Aristotelian Square of Opposition is based on the presupposition that the claims to which it is applied do have existential import.

The Aristotelian Interpretation also assumes that a universal affirmative claim such as "All hot dog fans are people who love Frank 'n' Stein" asserts *both* that "All hot dog fans are people who love Frank 'n' Stein" *and* that "Some hot dog fans are people who love Frank 'n' Stein." It also assumes that a universal negative claim such as "No LAPD detectives are crooks" asserts *both* that "No LAPD detectives are crooks" *and* that "Some LAPD detectives are not crooks."

---

[1]This is named after the English mathematician George Boole (1815-1864), who championed this interpretation, although he was not the first person to champion it.
[2]This is named after the ancient Greek philosopher Aristotle (384-322 B.C.E.), who was the first person known to carefully discuss categorical syllogisms. Aristotle assumed the Aristotelian interpretation.

The Aristotelian Square of Opposition
Aristotelian Interpretation

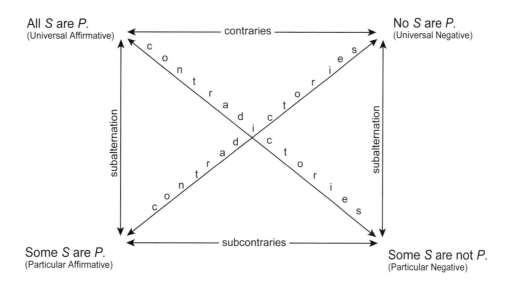

All *S* are *P*.
(Universal Affirmative)

No *S* are *P*.
(Universal Negative)

contraries

subalternation

contradictories

subalternation

subcontraries

Some *S* are *P*.
(Particular Affirmative)

Some *S* are not *P*.
(Particular Negative)

Corresponding claims are different claims with the same **subject** and predicate terms. For example, all the claims below are corresponding claims.

All people who work at Frank 'n' Stein stands are people under forty.

No people who work at Frank 'n' Stein stands are people under forty.

Some people who work at Frank 'n' Stein stands are people under forty.

Some people who work at Frank 'n' Stein stands are not people under forty.

In the Aristotelian interpretation, if a universal claim is true, the corresponding particular claims is true. This is called **subalternation**.

Examples of Subalternation Claims:

Universal Claims	Corresponding Particular Claims
All people who work at Frank 'n' Stein stands are people under forty.	Some people who work at Frank 'n' Stein stands are people under forty.
No people who work at Frank 'n' Stein stands are people under forty.	Some people who work at Frank 'n' Stein stands are not people under forty.

Subalternation only allows you to infer a particular given the truth of a universal. It does not allow you to infer the truth of a universal given its corresponding particular claim.

Two statements are **contraries** if it is possible for both to be false, but it is not possible for both to be true. In the Aristotelian interpretation, universal affirmative claims and universal negative claims are contraries.

Examples of Contrary Claims:

Universal Affirmative Claims	Universal Negative Claims
All Frank 'n' Stein customers are root beer fans.	No Frank 'n' Stein customers are root beer fans.
All Frank 'n' Stein customers are people who like chicken.	No Frank 'n' Stein customers are people who like chicken.

Note: The relation of contrariety *only* allows you to infer that one of a pair of corresponding universal claims is *false given that the other is true*. It *does not* allow you to draw any inferences if you are given that a universal claim is false.

Two statements are **subcontraries** if it is possible for both to be true, but it is not possible for both to be false. In the Aristotelian interpretation, particular affirmative claims and particular negative claims are subcontraries.

Examples of Subcontrary Claims:

Particular Affirmative Claims	Particular Negative Claims
Some Frank 'n' Stein employees are McGoo Candy employees.	Some Frank 'n' Stein employees are not McGoo Candy employees.
Some Frank 'n' Stein officers are hot dog fans.	Some Frank 'n' Stein officers are not hot dog fans.

Note: The relation of subcontrariety *only* allows you to infer that one of a pair of corresponding particular claims is *true given that the other is false*. It *does not* allow you to draw any inferences if you are given that a particular claim is true.

Aristotelian Contradictories are as they were under the Boolean interpretation. If a given claim is true, you can infer that its contradictory is false. If a given claim is false, you can infer that its contradictory is true.

Note: When using the Aristotelian Square of Opposition, the assumption is that the claims have existential import; in other words, the claims talk about things that really exist. When the claims are about things that do not exist, then the **existential fallacy** is committed. The existential fallacy occcurs whenever subalternation, contrary, and subcontrary relations are used correctly with claims about things that do *not* exist. Because of this the argument is invalid. For example:

> All vampires who eat chocolate are harmless creatures.
> So, some vampires who eat chocolate are harmless creatures.

This argument correctly uses subalternation. If vampires actually existed, then the argument would be valid; however, because vampires do not exist, the argument commits the existential fallacy and is invalid.

Sometimes we have an argument that appears to be valid, but we may not be sure that the things denoted by the critical term actually exist. For the argument to be valid, the critical term must denote at least one existing thing. In a categorical syllogism the critical term will be the subject term, the predicate term, or the middle term, depending upon the form of the argument.* The key here is that we may not have enough information to know if the things actually exist. In this case the argument is **conditionally valid** until we do know. Once we know, then we can determine if the argument is valid or commits the existential falacy and thus invalid. For example:

All space-sick astronauts are lazy people.
All lazy people are immoral people
_____
Some immoral people are space-sick astronauts.

Boolean Interpretation	Aristotelian Interpretation
The Boolean interpretation is neutral about existence, so whether or not space-sick astronauts exist is not important for the validoty of the argument. However, under the Boolean interpretation, this argument is invalid because the conclusion cannot be particular if both premises are universal. This violates Rule 6 which says that if there is a particular conclusion, then there must be exactly one particular premise. It also violates Rule 4 because it distributes the Major Term in the Major Premise, but the Predicate Term (the Major Term) is not distributed in the conclusion.	Under the Aristotelian interpretation, if some space-sick astronauts (our critical term in this argument) actually exist, then the argument is valid. If we do not now whether this is true, then the argument is conditionally valid. If we find out that no space-sick astronauts exist, then it commits the existential fallacy and is invalid. As we see, it is possible under the Aristotelian interpretation to have universal premises and a particular conclusion, but the argument must be about things that actually exist.

Examples of inferences using the Aristotelian square of opposition in Case 23:

a.	Given: "All Frank 'n' Stein employees are happy people" is true. It follows that "Some Frank 'n' Stein employees are happy people" by subalternation. It follows that its contrary, "No Frank 'n' Stein employess are happy people," is false. It follows that its contradictory, "Some Frank 'n' Stein employees are not happy people," is false.

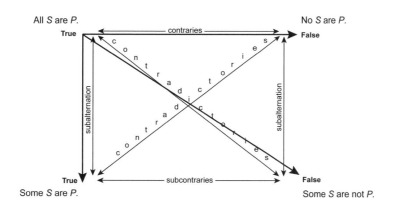

*Because we are only introducing the Aristotelian interpretation to you, it is not necessary to learn how to identify the critical term. What is important is that the Aristotelian interpretation allows for conditional validity.

b.	Given: "Some hot dog lovers are Frank 'n' Stein lovers" is true. It follows that its contradictory, "No hot dog lovers are Frank 'n' Stein lovers," is false. Nothing else follows. One cannot determine the truth-value of either "All hot dog lovers are Frank 'n' Stein lovers" or "Some hot dog lovers are not Frank 'n' Stein lovers."

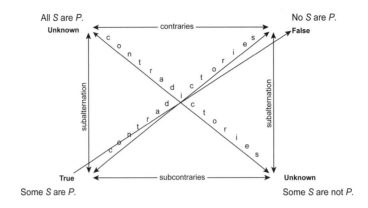

c.	Given: "No chicken lovers are Frank 'n' Stein lovers" is false. It follows that its contradictory, "Some chicken lovers are Frank 'n' Stein lovers," is true. Nothing else follows. One cannot determine the truth-value of either "All chicken lovers are Frank 'n' Stein lovers" or "Some chicken lovers are not Frank 'n' Stein lovers."

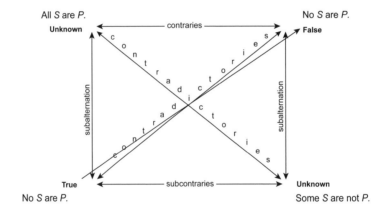

d.	Given: "Some Frank 'n' Stein lovers are not root beer lovers" is false. It follows that its subcontrary, "Some Frank 'n' Stein lovers are root beer lovers," is true. It follows that its contradictory, "All Frank 'n' Stein lovers are root beer lovers" is true. It follows that the contrary of "All Frank 'n' Stein lovers are root beer lovers," "No Frank 'n' Stein lovers are root beer lovers," is false.

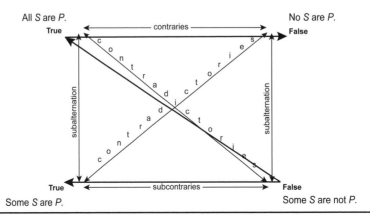

In Section 6.20 we will return to using the Boolean interpretation.

6.19 Exercise Given the Aristotelian Square of Opposition and given the truth-value of Claim 1, what can one infer regarding the truth value of Claim 2? Circle the correct answer. Writing the form of the claim is often helpful, but it is not required.

1. **Example:**
   1. "No Frank 'n' Stein officers are people who wear Dracula costumes to work" is true.
   2. "Some Frank 'n' Stein officers are not people who wear Dracula costumes to work."

   (a.) **Claim 2 is true.**
   b. Claim 2 is false.
   c. One can make no inference regarding the truth-value of Claim 2.

   No S are P.
   Some S are not P.

2.
   1. "Some people dressed like Dracula are not people who work at Frank 'n' Stein" is true.
   2. "Some people dressed like Dracula are people who work at Frank 'n' Stein."

   a. Claim 2 is true.
   b. Claim 2 is false.
   c. One can make no inference regarding the truth-value of Claim 2.

3.
   1. "All root beer lovers are people who would like Frank 'n' Stein" is true.
   2. "Some root beer lovers are people who would like Frank 'n' Stein."

   a. Claim 2 is true.
   b. Claim 2 is false.
   c. One can make no inference regarding the truth-value of Claim 2.

4.
   1. "Some people who wear monstrous costumes are people who work at Frank 'n' Stein" is true.
   2. "All people who wear monstrous costumes are people who work at Frank 'n' Stein."

   a. Claim 2 is true.
   b. Claim 2 is false.
   c. One can make no inference regarding the truth-value of Claim 2.

(Continued)

5. 1. "All Frank 'n' Stein fans are wild and crazy people" is true.
    2. "No Frank 'n' Stein fans are wild and crazy people."
    a. Claim 2 is true.
    b. Claim 2 is false.
    c. One can make no inference regarding the truth-value of Claim 2.

6. 1. "No Frank 'n' Stein fans are vegetarians" is true.
    2. "Some Frank 'n' Stein fans are vegetarians."
    a. Claim 2 is true.
    b. Claim 2 is false.
    c. One can make no inference regarding the truth-value of Claim 2.

7. 1. "Some vegetarians are people who might rob Frank 'n' Stein" is true.
    2. "Some vegetarians are not people who might rob Frank 'n' Stein."
    a. Claim 2 is true.
    b. Claim 2 is false.
    c. One can make no inference regarding the truth-value of Claim 2.

8. 1. "Some detectives are not people who find robbing a hot dog shop surprising" is true.
    2. "All detectives are people who find robbing a hot dog shop surprising."
    a. Claim 2 is true.
    b. Claim 2 is false.
    c. One can make no inference regarding the truth-value of Claim 2.

9. 1. "All Frank 'n' Stein employees are happy people" is false.
    2. "Some Frank 'n' Stein employees are happy people."
    a. Claim 2 is true.
    b. Claim 2 is false.
    c. One can make no inference regarding the truth-value of Claim 2.

10.   1. "No Frank 'n' Stein employees are people who
            carry swords" is false.
        2. "All Frank 'n' Stein employees are people who
            carry swords."
    a. Claim 2 is true.
    b. Claim 2 is false.
    c. One can make no inference regarding the truth-value
        of Claim 2.

11.   1. "Some robbers are people who hate root
            beer" is false.
        2. "Some robbers are not people who hate
            root beer."
    a. Claim 2 is true.
    b. Claim 2 is false.
    c. One can make no inference regarding the truth-value
        of Claim 2.

12.   1. "Some root beer salespeople are not people
            who like Frank 'n' Stein" is false.
        2. "No root beer salespeople are people who like
            Frank 'n' Stein."
    a. Claim 2 is true.
    b. Claim 2 is false.
    c. One can make no inference regarding the truth-value
        of Claim 2.

13.   1. "All root beer lovers are hot dog lovers"
            is false.
        2. "Some root beer lovers are not hot dog
            lovers."
    a. Claim 2 is true.
    b. Claim 2 is false.
    c. One can make no inference regarding the truth-value
        of Claim 2.

14.   1. "Some hot dog lovers are people who like
            fancy food" is false.
        2. "All hot dog lovers are people who like fancy
            food."
    a. Claim 2 is true.
    b. Claim 2 is false.
    c. One can make no inference regarding the truth-value
        of Claim 2.

(Continued)

15.
1. "Some people who dine at Frank 'n' Stein are not people who love squares of opposition" is false.

2. "Some people who dine at Frank 'n' Stein are people who love squares of opposition."

a. Claim 2 is true.

b. Claim 2 is false.

c. One can make no inference regarding the truth-value of Claim 2.

6.20 Toward Ordinary Language Syllogisms: Conversion, Obversion, and Contraposition Using the Boolean Interpretation

Two claims are **logically equivalent** if they are true under exactly the same circumstances. In this section we examine ways to change categorical claims. Some of these are logically equivalent to the original claims. Some are not.

To form the **converse** of a categorical claim, switch the positions of the subject and predicate terms. To decide whether a categorical claim is logically equivalent to its converse, look at a Venn diagram of the claim and its converse. If the claims are logically equivalent, the diagrams look alike.[3]

Claim	Claim's Converse
All humans are mammals.	All mammals are humans.
All S are P.	All P are S.
The converse of this claim is not logically equivalent to the claim.	

Claim	Claim's Converse
No humans are birds.	No birds are humans.
No S are P.	No P are S.
The converse of this claim is logically equivalent to the claim.	

---

[3] A categorical claim is logically equivalent to its converse if and only if either both terms are distributed in the claim or neither term is distributed in the claim.

Claim	**Claim's Converse**
Some humans are Texans.	Some Texans are humans.
Some S are P.	Some P are S.

The converse of the claim is logically equivalent to the claim.

Claim	**Claim's Converse**
Some humans are not Texans.	Some Texans are not humans.
Some S are not P.	Some P are not S.

The converse of the claim is not logically equivalent to the claim.

Conversion Summary

Form of claim	**Converse**
All S are P.	Not logically equivalent.
No S are P.	No P are S.
Some S are P.	Some P are S.
Some S are not P.	Not logically equivalent.

Examples of claims and their converses in Case 23:

a.	The converse of "All people who work in the Frank 'n' Stein stands are people who wear Frankenstein or Dracula costumes" is "All people who wear Frankenstein or Dracula costumes are people who work in the Frank 'n' Stein stands": " All S are F" is *not* ≡ "All F are S." The original claim is true (sentence 4). Its converse is false: Frankenstein and Dracula costumes are popular Halloween costumes. This shows that a universal affirmation claim is *not* logically equivalent to its converse.
b.	The converse of "No LAPD detectives are people who work in Frank 'n' Stein stands" is "No people who work in Frank 'n' Stein stands are LAPD detectives": "No L are P" ≡ "No P are L." Both claims say that the set of LAPD detectives is entirely distinct from the set of people who work in Frank 'n' Stein stands. The two claims are logically equivalent.
c.	The converse of "Some people who work in Frank 'n' Stein stands are people who wear Dracula costumes" is "Some people who wear Dracula costumes are people who work in Frank 'n' Stein stands": "Some F are D" ≡ "Some D are F." Both claims say that there is at least one thing that is both a person who works in a Frank 'n' Stein stand and a person who wears a Dracula costume. The two claims are logically equivalent.
d.	The converse of "Some hot dog stands are not Frank 'n' Stein stands" is "Some Frank 'n' Stein stands are not hot dog stands": "Some H are not F" is *not* ≡ "Some F are not H." The first claim is true. The second is false. A particular negative claim is *not* logically equivalent to its converse.

6.21 Exercise Is claim 1 logically equivalent to claim 2? Circle the correct answer. Writing the form of the claim is often helpful, but it is not required.

1. **Example:**
    1. Some Frank 'n' Stein employees are not McGoo Candy employees.
    2. Some McGoo Candy employees are not Frank 'n' Stein employees.
    a. Logically equivalent
    (b.) **Not logically equivalent**

Some S are not P.
Some P are not S.

2.
    1. All Frank 'n' Stein customers are people who like hot dogs.
    2. All people who like hot dogs are Frank 'n' Stein customers.
    a. Logically equivalent
    b. Not logically equivalent

3.
    1. No people who despise root beer are Frank 'n' Stein customers.
    2. No Frank 'n' Stein customers are people who despise root beer.
    a. Logically equivalent
    b. Not logically equivalent

4.
    1. Some robbers are Frank 'n' Stein employees.
    2. Some Frank 'n' Stein employees are robbers.
    a. Logically equivalent
    b. Not logically equivalent

5.
    1. No Frank 'n' Stein employees are employees of the LAPD.
    2. No employees of the LAPD are Frank 'n' Stein employees.
    a. Logically equivalent
    b. Not logically equivalent

6.
    1. Some Frank 'n' Stein customers are not hamburger fans.
    2. Some hamburger fans are not Frank 'n' Stein customers.
    a. Logically equivalent
    b. Not logically equivalent

7. 1. Some people who eat hot dogs are not health fanatics.
    2. Some health fanatics are not people who eat hot dogs.
a. Logically equivalent
b. Not logically equivalent

8. 1. All health food fanatics are people who avoid Frank 'n' Stein.
    2. All people who avoid Frank 'n' Stein are health food fanatics.
a. Logically equivalent
b. Not logically equivalent

9. 1. Some people who avoid hot dogs are people who do not watch their weight.
    2. Some people who do not watch their weight are people who avoid hot dogs.
a. Logically equivalent
b. Not logically equivalent

10. 1. No people who eat at Frank 'n' Stein are people who do not like root beer.
    2. No people who do not like root beer are people who eat at Frank 'n' Stein.
a. Logically equivalent
b. Not logically equivalent

The **complement of a set** is all things outside of that set. The complement of the set of all things that are hot dogs is the set of all things that are *not* hot dogs. The set of things that are not hot dogs includes hamburgers, tables, chairs, people, and anything else that is not a hot dog. The easiest way to form a **complementary term** is by adding the preface *non-* to a word. So, the complement of the term *hot dogs* is *non-hot dogs.*[4]

To form the **obverse of a claim,** change an affirmative claim to a negative claim or a negative claim to an affirmative claim *and* replace the predicate term with its complement. The obverse of any claim is logically equivalent to the original claim.

Claim	Claim's Obverse
Universal Affirmative	Universal Negative
All *S* are *P*.	No *S* are non-*P*.

Claim	Claim's Obverse
Universal Negative	Universal Affirmative
No *S* are *P*.	All *S* are non-*P*.

---

[4]Adding the prefaces *in-*, *im-*, and *un-* and the suffix *–less* often pick out the complement of a given class. For example, *incomplete* is the complement of the term *complete*. But *these* prefaces and suffixes do *not always* pick out the complement of a term. For example, *flammable* and *inflammable* are synonyms: They both pick out the class of objects capable of being burned. The term *invaluable* does *not* mean without value; rather it means extremely valuable, as does *priceless.*

Claim	Claim's Obverse
Particular Affirmative	Particular Negative
Some *S* are *P.*	Some *S* are not non-*P.*

Claim	Claim's Obverse
Particular Negative	Particular Affirmative
Some *S* are not *P.*	Some *S* are non-*P.*

Obversion Summary

Claim	Obverse Claim
All *S* are *P.*	No *S* are non-*P.*
No *S* are *P.*	All *S* are non-*P.*
Some *S* are *P.*	Some *S* are not non-*P.*
Some *S* are not *P.*	Some *S* are non-*P.*

Examples of obversion in Case 23:

a.	"All hot dog fans are people who like ketchup" is logically equivalent to its obverse, "No hot dog fans are non-people who like ketchup": "All H are P" ≡ "No H are non-P." The negative quantifier 'No' effectively negates the negative predicate 'non-people.'
b.	"No vegetarians are people who eat at Frank 'n' Stein" is logically equivalent to its obverse, "All vegetarians are non-people who eat at Frank 'n' Stein": "No V are P" ≡ "All V are non-P." Here the negative moves from the quantifier 'No' into the predicate 'non-P.'
c.	"Some hot dog lovers are mustard lovers" is logically equivalent to its obverse, "Some hot dog lovers are not non-mustard lovers": "Some H are M" ≡ "Some H are not non-M." Again, there is a double negation.
d.	"Some hot dog lovers are not mustard lovers" is logically equivalent to its obverse, "Some hot dog lovers are non-mustard lovers": "Some H are not M" ≡ "Some H are non-M." Here the 'not' in the given claim moves into the predicate 'non-M.'

Note: A speaker or writer can engage in both obversion and conversion with respect to a given categorical claim. Then the result might or might not be logically equivalent.

e.	"All Frank 'n' Stein fans are hot dog lovers" obverts to "No Frank 'n' Stein fans are non-hot dog lovers," which converts to "No non-hot dog lovers are Frank 'n' Stein fans": "All F are H" ≡ "No F are non-H" ≡ "No non-H are F." The initial observation yields a logically equivalent statement which is a universal negative. The converse of a universal negative is logically equivalent to the original universal negative. So, "All Frank 'n' Stein fans are hot dog lovers" is logically equivalent to "No non-hot dog lovers are Frank 'n' Stein fans": "All F are H" ≡ "No non-H are F."
f.	"Some Frank 'n' Stein fans are root beer lovers" obverts to "Some Frank 'n' Stein fans are not non-root beer lovers," which converts to "Some non-root beer lovers are not Frank 'n' Stein fans": "Some F are R" ≡ "Some F are not non-R" is *not* ≡ "Some non-R are not F." But a particular negative is *not* logically equivalent to its converse. So, "Some Frank 'n' Stein fans are root beer lovers" is *not* logically equivalent to "Some non-root beer lovers are not Frank 'n' Stein fans": "Some F are R" is *not* ≡ "Some non-R are not F."

6.22 Exercise Is the first claim logically equivalent to the second claim? Circle the correct answer. Writing the form of the claim is often helpful, but it is not required.

1. **Example:**
   No Frank 'n' Stein fans are vegetarians.
   All vegetarians are non-Frank 'n' Stein fans.
   (a.) **Logically equivalent**
   b. Not logically equivalent

   No S are P.
   All P are non-S.

2.   All Frank 'n' Stein regulars are young people.
   No Frank 'n' Stein regulars are non-young people.
   a. Logically equivalent
   b. Not logically equivalent

3.   Some Frank 'n' Stein employees are not robbers.
   Some robbers are non-Frank 'n' Stein employees.
   a. Logically equivalent
   b. Not logically equivalent

4.   Some people who wear Dracula costumes are hot dog sellers.
   Some people who wear Dracula costumes are not non-hot dog sellers.
   a. Logically equivalent
   b. Not logically equivalent

5.   All Frank 'n' Stein hot dogs are beef products.
   No Frank 'n' Stein hot dogs are non-beef products.
   a. Logically equivalent
   b. Not logically equivalent

6.   Some people who sell root beer are not Frank 'n' Stein employees.
   Some people who sell root beer are non-Frank 'n' Stein employees.
   a. Logically equivalent
   b. Not logically equivalent

(Continued)

7.	All vegetarians are people who avoid Frank 'n' Stein.
	No people who avoid Frank 'n' Stein are non-vegetarians.
	a. Logically equivalent
	b. Not logically equivalent

8.	Some people who wear Dracula costumes are not non-Frank 'n' Stein employees.
	Some Frank 'n' Stein employees are people who wear Dracula costumes.
	a. Logically equivalent
	b. Not logically equivalent

9.	Some root beer drinkers are not people who drink beer without the root.
	Some people who drink beer without the root are not non-root beer drinkers.
	a. Logically equivalent
	b. Not logically equivalent

10.	Some root beer drinkers are not hot dog eaters.
	Some non-hot dog eaters are root beer drinkers.
	a. Logically equivalent
	b. Not logically equivalent

To form the **contrapositive** of a categorical claim, replace *both* the subject and predicate terms with their complements and then convert the new claim. Some categorical claims are logically equivalent with their contrapositive and some are not.

You can see whether a categorical claim is logically equivalent to its contrapositive by comparing the Venn diagram of the claim and its contrapositive. If the claims are logically equivalent, the diagrams look alike.

Claim	Form	Claim's Contrapositive	Form
All ducks are birds.	All *S* are *P*.	All non-birds are non-ducks.	All non-*P* are non-*S*.
Logically Equivalent Claims			

Claim	Form	Claim's Contrapositive	Form
No dogs are birds.	No *S* are *P*.	No non-birds are non-dogs.	No non-*P* are non-*S*.
Not Logically Equivalent Claims			

Claim	Form	Claim's Contrapositive	Form
Some birds are little creatures.	Some *S* are *P*.	Some non-little creatures are non-birds.	Some non-*P* are non-*S*.
Not Logically Equivalent Claims			

Claim	Form	Claim's Contrapositive	Form
Some pigs are not large creatures.	Some *S* are not *P*.	Some non-large creatures are not non-pigs.	Some non-*P* are not non-*S*.

Logically Equivalent Claims

Contraposition Summary

Given claim	Contrapositive
All *S* are *P*.	All non-*P* are non-*S*.
No *S* are *P*.	Not logically equivalent.
Some *S* are *P*.	Not logically equivalent.
Some *S* are not *P*.	Some non-*P* are not non-*S*.

Examples of contraposition in Case 23:

a. "All hot dog lovers are ketchup fans" contraposes to "All non-ketchup fans are non-hot dog lovers," and the two claims are logically equivalent: "All H are K" ≡ "All non-K are non-H." The proof: "All hot dog lovers are ketchup fans" is logically equivalent to its obverse "No hot dog lovers are non-ketchup fans," which is logically equivalent to its converse "No non-ketchup fans are hot dog lovers," which is logically equivalent to its obverse "All non-ketchup fans are non-hot dog lovers": "All H are K" ≡ "No H are non-K" ≡ "No non-K are H" ≡ "All non-K are non-H."

b. "No hot dog lovers are vegetarians" contraposes to "No non-vegetarians are non-hot dog lovers," but the two claims are *not* logically equivalent: "No H are V" is *not* ≡ "No non-V are non-H." The proof: "No non-vegetarians are non-hot dog lovers is logically equivalent to its obverse "All non-vegetarians are hot dog lovers": "No non-V are non-H" ≡ "All non-V are H." Assume now that "No hot dog lovers are vegetarians": "No H are V" is true. But is "All non-V are H" also true? You probably know a person who is a non-vegetarian but does not like hot dogs. This means that "All non-V are H" is false and so is its equivalent "No non-V are non-H," which is the contraposition we started with. So, the contraposition cannot be logically equivalent to the given claim since the given claim is true and its contrapositive is false.

c. "Some hot dog lovers are ketchup fans" contraposes to "Some non-ketchup fans are non-hot dog lovers, but the two claims are *not* logically equivalent: "Some H are K" is *not* ≡ "Some non-K are non-H." While both the claim and its contrapositive might be true, they do *not* pick out the same objects. The first claim picks out something that is both a hot dog lover and a ketchup fan. The second claim picks out something that is neither a hot dog lover nor a ketchup fan.

d.	"Some hot dog lovers are not ketchup fans" contraposes to "Some non-ketchup fans are not non-hot dog lovers," and the two claims are logically equivalent: "Some H are not K" ≡ "Some non-K are not non-H." The proof: "Some hot dog lovers are not ketchun fans" is logically equivalent to its obverse "Some hot dog lovers are non-ketchup fans," which is logically equivalent to its converse "Some non-ketchup fans are hot dog lovers," which is logically equivalent to its obverse "Some non-ketchup fans are not non-hot dog lovers": "Some H are not K" ≡ "Some H are non-K" ≡ "Some non-K are H" ≡ "Some non-K are not non-H."

Note: As in example a and d above, a speaker or writer can engage in contraposition in conjunction with conversion and obversion.

e.	"Some hot dog lovers are not ketchup fans" is logically equivalent to "Some non-ketchup fans are hot dog lovers": "Some H are not K" ≡ "Some non-K are H." The proof: "Some hot dog lovers are not ketchup fans" is logically equivalent to its contrapositive "Some non-ketchup fans are not non-hot dog lovers," which is logically equivalent to its obverse "Some non-ketchup fans are hot dog lovers": "Some H are not K" ≡ "Some non-K are not non-H" ≡ "Some non-K are H."
f.	"No hot dog lovers are vegetarians" is *not* logically equivalent to "All non-vegetarians are hot dog lovers": "No H are V" is *not* ≡ "All non-V are H." The proof: "No hot dog lovers are vegetarians" is logically equivalent to its obverse "All hot dog lovers are non-vegetarians." But "All hot dog lovers are non-vegetarians" is *not* logically equivalent to "All non-vegetarians are hot dog lovers": "No H are V" ≡ "All H are non-V" is *not* ≡ "All non-V are H." So, since the obverse "All H are non-V" is *not* logically equivalent to "All non-V are H", its equivalent "No H are V", which is our original claim, cannot be logically equivalent to "All non-V are H" either.

6.23 Exercise Is Claim 1 logically equivalent to Claim 2? Circle the correct answer. Writing the form of the claim is often helpful, but it is not required.

1. **Example:**
   1. All Frank 'n' Stein employees are people who wear odd costumes.
   2. No non-people who wear odd costumes are Frank 'n' Stein employees.

   (a.) **Logically equivalent**
   b. Not logically equivalent

   All S are P.
   No non-P are S.

2.
   1. No Frank 'n' Stein employees are normal people.
   2. No non-normal people are non-Frank 'n' Stein employees.
   a. Logically equivalent
   b. Not logically equivalent

3.
   1. Some LAPD detectives are happy-go-lucky people.
   2. Some happy-go-lucky people are not non-LAPD detectives.
   a. Logically equivalent
   b. Not logically equivalent

4.
   1. Some LAPD detectives are not happy-go-lucky people.
   2. Some non-happy-go-lucky people are LAPD detectives.
   a. Logically equivalent
   b. Not logically equivalent

5.
   1. All Frank 'n' Stein employees are non-vegetarians.
   2. No vegetarians are Frank 'n' Stein employees.
   a. Logically equivalent
   b. Not logically equivalen

6.
   1. No Monster Dogs are small hot dogs.
   2. All small hot dogs are non-Monster Dogs.
   a. Logically equivalent
   b. Not logically equivalent

7.   1. Some Monster Dogs are complete meals.
        2. Some non-complete-meals are non-Monster Dogs.
  a. Logically equivalent
  b. Not logically equivalent

8.   1. Some Frank 'n' Stein officers are not happy-go-lucky people.
        2. Some happy-go-lucky people are not non-Frank 'n' Stein officers.
  a. Logically equivalent
  b. Not logically equivalent

9.   1. Some Frank 'n' Stein employees are not unhappy people.
        2. Some happy people are Frank 'n' Stein employees.
  a. Logically equivalent
  b. Not logically equivalent

10.   1. No unsolvable cases are cases the LAPD likes.
        2. All cases the LAPD likes are solvable cases.
  a. Logically equivalent
  b. Not logically equivalent

6.24 Ordinary Language Syllogisms

Categorical syllogisms in ordinary English can differ from standard form categorical syllogisms in three ways. (1) They might not contain standard form categorical claims. (2) They might contain more than three distinct terms, but can be restated so that they have exactly three terms. (3) They are not given in the standard order: Major Premise, Minor Premise, Conclusion. Restating an ordinary language syllogism in standard form is called **reducing** or **translating the syllogism to standard form**.

If the order in which a syllogism is stated is not Major Premise, Minor Premise, conclusion, it is easy to restate it in standard form. Find the conclusion. Identify the Major Term (**predicate term** of the conclusion) and the Minor Term (**subject term** of the conclusion). Determine which premise has each term. Restate the syllogism in standard form: Major Premise, Minor Premise, Conclusion.

Standard form categorical claims are stylistically stilted. They have a quantifier which is either *All*, *No*, or *Some*. They have a **subject term** and a **predicate term** which is either a noun or a noun with some modification (an adjective or a dependent clause). The **subject term** and **predicate term** are connected by a form of the verb *to be*. In ordinary English, categorical claims may lack any of these characteristics.

There are many ways to say *All*: *every, any, each, each and every*. If you find any of those words, replace the word with *All*. "Each and every robbery must have been an inside job" (sentence 17) is restated as "All robberies are events that must have been inside jobs." *A, An*, or *The* should be replaced by *All* if it is clear that the **subject term** refers to an entire set of objects. "A police detective is a police officer" means "All police detectives are police officers." Sometimes no quantifier is given: "LAPD detectives are police officers." In such a case, you need to find the intended meaning. Here it probably means "All LAPD detectives are police officers."[5]

None but and *only* also mark universal affirmative claims, *with a difference*. "None but police officers are LAPD detectives" means "All LAPD detectives are police officers." *Only* should be treated in the same way as *none but*, but with an *additional* difference. The claim "Only LAPD detectives are police officers" should *first* be restated as "All police officers are LAPD detectives." "All police officers are LAPD detectives" is false. So, convert the **subject** and **predicate term**s and ask whether the resulting claim is true. "All LAPD detectives are police officers" is true. So, "All LAPD detectives are police officers" is probably what was meant by "Only LAPD detectives are police officers." *Generally, determining whether a claim is true is a good guide to what is probably meant by a categorical claim that is not in standard form.*

There are several words that mean *No*: *not any, none, there is not a*. If you find any of these words, replace the word with *No*. "Not any active police officers are convicted criminals" is restated as "No active police officers are convicted criminals."

---

[5]The claim "LAPD detectives are police officers" is ambiguous. It could mean "All LAPD detectives are police officers" or "Some LAPD detectives are police officers." Both are true. Since the universal is true, one would typically assume the universal was meant. *The exception* to this general rule is when the claim is found in the context of an argument that would be valid only if the claim is interpreted as a particular affirmative. In *such a case* one should interpret it as "Some LAPD detectives are police officers."

There are several words that mean *Some*: *there is a*, *at least one*, *several*, *various*, *many*. If one finds any of those words, replace the word(s) with *Some*. "At least one Frank 'n' Stein employee is a robber" is restated as "Some Frank 'n' Stein employee is a robber." *A*, *An*, and *The* should be replaced by *Some* if the **subject term** *does not* pick out an entire set of things. "A Frank 'n' Stein employee is a robber" is restated as "Some Frank 'n' Stein employees are robbers."

In addition to the words for *Some*, there are several expressions that mean *Some ... are not*: *not every*, *not all*. "Not all Frank 'n' Stein employees are robbers" is restated as "Some Frank 'n' Stein employees are not robbers."

Some ordinary language quantifiers are complex. "All but (all except) company officers are robbery suspects" means *both* "All non-company-officers are robbery suspects" *and* "No company officers are robbery suspects." *Almost all*, *not quite all*, and *only some* mean both *some are* and *some are not*. So, "Almost all employees are robbery suspects" means *both* "Some employees are robbery suspects" and "Some employees are not robbery suspects."[6]

Some words make implicit reference to something. *Anyone* and *everyone* mean *all people*. *Someone* means *some people*. *Anytime* means *all times*. *Sometimes* means *some times*.

Examples of reducing quantifiers to standard form in Case 23:

a.	"Any Frank 'n' Stein employee is a robbery suspect" is restated as "All Frank 'n' Stein employees are robbery suspects."
b.	"Not any Monster Dogs are hamburgers" is restated as "No Monster Dogs are hamburgers."
c.	"At least one Monster Dog is a tasty treat" is restated as "Some Monster Dogs are tasty treats."
d.	"Not every Frank 'n' Stein officer is an honest person" is restated as "Some Frank 'n' Stein officers are not honest people."
e.	"Only some employees are robbery suspects" is restated as "Some employees are robbery suspects" and "Some employees are not robbery suspects."

Note: Some nonstandard quantifiers result in claims that do not include a form of the verb to be. In such a case one needs to restate the claim with a form of the verb to be and, perhaps, add a noun to the **predicate term**.

f.	"There is a glass of root beer that satisfies one's thirst" is restated as "Some glass of root beer is a thing that satisfies one's thirst."
g.	"There is not an employee who is not a suspect" is restated as "No employee is a person who is not a suspect." That statement obverts to "All employees are suspects."

---

[6]If a claim with a complex quantifier is the *premise* of a syllogism, one should choose whichever of the two claims made will yield a valid syllogism. If *neither* claim will yield a valid syllogism, one must show that *neither* will yield a valid syllogism. If a claim with a complex quantifier is the *conclusion* of an argument, disregard the claim that *does not follow* from the premises, since, *at most*, one claim follows from a pair of premises.

6.25 Exercise To which standard form categorical claim can the given claim be reduced? Circle the correct answer. Writing the form of the claim is often helpful, but it is not required.

1. **Example:**
   Given: Every Frank 'n' Stein employee is a happy person.
   (a.) **All Frank 'n' Stein employees are happy people.**
   b. No Frank 'n' Stein employees are happy people.
   c. Some Frank 'n' Stein employees are happy people.
   d. Some Frank 'n' Stein employees are not happy people.

   All S are P.

2. Given: Not every company officer is a happy person.
   a. All company officers are happy people.
   b. No company officers are happy people.
   c. Some company officers are happy people.
   d. Some company officers are not happy people.

3. Given: Not any company officer is a happy person.
   a. All company officers are happy people.
   b. No company officers are happy people.
   c. Some company officers are happy people.
   d. Some company officers are not happy people.

4. Given: Several employees are people who wear odd costumes.
   a. All employees are people who wear odd costumes.
   b. No employees are people who wear odd costumes.
   c. Some employees are people who wear odd costumes.
   d. Some employees are not people who wear odd costumes.

5. Given: Only some employees are suspects in the case.
   a. All suspects in the case are employees.
   b. Some employees are suspects in the case.
   c. Some employees are not suspects in the case.
   d. Both b and c

6. Given: None but workers at the stands are suspects in the case.
   a. All workers at the stands are suspects in the case.
   b. All suspects in the case are workers at the stands.
   c. No workers at the stands are suspects in the case.
   d. Some workers at the stands are not suspects in the case.

7. Given: There are not any police officers who are suspects in the case.
   a. All suspects in the case are not police officers.
   b. No police officers are suspects in the case.
   c. Some suspects in the case are not police officers.
   d. Some police officers are suspects in the case, and some police officers are not suspects in the case.

8. Given: Only some employees are robbery suspects.
   a. No employees are robbery suspects.
   b. Some employees are robbery suspects.
   c. Some employees are not robbery suspects.
   d. Both b and c

9. Given: Anyone who is employed by Frank 'n' Stein is a person who could have robbed the stands.
   a. All people who are employed by Frank 'n' Stein are people who could have robbed the stands.
   b. No people who are employed by Frank 'n' Stein are people who could have robbed the stands.
   c. Some people who are employed by Frank 'n' Stein are people who could have robbed the stands.
   d. Some people who are employed by Frank 'n' Stein are not people who could have robbed the stands.

10. Given: Every company officer is a person who would not have robbed the stands.
    a. All company officers are people who would have robbed the stands.
    b. No company officers are people who would have robbed the stands.
    c. Some company officers are people who would have robbed the stands.
    d. Some company officers are not people who would have robbed the stands.

Sometimes an ordinary language categorical claim does not contain a form of the verb *to be*. In such cases, add a form of the verb *to be*. This often requires you to add a noun to the resulting predicate or change the predicate to a noun phrase.

Examples of adding a form of to be in Case 23:

a.	"All Frank 'n' Stein employees love root beer" is restated as "All Frank 'n' Stein employees are people who like root beer" or as "All Frank 'n' Stein employees are root beer lovers."
b.	"Not any hot dog haters work at Frank 'n' Stein" is restated as "No hot dog haters are people who work at Frank 'n' Stein."
c.	"There is a robber who eats hot dogs" is restated as "Some robbers are hot dog eaters" or "Some robbers are people who eat hot dogs."
d.	"Not every Frank 'n' Stein employee enjoys standing for eight straight hours" is restated as "Some Frank 'n' Stein employees are not people who enjoy standing for eight hours."

6.26 Exercise To which standard form categorical claim can the given claim be reduced? Circle the correct answer. It is often helpful to write the form of the claim as you read each exercise, but it is not required.

1. **Example:**
   Given: Every Frank 'n' Stein employee drinks a gallon of root beer every day.
   All S are P.
   a. **All Frank 'n' Stein employees are people who drink a gallon of root beer every day.**
   b. All people who drink a gallon of root beer every day are Frank 'n' Stein employees.
   c. No Frank 'n' Stein employees are people who drink a gallon of root beer every day.
   d. Some people who drink a gallon of root beer every day are Frank 'n' Stein employees.

2. Given: Not any Frank 'n' Stein employees work for McGoo Candies.
   a. All Frank 'n' Stein employees are people who work for McGoo Candies.
   b. No Frank 'n' Stein employees are people who work for McGoo Candies.
   c. Some Frank 'n' Stein employees are people who work for McGoo Candies.
   d. Some Frank 'n' Stein employees are not people who work for McGoo Candies.

3. Given: Anyone who likes hot dogs will love eating at Frank 'n' Stein.
   a. All people who like hot dogs are people who will love eating at Frank 'n' Stein.
   b. No people who like hot dogs are people who will love eating at Frank 'n' Stein.
   c. Some people who like hot dogs are people who will love eating at Frank 'n' Stein.
   d. Some people who like hot dogs are not people who will love eating at Frank 'n' Stein.

4. Given: At least one LAPD detective enjoys dining at Frank 'n' Stein.
   a. All LAPD detectives are people who enjoy dining at Frank 'n' Stein.
   b. No LAPD detectives are people who enjoy dining at Frank 'n' Stein.
   c. Some LAPD detectives are people who enjoy dining at Frank 'n' Stein.
   d. Some LAPD detectives are not people who enjoy dining at Frank 'n' Stein.

(Continued)

5. Given: There is a robber who does not enjoy dining at Frank 'n' Stein.
    a. All robbers are people who enjoy dining at Frank 'n' Stein.
    b. No robbers are people who do not enjoy dining at Frank 'n' Stein.
    c. Some robbers are people who enjoy dining at Frank 'n' Stein.
    d. Some robbers are not people who enjoy dining at Frank 'n' Stein.

6. Given: Not all robbers enjoy root beer floats.
    a. No robbers are people who enjoy root beer floats.
    b. Some robbers are people who enjoy root beer floats.
    c. Some robbers are not people who enjoy root beer floats.
    d. Some people who enjoy root beer floats are not robbers.

7. Given: Many Frank 'n' Stein diners eat Monster Dogs to excess.
    a. All Frank 'n' Stein diners are people who eat too many Monster Dogs.
    b. No Frank 'n' Stein diners are people who eat too many Monster Dogs.
    c. Some Frank 'n' Stein diners are people who eat too many Monster Dogs.
    d. Some Frank 'n' Stein diners are not people who eat too many Monster Dogs.

8. Given: It is not the case that every robber eats hot dogs without mustard.
    a. All robbers are people who eat hot dogs with mustard.
    b. No robbers are people who eat hot dogs without mustard.
    c. Some robbers are people who eat hot dogs with mustard.
    d. Some robbers are not people who eat hot dogs with mustard.

9. Given: There are not any robbers who do not drink root beer.
   a. All robbers are root beer drinkers.
   b. No robbers are root beer drinkers.
   c. Some robbers are root beer drinkers.
   d. Some robbers are not root beer drinkers.

10. Given: Almost all robbers who dress in Frankenstein costumes look ridiculous.
   a. Some ridiculous-looking robbers are not people who dress in Frankenstein costumes.
   b. Some robbers who dress in Frankenstein costumes are people who look ridiculous.
   c. Some robbers who dress in Frankenstein costumes are not people who look ridiculous.
   d. Both b and c

Sometimes a categorical syllogism appears to have more than three terms, but some terms are synonyms or antonyms.* If there are synonyms, we can replace one synonym with the other. Sometimes we replace *near* synonyms with one another as in the case with canines and dogs. The set of canines includes wolves and fox and so is broader than the set of dogs. However, if we find a syllogism in which one premise refers to dogs and the other premise or conclusion refers to canines, then they should be treated as synonyms. Dealing with antonyms requires that we obvert (or convert and then obvert). Once we have obverted, we have a synonym.

Examples of syllogisms containing synonyms or antonyms in Case 23:

a.	All robbers are undesirable people. All people who steal from Frank 'n' Stein are crooks.<hr>So, no people who steal from Frank 'n' Stein are desirable people. *Robbers* and *crooks* are synonyms. So, one replaces *robbers* with *crooks*, or *crooks* with *robbers* . All robbers are undesirable people. All people who steal from Frank 'n' Stein are robbers.<hr>So, no people who steal from Frank 'n' Stein are desirable people. The major premise contains the term *undesirable people*. The conclusion contains the term *desirable people*. The two terms are complementary (antonyms). So, we obvert. If we obvert the major premise, the resulting syllogism is: No robbers are desirable people. All people who steal from Frank 'n' Stein are robbers.<hr>So, no people who steal from Frank 'n' Stein are desirable people. If we obvert the conclusion, the resulting syllogism is: All robbers are undesirable people. All people who steal from Frank 'n' Stein are robbers.<hr>So, all people who steal from Frank 'n' Stein are undesirable people. While both are acceptable, the first may be preferable. It is typically clearer if one reduces terms to a *positive* form (*desirable people*) rather than a negative form (*undesirable people*) when it is possible to do so. There are cases in which it is impossible to avoid the negative form of a term.

*A synonym is a word or phrase that means exatly the same or nearly the same as another word or phrase; for example, *shut* is a synonym of *close*. An antonym is a word that means the exact opposite of another word; for example, *good* is an antonym of *bad*.

b.	Anyone who robs Frank 'n' Stein is a desperate person. Anyone who does not steal from Frank 'n' Stein is happy. None but joyous people are not people in great need. *Anyone* means the premises are universal affirmative claims concerning people. *None but* means the conclusion is a universal affirmative, but we convert the terms. *Robs* and *steals* are synonyms, as are *happy people* and *joyous people*, and *desperate people* and *people in great need*. So, an initial step toward a reduction to standard form is: All people who rob Frank 'n' Stein are desperate people. All people who do not rob Frank 'n' Stein are happy people. All people who are not desperate are happy people. Of course, we still have five terms: *people who rob Frank 'n' Stein*, *people who do not rob Frank 'n' Stein*, *desperate people*, *people who are not desperate*, and *happy people*. If we contrapose the second premise and the conclusion, we reduce it to standard form: All people who rob Frank 'n' Stein are desperate people. All non-happy people are people who rob Frank 'n' Stein. All non-happy people are people who are desperate. The subject term is *non-happy people*. In *this* argument it is impossible to reduce all terms to positive form.
c.	**Singular propositions** concern one specific person or thing. "Stephanie Wise is a detective" is an example of a singular proposition. We treat singular propositions as if they are universal propositions. So, if we are given: All LAPD detectives are city employees. Stephanie Wise is an LAPD detective. So, Stephanie Wise is a city employee. We would treat both the minor premise and the conclusion as universal claims: All LAPD detectives are city employees. (All) Stephanie Wise is an LAPD detective. So, (all) Stephanie Wise is a city employee.

6.27 Exercise Circle the standard form categorical syllogism that matches the syllogism, then decide if the syllogism is valid. Writing the form of the claim is often helpful, but it is not required.

1. **Example:**
   Everyone who likes hot dogs will love Frank 'n' Stein.
   Someone who drinks root beer is a hot dog fan.
   ────────────────────────────────────
   So, there is a root beer drinker who will be very favorably disposed toward Frank 'n' Stein.

   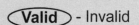

   All M are P.
   Some S are M.
   Some S are P.

   (a.) **All hot dog fans are people who will love Frank 'n' Stein.**
      Some root beer drinkers are hot dog fans.
      ────────────────────────────────────
      So, some root beer drinkers are people who will love Frank 'n' Stein.

   b. No hotdog fans are Frank 'n' Stein fans.
      Some root beer fans are hot dog fans.
      ────────────────────────────────────
      So, no root beer fans are Frank 'n' Stein fans.

   c. All people who love Frank 'n' Stein are hot dog fans.
      Some hot dog fans are root beer drinkers.
      ────────────────────────────────────
      So, some root beer fans are Frank 'n' Stein fans.

   d. All people who like hot dogs are people who will love Frank 'n' Stein.
      Some root beer fans are not hot dog fans.
      ────────────────────────────────────
      So, some root beer fans are not people who will love Frank 'n' Stein.

   This categorical syllogism is:

   (Valid) - Invalid

2. Everyone who works at Frank 'n' Stein loves hot dogs. Some Frank 'n' Stein employees also works at McGoo Candies.
_____
So, at least some McGoo Candies employees are hot dog fans.

a. No Frank 'n' Stein employees are hot dog fans. Some Frank 'n' Stein employees are McGoo Candies employees.
_____
So, some McGoo Candies employees are hot dog fans.

b. No Frank 'n' Stein employees are non-hot dog fans. All Frank 'n Stein employees are McGoo Candies employees.
_____
So, no McGoo Candies employees are non-hot dog fans.

c. All Frank 'n' Stein employees are hot dog fans. Some Frank 'n' Stein employees are McGoo Candies employees.
_____
So, some McGoo Candies employees are hot dog fans.

d. Some Frank 'n' Stein employees are not hot dog fans. Some Frank 'n' Stein employees are McGoo Candies employees.
_____
So, some McGoo Candies employees are not hot dog fans.

This categorical syllogism is:

Valid - Invalid

3. Every unemployed teen is a robber. There is an employed teen who is not a corporate executive.
_____
So, at least one corporate executive is not a crook.

a. No robbers are employed teens. Some employed teens are not corporate executives.
_____
So, some corporate executives are not robbers.

b. All non-robbers are employed teens. Some employed teens are not corporate executives.
_____
So, some corporate executives are non-robbers.

c. All robbers are unemployed teens. Some corporate executives are not unemployed teens.
_____
So, some corporate executives are not robbers.

d. Some employed teens are not robbers. Some employed teens are corporate executives.
_____
So, some corporate executives are not robbers.

This categorical syllogism is:

Valid - Invalid

(Continued)

4. No robbers are root beer fans.
    Some non-root beer fans are not non-Frank 'n' Stein employees.
    _____
    So, some Frank 'n' Stein employees are not robbers.

    a. All root beer fans are robbers.
        Some root beer fans are Frank 'n' Stein employees.
        _____
        So, some Frank 'n' Stein employees are not robbers.

    b. All non-root beer fans are robbers.
        Some non-root beer fans are not Frank 'n' Stein employees.
        _____
        So, some Frank 'n' Stein employees are not robbers.

    c. No robbers are root beer fans.
        Some Frank 'n' Stein employees are not root beer fans.
        _____
        So, some Frank 'n' Stein employees are not robbers.

    d. All robbers are non-root beer fans.
        Some non-root beer fans are not Frank 'n' Stein employees.
        _____
        So, some Frank 'n' Stein employees are not robbers.

This categorical syllogism is:

Valid - Invalid

5. There is no detective who is not puzzled.
    Everyone who is not a detective drinks root beer.
    _____
    So, anyone who doesn't drink root beer is puzzled.

    a. No detectives are puzzled people.
        All detectives are root beer drinkers.
        _____
        So, no root beer drinkers are puzzled people.

    b. All detectives are puzzled people.
        All non-root beer drinkers are detectives.
        _____
        So, all non-root beer drinkers are puzzled people.

    c. All detectives are puzzled people.
        No detectives are root beer drinkers.
        _____
        So, no root beer drinkers are puzzled people.

    d. No detectives are puzzled people.
        All root beer drinkers are detectives.
        _____
        So, no root beer drinkers are puzzled people.

This categorical syllogism is:

Valid - Invalid

6. There is a robber who left a fingerprint at a Frank 'n' Stein stand.
   Someone whose fingerprint was found at a Frank 'n' Stein stand is employed by Frank 'n' Stein.

   So, someone who works at Frank 'n' Stein does not refrain from theft.

   a. Some robber is a person who left a fingerprint at a Frank 'n' Stein stand.
      Some person who left a fingerprint at a Frank 'n' Stein stand is a Frank 'n' Stein employee.

      So, some Frank 'n' Stein employee is a robber.

   b. No robber is a person who left a fingerprint at a Frank 'n' Stein stand.
      Some person who left a fingerprint at a Frank 'n' Stein stand is a Frank 'n' Stein employee.

      So, some Frank 'n' Stein employee is a robber.

   c. Some person who left a fingerprint at a Frank 'n' Stein stand is a robber.
      Some Frank 'n' Stein employee is a person who left a fingerprint at a Frank 'n' Stein stand.

      So, some Frank 'n' Stein employee is a robber.

   d. All people who left a fingerprint at a Frank 'n' Stein stand are robbers.
      Some people who left a fingerprint at a Frank 'n' Stein stand is a Frank 'n' Stein employee.

      So, some Frank 'n' Stein employees are robbers.

This categorical syllogism is:

Valid - Invalid

(Continued)

7. Any wiener sold at Frank 'n' Stein makes one's mouth water.
   Not any frankfurter that causes salivation is untasty.
   _____
   Hence, every delicious hot dog is a frankfurter that can be purchased at Frank 'n' Stein.

   a. All hot dogs that make one's mouth water are hot dogs sold at Frank 'n' Stein.
      All tasty hot dogs are hot dogs that make one's mouth water.
      _____
      Hence, all tasty hot dogs are hot dogs sold at Frank 'n' Stein.

   b. No frankfurters sold at Frank 'n' Stein are frankfurters that make one's mouth water.
      No frankfurters that make one's mouth water are untasty.
      _____
      Hence, no untasty frankfurters are frankfurters sold at Frank 'n' Stein.

   c. All hot dogs sold at Frank 'n' Stein are hot dogs that make one's mouth water.
      No hot dog that makes one's mouth water is tasty.
      _____
      Hence, all tasty hot dogs are hot dogs sold at Frank 'n' Stein.

   d. All hot dogs sold at Frank 'n' Stein are hot dogs that make one's mouth water.
      All hot dogs that makes one's mouth water are delicious hot dogs.
      _____
      Hence, all delicious hot dogs are hot dogs sold at Frank 'n' Stein.

This categorical syllogism is:

Valid - Invalid

8. There is a crook who robs hot dog stands.
    Any robber who pulls stickups at wiener emporiums is desperate.
    _____
    Ergo, a person beyond hope is a crook.

    a. All crooks who rob hot dog stands are robbers.
        All crooks who rob hot dog stands are desperate people.
        _____
        Ergo, all desperate people are robbers.

    b. Some crooks are people who rob hot dog stands.
        All people who rob hot dog stands are desperate people.
        _____
        Ergo, some desperate people are crooks.

    c. Some crook is a crook who robs hot dog stands.
        All crooks who rob hot dog stands are desperate people.
        _____
        Ergo, all desperate people are crooks who rob hot dog stands.

    d. All crooks who rob hot dog stands are crooks.
        Some crooks who rob hot dogs stands are people who are beyond hope.
        _____
        Ergo, some people who are beyond hope are crooks.

This categorical syllogism is:

Valid - Invalid

(Continued)

9. There is not a purveyor of fast food who does not covet riches.
    Anyone who wants to be rich is an unscrupulous scoundrel.
    ───
    So, some persons restrained by a sense of right and wrong are people who sell fast food.

    a. No person who sells fast food is a person who wants to be rich.
        All persons who want to be rich are unscrupulous scoundrels.
        ───
        So, some unscrupulous scoundrels are persons who want to be rich.

    b. All persons who sell fast food are persons who covet riches.
        No persons who covet riches are unscrupulous people.
        ───
        So, some unscrupulous people are not persons who sell fast food.

    c. Some persons who sell fast food are not people who covet riches.
        All people who covet riches are unscrupulous scoundrels.
        ───
        So, some unscrupulous scoundrels are not people who sell fast food.

    d. All people who sell fast food are people who want to be rich.
        No people who want to be rich are people restrained by a sense of right and wrong.
        ───
        So, some people who are restrained by a sense of right and wrong are people who sell fast food.

This categorical syllogism is:

Valid - Invalid

© 2011 The Critical Thinking Co.™ • www.CriticalThinking.com • 800-458-4849

10. Almost all LAPD detectives are honest people.
No people whose morals are arrow-straight are
disreputable people.

So, there is a person of good repute who is an
LAPD detective.

   a. Some LAPD detectives are not honest people.
No honest people are people with a good reputation.

So, some people with a good reputation are
LAPD detectives.

   b. Some LAPD detectives are honest people.
All honest people are people with a good reputation.

So, some people with a good reputation are
LAPD detectives.

   c. All LAPD detectives are honest people.
All honest people are people with a good reputation.

So, all people with a good reputation are
LAPD detectives.

   d. No LAPD detectives are honest people.
All people with a good reputation are honest people.

So, no people with a good reputation are
LAPD detectives.

This categorical syllogism is:

Valid - Invalid

Some ordinary language syllogisms have universal premises and a particular conclusion.

Example 1: Terms have no existential import   Example 2: Terms have existential import

All mermaids are half-human sea creatures.   All cats are animals.

No unicorns are half-human sea creatures.   All lions are cats.
_____   _____

Some unicorns are not mermaids.   Some lions are animals.

According to the **Boolean interpretation**, which follows the rules in Section 6.6 and Venn diagrams in section 6.11, no such syllogism is valid. This means that both Examples 1 and 2 are invalid because a particular conclusion cannot follow from two universal premises.[1]

According to the **Aristotelian interpretation**, if all the terms in the syllogism refer to things that exist,[2] then it is possible that a particular conclusion *might* follow from universal premises and we can proceed to test the syllogism for validity. This is sometimes called conditional validity.

Example 1: Terms have no existential import
This syllogism is invalid since mermaids, half-human sea creatures, and unicorns do not exist. This is an example of an argument committing the existential fallacy. We have no need to test for validity since we know that the lack of existential import makes the argument invalid.

Example 2: Terms have existential import
Because these terms refer to things that exist, we can test the syllogism for validity. To do this we will need to treat one of the universal premises as *if* it was a particular premise. We are concerned about the correct distribution of the terms:[3]

1. Check the conclusion to see if the Subject Term and the Predicate Term are distributed.
2. Check the premises to see that the Major Term and the Minor Term have the same distribution as in the conclusion.
3. Check the Middle Term to see if it is distributed only once.
4. Which premise has the problem? The troublesome premise will be the one we change. Our goal is correct distribution. This may mean using conversion, obversion, or contraposition. The argument is valid **only** if we have correct distribution of the terms. If we do not have correct distribution, then the argument is invalid.

In Example 2:
1. Neither the Subject Term (lions) nor the Predicate Term (animals) is distributed.
2. In the Major Premise, the Major Term (animals) is not distributed. Correct.
   In the Minor Premise, the Minor Term (lions) is distributed. Wrong!
3. The Middle Term (cats) is distributed only once. Correct
4. The premise with the problem is the Minor Premise, so we need to change this premise to its corresponding particular premise, in this case, a particular affirmative premise:
   Some lions are cats. The test shows us that Example 2 is a valid argument.

_____

[1] See Rule 6 on page 320.
[2] There must be at least one member in each of the classes identified in the claims.
[3] See pages 313–315.

Examples of conditionally valid categorical syllogisms in Case 23:

a. All LAPD detectives are honest people.
All honest people are trustworthy people.

So, some trustworthy people are LAPD detectives.

All (L) are H.   L is distributed, but it should not be distributed.

All (H) are T.   H is distributed only once. No problem.

Some T are L.   Neither T nor L are distributed.

The problem is found in the Major Premise because the Major Term (L) is distributed when it should not be distributed. So, we replace the Major Premise with its corresponding particular claim, which is a particular affirmative claim, as follows:

Some LAPD detectives are honest people.   Some L are H.
All honest people are trustworthy people.   All H are T.
Some trustworthy people are LAPD detectives.   Some T are L.

The argument is **valid**.

b. All people who rob Frank 'n' Stein are Frank 'n' Stein employees.
No Frank 'n' Stein employees are people who make minimum wage.

Some people who make minimum wage are not people who rob Frank 'n' Stein.

All (R) are E.   R is distributed, and it should be distributed.

All (E) are (M).   E is distributed only once. M should not be distributed.

Some M are not (R).   R is distributed, so it must be distributed in the Major Premise.

The problem occurs in the Minor Premise because the Minor Term (M) should not be distributed. We need a particular negative claim, but we will need to convert the premise so that the Middle Term (E) remains distributed:

All people who rob Frank 'n' Stein are Frank n' Stein employees.   All R are E.
Some people who make mimimum wage are not Frank 'n' Stein employees.   Some M are not E.
Some people who make minimum wage are not people who rob Frank 'n' Stein.   Some M are not A.

The argument is **valid**.

6.28 Exercise Using the Aristotelian interpretation and assuming that Case 23 (p. 357) is about things that actually exist, which of the following can be treated as valid categorical syllogisms in everyday contexts? Circle the correct answer. Writing the form of the claim is often helpful, but it is not required.

1. **Example:**
   All LAPD detectives are city employees.
   All police investigating the Frank 'n' Stein robberies are LAPD detectives.
   So, some police investigating the Frank 'n' Stein robbers are city employees.
   a. **Valid**
   b. Invalid

All M are P.
Some S are M.*
Some S are P.

*S should not be distributed, so the Minor Premise was replaced by its correspondingly particular claim.

2. All LAPD detectives are intelligent people.
   All LAPD detectives are city employees.
   So, some city employees are intelligent people.
   a. Valid
   b. Invalid

3. No LAPD detectives are zgwufs.
   All zgwufs are trolls.
   So, some trolls are LAPD detectives.
   a. Valid
   b. Invalid

4. No Frank 'n' Stein employees work for the LAPD.
   All LAPD employees are city employees.
   So, some city employees are not Frank 'n' Stein employees.
   a. Valid
   b. Invalid

5. Not any Frank 'n' Stein employees are police officers.
   Every Frank 'n' Stein employee is a teenager.
   So, there is a teenager who is not a police officer.
   a. Valid
   b. Invalid

6. There is no zigwuff that works for the LAPD.
   Every agelgas works for the LAPD.
   So, some agelgas is a zigwuff.
   a. Valid
   b. Invalid

7. Not any homeless people work for the LAPD.
    Every LAPD detective works for the LAPD.
    _____
    So, some LAPD detective is not a homeless person.
    a. Valid
    b. Invalid

8. Not every homeless person is a Frank 'n'
    Stein employee.
    There is not a homeless person who works for
    the LAPD.
    _____
    So, there is a person who works for the LAPD who is
    not a Frank 'n' Stein employee.
    a. Valid
    b. Invalid

9. No Frank 'n' Stein employees are mischievous spirits.
    All goblins are mischievous spirits.
    _____
    So, there is a goblin that is not a Frank 'n' Stein
    employee.
    a. Valid
    b. Invalid

10. Not any teenager is employed by the LAPD.
    Each and every Frank 'n' Stein waitperson is
    a teenager.
    _____
    Ergo, at least one Frank 'n' Stein waitperson is not
    employed by the LAPD.
    a. Valid
    b. Invalid

| CASE 24 | City of Los Angeles Police Department |

[1]There was a series of robberies at all the high school band rooms throughout the city the day before the football games. [2]Mrs. North, the City School superintendent, said, "In each break-in, two people entered the room. [3]The fat one was dressed like the tuba player and carried a tuba, and the thin one was dressed like a drum major. [4]No one thought much of the outfits, since that's how all the band students dress. [5]Sometimes they'd come shortly before the change of classes. [6]They'd bring a note from the school principal, dismissing them from class early and take all the musical instruments onto a rented truck to be taken to the next football game. [7]Sometimes they posed as new students who were applying to get into the band. [8]Only in the last two break-ins did they use guns and demand all the money from the band boosters' barbecued chicken sales."

[9]Detective Wise interviewed Mr. Musicmaker, the director of band at North City High School. [10]"All our robberies were events that occurred during the afternoon. [11]So, all cases in which band instruments and receipts from chicken sales were taken were events that occurred during the afternoon."

[12]Martin Soprano, who was the assistant to the director of band at South City High School, said, "No robberies were events that occurred during the morning or lunch practice times. [13]But some events that occurred during the morning and lunch practice times were events in which tuba players and drum majors were present. [14]So, I'll let you draw your own conclusions."

[15]Violet Scale, the director of band at West City High School, pointed out in a strong voice, "No break-in was carefully planned. [16]No break-in could be carelessly planned unless it was an outside job. [17]So, each and every break-in must have been an outside job."

[18]Detective Wise considered all the evidence. [19]All the band members practice in their band uniforms the day before football games. [20]So, at least some of the students were in their band uniforms that day for practice. [21]No students dress in the typical clothing worn by teachers. [22]So, it is not the case that some students were practicing in clothing typically worn by teachers. [23]If we know that some of the students were not the criminals, does it follow that no students were criminals?

6.29 Review Exercise Circle the answer that follows from each argument.

1. **Example:**
   All criminals are worthy of punishment.
   Some jewel thieves are criminals.
   _____
   So, ...
   a. **some jewel thieves are worthy of punishment.**
   b. some jewel thieves are not worthy of punishment.
   c. all jewel thieves are worthy of punishment.
   d. nothing follows.

   All M are P.
   Some S are M.
   Some S are P.

2. Some robbers are people who wear band uniforms.
   Some people who wear band uniforms are
   not musicians.
   _____
   So, ...
   a. some musicians are not robbers.
   b. some robbers are not musicians
   c. some robbers are musicians.
   d. nothing follows.

3. No robbers are high school principals.
   All high school principals are people with
   graduate degrees.
   _____
   So, ...
   a. no robbers are people with graduate degrees.
   b. all people people with graduate degrees are robbers.
   c. some robbers are not people with graduate degrees.
   d. nothing follows.

4. Some robbers are not punished.
   All robbers are lawbreakers.
   _____
   So, ...
   a. no lawbreakers are punished.
   b. some people who are punished are not law-
      breakers.
   c. some lawbreakers are not punished.
   d. nothing follows.

5. Some people in jail are not troublemakers.
   No people in jail are people who are wearing
   band uniforms.
   _____
   So, ...
   a. some people wearing band uniforms are
      not troublemakers.
   b. some people wearing band uniforms are troublemakers.
   c. all people wearing ban uniforms are people in jail.
   d. nothing follows.

(Continued)

6. Some football fans are people in band uniforms.
   All football fans are people who love touchdowns.

   So, ...
   a. all people who love touchdowns are people in band uniforms.
   b. some people in band uniforms are not people who love touchdowns.
   c. some people who love touchdowns are people in band uniforms.
   d. nothing follows.

7. Some people who enjoy kicking soccer balls are not football fans.
   All people who love soccer are people who enjoy kicking soccer balls.

   So, ...
   a. some people who enjoy kicking soccer balls are not football fans.
   b. some football fans are not people who enjoy kicking soccer balls
   c. some people who enjoy kicking soccer balls are football fans.
   d. nothing follows.

8. No vegetarians are people who eat meat.
   Some people who eat vegetables are people who eat meat.

   So, ...
   a. some people who eat vegetables are people who eat meat.
   b. some people who eat vegetables are not vegetarians.
   c. some vegetarians are not people who eat vegetables.
   d. nothing follows.

9. All band members are people who dress in band uniforms.
   No phone company workers are people who dress in band uniforms

   So, ...
   a. no phone company workers are band members.
   b. all band members are phone company workers.
   c. some phone company workers are band members.
   d. nothing follows.

10. All people who dress in band uniforms are music lovers.
    Some electricians are not people who dress in
    band uniforms.
    So, ...
    a. some electricians are not music lovers.
    b. some music lovers are not electricians.
    c. no electricians are music lovers.
    d. nothing follows.

6.30 Review Exercise Circle the missing premise that will produce a valid categorical
        syllogism, or circle "d."

1. **Example**:
   All band members are music lovers.
   So, some music lovers are not football players.
   a. Some high school students are not band members.
   b. **Some band members are not football players.**
   c. No band members are football players.
   d. No premise will yield a valid syllogism.

   All M are S.
   Some M are not P.
   Some S are not P.

2. No drum major is a person who hates a baton.
   So, some high school student is not a person who hates
   a baton.
   a. Some drum major is a high school student.
   b. No drum major is a high school student.
   c. Some high school student is not a drum major.
   d. No premise will yield a valid syllogism.

3. All band members are suspects in the robberies.
   So, some band members are people who will
   be questioned.
   a. Some people who will be questioned are suspects in
      the robberies.
   b. Some suspects in the robberies are not people who
      will be questioned.
   c. All people who will be questioned are suspects in
      the robberies.
   d. No premise will yield a valid syllogism.

4. Some soccer players are football players.
   So, no football player is a trombone player.
   a. No trombone player is a soccer player.
   b. Some trombone player is not a soccer player.
   c. All soccer players are trombone players.
   d. No premise will yield a valid syllogism.

(Continued)

5. Some crooks are robbers.

   So, some robbers are devious people.
   a. All devious people are crooks.
   b. All crooks are devious people.
   c. Some crooks are devious people.
   d. No premise will yield a valid syllogism.

6. No devious people are honest people.

   So, no truthful people are devious people.
   a. Some truthful people are honest.
   b. All honest people are truthful people.
   c. All truthful people are honest people.
   d. No premise will yield a valid syllogism.

7. No college students are members of the high school band.

   So, some members of the high school band are not tuba players.
   a. All college students are tuba players.
   b. Some tuba players are college students.
   c. Some tuba players are not college students.
   d. No premise will yield a valid syllogism.

8. Some musicians are not composers.

   So, some musicians are not writers of their own music.
   a. All writers of their own music are composers.
   b. All composers are writers of their own music.
   c. No writers of their own music are composers.
   d. No premise will yield a valid syllogism.

9. No teachers at North City HS are robbers.

   So, no English teachers at North City HS are robbers.
   a. Some English teachers at North City HS are teachers at North City HS.
   b. All teachers at North City HS are English teachers at North City HS.
   c. All English teachers at North City HS are teachers at North City HS.
   d. No premise will yield a valid syllogism.

10. All musicians are creative people.

    So, all tuba players are musicians.
    a. All tuba players are creative people.
    b. All creative people are tuba players.
    c. Some tuba players are not creative people.
    d. No premise will yield a valid syllogism.

6.31 Review Exercise Given the Boolean Square of Opposition and given the truth-value of the first claim, what should you infer regarding the truth value of the second claim? Circle the correct answer.

1. **Example:**
    "Some musicians are tuba players" is true.
    "All musicians are tuba players."
    a. Claim 2 is true.
    b. Claim 2 is false.
    c. **One can make no inference regarding the truth-value of Claim 2.**

    Some S are P.
    All S are P.

2.   "Some musicians are not trombone players" is true.
        "All musicians are trombone players."
    a. Claim 2 is true.
    b. Claim 2 is false.
    c. One can make no inference regarding the truth-value of Claim 2.

3.   "No football players are band members" is true.
        "Some football players are band members."
    a. Claim 2 is true.
    b. Claim 2 is false.
    c. One can make no inference regarding the truth-value of Claim 2.

4.   "All band members are creative" is true.
        "No band members are creative."
    a. Claim 2 is true.
    b. Claim 2 is false.
    c. One can make no inference regarding the truth-value of Claim 2.

5.   "All people who wear uniforms are police officers" is false.
        "Some people who wear uniforms are not police officers."
    a. Claim 2 is true.
    b. Claim 2 is false.
    c. One can make no inference regarding the truth-value of Claim 2.

(Continued)

6. "Some band uniforms are not clean" is false.
"All band uniforms are clean."
a. Claim 2 is true.
b. Claim 2 is false.
c. One can make no inference regarding the truth-value of Claim 2.

7. "Some band uniforms are not blue" is false.
"Some band uniforms are blue."
a. Claim 2 is true.
b. Claim 2 is false.
c. One can make no inference regarding the truth-value of Claim 2.

8. "No college teachers are high school teachers" is true.
"Some college teachers are not high school teachers."
a. Claim 2 is true.
b. Claim 2 is false.
c. One can make no inference regarding the truth-value of Claim 2.

9. "All teachers are certified" is true.
"Some teachers are certified."
a. Claim 2 is true.
b. Claim 2 is false.
c. One can make no inference regarding the truth-value of Claim 2.

10. "No police detectives are curious people" is false.
"Some police detectives are curious people."
a. Claim 2 is true.
b. Claim 2 is false.
c. One can make no inference regarding the truth-value of Claim 2.

6.32 Review Exercise Given the Aristotelian Square of Opposition and given the truth-value of the first claim, what should you infer regarding the truth value of the second claim? Circle the correct answer.

1. **Example:**
   "No detectives are band members" is true.
   "Some detectives are not band members."
   a. **Claim 2 is true.**
   b. Claim 2 is false.
   c. One can make no inference regarding the truth-value of Claim 2.

   No S are P.
   Some S are not P.

2.   "Some band uniforms are not clean" is true.
        "Some band uniforms are clean."
   a. Claim 2 is true.
   b. Claim 2 is false.
   c. One can make no inference regarding the truth-value of Claim 2.

3.   "All crooks are devious" is true.
        "Some crooks are devious."
   a. Claim 2 is true.
   b. Claim 2 is false.
   c. One can make no inference regarding the truth-value of Claim 2.

4.   "Some tuba players are suspects" is true.
        "All tuba players are suspects."
   a. Claim 2 is true.
   b. Claim 2 is false.
   c. One can make no inference regarding the truth-value of Claim 2.

5.   "All musicians are creative" is true.
        "No musicians are creative."
   a. Claim 2 is true.
   b. Claim 2 is false.
   c. One can make no inference regarding the truth-value of Claim 2.

6.   "No police detective are suspects" is true.
        "Some police detectives are suspects."
   a. Claim 2 is true.
   b. Claim 2 is false.
   c. One can make no inference regarding the truth-value of Claim 2.

(Continued)

7.   "Some criminals are burglars" is true.
      "Some criminals are not burglars."
   a. Claim 2 is true.
   b. Claim 2 is false.
   c. One can make no inference regarding the truth-value
      of Claim 2.

8.   "Some criminals are not thieves" is true.
      "All criminals are thieves."
   a. Claim 2 is true.
   b. Claim 2 is false.
   c. One can make no inference regarding the truth-value
      of Claim 2.

9.   "All detectives are lazy people" is false.
      "Some detectives are not lazy people."
   a. Claim 2 is true.
   b. Claim 2 is false.
   c. One can make no inference regarding the truth-value
      of Claim 2.

10.   "No criminals are unpunished people" is false.
      "All criminals are unpunished people."
   a. Claim 2 is true.
   b. Claim 2 is false.
   c. One can make no inference regarding the truth-value
      of Claim 2.

11.   "Some band directors are not teachers" is false.
      "Some band directors are teachers."
   a. Claim 2 is true.
   b. Claim 2 is false.
   c. One can make no inference regarding the truth-value
      of Claim 2.

12.   "Some rental trucks are not trucks" is false.
      "No rental trucks are trucks."
   a. Claim 2 is true.
   b. Claim 2 is false.
   c. One can make no inference regarding the truth-value
      of Claim 2.

13.   "All musicians are band directors" is false.
        "Some musicians are not band directors."
   a. Claim 2 is true.
   b. Claim 2 is false.
   c. One can make no inference regarding the truth-value
      of Claim 2.

14.   "Some football players are band members" is
        false.
        "All football players are band members."
   a. Claim 2 is true.
   b. Claim 2 is false.
   c. One can make no inference regarding the truth-value
      of Claim 2.

15.   "Some band members are not absent" is false.
        "Some band members are absent."
   a. Claim 2 is true.
   b. Claim 2 is false.
   c. One can make no inference regarding the truth-value
      of Claim 2.

6.33   Review Exercise   Is the second claim logically equivalent to the first claim? Circle the
correct answer.

1. **Example:**
        Some students are not band members.
        Some band members are not students.
   a. Logically equivalent
   (b.) **Not logically equivalent**

   Some S are not P.
   Some P are not S.

2.   All detectives are police officers.
        All police officers are detectives.
   a. Logically equivalent
   b. Not logically equivalent

3.   No detectives are suspects.
        No suspects are detectives.
   a. Logically equivalent
   b. Not logically equivalent

(Continued)

4.   Some crooks are burglars.
       Some burglars are crooks.
    a. Logically equivalent
    b. Not logically equivalent

5.   No teachers at North City HS are high
       school students.
       No high school students are teachers at North
       City HS.
    a. Logically equivalent
    b. Not logically equivalent

6.   Some trucks are not rental trucks.
       Some rental trucks are not trucks.
    a. Logically equivalent
    b. Not logically equivalent

7.   Some mammals are not musicians.
       Some musicians are not mammals.
    a. Logically equivalent
    b. Not logically equivalent

8.   All band members at North City HS are high
       school students.
       All high school students are band members at
       North city HS.
    a. Logically equivalent
    b. Not logically equivalent

9.   Some students who are not debaters are
       band members.
       Some band members are students who are
       not debaters.
    a. Logically equivalent
    b. Not logically equivalent

10.   No mystery lovers are readers who do not enjoy
       reading Sherlock Holmes.
       No readers who do not enjoy Sherlock Holmes
       are mystery lovers.
    a. Logically equivalent
    b. Not logically equivalent

6.34   Review Exercise   Is the second claim logically equivalent to the first claim? Circle the correct answer.

1. **Example:**
    No detectives are high school students.
    All high school students are non-detectives.
    a. **Logically equivalent**
    b. Not logically equivalent

    No S are P.
    All P are non-S.

2.   All band directors are experienced teachers.
        No band directors are non-experienced teachers.
    a. Logically equivalent
    b. Not logically equivalent

3.   Some trucks are not rental trucks.
        Some rental trucks are non-trucks.
    a. Logically equivalent
    b. Not logically equivalent

4.   Some trucks are rental trucks.
        Some rental trucks are not non-trucks.
    a. Logically equivalent
    b. Not logically equivalent

5.   All rental trucks are trucks.
        No trucks are non-rental trucks.
    a. Logically equivalent
    b. Not logically equivalent

6.   Some trucks are not rental trucks.
        Some trucks are non-rental trucks.
    a. Logically equivalent
    b. Not logically equivalent

7.   All high schools are things bigger than
        one classroom.
        No things bigger than one class room are non-
        high schools.
    a. Logically equivalent
    b. Not logically equivalent

(Continued)

8.   Some baseball players are not non-athletes
        Some athletes are baseball players.
   a. Logically equivalent
   b. Not logically equivalent

9.   Some trucks are not rental trucks.
        Some rental trucks are not non-trucks.
   a. Logically equivalent
   b. Not logically equivalent

10.   Some high school students are not band
        members.
        Some non-band members are high school
        students.
   a. Logically equivalent
   b. Not logically equivalent

6.35 Review Exercise Is the second claim logically equivalent to the first claim? Circle the
correct answer..

1. **Example:**
        All detectives are police officers.
        No non-police officers are detectives.
   a. **Logically equivalent**
   b. Not logically equivalent

All S are P.
No non-P are S.

2.   No crooks are honest people.
        No non-honest people are non-crooks.
   a. Logically equivalent
   b. Not logically equivalent

3.   Some students are band members.
        Some band members are not non-students.
   a. Logically equivalent
   b. Not logically equivalent

4.   Some students are not band members.
          Some non-band members are students.
     a. Logically equivalent
     b. Not logically equivalent

5.   All football players are non-band members.
          No band members are football players.
     a. Logically equivalent
     b. Not logically equivalent

6.   No detectives are army generals.
          All army generals are non-detectives.
     a. Logically equivalent
     b. Not logically equivalent

7.   Some students are suspects.
          Some non-suspects are non-students.
     a. Logically equivalent
     b. Not logically equivalent

8.   Some trucks are not Avis trucks.
          Some non-Avis-trucks are not non-trucks.
     a. Logically equivalent
     b. Not logically equivalent

9.   Some A students are not non-band-members
          Some band members are A students.
     a. Logically equivalent
     b. Not logically equivalent

10.   No unstoppable teams are weak teams.
          All weak teams are stoppable teams.
     a. Logically equivalent
     b. Not logically equivalent

6.36 Review Exercise To which standard form categorical claim can the given claim be reduced? Circle the correct answer.

1. **Example:**
   Given: Only some students are band members.
   a. All students are band members.
   b. Some students are band members.
   c. Some students are not band members.
   (d.) **Both b and c**

   Some S are P.
   Some S are not P.

2. Given: Not any college student is a member of the high school band.
   a. All college students are members of the high school band.
   b. No college students are members of the high school band.
   c. Some college students are members of the high school band.
   d. Some college students are not members of the high school band.

3. Given: Not every musician is a member of the high school band.
   a. All musicians are members of the high school band.
   b. No musicians are members of the high school band.
   c. Some musicians are members of the high school band.
   d. Some musicians are not members of the high school band.

4. Given: Several teachers are people who enjoy band music.
   a. All teachers are people who enjoy band music.
   b. No teachers are people who enjoy band music.
   c. Some teachers are people who enjoy band music.
   d. Some teachers are not people who enjoy band music.

5. Given: Each and every band member is a musician.
   a. All band members are musicians.
   b. Some band members are musicians.
   c. Some band members are not musicians.
   d. Both b and c

6. Given: None but musicians are band members.
   a. All musicians are band members.
   b. All band members are musicians.
   c. No musicians are band members.
   d. Both a and b

7. Given: There isn't any principal who is a robber.
   a. All principals are robbers.
   b. No principals are robbers.
   c. Some robbers are not principals.
   d. Some principals are not robbers.

8. Given: Not all musicians are violinists.
   a. No musicians are violinists.
   b. Some musicians are violinists.
   c. Some musicians are not violinists.
   d. Both b and c

9. Given: Any crook is a person who can benefit from jail.
   a. Some crooks are persons who can benefit from jail.
   b. No crooks are persons who can benefit from jail.
   c. Some crooks are persons who can benefit from jail.
   d. All crooks are persons who can benefit from jail.

10. Given: Musicians are sometimes band members.
    a. All musicians are band members.
    b. Some musicians are band members.
    c. Some musicians are not band members.
    d. Both b and c

6.37 Review Exercise To which standard form categorical syllogism can the given syllogism be reduced? Is the syllogism valid? Circle the correct answers.

1. **Example:**
   Everyone who likes football loves a touchdown.
   Someone who is a band member likes football.
   So, there is a band member who is crazy about touchdowns.

   All M are P.
   Some S are M.
   Some S are P.

   a. No football fans are people who love touchdowns.
   Some band members are football fans.

   So, some band members are not people who love touchdowns.

   b.) **All football fans are people who love touchdowns.**
   Some band members are football fans.

   So, some band members are people who love football.

   c. All people who love touchdowns are football fans.
   Some football fans are band members.

   So, some band members are people who love touchdowns.

   d. All football fans are people who love touchdowns.
   Some band members are football fans.

   So, some band members are not people who love touchdowns.

   This categorical syllogism is:

   (Valid) - Invalid

2. Everyone who attends football camp is a sports fanatic.
   Some attendees at football camp also are baseball players.

   So, at least some baseball players are sports fanatics.

   a. No football camp attendees are sports fanatics.
   Some football camp attendees are baseball players.

   So, some baseball players are not sports fanatics.

   b. No football camp attendees are non-sports fanatics.
   All baseball players are football camp attendees.

   So, no baseball players are non-sports fanatics.

   c. All football camp attendees are sports fanatics.
   Some football camp attendees are baseball players.

   So, some baseball players are sports fanatics.

   d. Some football camps attendees are sports fanatics.
   Some football camp attendees are not baseball players.

   So, some baseball players are not sports fanatics.

   This categorical syllogism is:

   Valid - Invalid

3. Every non-union musician is hopeful.
    There is a union musician who is not a trumpet player.
    So, at least one trumpet player is unhopeful.
    a. No hopeful people are non-union musicians.
        Some non-union musicians are not trumpet players.
        So, some trumpet players are not hopeful people.

    b. All unhopeful people are union musicians.
        Some union musicians are not trumpet players.
        So, some trumpet players are unhopeful people.

    c. All hopeful people are union musicians.
        Some trumpet players are not hopeful people.
        So, some trumpet players are union musicians.

    d. Some unhopeful people are union musicians.
        Some hopeful people are not trumpet players.
        So, some union musicians are not trumpet players.

This categorical syllogism is:

Valid - Invalid

4. No football players are wrestlers.
    Some non-wrestlers are non-starters.
    So, some starters are not football players.
    a. All wrestlers are football players.
        Some wrestlers are starters.
        So, some starters are football players.

    b. No wrestlers are football players.
        Some wrestlers are not starters.
        So, some starters are not football players.

    c. No football players are wrestlers.
        Some starters are football players.
        So, some wrestlers are not starters.

    d. All football players are non-wrestlers.
        Some non-wrestlers are not starters.
        So, some starters are not football players.

This categorical syllogism is:

Valid - Invalid

(Continued)

5. No Honors Physics student is incurious.
    Anyone who is not an Honors Physics student is a
    pizza fanatic.
    So, everyone who is not a pizza fanatic is curious.
    a. No Honors Physics students are curious.
        All Honors Physics students are pizza fanatics.
        So, no pizza fanatics are curious.

    b. All Honors Physics students are curious.
        All non-pizza fanatics are Honors Physics students.
        So, all non-pizza fanatics are curious.

    c. All Honors Physics students are curious.
        No Honors Physics students are pizza fanatics.
        So, no pizza fanatics are curious.

    d. No Honors Physics students are incurious.
        All Honors Physics students are pizza fanatics.
        So, no pizza fanatics are incurious.

This categorical syllogism is:

Valid - Invalid

6. At least one band director is ambidextrous.
    Some ambidextrous person can write with the left hand.
    So, someone who writes with the left hand is not the
    opposite of the leader of the band.
    a. Some band directors are ambidextrous persons.
        Some ambidextrous persons are persons who can
        write with the left hand.
        So, some persons who can write with the left hand are
        band directors.

    b. No band directors are ambidextrous.
        Some ambidextrous persons are persons who can
        write with the left hand.
        So, some persons who can write with the left hand are
        band directors.

    c. Some ambidextrous persons are band directors.
        Some ambidextrous persons are persons who can
        write with the left hand.
        So, some persons who can write with the left hand are
        band directors.

    d. All ambidextrous persons are band directors.
        Some ambidextrous persons are persons who can
        write with the left hand.
        So, some persons who can write with the left hand are
        band directors.

This categorical syllogism is:

Valid - Invalid

(Continued)

7. Any rental truck is a truck.
    No truck is a vehicle with a small motor.
    Hence, every vehicle with a large motor is a rental truck.
    a. All trucks are rental trucks.
        All trucks are vehicles with large motors.
        Hence, all trucks with large motors are rental trucks.

    b. No trucks are non-rental trucks.
        All trucks are vehicles with large motors.
        Hence, No trucks with large motors are non-
        rental trucks.

    c. All trucks are rental trucks.
        All trucks are vehicles with motors that are not small.
        Hence, all trucks with motors that are not small are
        rental trucks.

    d. All rental trucks are trucks.
        All trucks are vehicles with a large motor.
        Hence, all vehicles with a large motor are rental trucks.

This categorical syllogism is:

Valid - Invalid

8. There are some students who love music.
    No lovers of music hate marching bands.
    So, some lovers of marching bands are students.
    a. Some students are not lovers of music.
        All lovers of music are lovers of marching bands.
        So, some lovers of marching bands are students.

    b. Some students are lovers of music.
        All lovers of music are lovers of marching bands.
        So, some lovers of marching bands are students.

    c. Some students are lovers of music.
        No lovers of music are haters of marching bands.
        So, some lovers of marching bands are students.

    d. Some students are lovers of music.
        All lovers of music are lovers of marching bands.
        So, some lovers of marching bands are not lovers of music.

This categorical syllogism is:

Valid - Invalid

(Continued)

9. There isn't any crook who does not detest the police.
    Everyone who does likes the police loves order in
    the city.
    _____
    So, some people who love disorder are crooks.

    a. Some crooks are people who like the police.
        All people who like the police are people who love
        order in the city.
        _____
        Hence, some people who like order in the city are
        not crooks.

    b. No crook is a person who loves the police.
        All people who love the police are people who love
        order in the city.
        _____
        Hence, some people who love order in the city
        are crooks.

    c. All crooks are people who detest the police. All
        people who detest the police are people who like
        order in the city.
        _____
        Hence, some people who like order in the city
        are crooks.

    d. Some crooks are people who detest the police. All
        people who like disorder in the city are people who
        detest the police.
        _____
        Hence, some people who like disorder in the city
        are crooks.

This categorical syllogism is:

Valid - Invalid

10. Many crooks are people without honor among thieves.
    All people without honor among thieves
    are untrustworthy.
    ―――――――――――――――――――
    Hence, there is not a trustworthy person who is
    a crook.

    a. Some crooks are not people without honor
       among thieves.
       All people without honor among thieves are
       untrustworthy persons.
       ―――――――――――――――――――
       Hence, some untrustworthy persons are crooks.

    b. Some crooks are people without honor among
       thieves.
       All people without honor among thieves are
       untrustworthy persons.
       ―――――――――――――――――――
       Hence, some untrustworthy persons are crooks.

    c. All crooks are people without honor among thieves.
       All people without honor among thieves are
       untrustworthy persons.
       ―――――――――――――――――――
       Hence, all untrustworthy persons are crooks.

    d. Some crooks are people with honor among thieves.
       All people with honor among thieves are
       trustworthy persons.
       ―――――――――――――――――――
       Hence, some trustworthy persons are crooks.

This categorical syllogism is:

Valid - Invalid

6.38 Review Exercise Which of the following are valid categorical syllogisms in the Aristotelian interpretation? Circle the correct answer.

1. **Example:**
   All teachers at city high schools are in the state
   retirement plan.
   All band directors at city high schools are teachers at
   city high schools.
   ―――――――――――――――――――
   So, some band directors at city high schools are in the
   state retirement plan.
   (a.) **Valid**
   b. Invalid

   All M are P.
   Some S are M.*
   ―――――――――
   Some S are P.

   *S should not be distributed, so the Minor Premise was replaced by its correspondingly particular claim.

2. All band students are hard-working.
   All band students are musical people.
   ―――――――――――――――――――
   So, some musical people are hard-working.
   a. Valid
   b. Invalid

(Continued)

3. No band directors are crooks.
    All crooks are dishonest people.
    So, some dishonest people are not band directors.
    a. Valid
    b. Invalid

4. No students are band directors.
    All band directors are music lovers.
    So, some music lovers are students.
    a. Valid
    b. Invalid

5. Some band member is not a student on the honor roll.
    Not every student is a band member.
    So, there is a student who is not a student on the
    honor roll.
    a. Valid
    b. Invalid

6. All drum majors are students.
    No drum majors are valedictorians.
    So, some valedictorians are students.
    a. Valid
    b. Invalid

7. Every dishonest person is a crook.
    Not any students are crooks.
    So, some students are not dishonest.
    a. Valid
    b. Invalid

8. Not every crook is a robber of high school bands.
    Not every crook is a man.
    So, some man is a robber of high school bands.
    a. Valid
    b. Invalid

9. No swimming instructors are band directors.
    All lifeguards at city high school are also
    swimming instructors .
    So, some lifeguards are not band directors.
    a. Valid
    b. Invalid

10. Not any debater is a band member.
    Each and every student leader is a debater.
    Hence, at least one student leader is not a band
    member.
    a. Valid
    b. Invalid

Chapter 6 Quiz

Choose the best answer for each of the following questions.

1. Categorical claims state:
   a. relations between persons.
   b. relations between sets of things.
   c. relations that always hold.
   d. relations that never hold.
   e. both a and c

2. Every categorical claim in standard form:
   a. contains a subject term.
   b. contains a predicate term.
   c. contains a quantifier.
   d. contains a form of the verb to be.
   e. all of the above

3. A claim of the form "No S are P" is:
   a. a universal affirmative claim.
   b. a universal negative claim.
   c. a particular affirmative claim.
   d. a particular negative claim.
   e. none of the above

4. Standard form categorical syllogisms always contain:
   a. exactly three terms that are used with the same meaning throughout.
   b. universal and particular claims.
   c. universal claims that are true only if their corresponding particular claims are true.
   d. at least three premises.
   e. the relation of validity between the premises and the conclusion.

5. The Major Term of a categorical syllogism is:
   a. the subject term of the conclusion.
   b. the predicate term of the conclusion.
   c. the subject term of the Major Premise.
   d. the term that is in both premises but not in the conclusion.
   e. a form of the verb to be.

6. The obverse of a categorical claim is:
   a. formed by changing claim from affirmative to negative or negative to affirmative and replacing the predicate term with its complement.
   b. formed by changing claim from affirmative to negative or negative to affirmative and replacing the subject term with its complement.
   c. logically equivalent to the given claim only for universal affirmatives and particular negatives.
   d. always logically equivalent to the given claim.
   e. both a and d

7. A categorical syllogism with a particular premise and a universal conclusion is:
    a. valid only when both premises are negative.
    b. valid only when one of the premises is negative and the conclusion is affirmative.
    c. valid only if both premises are particular.
    d. valid only if there are four terms in the syllogism.
    e. never valid.

8. In the Boolean interpretation of categorical claims, if we are given that a universal affirmative proposition is true, we can immediately infer:
    a. only that the corresponding particular negative is false.
    b. only that the corresponding particular affirmative is true.
    c. that the corresponding particular affirmative is true, and that the corresponding universal negative and particular negative are both false.
    d. that the corresponding particular affirmative is false, and that the corresponding universal negative and particular negative are both true.
    e. we can make no inferences regarding the truth value of any other categorical claims.

9. As found in ordinary English, a categorical syllogism with four terms:
    a. is always invalid.
    b. might be valid if the four terms can be reduced to three terms.
    c. is valid whenever the four terms can be reduced to three terms.
    d. must be treated as two distinct syllogisms.
    e. is never found, since ordinary English syllogisms must have exactly three terms.

10. If a categorical claim contains a premise of the form, "Only some S are M," this means:
    a. there is exactly one S that is M.
    b. only that there is at least one S that is M.
    c. only that there is at least one S that is not M.
    d. both "Some S are M" and "No S are M."
    e. both "Some S are M" and "Some S are not M."

CHAPTER 7

- Inductive Arguments
- Review

Overview

Inductive arguments with true premises may provide *some*, but *not* conclusive, evidence for the truth of their conclusions.

CASE 25	City of Los Angeles Police Department

[1]There was a robbery at the Consolidated Bank right after the bank opened in the morning on Tuesday. [2]Detective Wise was called to the bank to investigate.

[3]Detective Wise asked the bank tellers how many robbers there were. [4]Five bank tellers all agreed that there were four bank robbers. [5]Three tellers said that all the robbers were men who wore Halloween masks. [6]Two other tellers said that there were two men and two women who were dressed in men's clothing and wore Halloween masks. [7]The detective wondered which statements were true. [8]She thought about another bank robbery that had occurred in the city eight days ago right after the bank had opened in the morning. [9]There were four robbers involved in that robbery. [10]The tellers in that previous bank robbery had agreed that the robbers were men who wore Halloween masks. [11]Detective Wise concluded from the similarity of the two robberies that all the robbers in this last bank robbery were probably men.

[12]Detective Wise asked whether there were any weapons involved. [13]The bank president said that he did not see any weapons in the Tuesday robbery but that he only heard the robbers make threats against the bank employees. [14]The detective remembered that the bank robbery eight days ago also did not involve any weapons but only threats against the employees. [15]Detective Wise concluded even more strongly that the same robbers were involved.

[16]A police officer came in to the bank and said that he had found SUV tire marks from the get-away car. [17]Detective Wise remembered that the bank robbery eight days ago was done by four robbers who escaped on motorcycles. [18]The detective wondered if this robbery on Tuesday was a copycat robbery of the one done eight days ago and not one done by the same band of crooks.

[19]They found a woman's wig and mask, apparently dropped by one of the robbers outside the bank, that matched the hair color and mask worn by one of the robbers. "[20]Detective Wise remembered that no wigs or masks were found after the bank robbery eight days ago. [21]The detective was puzzled and thought that maybe the same robbers were involved in both robberies but that they were getting careless in leaving their disguises behind.

[22]Detective Wise asked how the bank robbery was committed. [23]The president replied that the robbers planned like engineers, carefully plotting out every move in the robbery. [24]A teller said that the robbers disguised their voices by speaking like ventriloquists through dummies.

[25]Detective Wise asked how the robbers were dressed. [26]One teller said that they were dressed like businesspeople even though they wore masks. [27]A second teller said that they were dressed like models for a men's fashion show. [28]A third teller said that they were dressed like salesmen at an expensive men's clothing store. [29]Detective Wise remembered that in the robbery eight days ago the robbers were dressed like members of a motorcycle gang with leather jackets and leather pants. [30]The detective concluded that because of the dissimilarity of clothing worn by the robbers in the two bank robberies that there were two different gangs involved.

7.1 Argument by Analogy*

Analogies are comparisons that state a similarity between two or more things.

There are **three kinds of analogies:**

Descriptive Analogies	Explanation Analogies	Analogy Arguments
Some analogies are simply *descriptions*:	Other analogies are *comparisons* that help to explain one thing by comparing it to another thing. These analogies can be used to explain how to do something or how something happens or works.	Finally, other analogies are *used to argue*. When we argue by analogy, we claim that because two or more things are similar in a number of ways, it is likely that they are similar in yet another way. They are inductive arguments that may properly conclude only that the conclusion is probably true.
Examples: "One teller said that they were dressed like businesspeople even though they wore masks."		
	Examples: When the president said that "the robbers planned like engineers, carefully plotting out every move in the robbery," he made a comparison, which is an analogy, that helps to explain how the robbery happened (sentence 23).	**Examples:** **First similarity:** Both robberies occurred in the morning.
"A second teller said that they were dressed like models for a men's fashion show."		**Second similarity:** Both robberies involved four robbers.
"A third teller said that they were dressed like salesmen at an expensive men's clothing store" (sentences 26-28).		**Third similarity:** All robbers in both robberies wore men's clothing.
	When a teller said that "the robbers disguised their voices by speaking like ventriloquists through dummies," she made a comparison, an analogy, that helps explain how the robbers disguised their voices (sentence 24).	**Fourth point:** The robbers in the first robbery were men.
		Conclusion: Therefore, the robbers in the second robbery were probably men.

*See page 169 to review the initial lesson on arguments by analogy.

> **7.2   Exercise** Identify each analogy as a descriptive analogy, an explanation analogy, or an argument by analogy. Circle the correct answer.

1. **Example**:
    The first robber's footwear looked like army boots.
    a. **Descriptive analogy**
    b. Explanation analogy
    c. Argument by analogy

2. Because the robbers in both crimes were four in number and the robberies took place right after the bank opened, we can say that the same crooks were involved.
    a. Descriptive analogy
    b. Explanation analogy
    c. Argument by analogy

3. In both robberies there were four robbers who all wore Halloween masks. So, it was the same gang that did the two robberies.
    a. Descriptive analogy
    b. Explanation analogy
    c. Argument by analogy

4. The teller said that the robbers were dressed like motorcyclists.
    a. Descriptive analogy
    b. Explanation analogy
    c. Argument by analogy

5. The robbers spoke in a squeaky voice by disguising their voices as if they were ventriloquists.
    a. Descriptive analogy
    b. Explanation analogy
    c. Argument by analogy

6. The robbers were the same in both robberies because in both robberies they wore wigs and masks and they did not use weapons.
    a. Descriptive analogy
    b. Explanation analogy
    c. Argument by analogy

7.3 Evaluating Arguments by Analogy

There are **six rules** we use to evaluate arguments by analogy:

> **Rule 1: The greater the number of similarities, the stronger the argument.**
>
> If there is only similarity between the two bank robberies that suggests that the same gang is involved, then the conclusion is weak. The greater the number of similar properties between the things compared, the stronger the argument.

> **Rule 2: The similarities must be relevant.**
>
> Cause and effect connections between the properties and the conclusion are often what we seek in looking for relavant similarities. For example, if the vocabulary used by the robbers in the different bank robberies is similar, then this factor is relevant to the conclusion that the same gang is involved; but if the robbers all like to listen to the Beatles, this similarity is not relavant to the conclusion.

> **Rule 3: The more things compared, the stronger the argument.**
>
> For example, if we are comparing five bank robberies that are similar instead of only two bank robberies, then the conclusion that the same gang is involved is stronger.

> **Rule 4: The fewer dissimilarities there are among the things compared, the stronger the argument.**
>
> For example, when the two bank robberies have many dissimilarities such as a different number of robbers, different weapons, different speech patterns, and different escape vehicles, then the conclusion that the same gang committed the robberies is unlikely. But when the two bank robberies do not have many dissimilarities, for example, they do not have a different number of robbers, do not have different weapons, do not have different speech patterns, and do not have different escape vehicles, then the conclusion that it is the same gang is more likely.

Rule 5:   If many things are being compared, there are times when dissimilarities strengthen the argument.

For example, assume there was a series of bank robberies. The police conclude that the same robbers committed each crime, because in each bank they found an engraved note saying, *"Thank you ever so much! The Robbers."* But the robberies differed from one another in many ways. Some banks had elaborate security systems; others did not. Some robberies were committed during the day. During those, the robbers sometimes threatened violence with guns and sometimes they threatened violence with explosives. The robbers sometimes bored into the bank vault from underground. In each case there was a thank you note, and the robbers stole at least a quarter million dollars. Given these differences, the police might conclude that the robbers are very good at what they do, since it makes little difference how they go about doing it.

Rule 6: An overstated or overconfident conclusion weakens the argument.

Inductive arguments conclude probability — not certainty. When we state an inductive conclusion as certain or almost certain, we overstate the conclusion and thereby weaken the inductive argument. Greater certainty and greater specificity in the conclusion demands stronger evidence and is easier to falsify than a less certain and broader conclusion. For example, if Detective Wise concludes that it is practically certain that the same gang was involved in both robberies, she weakens her argument because she ignores the evidence that the robbers used different escape vehicles in the two robberies and that they also wore very different kids of clothing each time.

Example

Josh went hiking in the Rocky Mountains and he liked it.

He went hiking along the Mississippi River and he liked it.

He went hiking in Death Valley and he liked it.

He's planning to go hiking in the Blue Ridge Mountains, and he expects he'll like it.

Evaluating this affirmative claim using the six rules:

a.	What if Josh concludes his hike in the Blue Ridge Mountains will certainly be the best he ever took. The argument is weaker because of Rule 6. Josh is stating his conclusion too strongly.	Rule 6
b.	What if Josh had never gone hiking on a cold and snowy day, and this hike will be on a cold and snowy day? The argument is weaker because of Rule 4. Josh is ignoring a key dissimilarity, the snow, which was not present in any of his other hikes.	Rule 4
c.	What if all Josh's earlier hikes had been during the daytime and this one will be at night? The argument is weaker because of Rule 4.	Rule 4
d.	What if Josh is going to wear the same jacket he wore when hiking in the Rockies? The argument is neither stronger nor weaker because of Rule 2.	Rule 2
e.	What if Josh had also hiked in woodlands in Europe and Asia and liked it? The argument is stronger because of Rule 5. The many different places where Josh has hiked show that his enjoyment of hiking does not depend on the place, but simply on the exercise of walking itself.	Rule 5
f.	What if Josh had gone on three additional hikes and each time he enjoyed it? The argument is stronger because of Rule 3. The more things compared (hikes), the stronger the argument.	Rule 3
g.	What if Josh's best friend Peter went with him on all the previous hikes and will go on the next hike as well? The argument is stronger because this is an additional similarity. Having his best friend along adds to the enjoyment that Josh experiences when he goes hiking.	Rule 1
h.	What if it had been raining when Josh hiked in the Rockies, it had been snowing when he hiked along the Mississippi, and it had been over 100 degrees and sunny when he hiked in Death Valley? The many different weather conditions in which Josh has hiked show that his enjoyment of hiking does not depend so much on the external conditions that would bother other people, but simply on the exercise of walking itself for Josh.	Rule 5
i.	What if he had never hiked in an area where there were many bears, but there are many bears in the Blue Ridge Mountains? Josh is ignoring a key dissimilarity, the many bears which were not present in any of his other hikes. Bears can attack hikers.	Rule 4

7.4 **Exercise** Circle the correct application of the rules for evaluating arguments by analogy.

Case 25 Excerpt

Detective Wise asked the bank tellers how many robbers there were. Five bank tellers all agreed that there were four bank robbers. Three tellers said that all the robbers were men who wore Halloween masks. Two other tellers said that there were two men and two women who were dressed in men's clothing and wore Halloween masks. The detective wondered which statements were true. She thought about another bank robbery that had occurred in the city eight days ago right after the bank had opened in the morning. There were four robbers involved in that robbery. The tellers in that previous bank robbery had agreed that the robbers were men who wore Halloween masks. Detective Wise concluded from the similarity of the two robberies that all the robbers in this last bank robbery were probably the same men.

1. **Example**:
   What if Detective Wise had concluded that it was almost certain, based on the similarity of the two robberies, that all the robbers in this last bank robbery were men?
   a. The argument is stronger because it follows Rule 2, the similarities must be relevant.
   (b.) **The argument is weaker because it breaks Rule 6, an overstated conclusion weakens the argument.**
   c. The argument is neither stronger nor weaker because of Rule 3, the more things compared, the stronger the argument.

2. What if there were four bank robberies with all the same characteristics?
   a. The argument is stronger because it follows Rule 3, the more things compared, the stronger the argument.
   b. The argument is weaker because breaks Rule 6, an overstated conclusion weakens the argument.
   c. The argument is neither stronger nor weaker because of Rule 3, the more things compared, the stronger the argument.

3. What if the tellers in one bank robbery said the four robbers were women but in the other, the bank tellers said the four robbers were men?
   a. The argument is stronger because it follows Rule 3, the more things compared, the stronger the argument.
   b. The argument is weaker because it breaks Rule 4, the fewer dissimilarities there are among the things compared, the stronger the argument.
   c. The argument is neither stronger nor weaker because of Rule 6, an overstated conclusion weakens the argument.

4. What if the bank robbers also all wore similar basketball shoes in both robberies?
   a. The argument is stronger because it follows Rule 1, the greater the number of similarities, the stronger the argument.
   b. The argument is weaker because it breaks Rule 6, an overstated conclusion weakens the argument.
   c. The argument is neither stronger nor weaker because of Rule 3, the more things compared, the stronger the argument.

5. What if the bank robbers spoke fluent English in one robbery, but fluent Romanian in the other robbery?
   a. The argument is stronger because it follows Rule 3, the more things compared, the stronger the argument.
   b. The argument is weaker because it breaks Rule 4, the fewer dissimilarities there are among the things compared, the stronger the argument.
   c. The argument is neither stronger nor weaker because of Rule 6, an overstated conclusion weakens the argument.

6. What if the robbers used weapons in the first robbery but no weapons in the second robbery?
   a. The argument is stronger because it follows Rule 4, the fewer dissimilarities there are among the things compared, the stronger the argument.
   b. The argument is weaker because it breaks Rule 4, the fewer dissimilarities there are among the things compared, the stronger the argument.
   c. The argument is neither stronger nor weaker because of Rule 6, an overstated conclusion weakens the argument.

7. What if the first bank robbery took place in banking hours during the day, but the second bank robbery took place in the middle of the night?
   a. The argument is stronger because it follows Rule 1, the greater the number of similarities, the stronger the argument.
   b. The argument is weaker because it breaks Rule 4, the fewer dissimilarities there are among the things compared, the stronger the argument.
   c. The argument is stronger because of Rule 3, the more things compared, the stronger the argument.

8. What if a police officer came into the bank and said that he had found SUV tire marks from the getaway car, but the bank robbery eight days ago was done by four robbers who escaped on motorcycles?
   a. The argument is stronger because of Rule 3, the more things compared, the stronger the argument.
   b. The argument is stronger because it follows Rule 1, the greater the number of similarities, the stronger the argument.
   c. The argument is weaker because it breaks Rule 4, the fewer dissimilarities there are among the things compared, the stronger the argument.

9. What if in both bank robberies the robbers wore business attire rather than motorcycle clothing in one and business attire in the other?
   a. The argument is stronger because of Rule 3, the more things compared, the stronger the argument.
   b. The argument is stronger because it follows Rule 1, the greater the number of similarities, the stronger the argument.
   c. The argument is weaker because it breaks Rule 4, the fewer dissimilarities there are among the things compared, the stronger the argument.

(Continued)

10. What if, in both bank robberies weapons had been used rather than weapons in one robbery and no weapons in the other?
    a. The argument is weaker because it breaks Rule 3, the more things compared, the stronger the argument.
    b. The argument is weaker because Rule 6 is broken, an overstated conclusion weakens the argument.
    c. The argument is stronger because it follows Rule 1, the greater the number of similarities, the stronger the argument.

7.5 Inductive Generalizations*

Some **inductive arguments** reach general conclusions. For example, we might conclude that since all the crows we've seen are black, most or even all crows are black. These arguments go from claims about particular examples which have a property to a generalization about all or most such things having the same property.

Notice how these arguments are like analogies and how they are different. In an analogy, we go directly from properties of individual objects to properties of another object. In a generalization, we go from a property that is true of a number of objects to a general claim about all or most such objects. Generalizations also assume there are similarities. They often assume that future situations will be similar to past situations.

There are three basic rules to help us judge the strength of inductive generalizations:

> **Rule 1: As the number of cases we examine increases, the generalization becomes stronger.**
>
> For example, if we know that ten different bank robberies were done by the same four robbers, then we could conclude that probably all or most of the 20 bank robberies in this last year, were done by the same four robbers.

> **Rule 2: As the diversity of the cases increases, the generalization is strengthened.**
>
> For example, assume Detective Wise concluded that explosives are the threat of choice among California bank robbers this year. She has some evidence for this if all the bank robbers in Los Angeles threatened their victims with explosives. But California is a big state. Her conclusion would be much stronger if the sample from which she generalized included bank robberies from all over the state: San Francisco, San Diego, Eureka, Sacramento, and so forth.

> **Rule 3: An overstated or overconfident conclusion weakens the argument.**
>
> We used this same rule in evaluating arguments by analogy. Arguments by analogy and inductive generalizations conclude with probability, not certainty. When an inductive argument is used to conclude with certainty or near-certainty, then the conclusion is being stated too strongly. Consequently, since the evidence for the conclusion is the same, but one concludes, that "All X are Y," rather than "Many X are Y," the overall argument is weakened. For example, if we argue from the fact that ten bank robberies in one city were done by the same four robbers to the conclusion that all bank robberies in the last year in all the entire country must have been done by the same four robbers, then we have overstated the conclusion. There are hundreds of bank robberies every year, so it is nearly impossible for one gang to commit all those robberies.

*See page 166 to review the initial lesson on inductive generalizations.

Example

Maria had a great time swimming last summer in the Atlantic Ocean. She also had fun swimming last summer in the Pacific Ocean and the Mediterranean Sea. Maria concludes that she will probably enjoy swimming again in the summer.

Evaluating this inductive generalization using the three rules:

a.	What if Maria concludes that she will absolutely enjoy swimming all her life in all kinds of weather? It may be likely that she will enjoy swimming in the summer in other places, but not that she will definitely enjoy swimming in all kinds of weather.	Rule 3
b.	What if Maria has swum in summer, fall, winter, and spring under many different weather conditions, and she has enjoyed swimming all these times, and then she concludes that she will probably enjoy swimming in the future in many different places under many different conditions? Since Maria has swum under many varied conditions and in many different places, the conclusion is strengthened because we know it is not the place or the weather that Maria enjoys so much as it is simply the swimming itself.	Rule 2
c.	What if Maria has also swum during the summer in many lakes and rivers in addition to the original cases mentioned above, and has enjoyed all those occasions of swimming, and she concludes that she will probably enjoy swimming during the summer in many different places? A few cases in the premises may indicate some probability of the truth of the conclusion. Many more cases in the premises offer more support for the inductive generalization.	Rule 1

7.6   Exercise Read the information below, then evaluate each inductive generalization using the three rules. Circle the correct answer.

On December 31, Detective Wise thought about the bank robberies that had occurred in the city that year. There had been twenty robberies. She had investigated ten of them. Four of the robberies she investigated were committed by four men in Halloween masks. Three robberies were committed by five people in ski masks. Two cases were tunnel jobs, and the crime scene folks concluded that it would have taken at least six strong people to tunnel from the sewer to the banks in the time following the last sewer inspection. And then there was Granny Smead's "Daring Daylight Holdup," to quote the *Times*. It was the middle of the day. She wore no disguise. She used a .22 pistol whose "bullets" were made of bubble gum. She was picked up three minutes after the robbery, gun in hand, calmly walking down the street: She just wanted to go back home to prison. Given the nine serious robberies she'd investigated, Detective Wise concluded that it's likely every serious bank job that year involved at least three crooks.

1. **Example:**
    What if Detective Wise had concluded that it was almost certain that all the serious bank robberies were committed by at least four crooks?
    a. As the number of cases we examine increases, the generalization becomes stronger.
    b. As the diversity of the cases increases, the generalization is strengthened.
    c. **An overstated conclusion weakens the argument.**

2. What if she discovered that eight of the ten robberies she hadn't investigated involved at least four robbers?
    a. As the number of cases we examine increases, the generalization becomes stronger.
    b. As the diversity of the cases increases, the generalization is strengthened.
    c. An overstated conclusion weakens the argument.

3. What if Detective Wise had investigated only three serious bank robberies this year?
    a. The argument is weakened because this rule is broken: As the number of cases we examine increases, the generalization becomes stronger.
    b. The argument is weakened because this rule is broken: As the diversity of the cases increases, the generalization is strengthened.
    c. An overstated conclusion weakens the argument.

4. What if the robberies Detective Wise had investigated were committed in ten different sections of the city?
    a. As the number of cases we examine increases, the generalization becomes stronger.
    b. As the diversity of the cases increases, the generalization is strengthened.
    c. An overstated conclusion weakens the argument.

5. What if one of the bank robberies was in January, two were in March, three were in August, one was in October, and two were in December?
    a. As the number of cases we examine increases, the generalization becomes stronger.
    b. As the diversity of the cases increases, the generalization is strengthened.
    c. An overstated conclusion weakens the argument.

(Continued)

6. What if Detective Wise concludes that a serious bank job requires at least four robbers?
    a. As the number of cases we examine increases, the generalization becomes stronger.
    b. As the diversity of the cases increases, the generalization is strengthened.
    c. An overstated conclusion weakens the argument.

7. What if all the bank robberies Detective Wise investigated happened in Chinatown?
    a. The conclusion is weakened, because fewer cases are considered.
    b. The conclusion is weakened because the sample is less diverse.
    c. The conclusion is stronger, so there is less evidence that the conclusion is true.

8. What if Detective Wise investigated only five bank robberies this year?
    a. The argument is weakened because this rule is broken: As the number of cases we examine increases, the generalization becomes stronger.
    b. The argument is weaker because this rule is broken: As the diversity of the cases increases, the generalization is strengthened.
    c. An overstated conclusion weakens the argument.

9. What if Detective Wise concludes that all serious bank robberies in Southern California involve at least three crooks?
    a. As the number of cases we examine increases, the generalization becomes stronger.
    b. As the diversity of the cases increases, the generalization is strengthened.
    c. An overstated conclusion weakens the argument.

10. What if Detective Wise generalized from only the three cases she investigated in the past four months?
    a. The argument is weakened because as the number of cases we examine decreases, the evidence for the conclusion becomes weaker.
    b. The argument is weakened because the sample is less diverse.
    c. The evidence for the conclusion is weaker because the conclusion itself is stronger.

CASE 26	City of Los Angeles Police Department

[1]A building on the corner of East Cesar E. Chavez Avenue and Lyon Street disappeared. [2]It was a spectacular disappearance. [3]There was a loud explosion, and the building spread in all directions. [4]Traffic on Chavez and Lyon was stopped. [5]Several drivers were injured. [6]Detective Wise led the team investigating the explosion.

[7]Why had the building exploded? [8]If it had been a planned professional demolition, papers would have been filed at city hall. [9]No papers were filed. [10]Alberto Sanchez, the fire inspector, said that the pattern of the explosion was consistent with igniting a massive gas leak, but no gas mains go to the building. [11]Sanchez's investigation concluded that the explosion was caused by several hundred pounds of dynamite located at various parts of the building. [12]It had been no accident. [13]Who would do such a thing?

[14]The building was owned by Smyth Industries. [15]The company filed for bankruptcy six months ago. [16]The building was deserted. [17]"Could the company officers have destroyed the building to collect the insurance?" Detective Wise wondered. [18]"But why would they have done such a clumsy job?"

[19]Two days after the explosion, a letter appeared at police headquarters. [20]"We blew up the Smyth building. [21]The city has one week to make serious steps to care for its stray cats or other buildings will fall." [22]The note was signed "The Feral Cat League."

[23]The Feral Cat League is a group of cats' rights advocates. [24]No police know who is involved in the league. [25]Cats' rights posters mysteriously appear on buildings. [26]Ads appear in newspapers. [27]The league pays for the ads by dropping common, cash-filled, fingerprint-free envelopes in the newspapers' drop boxes. [28]The envelopes cannot be traced. [29]And there are the bombings. [30]In the past three months, buildings were destroyed in New York City, Cleveland, El Paso, Chicago, and Seattle. [31]Each time, the Feral Cat League claimed responsibility and demanded protection for stray cats.

[32]"It fits the pattern, right down to those elements the police didn't release to the newspapers," thought Detective Wise. [33]"If the city does nothing and another building drops, we'll have even more evidence that the league is behind this. [34]At least they always choose deserted buildings. [35]But they're such messy bombers that people get hurt. [36]They have to be stopped!"

7.7 Argument to the Best Explanation*

The argument to the best explanation argues that the best explanation for a set of facts is probably true. We learned in Chapter 4 that explanations tell us why or how something happened. A hypothesis is a potential explanation. Some hypothesis are better than others. It is important to figure out which hypothesis is the best. This is important because the strength of our argument depends upon our evaluation of the hypothesis. How do we determine which hypothesis – explanation – is the best and most probably true?

There are **six rules** for evaluating hypotheses:

> **Rule 1: A hypothesis should be testable.**
>
> If a hypothesis is true, you should be able to predict that some event will occur or that something has occurred. If the predicted event does not occur or did not occur, this shows that the hypothesis is false.

Examples of testable hypotheses in Case 26:

a.	**Hypothesis:** The building's destruction was caused by a professional demolition company. If the building's demolition was caused by a professional demolition company, then papers would have been filed at city hall. Papers were not filed at city hall. So, the building's demolition was not caused by a professional demolition company (sentences 8-9).
b.	**Hypothesis:** The building's destruction was caused by a gas leak. If the building's destruction was caused by a gas leak, then one should find gas mains leading to the building. No gas mains lead to the building. So the building's destruction was not caused by a gas leak (sentence 10).
c.	**Hypothesis:** Smyth Industries destroyed the building to collect insurance. If Smyth Industries destroyed the building to collect insurance, they would have insurance to pay for the damages. However, if they do not have an insurance policy to pay for damage to the building, then Smyth Industries did not destroy the building to collect insurance.
d.	**Hypothesis:** The building was destroyed by the Feral Cat League. If the building was destroyed by the Feral Cat League, and then if the city does nothing to help stray cats within the next week, then another building will be destroyed. Having the city do nothing and seeing whether another building is destroyed is a way to test the hypothesis (sentence 33).

*See page 173 to review the initial lesson on Arguments to the Best Explanation.

> **Rule 2: If predictions based upon a hypothesis come true, this tends to show that the hypothesis is true.**
>
> If a prediction based on a hypothesis comes true, this is evidence to believe the hypothesis. However, this is an inductive argument so it is always possible that the hypothesis is false even though the predictions come true.

Examples of predictions based on a hypothesis in Case 26:

a.	**Hypothesis:** The Feral Cat League is behind the bombing.
	If the Feral Cat League is behind the bombings and the city does nothing to improve the fate of stray cats within a week, then another building will be bombed. Assume that the city does nothing to improve the fate of stray cats and another building is bombed. This new bombing is evidence that the Feral Cat League is behind the bombing.
b.	**Hypothesis:** Smyth Industries is behind the bombing.
	If Smyth Industries is behind the bombing, then the company officers will receive a large insurance settlement. Assume the company officers do receive a large insurance settlement. This is evidence that Smyth Industries is behind the bombing.
c.	**Hypothesis:** The Feral Cat League is behind the bombing.
	If the Feral Cat League is behind the bombing, then they will take responsibility for the bombing. The Feral Cat League takes responsibility for the bombing. This is evidence that the Feral Cat League is behind the bombing.
d.	**Hypothesis:** Detective Wise arranged the bombing.
	If Detective Wise arranged the bombing, then her romantic ties with Archy Smyth, president of Smyth Industries, ended last week. Assume Detective Wise's romantic ties with Archy Smyth ended last week. This is evidence that Detective Wise arranged the bombing.

It is reasonable to believe that hypotheses a, b, and c above are far more plausible than hypothesis d. Why? There are independent reasons to believe that the hypotheses might be true. Examining Example A, the action is similar (analogous) to actions in other cities for which the Feral Cat League claimed responsibility. Examining Example B, people have been known to destroy their own property to collect insurance. Examining Example C, groups that engage in violent acts to further a cause often take responsibility for their actions. There is no known evidence that Detective Wise is a bomber.

Rule 3: A hypothesis is plausible if it is consistent with the best theoretical explanations available.

Examples in which the plausibility of the hypothesis is considered in Case 26:

a.	**Hypothesis:** The Feral Cat League committed the crime.
	This is a plausible hypothesis because the Feral Cat League claimed responsibility for the crime as well as similar crimes in other cities, and groups that claim responsibility for violent crimes are often the groups that commit them.
b.	**Hypothesis:** The Sons of Norway committed the crime.
	This hypothesis is not plausible. The Sons of Norway is an organization that celebrates its Norwegian-American heritage. They're generally a gentle group. There is no evidence that they engage in violent actions. (Enthusiastically attacking a plate of lutefisk does not count as a violent action.)
c.	**Hypothesis:** The Smyth building was bombed by a group of invisible gremlins.
	The hypothesis is not plausible because there is no reason to believe that gremlins exist.

Rule 4: A hypothesis is more probably true if it is broad in scope; that is, if it explains more events than alternative hypotheses.

Examples taking hypothetical broadness into account in Case 26:

a.	**Hypothesis:** The Feral Cat League committed the crime.
	This hypothesis explains both the bombing and the fact that a note was received from the Feral Cat League, claiming responsibility for the crime.
b.	**Hypothesis:** Smyth Industries bombed its own building.
	This could explain the bombing, but it would not explain why the police received a note from the Feral Cat League that claimed responsibility for the crime.
c.	**Hypothesis:** The First Methodist Church choir bombed the building so they'd feel safer walking from the church parking lot (which was beside the building) into the church.
	This might explain the bombing, but it would not explain the note from the Feral Cat League to the police. It is probably not a plausible hypothesis, because most Methodist choir members are not violent people. It's also likely that choir members would be concerned about potential damage to the church building if they bombed a neighboring building.

Rule 5: **When choosing between two hypotheses, the simplest explanation is more probably true.**

This is known as the **principle of parsimony** or **Ockham's Razor**, after the 14th century English philosopher, William of Ockham (c.1285-1349). It basically says that simpler explanations are better than complex explanations. It assumes that similar effects have similar causes.

Examples of taking simplicity into account in Case 26:

a.	**Hypothesis:** Bombings in Los Angeles, New York City, Cleveland, El Paso, Chicago, and Seattle are similar to one another. So, it is more likely that they have a common cause than that a different group is responsible in each case.
b.	**Hypothesis:** One might be able to explain the bombing in Los Angeles on the basis of a conspiracy between Smyth Industries and the Feral Cat League. It is more likely that either Smyth Industries or the Feral Cat League is responsible without conspiring.

Rule 6: **A hypothesis is more probably true if it correctly predicts previously unknown events.**

This is known as the **fruitfulness of a hypothesis.**

Examples of fruitful hypotheses in Case 26:

a.	If a hypothesis correctly predicted the city in which the Feral Cat League will bomb next, it increases the probability that the hypothesis is true.
b.	If a hypothesis correctly predicted the next building in the city that would be bombed, it increases the probability that the hypothesis is true.
c.	A classic and real example of Rule 5 is Einstein's General Theory of Relativity, which predicted that during an eclipse a star's true location would differ from its perceived location. During a solar eclipse in 1919, this prediction was demonstrated to be true, further evidence for Einstein's General Theory of Relativity.

We can use these six rules to help identify the best hypothesis to explain an event or set of facts. The best hypothesis might not receive good marks regarding all the rules, but we generally use the rules to identify the best plausible hypothesis. Remember, what might at first seem to be an implausible hypothesis, might become more plausible as we gather evidence. As one of Detective Wise's ancestors once said, "When all other contingencies fail, whatever remains, however improbable, must be the truth." (Sherlock Holmes)

7.8   Exercise Evaluate each hypothesis using the six rules. Circle the correct answer.

1. **Example:**
   Hypothesis: The Smyth building was bombed by the Four Monotones, a barbershop quartet. The citywide barbershop singing contest is next week, and the Four Monotones' chief rivals, the Happy Notes, regularly practice at the church next to the Smyth building. By bombing the Smyth building, they figured the Happy Notes would be rattled and unable to practice for the contest.
   a. This is a plausible hypothesis, and it is simpler than suggesting the building was bombed by the Feral Cat League.
   b. This is a plausible hypothesis, and it is broad enough to explain the note to the police as well as similar bombings in other cities.
   c. **This is not a plausible hypothesis. Barbershop singers are not typically bombers. It does not explain the note received by the police. It cannot explain similar bombings in other cities.**
   d. This is not a plausible hypothesis. Although barbershop singers are not known for their violence, it is not a testable hypothesis.

2. Hypothesis: It was a copycat crime. Some group, as yet unknown, thought the Feral Cat League made headlines, so they decided to copy the league's bombings to gain publicity.
   a. This is a plausible hypothesis and it is both broader and simpler than the hypothesis that the Feral Cat League committed the crime.
   b. This is a plausible hypothesis because it could not have been predicted given all the earlier evidence.
   c. This is not a plausible hypothesis because it is not testable.
   d. This is not a plausible hypothesis because it does not explain why the note to the police claimed that the Feral Cat League committed the crime. Indeed, since the copycat group allegedly wanted publicity, it could not obtain that if the Feral Cat League claimed responsibility.

3. Hypothesis: It was a copycat crime committed by the officers of Smyth Industries to collect the insurance on the building.
   a. This is a plausible hypothesis because crimes are sometimes committed to collect insurance.
   b. This is a plausible hypothesis because it explains both why the building was bombed and why the police received a note claiming that the Feral Cat League took responsibility for   the crime.
   c. This is not a plausible hypothesis because it does not explain how the elements of the earlier crimes that were known only to the police could have been copied.
   d. This is not a plausible hypothesis because Smyth Industries would have sold the building before declaring bankruptcy.

4. Hypothesis: The city took no actions to improve the fate of stray cats after the Smyth building was bombed. A week later, an empty building on Sunset Boulevard was bombed and the Feral Cat League claimed responsibility for the bombing.
    a. This increases the plausibility that the Feral Cat League was responsible for the crime since it fulfills a prediction based upon the hypothesis that they did it.
    b. This increases the plausibility that the Feral Cat League was responsible for the crime, since it shows that the hypothesis that they did it is fruitful. The hypothesis predicted an event that would not have been predicted on the basis of any other hypothesis.
    c. This does not increase the plausibility that the Feral Cat League was responsible for the crime since it is implausible that group would claim responsibility for several crimes.
    d. This does not increase the plausibility that the Feral Car League was responsible for the crime since it is a simpler hypothesis to suggest that different groups were responsible for the two bombings.

5. Hypothesis: Three days after the bombing, a large ad was placed in the *Los Angeles Times* featuring a picture of the bombed building saying, "We did it. Which building's next? The Feral Cat League."
    a. This gives more reason to accept the hypothesis that the Feral Cat League committed the bombing because that hypothesis allows one to predict that they'd run an ad claiming responsibility.
    b. This gives more reason to accept the hypothesis that the Feral Cat League committed the bombing because the ad provides another fact that is explained by that hypothesis.
    c. This gives less reason to accept the hypothesis that the Feral Cat League committed the bombing because it is a simpler explanation to claim that the Feral Cat League was responsible for both the bombing and the newspaper ad.
    d. This gives less reason to accept the hypothesis that the Feral Cat League committed the bombing because no one could have predicted the newspaper ad based on that hypothesis.

6. Hypothesis: Four days after the bombing, an occupied downtown skyscraper was bombed. Responsibility was claimed by the Beagle Bomber Brigade. They demanded the restoration of more World War I airplanes.
    a. It is likely that the Feral Cat League was responsible for the bombing since it is a simpler hypothesis that they were responsible for all the bombings than only some of them.
    b. It is likely that the Feral Cat League was responsible for the bombing since that hypothesis is testable, while any hypothesis concerning the Beagle Bombers Brigade is not testable.
    c. It is not likely that the Feral Cat League was responsible for the bombing since that hypothesis will not explain why there was a change from unoccupied buildings to occupied buildings or why there was a change in the name and demands of the bombers.
    d. It is not likely that the Feral Cat League was responsible for the bombing since it is implausible that restoring old airplanes could help stray cats.

(Continued)

7. Hypothesis: The city officials decided to "take care" of its stray cats by having police officers shoot them on sight. Several hundred cats were killed within five days. On the night of the fifth day, a large abandoned building on Wilshire was bombed. The next day, the police received a note reading, "That's not what we meant by *take care*. Be nice to the kitties or buildings will start dropping daily. The Feral Cat League."
   a. This strengthens the evidence for the hypothesis that the Feral Cat League is behind the bombings because that hypothesis explains both the second bombing and the second note.
   b. This strengthens the evidence for the hypothesis that the Feral Cat League is behind the bombings because the latest bombing could not have been predicted.
   c. This weakens the evidence for the hypothesis that the Feral Cat League is behind the bombings because it will not explain the actions of the city officials.
   d. This weakens the evidence for the hypothesis that the Feral Cat League is behind the bombings because that hypothesis is too broad to explain the latest bombing.

8. Hypothesis: The city did nothing to improve the fate of stray cats. Two weeks after the Smyth building was bombed, no other buildings had been bombed.
   a. This strengthens the evidence for the hypothesis that the Feral Cat League was responsible for bombing the Smyth building since only that hypothesis is broad enough to explain why the building was bombed.
   b. This strengthens the evidence for the hypothesis that the Feral Cat League was responsible for bombing the Smyth building since that hypothesis is simpler than alternative hypotheses.
   c. This weakens the evidence for the hypothesis that the Feral Cat League was responsible for bombing the Smyth building since that hypothesis was not fruitful.
   d. This weakens the evidence for the hypothesis that the Feral Cat League was responsible for bombing the Smyth building since predictions made on the basis of that hypothesis were false.

9. Hypothesis: An examination of building plans showed that the Smyth building was once connected by a tunnel to the Shomo building across Lyon Street. While the tunnel had been sealed in 1956, it had recently been opened. In the Shomo building, the entrance to the tunnel was in a suite of offices rented by the McGoogel Corporation. The McGoogel office was empty except for a crumpled cats'-rights poster, and no evidence of the existence of the McGoogel Corporation was found.

    a. This strengthens the evidence for the hypothesis that the Feral Cat League was responsible for bombing the Smyth building, since it would explain how the Feral Cat League gained entrance to the Smyth building and it would explain how the poster got into the McGoogel office.

    b. This strengthens the evidence for the hypothesis that the Feral Cat League was responsible for bombing the Smyth building, since taking over the McGoogel office was predictable on the basis of the hypothesis that the Feral Cat League was responsible for bombing the Smyth building.

    c. This weakens the evidence for the hypothesis that the Feral Cat League was responsible for bombing the Smyth building, since the Feral Cat League is not a registered corporation.

    d. This weakens the evidence for the hypothesis that the Feral Cat League was responsible for bombing the Smyth building, since it would be a simpler hypothesis to claim that the McGoogel Corporation bombed the Smyth building.

10. Hypothesis: Five days after the bombing, George Chow came to the police station and said he bombed the Smyth building. After two hours of questioning, the police released him because he knew no details of the bombing of the building.

    a. This strengthens the evidence for the hypothesis that the Feral Cat League was responsible for the bombing, since the police discarded the hypothesis that George Chow bombed the building.

    b. This weakens the evidence for the hypothesis that the Feral Cat League was responsible for the bombing, since it shows that there is an equally plausible hypothesis.

    c. This neither strengthens nor weakens the evidence for the hypothesis that the Feral Cat League was responsible for the bombing, since the truth of George's confession is irrelevant to the truth of the hypothesis.

    d. This neither strengthens nor weakens the evidence for the hypothesis that the Feral Cat League was responsible for the bombing, since the police concluded that there was no evidence that George Chow committed the crime.

CASE 27	City of Los Angeles Police Department

[1]There was a burglary at the night in a Wells Fargo office. [2]Detective Wise was called to the building to investigate.

[3]Detective Wise examined the evidence left by the crook or crooks. [4]There were two pairs of plastic gloves, both the same size. [5]The manufacturer of the gloves was Hospital Supply Corporation. [6]There was one stethoscope, apparently used to listen to the tumblers in the lock of the safe. [7]A Google earth map was on the floor with the building of Wells Fargo circled. [8]The detective found out that these items did not belong to any employees. [9]She thought about another safe-cracking burglary of another Wells Fargo office that had occurred in the city three days ago. [10]All the same evidence was found, two pairs of plastic gloves, the same manufacturer of the gloves, a Google earth map of the office, and a stethoscope. [11]Detective Wise concluded from the similarity of the two burglaries that the same criminal or criminals were involved. [12]What she was unsure of was whether there were two burglars or only one burglar who had used two pairs of gloves.

[13]Detective Wise also wondered how the night watchman in each building had not heard the burglary. [14]The detective wondered if this burglary was committed by someone walking around on tiptoe like a ballet dancer. [15]She wondered whether the criminals, if there were two burglars, used text-messaging the way that experienced users of cell phones would, to talk to each other, even though they were in the same room.

[16]Then one of police officers found two pairs of green surgical booties, such as those used by surgeons in an operating room to reduce friction, in the alley behind the building of the most recent burglary. [17]The manufacturer of the booties was the same company that made the plastic gloves. [18]Detective Wise concluded that it was almost certain now that two burglars had been involved. [19]Then the detective got a call from police headquarters and heard from her supervisor that a witness had turned up who had seen two motorcycles behind the building on the night of the burglary. [20]The detective concluded that it was even more likely that two burglars were involved.

7.9   Review Exercise Identify each as a descriptive analogy, an explanation analogy, or an argument by analogy. Circle the correct answer.

1. **Example:**
    The burglars' foot coverings looked like green surgical booties.
    (a.) **Descriptive analogy**
    b. Explanation analogy
    c. Argument by analogy

2. Because much of the evidence was the same in both burglaries, such as green booties, stethoscopes, and Google earth maps, we can affirm that the same crooks were involved.
    a. Descriptive analogy
    b. Explanation analogy
    c. Argument by analogy

3. In both robberies there were many similarities. So, it was the same criminals who burglarized the safes of Wells Fargo.
    a. Descriptive analogy
    b. Explanation analogy
    c. Argument by analogy

4. The detective thought the burglars were quiet, like mice.
    a. Descriptive analogy
    b. Explanation analogy
    c. Argument by analogy

5. There were two burglars who used text-messaging the way that experienced cell phone users do so they could communicate without being heard.
    a. Descriptive analogy
    b. Explanation analogy
    c. Argument by analogy

6. There were probably two criminals involved in the burglaries because there were two pairs of gloves, two pairs of booties in two of the robberies, and two motorcycles probably involved in one of the burglaries.
    a. Descriptive analogy
    b. Explanation analogy
    c. Argument by analogy

7.10 Review Exercise Circle the correct application of the rules for evaluating arguments by analogy.

1. **Example:**
What if the burglars used weapons in the first crime, but used no weapons in the second robbery because the watchman heard no noise whatsoever?
   a. The argument is stronger because it follows Rule 4, the fewer dissimilarities there are among the things compared, the stronger the argument.
   b. **The argument is weaker because it breaks Rule 4, the fewer dissimilarities there are among the things compared, the stronger the argument.**
   c. The argument is neither stronger nor weaker because of Rule 6, an overstated conclusion weakens the argument.

2. What if Detective Wise concluded that it was certain now that two burglars had been involved?
   a. The argument is stronger because it follows Rule 2, the similarities must be relevant.
   b. The argument is weaker because it breaks Rule 6, an overstated conclusion weakens the argument.
   c. The argument is neither stronger nor weaker because of Rule 3, the more things that are compared, the stronger the argument.

3. What if there were four bank burglaries with all the same characteristics?
   a. The argument is stronger because it follows Rule 3, the more things compared, the stronger the argument.
   b. The argument is weaker because it breaks Rule 6, an overstated conclusion weakens the argument.
   c. The argument is neither stronger nor weaker because of Rule 3, the more things compared, the stronger the argument.

4. What if the evidence in one burglary had two sets of plastic gloves, two sets of booties, and two motorcycles, but the evidence in the other burglary had only one set of gloves, one set of booties, and one motorcycle?
   a. The argument is stronger because it follows Rule 3, the more things compared, the stronger the argument.
   b. The argument is weaker because it breaks Rule 4, the fewer dissimilarities there are among the things compared, the stronger the argument.
   c. The argument is neither stronger nor weaker because of Rule 6, an overstated conclusion weakens the argument.

5. What if the burglars had wiped away any fingerprints in the office and also left the rear window open in both burglaries?
   a. The argument is stronger because it follows Rule 1, the greater the number of similarities, the stronger the argument.
   b. The argument is weaker because it breaks Rule 6, an overstated conclusion weakens the argument.
   c. The argument is neither stronger nor weaker because of Rule 3, the more things compared, the stronger the argument.

6. What if the burglars used small explosives in one burglary, but in the other, had used a stethoscope, even though the two safes were of the same make and size?
   a. The argument is stronger because it follows Rule 3, the more things compared, the stronger the argument.
   b. The argument is weaker because it breaks Rule 4, the fewer dissimilarities there are among the things compared, the stronger the argument.
   c. The argument is neither stronger nor weaker because of Rule 6, an overstated conclusion weakens the argument.

7. What if the first burglary had 10 pairs of plastic gloves and ten pairs of green booties, but the second burglary had no plastic gloves and no pairs of booties?
   a. The argument is stronger because it follows Rule 1, the greater the number of similarities, the stronger the argument.
   b. The argument is weaker because it breaks Rule 4, the fewer dissimilarities there are among the things compared, the stronger the argument.
   c. The argument is stronger because of Rule 3, the more things compared, the stronger the argument.

8. What if the crime lab discovered that there were the same fingerprints left in five earlier burglaries and Detective Wise concluded that the sixth burglary was done by the same criminals since the same fingerprints were found?
   a. The argument is stronger because of Rule 3, the more things compared, the stronger the argument.
   b. The argument is stronger because it follows Rule 1, the greater the number of similarities, the stronger the argument.
   c. The argument is weaker because it breaks Rule 4, the fewer dissimilarities there are among the things compared, the stronger the argument.

9. What if, in both burglaries, the two criminals had been seen dressed in green surgical garments with white masks over their faces?
   a. The argument is stronger because of Rule 3, the more things compared, the stronger the argument.
   b. The argument is stronger because it follows Rule 1, the greater the number of similarities, the stronger the argument.
   c. The argument is weaker because it breaks Rule 4, the fewer dissimilarities there are among the things compared, the stronger the argument.

10. What if, in both burglaries, the burglars had left notes that mocked the police department?
    a. The argument is weaker because it breaks Rule 3, the more things compared, the stronger the argument.
    b. The argument is neither stronger nor weaker because Rule 6 is broken, an overstated conclusion weakens the argument.
    c. The argument is stronger because it follows Rule 1, the greater the number of similarities, the stronger the argument.

7.11 Review Exercise Read the information below, then evaluate the following inductive generalizations by the three rules. Circle the correct answer.

> Detective Wise is an avid birdwatcher. One morning she looks out her window and sees ten ravens. They're all black. She jumps to the conclusion that most ravens are black.

1. **Example:**
    What if Detective Wise had concluded that all ravens are black?
    a. As the number of cases we examine increases, the generalization becomes stronger.
    b. As the diversity of the cases increases, the generalization is strengthened.
    c. An overstated conclusion weakens the argument.

2. What if there were twenty ravens in her yard and they were all black?
    a. As the number of cases we examine increases, the generalization becomes stronger.
    b. As the diversity of the cases increases, the generalization is strengthened.
    c. An overstated conclusion weakens the argument.

3. What if she had based her conclusion on ten ravens observed at different places in Los Angeles, all of which were black?
    a. The number of cases is increased, so the conclusion is strengthened.
    b. The sample is more diverse, so the conclusion is strengthened.
    c. An overstated conclusion weakens the argument.

4. What if on vacation Detective Wise observes fifty more ravens, and they're also black?
    a. As the number of cases we examine increases, the generalization becomes stronger.
    b. As the diversity of the cases increases, the generalization is strengthened.
    c. An overstated conclusion weakens the argument.

5. What if she travels to England and observes two hundred black ravens near Buckingham Palace?
    a. As the number of cases we examine increases, the generalization becomes stronger.
    b. As the diversity of the cases increases, the generalization is strengthened.
    c. An overstated conclusion weakens the argument.

6. What if her sample includes both Los Angeles and Australian ravens, which are black?
    a. As the number of cases we examine increases, the generalization becomes stronger.
    b. As the diversity of the cases increases, the generalization is strengthened.
    c. An overstated conclusion weakens the argument.

7. What if she scoured history books and discovered that all references to ravens were references to black birds?
    a. As the number of cases we examine increases, the generalization becomes stronger.
    b. As the diversity of the cases increases, the generalization is strengthened.
    c. An overstated conclusion weakens the argument.

8. What if Detective Wise observes only four ravens from her breakfast nook before concluding that most ravens are black?
    a. The argument is weakened because the number of cases examined is decreased.
    b. The argument is weaker because her sample is less diverse.
    c. An overstated conclusion weakens the argument.

9. What if she concluded that most ravens in her neighborhood are black?
    a. As the number of cases we examine increases, the generalization becomes stronger.
    b. As the diversity of the cases increases, the generalization is strengthened.
    c. An overstated conclusion weakens the argument.

10. What if Detective Wise observes three black ravens and five black crows, concluding that all ravens are black?
    a. The argument is weakened because because the sample is smaller.
    b. The argument is weakened because this rule is broken: As the diversity of the cases increases, the generalization is strengthened.
    c. An overstated conclusion weakens the argument.

7.12 Review Exercise Evaluate the following hypotheses. Circle the best answer.

1. **Example:**
   Hypothesis: Legionnaires' Disease, a severe type of pneumonia at the City Hotel, is caused by bad luck.
    a. This is a plausible hypothesis and it is simpler than suggesting that the illness was caused by the simultaneous occurrence of 20 viruses.
    b. This is a plausible hypothesis and it is broad enough to explain many other forms of pneumonia occur.
    c. **This is not a plausible hypothesis. Bad luck could explain why everything bad happens, and so it doesn't explain why any particular thing which is bad would happen.**
    d. This is a plausible hypothesis. Unpredictable events do occur, and scientific hypotheses need to explain unpredictable events.

2. Hypothesis: Legionnaires' Disease at the City Hotel was caused by the red hair of the people who became ill.
    a. This is a plausible hypothesis because many other forms of pneumonia are caused by red hair.
    b. This is a plausible hypothesis because it would explain why some people with blond hair at the hotel did not become ill but other people with blond hair did become ill.
    c. This is not a plausible hypothesis because it is not testable.
    d. This is not a plausible hypothesis because it does not explain why some people with red hair at the hotel did not become ill, but others with red hair did.

(Continued)

3. Hypothesis: The Legionnaires' Disease at City Hotel was caused by a terrorist group.
   a. This is a plausible hypothesis because crimes by terrorist groups are possible with biological or chemical agents.
   b. This is a plausible hypothesis because it explains why the people got sick at only one hotel and not at other places in the city.
   c. This is not a plausible hypothesis because it does not explain why no terrorist group has taken responsibility for the crime, nor does it explain why the biological or chemical agent cannot yet be identified. However, it would be reasonable to expect that any terrorist group would work with some well-known biological or chemical agent to cause the illness.
   d. This is not a plausible hypothesis because it is not testable.

4. Hypothesis: Since many other pneumonias are caused by viruses or bacteria, it is likely that Legionnaires' Disease, a severe form of pneumonia, is caused by a virus or bacterium.
   a. This hypothesis is plausible because it fits in with other well-verified hypotheses about different kinds of pneumonia.
   b. This hypothesis is plausible because it predicts an event, a new form of pneumonia, that would not have been predicted on the basis of any other hypothesis.
   c. This hypothesis does not increase the plausibility that all pneumonias are caused by viruses or bacteria.
   d. This hypothesis does not increase the plausibility that the viruses or bacteria are responsible for Legionnaires' Disease because it is a simpler hypothesis to hold that all pneumonias are caused by viruses.

5. Hypothesis: One year after the new outbreak of Legionnaires' Disease had occurred, two other previously unknown kinds of pneumonia occurred. One was caused by a virus; the other was caused by a bacterium.
   a. This gives more reason to accept the hypothesis that Legionnaires' Disease is caused by a virus or bacterium because the hypothesis allows one to predict that new forms of pneumonia will develop as the earth's climate warms.
   b. This gives more reason to accept the hypothesis that Legionnaires' Disease is caused by a virus or bacterium because the hypothesis fits in with other well-verified hypotheses about pneumonia.
   c. This gives less reason to accept that Legionnaires' Disease is caused by a virus or bacterium because the hypothesis does not explain why only 10 percent of the people at City Hotel came down with Legionnaires' Disease.
   d. This gives less reason to accept that Legionnaires' Disease is caused by a virus or bacterium because no one could have predicted the development of new forms of pneumonia.

6. Hypothesis: An unknown group calling themselves Vigilantes for Vegetables sent the police a note claiming responsibility for the Legionnaires' Disease at City Hotel. They also sent a package with a new kind of virus, which they called the XYZ Virus, claiming that this virus had caused the disease. But when the police tested the virus in five different experiments using groups of mice, no mice in any group had pneumonia-like symptoms.
   a. This would strengthen the evidence for the hypothesis that no virus whatsoever was the cause of the illness since no mice came down with symptoms.
   b. This would strengthen the evidence for the hypothesis that the XYZ Virus was not the cause of the illness since no mice came down with symptoms.
   c. This would weaken the evidence for the hypothesis that the XYZ virus was not the cause of the illness. Since the police would not want the public to be scared, they cannot be trusted to conduct a fair test of the virus.
   d. This would weaken the hypothesis that no virus was the cause of the illness. Since the police would not want the public to be scared, they cannot be trusted to conduct a fair test of the virus.

7. Hypothesis: A new virus was found in the potato salad served at City Hotel, and this virus was given to a first group of 50 mice and withheld from a second group of 50 mice. Both groups were very similar except for receiving the virus, but neither group came down with pneumonialike symptoms.
   a. This strengthens the evidence for the hypothesis that Legionnaires' Disease is neither caused by a virus nor a bacterium because neither group of mice came down with pneumonialike symptoms.
   b. This weakens the evidence for the hypothesis that Legionnaires' Disease is neither caused by a virus nor a bacterium because the hypothesis that Legionnaires' Disease is caused by a bacterium is simpler than alternative hypotheses.
   c. This weakens the evidence for the hypothesis that Legionnaires' Disease is caused by a virus or a bacterium because that hypothesis was not fruitful in bringing about pneumonialike symptoms in either group of mice.
   d. This weakens the evidence for the hypothesis that Legionnaires' Disease is caused by the new virus because predictions made on the basis of that hypothesis were false.

(Continued)

8. Hypothesis: A new form of bacterium was found in the unpurified water of City Hotel's air conditioning system. This bacterium was given to 50 mice and withheld from 50 other mice. Both groups of mice were similar except for the fact that the first group of 50 received the new bacterium, and all 50 of this first group came down with pneumonialike symptoms.

   a. This strengthens the evidence for the hypothesis that Legionnaires' Disease is caused by the new bacterium because the hypothesis was verified by the experiment.

   b. This weakens the hypothesis that Legionnaires' Disease is caused by a virus or bacterium because the 50 mice not receiving the bacterium did not come down with pneumonialike symptoms,

   c. This both strengthens and weakens the evidence for the hypothesis that Legionnaires' Disease is caused by a virus or bacterium because the first group of 50 mice had pneumonialike symptoms but the second group of 50 did not have pneumonialike symptoms.

   d. This weakens the evidence for the hypothesis that Legionnaires' Disease is caused by a virus or bacterium because it would be a simpler hypothesis to claim that a virus was the cause of Legionnaires' Disease.

9. Hypothesis: Ten months after the outbreak of Legionnaires' Disease at City Hotel, 100 people became ill with Legionnaires' Disease at the Good Luck Casino in another state.

   a. This strengthens the evidence for the hypothesis that Legionnaires' Disease is caused by a virus or bacterium because we now have more evidence in the form of diseased lung tissue which we can test for the presence of an unknown bacterium or virus.

   b. This weakens the evidence for the hypothesis that Legionnaires' Disease is caused by a virus or bacterium because it shows that there is an equally plausible hypothesis that someone is deliberately spreading a virus or bacterium around.

   c. This would strengthen the evidence for the hypothesis that Legionnaires' Disease is caused by a virus or bacterium if testing in both cases at City Hotel and at the Good Luck Casino had eliminated any other possible causes of the pneumonias other than a virus or a bacterium.

   d. This weakens the evidence for the hypothesis that Legionnaires' Disease is caused by a virus or bacterium because the scientists now have too many pieces of evidence to analyze.

10. Hypothesis: A previously unknown virus and a previously unknown bacterium have been found at City Hotel. Either the virus or the bacterium or both may be the cause of Legionnaires' Disease

   a. The hypothesis that both are involved in causing the disease is unlikely since it almost never happens that both a virus and a bacterium work together to produce a disease.

   b. There is no way of testing whether the virus is responsible or the bacterium is responsible for causing the disease.

   c. No scientific experiment can ever conclusively prove any hypothesis.

   d. A scientific experiment can only disprove a hypothesis when it fails to bring about the expected results.

7.13 Appendix: Surveys

A **survey** is an inductive argument that gives you a snapshot of how something is in the world at a particular time. It involves an inductive generalization. Like any inductive generalization, there is usually a small sample from which you reach a general conclusion. So, the three criteria for evaluating inductive arguments apply to surveys as well. As we shall see, there are some additional questions you'll often want to ask. Let's start with a simple case.

Every ten years, the United States conducts a census. This survey is an attempt to get basic information about the population of the United States. Everyone is supposed to fill out a census, but not everyone does. Some census forms are misplaced. Some people forget to send them. Some people don't receive a form. Some people refuse to supply the private information. Most people receive a short form. It asks how many people are in your household. One household out of ten receives a long form. The long form asks more questions. Do you rent your home or own it? How many years did you go to school? What is your family income? And so forth. After the Census Bureau compiles all the data from the survey, there is a great deal of information about life in the United States.

If everyone in the United States filled out the census forms, we could be certain of the conclusions reached. Since some people don't fill out the forms, the Census Bureau sends out people to check on the forms that were not returned. By doing this, they can become fairly certain of the number of people in the United States on April 1 of that year. In 2000, they concluded that the population of the United States was approximately 280 million people.

The more interesting questions are on the long form. What portion of the population is Hispanic? What portion of the population has an annual family income of less than $20,000? What portion of the population lives on farms? But the long forms are only sent to one family out of ten. How can they be certain of their conclusions?

The conclusions drawn from the long form survey are a collection of inductive generalizations. Ten percent of the population is a large portion of the population. When we were wondering about the color of swans, we didn't observe nearly ten percent of all swans. But what if all the people who got the long forms were in New York City or Los Angles? The folks in the Midwest don't consider people on either coast "average Americans." The census takers want to find out who the "average Americans" are — average income, average number of children, and so forth. So, they want to make sure that the sample is diverse. They want to make sure their sample is **random.** A sample is random if every person in the population has an equal chance of being included in it. Randomness is an ideal. No survey is perfectly random. What does the Census Bureau do to obtain a random sample? They might send a long form to every tenth address on their mailing list. There are more O'Meara households than Flage households, so the number of O'Mearas who receive the long form will be greater. The number of people in cities will be larger than the number in small towns. This allows the Census Bureau to generalize on the basis of about ten percent of the population.

"But," you say, "it's not only the Census Bureau that makes general claims about the people in the United States. Almost every day on the news, we hear that the president's approval rating has gone up or down or that 58 percent of Americans don't like the proposed Social Security reforms. How do they know that? Do they interview about 280 million people, like the Census Bureau?"

Taking the census is very costly. ABC News or the Gallup Organization could not afford to interview 280 million people to see whether they approve of the president's activities or proposed bills. They usually interview about a thousand people. "How can a thousand people tell us anything about the views of 280 million people?" you ask. *As the number of people interviewed decreases, the importance of randomness increases.* Long experience has taught the poll takers that if they interview a thousand people, they will be accurate within 4 percent about 95 percent of the time. So, if we hear that the president's approval rating has dropped to 40 percent, it will be stated as 40 percent, plus or minus 4 percent. That means that between 36 and 44 percent of the population approves of what the president is doing.

How do the poll takers try to assure randomness? They use a method that is available to most people. Today, most polls are taken by telephone. Almost everyone has a telephone. Then they phone numbers at random. These numbers might be generated by computers. They also need to be sure their questions are neutral. For example, if you were asked, "You don't approve of what the president's doing, do you?" you might believe that the *correct* answer is "no." A more neutral question would be something like, "Do you approve of the president's policies?"

How the survey is taken is important. In 1936, *Literary Digest* took a poll to see who was preferred for president: Franklin Roosevelt or Alf Landon. The poll was taken by telephone. In 1936, having a telephone was more of a luxury than it is today. The survey data predicted that Alf Landon would be elected president, but that prediction proved false. Should you trust a poll taken today that is taken over the Internet? Why or why not?

There are companies that take surveys to measure public opinion. The Gallup Organization is one. The Harris Poll is another. If you hear that such a well-known company has taken a survey, should you trust the results? Probably. It's their business. They know what should be done to approach randomness. They have reputations to maintain. They often take polls before elections. If their predictions were regularly wrong, they'd lose business. It's in their best interest to get things right.

There are other surveys that you might want to question. Let's say a soft-drink maker tells you that it conducted a nationwide survey. More people preferred the taste of their brand than that of their leading competitor. When we hear claims like these, we should ask how the survey was conducted. Were the questions neutral? That is, were there questions that suggested choosing their brand the "correct answer?" If these were "taste tests," were they conducted in a neutral environment? If they were conducted in front of a "Drink Coke!" sign, that wouldn't be neutral. How many people were involved? In what parts of the country were the surveys made? Unfortunately, we won't find answers to most of those questions. So, as a good consumer, we should be a bit doubtful.

> About fifty years ago, a cigarette maker advertised that a nationwide survey had shown that more doctors smoked their brand than any other. One of the authors wrote the company a few years ago to see how the survey had been conducted. He's still waiting for an answer.

Have you ever noticed that manufacturers, political parties, and organizations representing specific groups of people often conduct surveys? Have you noticed that the reported surveys are always favorable to the views of those reporting them? Do you find that surprising? Does it make you wonder whether they report all the surveys they take? Does it make you wonder whether the surveys attempt to be random?

Chapter 7 Quiz

Choose the best answer for each of the following questions.

1. Inductive arguments:
   a. provide conclusive evidence for their conclusions.
   b. always reach a general conclusion.
   c. are sometimes deductively valid.
   d. provide only some evidence for their conclusions.
   e. always begin with premises referring to individuals.

2. Arguments by analogy:
   a. assume general conclusions are false.
   b. can proceed directly from individual cases to individual cases.
   c. are based on similarities among objects.
   d. are a type of deductive argument.
   e. both b and c

3. When the conclusion of an analogy or generalization becomes stronger:
   a. the evidence for it becomes weaker.
   b. it is easier to show that the conclusion is false.
   c. the argument is strengthened.
   d. it is also an argument to an explanation.
   e. both a and b

4. The diversity of a sample for an inductive generalization increases if the sample:
   a. is larger.
   b. is taken from more places in space and time.
   c. includes people of all races and religions.
   d. is consistent with the best scientific explanations.
   e. is approved by the National Science Foundation.

5. One of two explanations is more parsimonious if:
   a. it is based on a larger sample.
   b. it includes fewer distinct kinds of objects.
   c. it allows one to correctly predict events in the supernatural world.
   d. it is consistent with the best scientific explanations.
   e. compares more distinct properties of objects.

6. Other things being equal, one of two explanations is better if:
   a. it compares more distinct properties of objects.
   b. it proceeds from a larger sample.
   c. it has a stronger conclusion.
   d. it allows one to correctly predict previously unknown events.
   e. it allows one to include it in a deductive argument.

(Continued)

7. Some inductive arguments:
    a. reach general conclusions.
    b. reach conclusions about individual objects.
    c. give reasons to believe that a hypothesis is true.
    d. assume that conclusions reached by other inductive arguments are true.
    e. all of the above

8. In claiming that a hypothesis is testable one assumes:
    a. that the hypothesis is true.
    b. that one can make observations that tend to show that the hypothesis is true or false.
    c. that it is based upon a very large sample.
    d. that it is parsimonious.
    e. that it provides the best explanation of an event.

9. A conclusion of an inductive generalization that holds that most things of kind A are things of kind B:
    a. is stronger than a conclusion that all things of kind A are things of kind B.
    b. is the typical conclusion of a random survey.
    c. is better supported by the evidence than a conclusion that all things of kind A are things of kind B.
    d. is an instance of an argument to the best explanation.
    e. is unwarranted unless it follows as the conclusion of a sound deductive argument.

10. No inductive argument:
    a. is a valid deductive argument.
    b. proceeds from properties of individual objects to a general conclusion.
    c. concludes that one explanation is better than another explanation.
    d. compares objects directly.
    e. all of the above

CHAPTER 8

- Informal Fallacies
- Review

Overview

Informal fallacies are common errors in argument. Some of these errors are based on reasoning. Some are based upon false premises or weak premises. Some are based upon shifts in meaning.

CASE 28	City of Los Angeles Police Department

[1]Dectective Wise was called to the witness stand to testify about five bank robberies that had occurred in the city. [2]The person on trial was a man about 30 years old.

[3]The defense attorney asked the detective what was the evidence linking the accused to any of the robberies. [4]The detective replied that the fingerprints of the accused were found on the bank counter after the first robbery, but not after any of the other robberies. [5]The detective said that she assumed that the robber was the same because the same method of robbery had been followed in each case. [6]The defense attorney objected to the assumption, stating that the detective had made a hasty generalization that all the robberies were therefore done by the same person.

[7]The next question to the detective was whether she was an expert in fingerprint identification. [8]The detective admitted that she was not. [9]So the defense attorney objected to the detective's identification of the fingerprints as belonging to the accused. [10]But the detective replied that the defense attorney could call the fingerprint expert to the witness stand to find out the evidence.

[11]The defense attorney asked where the accused was arrested. [12]Detective Wise replied that the accused was arrested one block away from the fifth bank that had been robbed about 15 minutes after the robbery. [13]The defense attorney asked whether any bank money was found or any weapons. [14]The detective replied that no evidence from the fifth bank robbery was found on the accused. [15]The defense attorney argued that the accused was guilty of the first robbery but not of any of the others, because the detective was wrong in concluding that the accused had committed the fifth robbery just because he was found near the scene of the crime 15 minutes afterward.

8.1 Fallacies of Weak Induction

Fallacies of weak induction are found in arguments that provide some evidence, but not enough evidence to make the conclusion highly probable.   Here are four common fallacies of weak induction:

> **Fallacy 1: Hasty Generalization***
> This fallacy produces an unsupported conclusion when we base it on a sample which is either atypical, too small, or not diverse enough. Hasty generalizations can also play a part in prejudice and stereotypes.

Examples of hasty generalization:

a.	Based on one warm season at the North Pole, a news reporter draws the conclusion that global warming has arrived. It may or may not be the case that global warming has arrived, but concluding it has because of one warm season at the North Pole is unjustified.
b.	The defense attorney asked the detective what was the evidence linking the accused to any of the robberies. The detective replied that the fingerprints of the accused were found on the bank counter after the first robbery, but not after any of the other robberies. The detective said that she assumed that the robber was the same because the same method of robbery had been followed in each case. The defense attorney objected to the assumption, stating that the detective had made a hasty generalization that all the robberies were therefore done by the same person (sentences 3-6).
c.	A major of a very large city reads a report filed by the child of police that there have been three attacks by pit bulls in the last two years that resulted in serious bodily injury to people and concludes that all pit bulls are vicious and must be banned within city limits. The major is making a decision based on a sample that is too small and has stereotyped all pit bulls because of this hasty generalization.

> **Fallacy 2: Fallacious Appeal to Authority**
> Appeal to authority is fallacious when the authority appealed to is not a true authority in the field.

Examples of fallacious appeal to authority:

a.	In an advertisement, a movie star says one should buy a Cadillac, because they are wonderful cars. Movie stars are not experts about cars and their quality. *Consumer Reports* would be a good expert on the value of cars.
b.	The next question to the detective was whether she was an expert in fingerprint identification. The detective admitted that she was not. So the defense attorney objected to the detective's identification of the fingerprints as belonging to the accused. But the detective replied that the defense attorney could call the fingerprint expert to the witness stand to find out the evidence (sentences 7-10).
c.	A Nobel Prize winner in physics argues that taking vitamin C will prevent colds. A great physics professor is a good authority in physics, but not in biology and medicine.

*See our discussion about inductive generalizations on pages 463-464.

Fallacy 3: False Cause

The fallacy of False Cause occurs when we identify something as a cause that is not a cause. Simply because things happen together or because one thing follows another does not necessarily meanh that they are related as cause and effect. They might be; they might not. At most, they *might* suggest a casual connection. Another type of false cause is an oversimplified cause. This is when an effect is the result of a number of causes but only one of these causes is concluded to be the sole cause.

Examples of false cause:

a.	If I conclude that vitamin C prevents colds because I took it for a week and didn't get a cold, I have only a few correlations or for claiming a causal connection. Much more evidence would be needed to justify this conclusion.
b.	Joe always rubs his hands together with dirt before he goes to bat because he did that in one game and git five hits out of five at bats. Joe's faulty assumption is the basis for his superstitious actions. Rubbing his hands with dirt is not really a cause of his good hitting.
c.	A member of Congress argues that the amount of electricity consumed in the United States has increased because more people are playing games like Wii and XBox and consequently Congress should pass a special sales tax to help offset the cost of electricity. Despite the fact that games like Wii and XBox are very popular and use electricity, there are other reasons besides playing Wii and XBox for the increase in electric consumption.

Fallacy 4: Weak Analogy*

This fallacy occurs when the conclusion of an argument is based on a comparison between two things that are dissimilar in important ways.

Examples of weak analogy:

a.	If the robberies of the five banks had been done in different ways with different weapons, different escape cars, and different threats, but Detective Wise concluded that they had all been done by the same robbers, then she would commit the fallacy of weak analogy. Because there are significant differences among the five bank robberies, the analogy does not provide enough support to make it likely that the conclusion is true.
b.	Adults can publish what they wish in the newspaper, and since high school students are like adults, high school students should be able to publish what they wish. This is a weak analogy because high school students are different from adults in a number of important ways; for example, their brains are still developing and as a result there are differences in maturity, judgment, and impulse control. High school students also do not have the same rights and privileges as adults as seen in the decision by the Supreme Court to limit the speech and writing of high school students in order to prevent the advocacy of illegal actions.

*See our discussion about Evaluating Arguments by Analogy, pp. 457–459.

| 8.2 | **Exercise** Circle the probable fallacy involved in the arguments. |

1. **Example:**
   My 1997 Toyota Camry is unreliable. Therefore, all Toyotas are unreliable.
   a. **Hasty generalization**
   b. Fallacious appeal to authority
   c. False cause
   d. Weak analogy
   e. Probably not a fallacious argument

2. George Washington always smoked Virginia tobaccos in his pipe. So, Virginia tobaccos are the best in the world.
   a. Hasty generalization
   b. Fallacious appeal to authority
   c. False cause
   d. Weak analogy
   e. Probably not a fallacious argument

3. Getting an education is not important. Look at the billionaire owner of the new search engine for the Internet. He dropped out of college but made a billion dollars with his new search engine. Hence, education is not important for any students.
   a. Hasty generalization
   b. Fallacious appeal to authority
   c. False cause
   d. Weak analogy
   e. Probably not a fallacious argument

4. You should make 20 copies of this letter and pass them on to your friends so that you will have good luck, because I had good luck guessing the winner of the Kentucky Derby after I sent out 20 copies of the letter. I conclude that the letter obviously brought about the result of the good luck.
   a. Hasty generalization
   b. Fallacious appeal to authority
   c. False cause
   d. Weak analogy
   e. Probably not a fallacious argument

5. Einstein said that the speed of light was about 186,000 miles per second. So that is the speed of light.
   a. Hasty generalization
   b. Fallacious appeal to authority
   c. False cause
   d. Weak analogy
   e. Probably not a fallacious argument

(Continued)

6. I have been observing crows all over the U.S. for 50 years and they have all been black. So I conclude that the vast majority of crows in the U.S. are black.
   a. Hasty generalization
   b. Fallacious appeal to authority
   c. False cause
   d. Weak analogy
   e. Probably not a fallacious argument

7. A hamburger is like a time bomb because if you eat it, it will eventually blow up, destroying your heart. So, don't eat a hamburger.
   a. Hasty generalization
   b. Fallacious appeal to authority
   c. False cause
   d. Weak analogy
   e. Probably not a fallacious argument

8. The detective testified that the cause of death was arsenic poisoning. So arsenic was the cause of death.
   a. Hasty generalization
   b. Fallacious appeal to authority
   c. False cause
   d. Weak analogy
   e. Probably not a fallacious argument

9. The medical examiner testified that the cause of death was arsenic poisoning. So arsenic was the cause of death.
   a. Hasty generalization
   b. Fallacious appeal to authority
   c. False cause
   d. Weak analogy
   e. Probably not a fallacious argument

10. Labor Day is a legal holiday. All legal holidays have no mail delivery. So, Labor Day has no mail delivery.
    a. Hasty generalization
    b. Fallacious appeal to authority
    c. False cause
    d. Weak analogy
    e. Probably not a fallacious argument

CASE 29	City of Los Angeles Police Department

[1]Dectective Wise was sitting next to the prosecuting attorney as the defense attorney questioned the witness in the bank robbery case. [2]The prosecuting attorney wanted the detective to advise him.

[3]The defense attorney asked the witness whether she had stopped lying about the evidence in the case. [4]Before the witness could answer, the detective whispered to the prosecutor to object because the defense attorney's question assumed another question had been answered. [5]One question was, "Were you lying?" [6]The second question was, "Did you stop lying?" [7]The defense attorney was presuming that the answer to the first question was yes.

[8]The questioning continued as the defense attorney asked the witness whether she was telling all truths or all lies. [9]Detective Wise whispered to the prosecutor to object because the question presumed a false dichotomy. [10]The detective explained that there are more than two alternatives than either all truths or all lies; that some statements could be true but others false.

[11]The questioning continued as the prosecuting attorney asked the witness what she saw clearly during the bank robbery. [12]The witness said that she saw clearly that the robber had a mustache. [13]Detective Wise whispered to the prosecuting attorney that the witness was suppressing the evidence that her eyesight was very poor at the distance between herself and the robber. [14]The detective explained that the suppressed evidence contradicted the witness's claim that she "saw clearly that the robber had a mustache."

[15]The defense attorney continued to question the witness, asking if the "guilty robber" committed the crime. [16]Detective Wise whispered to the prosecutor to object because the question presumed the defendant was guilty of robbery. [17]The detective explained that asking whether the "guilty person" was guilty was fallacious because the answer was assumed in the characterization "guilty person."

8.3 Fallacies of Presumption

In **Fallacies of Presumption**, either the argument presumes something in the premises that is part or all of the conclusion, or the argument presumes that all the information is stated in the premises when, in fact, information is missing.

Fallacy 1: Begging the Question
This fallacy occurs when we assume in the premises the very point we are trying to conclude by either restating the conclusion in the premise or by arguing in a circle.

Examples of begging the question:

a.	A politician argues, "My opponent, Mrs. HoHum, is unqualified to be a senator and does not deserve your vote because she does not have the necessary experience and accomplishments to be elected to the Senate." To be unqualified for a job means the same thing as to not have the necessary qualities or accomplishments for a particular job. The premise merely restates the conclusion.
b.	The defense attorney continued to question the witness, asking if the guilty robber was guilty. Detective Wise whispered to the prosecuting attorney to object because the question presumed exactly what it hoped to prove, namely, that the robber was guilty. The detective explained that asking whether the guilty person was guilty was fallacious because guilt was used in the premise to prove guilt in the conclusion (sentences 15-17).
c.	Someone argues that Joe is brave because he is good and that Joe is good because he is brave. This is a circular argument because bravery is used to prove goodness and goodness is used to prove bravery.
d.	A Michael Jackson fan argues, "Michael Jackson is the greatest superstar of all time. He has sold more albums than anyone else and his music continues to be number one today. The reason Michael Jackson's music continues to be at the top of the charts is because more people have bought his albums than any other artist. People buy his albums because he is the greatest superstar of all time." This argument involves circular reasoning. These types of arguments can be convincing when they are long and complex because it can be easy to lose track of the circular reasoning.

Fallacy 2: Complex (loaded) Question

A complex or loaded question includes an assumption about something that is still in question. The question also puts the respondent in a bad light no matter how the question is answered.   For example, if someone asks you, "Have you quit beating your dog yet?" the question assumes you beat your dog. If you answer "yes," then listeners will infer that you did beat your dog, but have now stopped. If you answer "no," then listeners will assume that you still beat your dog.

Note: A complex question is not really a fallacy, since it's not an argument. It is listed as an informal fallacy, since in answering the question one draws a conclusion. Notice also that there are nonfallacious complex questions. If I ask, "Where were you Saturday night?" I'm assuming you were somewhere Saturday night, but that assumption is unquestionably true.

Examples of fallacious complex questions:

a.	If a person asks, "Have you stopped cheating on your taxes?" the question assumes that you cheat on your taxes.
b.	The defense attorney asked the witness when did the witness stop lying about the evidence in the case. Before the witness could answer, the detective whispered to the prosecuting attorney to object because the other attorney was asking two questions at the same time. One question was, "Were you lying?" The second question was, "When did you stop lying?" The attorney was presuming that the answer to the first question was yes (sentences 3-7).
c.	"Where were you last Saturday night?" The question is complex, since is assumes that the answer to the question "Were you somewhere Saturday night?" is "Yes." If you're old enough to be asked the complex question, you had to be somewhere or other on Saturday night (although not necessarily anywhere special). So, there is no fallacy.

Fallacy 3: Suppressed Evidence

The fallacy of suppressed evidence occurs whenever information which may be relevant to determining the truth or falsity of a conclusion is intentionally withheld.

Examples of the fallacy of suppressed evidence:

a.	A salesperson affirms that you should buy this 15-year-old car because it has only 20,000 miles on the odometer. But what is suppressed in this case is the relevant evidence that the odometer has been changed. We could find out the true mileage by checking with CARFAX.
b.	The questioning continued as the defense attorney asked the witness what the witness saw clearly during the bank robbery. The witness said that she saw clearly that the robber had a mustache. Detective Wise whispered to the prosecuting attorney to object because the witness was suppressing the evidence that her eyesight was very poor at the distance between herself and the robber. The detective explained that the suppressed evidence contradicted the witness's claim that she "saw clearly that the robber had a mustache" (sentences 11-14).

Fallacy 4: False Dichotomy (False Dilemma)

A false dichotomy is a disjunctive syllogism with a false disjunctive (either ... or ...) premise. These choices are presented as if they were the only possible choices when they are not. For example, the claim, "Either Detective Wise is 25 or she's 92" is false if she is actually 34. We would not want to conclude that since she is not 25, then she must be 92.

Examples of the fallacy of false dichotomy:

a.	The questioning continued as the defense attorney asked the witness whether the witness was telling all truths or all lies. Detective Wise whispered to the prosecuting attorney to object because the question presumed a false dichotomy. The detective explained that there are more than two alternatives than either all truths or all lies, that some statements could be true but others false (sentences 8-10).
b.	Someone argues that given the problems of global warming, we must either stop using fossil fuels or else we will turn the whole planet into a desert. Obviously, there are more alternatives than the two listed. Fossil fuels could be used moderately along with solar energy and wind energy and tidal energy.

8.4   Exercise Circle the fallacy of presumption involved in the arguments.

1. **Example:**
   Let's discuss buying a new car. Shall we buy a Japanese car or an American car?
   a. Begging the question
   b. Complex question
   c. Suppressed evidence
   (d.)**False dichotomy***
   e. Not a fallacious argument
   *Because there are many more kinds of cars than Japanese and American cars.

2. Eating high-cholesterol foods is dangerous to your health because such foods are a danger to your body's functioning.
   a. Begging the question
   b. Complex question
   c. Suppressed evidence
   d. False dichotomy
   e. Not a fallacious argument

3. Voting for more taxes for more roads is wrong because taxation is theft.
   a. Begging the question
   b. Complex question
   c. Suppressed evidence
   d. False dichotomy
   e. Not a fallacious argument

4. Why did you lie under oath?
   a. Begging the question
   b. Complex question
   c. Suppressed evidence
   d. False dichotomy
   e. Not a fallacious argument

5. You should obey your parents because it is the respectful thing to do. And it is the respectful thing to do because you will be obeying your parents.
   a. Begging the question
   b. Complex question
   c. Suppressed evidence
   d. False dichotomy
   e. Not a fallacious argument

(Continued)

6. We should vote for the referendum to legalize casinos because it provides for better schools without raising our taxes.
    a. Begging the question
    b. Complex question
    c. Suppressed evidence
    d. False dichotomy
    e. Not a fallacious argument

7. All Greeks are mortal because all Greeks are human and all humans are mortal.
    a. Begging the question
    b. Complex question
    c. Suppressed evidence
    d. False dichotomy
    e. Not a fallacious argument

8. Either study hard in high school and college or get a poor-paying job.
    a. Begging the question
    b. Complex question
    c. Suppressed evidence
    d. False dichotomy
    e. Not a fallacious argument

9. This year you must either vote for the Republican candidate or not vote at all. The Democrat isn't worth the time of day.
    a. Begging the question
    b. Complex question
    c. Suppressed evidence
    d. False dichotomy
    e. Not a fallacious argument

10. Have you stopped taking drugs?
    a. Begging the question
    b. Complex question
    c. Suppressed evidence
    d. False dichotomy
    e. Not a fallacious argument

8.5 Fallacies of Relevance, Part I

Fallacies of relevance occur when the evidence in the premises does not support the conclusion. We will take up four such fallacies in which irrelevant considerations are offered in the premises in Part I and another four such fallacies in Part II.

> **Fallacy 1: Appeal to Force**
> Appeal to force is an unjustified appeal to harm or a threat of harm in order to get a conclusion accepted.
>
> Note: Some appeals to force are not fallacious. The police officer who threatens to take away your driver's license if you don't make sure your driving obeys the traffic laws is acting within her role as a police officer. It is a justified appeal to force.

Examples of appeal to force:

a.	Candidate to voter: "I am sure you will want to vote for me for mayor because I wouldn't want it to come out that you cheat on your taxes." The threat of harm does not provide genuine evidence for the conclusion; it is irrelevant to the conclusion and therefore commits the Appeal to Force fallacy. However, if the candidate argued, "I am sure you will want to vote for me for mayor. I have served as a city council person for the last seven years and for three of those years I was chair of the budget committee," then the reason given would be relevant to the conclusion.
b.	You should vote for me for class president, so we can remain friends.
c.	Give me a raise or else something bad may happen to the company's computer system.
d.	Teacher: "If I catch you cheating on the test, you will fail the course." This is not a fallacious appeal to force.

> **Fallacy 2: Appeal to Pity**
> Emotional states are never reasons to accept a claim as true. The fallacy of appeal to pity is an appeal to one's sorry state as if it were a reason to believe that a statement is true.

Examples of the fallacy of appeal to pity:

a.	A drunk driver claims his violation of the law should be overlooked because his wife had just died.
b.	"I am the most qualified applicant for the job, because if I don't get the job, my family will starve." There is a moral principle that requires that we help those in need, but it is not relevant to whether this applicant is the most qualified applicant.
c.	Teacher, you must give me an A for this course because I will not be able to graduate if I get anything lower than an A.

Fallacy 3: Mob Appeal
The fallacy of mob appeal plays on our desire to be special, popular, or accepted in order to get us to accept the conclusion that is being proposed.

Examples of mob appeal:

a.	"You should vote for candidate Smith because she is a true American." The suggestion is that by voting for Smith you will be a member of the group of "true Americans"—whatever that means.
b.	An ad features a group of hip, attractive people drinking Maximum Cola. The caption reads, "Wouldn't you rather be a Maximum drinker?" The suggestion is that by drinking Maximum Cola, you would be one of the hip people.
c.	"Fudd Funeral Homes: The choice of discriminating families for more than a hundred years." This is sometimes called "snob appeal."

Fallacy 4: Straw Person
A straw person fallacy involves an attack on an argument that has been misrepresented in a way to make it easier to defeat. The straw person fallacy either focuses on an (allegedly) unstated premise or a distortion of the conclusion.

Examples of the straw person fallacy:

a.	Dr. Hernandez argues that national health insurance would provide for good medical care for all people because no one would be turned away from medical centers. Congressman Mertle attacks his argument by claiming that Dr. Hernandez's argument is correct if you believe that people should not be able to choose their health-care center.
b.	Candidate J.J. Smith wants people to vote for her because she will support tax cuts for the middle class. Candidate Booth replies that Smith's proposal means that she supports raising taxes on the poor.
c.	Mr. Jones argues that new taxes are needed to build a new elementary school, since the elementary schools are currently overcrowded. Ms. Wilson responds that the new taxes would "tax everyone out of their home." (Property taxes would go up. It is unlikely that they would force everyone to sell his or her home.)

8.6   Exercise Circle the fallacy involved in the arguments.

1. **Example:**
Showing a picture of a child suffering from severe malnutrition, the mailing from Worldwide Charity asks the receiver to send $25 or else this child and many others will die because of famine.
   a. Appeal to force
   (b.) **Appeal to pity***
   c. Mob appeal
   d. Straw person
   e. Probably not a fallacious argument
   *We might have an obligation to aid the poor, but that does not necessarily imply that we should give to Worldwide Charity. One issue is whether the money we give—or what portion of the money we give—will actually go to aid the poor. Some portion of what we give to a charity—sometimes a fairly large portion—goes to advertising.

2. The father said to his son that he could go to graduate school for an advanced degree in business, but that if he didn't return to run the family business, he would be disinherited.
   a. Appeal to force
   b. Appeal to pity
   c. Mob appeal
   d. Straw person
   e. Probably not a fallacious argument

3. Sandra has concluded that the system of numerical grades should be changed. But her position assumes that there are no true differences amongst the students in their learning. So the system of numerical grades should not be changed.
   a. Appeal to force
   b. Appeal to pity
   c. Mob appeal
   d. Straw person
   e. Probably not a fallacious argument

4. "Dear teacher, you must accept this late term paper because I have been having a hard time working my 30 hours at the restaurant and keeping up with my homework."
   a. Appeal to force
   b. Appeal to pity
   c. Mob appeal
   d. Straw person
   e. Probably not a fallacious argument

(Continued)

5. All basketball players in this league are males. J.J. is a basketball player in this league.
    Hence, J.J. is a male.
    a. Appeal to force
    b. Appeal to pity
    c. Mob appeal
    d. Straw person
    e. Probably not a fallacious argument

6. Detective Wise has argued that the city should budget more money for the police
    department so that it can replace its outdated equipment. But her argument assumes that
    we can solve problems by just throwing more money at them—which is clearly false. So,
    we must reject her argument.
    a. Appeal to force
    b. Appeal to pity
    c. Mob appeal
    d. Straw person
    e. Probably not a fallacious argument

7. Gerardo has the same ethnic background as you have. So you should vote for Gerardo.
    a. Appeal to force
    b. Appeal to pity
    c. Mob appeal
    d. Straw person
    e. Probably not a fallacious argument

8. Hilda has argued that we should not pour used motor oil into the ground, for such actions
    will pollute the groundwater and damage our health. Her argument is reasonable only if
    we assume that polluted groundwater is the only cause of bad health, which it is not. So,
    we should reject Hilda's argument.
    a. Appeal to force
    b. Appeal to pity
    c. Mob appeal
    d. Straw person
    e. Probably not a fallacious argument

9. One country says to another that the second one better give them 10 million barrels of oil
    a year or else atomic bombs will be used in a war against the second country.
    a. Appeal to force
    b. Appeal to pity
    c. Mob appeal
    d. Straw person
    e. Probably not a fallacious argument

10. Vote for the Independent Party candidate, Isabel Stanton, because she is the most patriotic of all the candidates.
    a. Appeal to force
    b. Appeal to pity
    c. Mob appeal
    d. Straw person
    e. Probably not a fallacious argument

8.7 Fallacies of Relevance, Part II

Here are four additional fallacies of relevance that occur when the evidence in the premises is replaced by personal character attacks that do not support the conclusion.

Fallacy 1: Personal Attack (*Ad Hominem*, Against the Person)

A response to an argument that focuses on the personal character or circumstances of the arguer, rather than supporting an argument.

Examples of personal attack:

a.	Ms. Newton argues that a national health-care program would provide a better health-care system than the current system. Mr. March replied, "What else would you expect from her? She's a communist."
b.	Senator Mill said, "Mr. Barley has defended the decisions of the president in vetoing the bill that would raise taxes for better heath care for children. But what else would you expect from Mr. Barley, since he is a member of the president's political party?"
c.	Mr. Gonzalez argued that the city should hire Jones Recyclers to handle their recyclable materials, since it had provided a safe and economical service to three neighboring cities. Ms. Chevnok responded, "Mr. Gonzales suggests Jones Recyclers because he owns hundreds of shares of stock in Jones Recyclers." (Since Mr. Gonzalez would stand to make money if the city hired Recyclers, Inc., one should look at his argument very carefully. This is not a ground, however, for simply dismissing his arguments.)

Fallacy 2: Accident

We all make judgments on the basis of widely accepted principles. These include such principles as "we should not lie," "we should keep our promises," and "we should do what we can to help people in distress." An argument commits the fallacy of accident when it justifies an action by appealing to the less relevant of two or more principles.

Examples of the fallacy of accident:

a.	I promised to meet you for lunch at 12:30. On the way to lunch, the car in front of me drives into a tree. I drive by a person in need of medical help and justify my decision by appealing to the principle that "A good person should always keep his or her appointments."
b.	We're both taking a test. I don't know the answer to one of the test questions, so I ask you for help. You tell me the answer and justify your decision by telling people, "One should always help people who are in distress." (The principle, "One should always do one's own work on tests," is more important in this case.)
c.	Henry and Zoe are deeply in love. They both vow never to be separated. So, when Zoe went into the women's rest room during the football game, Henry followed.

Fallacy 3: Avoiding the Issue (Red Herring)

Red herrings are smelly fish. When training hunting dogs, they are sometimes dragged across the trail of a hunted animal to tempt the dogs to follow the wrong trail. An argument may commit this fallacy of red herring when it drags another issue into an argument to distract us from the real issue. The fallacy only occurs when responding to an argument.

Examples of the fallacy of avoiding the issue:

a.	Senator Snort argued against the national health-care bill saying that it, like many other government programs, would be little more than a large, inefficient bureaucracy. Senator Sniff replied, "But if we don't pass the bill, we will have a huge increase in crime because patients will be forced to steal to pay their medical bills."
b.	Nurse Betty argued that too many students are overweight and undernourished. She concluded that the menu in the cafeteria should be changed to low fat food. Cook Clara replied, "We try to make meals that the students enjoy eating. If we start serving broccoli and Brussels sprouts every day, the result will be more uneaten food."
c.	Mr. Friz argued that the local factory should be closed for six months and remodeled because there have been proportionately more accidents in the factory than similar factories of the same size. Ms. Frop replied, "We can't close the factory. It employs more people than any other business in town. Closing the factory for any length of time would force most families to beg for food."

Fallacy 4: Irrelevant Conclusion (Missing the Point)

An argument commits the fallacy of irrelevant conclusion when the premises lead to one conclusion but the arguer claims an unrelated conclusion.

Examples of irrelevant conclusion:

a.	Congresswoman DeGras argued, "We all know that we must repair the highway system in this country. Bridges have collapsed. Highways are disintegrating. The $16 billion that the budget allocated for these repairs is only half the money needed to fix the problem. So we should encourage the public to take trains instead of overtaxing our roadways further." The Congresswoman's conclusion does not follow from her argument. We would expect her to conclude that more money is needed for highway repairs.
b.	Doctor to a patient: "You know that red meat is high in cholesterol. Too much cholesterol causes heart disease. Yet, you eat steak every day. So, keep up the good work." (Typically, a doctor might suggest one cut back on these foods.)
c.	A student to his teacher: "College has gotten very expensive. With the cash problems the state is having, our tuition is raised every year, while there are fewer scholarships and less grants. So you shouldn't care if we cheat on exams!" The premises of the student's argument do not lead to the conclusion that the teacher should accept cheating on exams. We would expect that the conclusion would focus on reducing the price of tuition.

8.8   Exercise Circle the probable fallacy involved in the arguments.

1. **Example:**
   One person at a public hearing proposes that everyone should be required to drive small cars that get 40 miles per gallon, but an opponent argues in response that that first speaker has two gas-guzzling Hummers in his driveway.
   a. **Personal attack**
   b. Accident
   c. Avoiding the issue
   d. Irrelevant conclusion
   e. Probably not a fallacious argument

2. A corporation president has proposed that we should lease more ocean land off of the Atlantic and Pacific coasts for oil and gas drilling, but someone responds that this corporation president is the owner of a gas- and oil-drilling company.
   a. Personal attack
   b. Accident
   c. Avoiding the issue
   d. Irrelevant conclusion
   e. Probably not a fallacious argument

3. A bank robber tells the teller to let him know what the combination to the safe is, because people should always tell the truth.
   a. Personal attack
   b. Accident
   c. Avoiding the issue
   d. Irrelevant conclusion
   e. Probably not a fallacious argument

4. Evidence gathered from the effect of diet on the health of the heart shows that diets low in cholesterol and animal fats help people to live a long life. So, if you desire a long life, you should put too much salt on your food.
   a. Personal attack
   b. Accident
   c. Avoiding the issue
   d. Irrelevant conclusion
   e. Probably not a fallacious argument

5. The dean of liberal arts said that courses in logic helped prepare students for law school better than any other course. But Joe argues that logic courses are puzzles wrapped up enigmas such as what happens when an irresistible force means an immovable object.
   a. Personal attack
   b. Accident
   c. Avoiding the issue
   d. Irrelevant conclusion
   e. Probably not a fallacious argument

6. Mr. Chou has argued that chewing tobacco is a disgusting practice that will give people cancer of the mouth, but many famous athletes chew tobacco. So we must reject Mr. Chou's argument.
    a. Personal attack
    b. Accident
    c. Avoiding the issue
    d. Irrelevant conclusion
    e. Probably not a fallacious argument

7. My teacher has argued this year that everyone should take a course in ethics in college, but last year, he argued that no one should take ethics in college because you needed to be ethical in character already by the time you were 18.
    a. Personal attack
    b. Accident
    c. Avoiding the issue
    d. Irrelevant conclusion
    e. Probably not a fallacious argument

8. Most people who enjoy Sudoku enjoy working out difficult solutions to puzzles, and most people who enjoy working out difficult solutions to puzzles enjoy the challenge of a logic course. So it is probable that some people who enjoy Sudoku enjoy the challenge of a logic course.
    a. Personal attack
    b. Accident
    c. Avoiding the issue
    d. Irrelevant conclusion
    e. Probably not a fallacious argument

9. Most people who enjoy Sudoku enjoy working out difficult solutions to puzzles, and most people who enjoy working out difficult solutions to puzzles enjoy the challenge of a logic course. So people have to be really weird nerds in order to enjoy a logic course.
    a. Personal attack
    b. Accident
    c. Avoiding the issue
    d. Irrelevant conclusion
    e. Probably not a fallacious argument

10. All fruits are a key part of a healthy diet. So rotten apples are a key part of a healthy diet.
    a. Personal attack
    b. Accident
    c. Avoiding the issue
    d. Irrelevant conclusion
    e. Probably not a fallacious argument

8.9 Fallacies of Ambiguity

When an argument shifts from one meaning of a word to another meaning, or when the meaning of a sentence can be interpreted in more than one way, then an argument might commit a fallacy of ambiguity.

Fallacy 1: Equivocation
When the meaning of a word changes in the course of an argument and the conclusion depends on the changed meaning, then the argument commits the fallacy of equivocation.

Examples of fallacy of equivocation:

a.	Boss: "I promised you a quarterly raise. I always keep my promises. So, here's twenty-five cents."
b.	All plants produce oxygen. The Toyota plant is three miles down the road. So, the Toyota plant produces oxygen.
c.	All dogs bark. This television is a real dog. So, this television barks.

Fallacy 2: Amphiboly
This fallacy occurs when poor grammatical sentence structure clouds the meaning of a statement so it can be interpreted in two or more different ways.

Examples of fallacy of amphiboly:

a.	Professor Smith gave a lecture on viruses that cause disease in the Science Building. So, we should avoid the Science Building.
b.	Joe started the car in the house. So, the car was in the house.

Fallacy 3: Accent
The fallacy of accent occurs when we emphasize different words in a statement or when a sentence is incompletely quoted out of context.

Examples of fallacy of accent:

a.	It's a general principle that *you* should not bear false witness. So, it's okay if *I* tell a few fibs.
b.	American criminals are very well-treated, for the Eighth Amendment to the Constitution says, " ... bail shall not be required, nor ... fines imposed, nor ... punishments inflicted."
c.	Senator Blower argued, "It is not in the national interest to go to war against the Canary Islands. The war cannot be justified." Senator Sucker replied, "We must invade the Canary Islands. Why, even Senator Blower used the word, 'justified' when talking about the war."

Fallacy 4: Composition

This fallacy occurs when we unreasonably conclude that something which is true of a part or parts is also of the whole.

Examples of fallacy of composition:

a.	Every part of my car weighs less than 500 pounds. So, my car weighs less than 500 pounds.
b.	Every member of St. Sinbad's Church is a weathy person. So, St. Sinbad's is a wealthy church.
c.	Every part of the Big Ben clock is small enough to hold in your hands. So, the Big Ben clock is small enough to hold in your hands.

Note: Some arguments from part to whole can be good arguments. For example, because every part of this machine is made from carbon compounds, we can conclude the whole machine is made from carbon compounds.

Fallacy 5: Division

This fallacy is the reverse of the fallacy of composition. This fallacy of division occurs when we unreasonably argue from the whole to the part.

Examples of fallacy of division:

a.	This car was made in the United States. Therefore, every part was made in the United States. (American-made cars have parts from all over the world.)
b.	The grade point average (GPA) of the senior class is 2.9. Martin Cruz is in the class, so he has a GPA of 2.9.
c.	The Salvation Army receives millions of dollars each year. So, every Salvation Army volunteer receives millions of dollars every year.

Note: Some arguments from whole to parts are legitimate. For example, if my computer weighs less than 12 pounds, I can correctly conclude that every part of my computer weighs less than 12 pounds.

8.10 Exercise Circle the fallacy of ambiguity in the arguments.

1. **Example:**
   The school teachers in the city are overpaid. So, Mr. Jones, a teacher who works 60 hours a week, is overpaid.
   a. Equivocation
   b. Amphiboly
   c. Accent
   d. Composition
   (e.) **Division**

2. Mr. Smith's average salary as a teacher in the last three years was $35,000 a year. Therefore the average salary of all teachers in the city in the last three years was $35,000 a year.
   a. Equivocation
   b. Amphiboly
   c. Accent
   d. Composition
   e. Division

3. A telegram answers the question whether Maria should buy an expensive car by the following words: "no expense too great." Maria concludes that she should buy the expensive car.
   a. Equivocation
   b. Amphiboly
   c. Accent
   d. Composition
   e. Division

4. Some musicians are felines since some musicians are cool cats and all cats are felines.
   a. Equivocation
   b. Amphiboly
   c. Accent
   d. Composition
   e. Division

5. Cars on the road are safer than they were ten years ago. So my car, a 1949 Hudson, is safer than it was ten years ago.
   a. Equivocation
   b. Amphiboly
   c. Accent
   d. Composition
   e. Division

6. Each flower in the arrangement is small, so the flower arrangement as a whole is small.
   a. Equivocation
   b. Amphiboly
   c. Accent
   d. Composition
   e. Division

7. On the stage where the debate of the candidates is taking place, Rosa is to the left of Maria. So Rosa is more liberal than Maria.
   a. Equivocation
   b. Amphiboly
   c. Accent
   d. Composition
   e. Division

8. President Kennedy said, "Ask not what your country can do for you. Ask what you can do for your country." So you should ask what your country can do to cut your taxes because Kennedy said, "Ask . . . what your country can do for you. . . ."
   a. Equivocation
   b. Amphiboly
   c. Accent
   d. Composition
   e. Division

9. Every stamp in Daniel's collection is 30 years old or older. So Daniel, who is 21, has a stamp collection that is more than 30 years old.
   a. Equivocation
   b. Amphiboly
   c. Accent
   d. Composition
   e. Division

10. Someone argues that no one really disbelieves in God or is an atheist because everyone believes in something and that something is the equivalent of God.
    a. Equivocation
    b. Amphiboly
    c. Accent
    d. Composition
    e. Division

(Continued)

11. The family room in the house I am planning to buy is very large. So the house I am planning to buy is very large.
    a. Equivocation
    b. Amphiboly
    c. Accent
    d. Composition
    e. Division

8.11 Review Exercise Circle the probable fallacy of weak induction involved in the arguments.

1. **Example:**
    A famous science fiction author has said that we will have people living on Mars by the year 2050. So, we should all agree that people will live on Mars by the year 2050.
    a. Hasty generalization
    (b.) **Fallacious appeal to authority**
    c. False cause
    d. Weak analogy
    e. Probably not a fallacious argument

2. I have seen 10 swans at the city zoo that are white. So we may conclude that the vast majority of swans are white.
    a. Hasty generalization
    b. Fallacious appeal to authority
    c. False cause
    d. Weak analogy
    e. Probably not a fallacious argument

3. It is not a crime to test an atomic weapon underground. So it is not a crime to test an atomic weapon in the atmosphere.
    a. Hasty generalization
    b. Fallacious appeal to authority
    c. False cause
    d. Weak analogy
    e. Probably not a fallacious argument

4. Robert ate pizza and got an A on his math test the next day, The same thing happened to Maria and Julio. So we should all eat pizza whenever we want to get A's on our math tests.
    a. Hasty generalization
    b. Fallacious appeal to authority
    c. False cause
    d. Weak analogy
    e. Probably not a fallacious argument

5. Joe was driving home from college his first day at the school when another driver from out of state cut him off from switching lanes, even after Joe had made a proper signal to change lanes. Joe concluded that all out-of-state drivers are bad drivers.
    a. Hasty generalization
    b. Fallacious appeal to authority
    c. False cause
    d. Weak analogy
    e. Probably not a fallacious argument

(Continued)

6. One hundred samples of ocean saltwater were tested, and they did not freeze at 0 degrees Centigrade. So ocean saltwater does not freeze at 0 degrees Centigrade.
    a. Hasty generalization
    b. Fallacious appeal to authority
    c. False cause
    d. Weak analogy
    e. Probably not a fallacious argument

7. Joe's Toyota Prius gets 40 miles per gallon of gas. So my Toyota SUV will also get 40 miles per gallon of gas.
    a. Hasty generalization
    b. Fallacious appeal to authority
    c. False cause
    d. Weak analogy
    e. Probably not a fallacious argument

8. Joe's Toyota Prius gets 40 miles per gallon of gas. So my Toyota Prius will also get 40 miles per gallon of gas.
    a. Hasty generalization
    b. Fallacious appeal to authority
    c. False cause
    d. Weak analogy
    e. Probably not a fallacious argument

9. I forgot to step on second base when I went out to play center field. I made two errors during that inning. So, I will never fail to step on second base when I go out to play center field.
    a. Hasty generalization
    b. Fallacious appeal to authority
    c. False cause
    d. Weak analogy
    e. Probably not a fallacious argument

8.12 Review Exercise Circle the probable fallacy of presumption involved in the arguments.

1. **Example:**
   Let's decide where we will go on vacation. Shall we go to New York or to California?
   a. Begging the question
   b. Complex question
   c. Suppressed evidence
   (d.) **False dichotomy**
   e. Not a fallacious argument

2. James is a man; hence James is a male.
   a. Begging the question
   b. Complex question
   c. Suppressed evidence
   d. False dichotomy
   e. Not a fallacious argument

3. The athlete who had recenty discovered he had a serious heart condition said, "Put me in Coach, I'm the best athlete you have available and I'm ready to go."
   a. Begging the question
   b. Complex question
   c. Suppressed evidence
   d. False dichotomy
   e. Not a fallacious argument

4. Prosecutor: "Where did you put the money that you took out of cash register?"
   Defendant: "In my workroom locker?"
   a. Begging the question
   b. Complex question
   c. Suppressed evidence
   d. False dichotomy
   e. Not a fallacious argument

5. Telling the truth is the most practical thing to do in the long run because the most practical thing to do in the long run is telling the truth.
   a. Begging the question
   b. Complex question
   c. Suppressed evidence
   d. False dichotomy
   e. Not a fallacious argument

(Continued)

6. We should dump the radioactive waste into the ocean 200 miles offshore because that method will be the cheapest way to dispose of the problem.
   a. Begging the question
   b. Complex question
   c. Suppressed evidence
   d. False dichotomy
   e. Not a fallacious argument

7. If Martina has good SAT scores and high grades, then she should go to college if she can finance it without heavy debt. Martina does have good SAT scores and high grades and can finance going to college without heavy debt. So she should go to college.
   a. Begging the question
   b. Complex question
   c. Suppressed evidence
   d. False dichotomy
   e. Not a fallacious argument

8. Either eat in moderation or become grossly overweight.
   a. Begging the question
   b. Complex question
   c. Suppressed evidence
   d. False dichotomy
   e. Not a fallacious argument

9. Either the Democratic candidate or the Independent candidate will win the election. The Democratic candidate will not win. So the Independent candidate will win.
   a. Begging the question
   b. Complex question
   c. Suppressed evidence
   d. False dichotomy
   e. Not a fallacious argument

10. When did you decide to be a quitter?
    a. Begging the question
    b. Complex question
    c. Suppressed evidence
    d. False dichotomy
    e. Not a fallacious argument

8.13 Review Exercise Circle the probable fallacy of relevance involved in the arguments.

1. **Example:**
   Buy Mrs. Magnowitz's Select Soups because Select Soups are the selection of most selective people.
   a. Appeal to force
   b. Appeal to pity
   (c.) **Mob appeal**
   d. Straw person
   e. Probably not a fallacious argument

2. Giving evidence of many cases in which people have been denied medical care and thereby died because of unfair practices of heath maintenance organizations, Mr. Fair has argued that significant reforms need to be made to the health system in the country.
   a. Appeal to force
   b. Appeal to pity
   c. Mob appeal
   d. Straw person
   e. Probably not a fallacious argument

3. The mother yelled at her daughter, "Go ahead and marry anyone you choose, but if you marry Mr. Smith, I will never speak with you again."
   a. Appeal to force
   b. Appeal to pity
   c. Mob appeal
   d. Straw person
   e. Probably not a fallacious argument

4. Mrs. Smith has argued that our country should devote 3% of our budget to foreign aid to help prevent starvation and terrible illness in poor countries. But her argument assumes that this would make all those people healthy, wealthy, and wise, which it certainly wouldn't. So, we must reject her argument.
   a. Appeal to force
   b. Appeal to pity
   c. Mob appeal
   d. Straw person
   e. Probably not a fallacious argument

5. "Even though I stole money from my company, have mercy on me because my wife will miss me if I have to go to prison."
   a. Appeal to force
   b. Appeal to pity
   c. Mob appeal
   d. Straw person
   e. Probably not a fallacious argument

(Continued)

6.   I chatted with Selma during Mr. Smith's history lecture. Mr. Smith stopped and said
     to us, "You two shall be silent, or I shall sentence you both to a week of detention after
     school." Since I'd studied informal fallacies, I could only smile, for Ms. Smith had clearly
     committed the fallacy of:
     a. Appeal to force
     b. Appeal to pity
     c. Mob appeal
     d. Straw person
     e. Probably not a fallacious argument

7.   Fiona has argued that the government should prevent insurance companies from refusing
     to insure people who are already ill. Her conclusion entails that the government should
     take over the health care system. But a government-run medical system is certain to be
     expensive and inefficient. So, we must reject Fiona's argument for the regulation of the
     medical inurance industry.
     a. Appeal to force
     b. Appeal to pity
     c. Mob appeal
     d. Straw person
     e. Probably not a fallacious argument

8.   The Chicago Cubs play for your home city. So you should root for the Cubs.
     a. Appeal to force
     b. Appeal to pity
     c. Mob appeal
     d. Straw person
     e. Probably not a fallacious argument

9.   Do not drink the water without boiling it for 20 minutes, the Health Commissioner said, or
     else you will suffer a water-caused disease.
     a. Appeal to force
     b. Appeal to pity
     c. Mob appeal
     d. Straw person
     e. Probably not a fallacious argument

10. Fred said to the teacher that he had better give him a good grade or else the teacher
    would receive a poor evaluation from Fred and his friends.
    a. Appeal to force
    b. Appeal to pity
    c. Mob appeal
    d. Straw person
    e. Probably not a fallacious argument

8.14 Review Exercise Circle the probable fallacy of relevance involved in the arguments.

1. **Example:**
Mr. Sanchez has testified before Congress that immigration should be greatly restricted, but Mrs. Wheat then testified that Mr. Sanchez's testimony was not worthwhile because he was an immigrant himself only 15 years ago.
   a. **Personal attack**
   b. Accident
   c. Avoiding the issue
   d. Irrelevant conclusion
   e. Probably not a fallacious argument

2. We have freedom of speech. So, it's okay to yell, "Fire" in a crowded theater.
   a. Personal attack
   b. Accident
   c. Avoiding the issue
   d. Irrelevant conclusion
   e. Probably not a fallacious argument

3. When Abraham Lincoln was in the House of Representatives, he voted in 1848 against going to war with Mexico, but his opponents argued that he was supporting the Mexicans who had killed many Americans at the Alamo.
   a. Personal attack
   b. Accident
   c. Avoiding the issue
   d. Irrelevant conclusion
   e. Probably not a fallacious argument

4. All collies are gentle animals. All gentle animals make good pets. So you should buy your young child a dog rather than a cat as a pet.
   a. Personal attack
   b. Accident
   c. Avoiding the issue
   d. Irrelevant conclusion
   e. Probably not a fallacious argument

5. Mr. Huxtable has argued that Congress should add more funding to NASA, the space agency, but his argument is a bad one because he is the chief administrator of NASA and only wants to expand his budget and his salary.
   a. Personal attack
   b. Accident
   c. Avoiding the issue
   d. Irrelevant conclusion
   e. Probably not a fallacious argument

(Continued)

6. The faculty of the college argued that the star quarterback of the university's football team had disgraced the university by failing all his courses in the spring, thereby failing to graduate. However, the coach responded by saying that you could find star football players who had failed to graduate at every top football program in the country.
    a. Personal attack
    b. Accident
    c. Avoiding the issue
    d. Irrelevant conclusion
    e. Probably not a fallacious argument

7. Mr. Roberts has argued that all citizens should have a right to a lawyer when they are accused of a crime, but Mr. Jones responds that Mr. Roberts is a card-carrying member of the ACLU, the American Civil Liberties Union, a notorious liberal organization.
    a. Personal attack
    b. Accident
    c. Avoiding the issue
    d. Irrelevant conclusion
    e. Probably not a fallacious argument

8. All those who love working on computers have good math skills, and all those who have good math skills have good skills of problem-solving, So it follows that all those who love working on computers have good skills of problem-solving.
    a. Personal attack
    b. Accident
    c. Avoiding the issue
    d. Irrelevant conclusion
    e. Probably not a fallacious argument

9. Whenever the barometer drops rapidly, a terrible storm is developing. The barometer is dropping rapidly. So it is a good time to go surfing because the waves will be gigantic.
    a. Personal attack
    b. Accident
    c. Avoiding the issue
    d. Irrelevant conclusion
    e. Probably not a fallacious argument

10. Mr. Robertson has argued against allowing people to have unlimited purchases of handguns because of the terrible result that these guns are taken across state lines to be sold to criminals. However, Mr. Tex responds that there can be no restriction of gun purchases because all citizens have an individual right to gun ownership because of the Second Amendment to the Constitution.
    a. Personal attack
    b. Accident
    c. Avoiding the issue
    d. Irrelevant conclusion
    e. Probably not a fallacious argument

8.15 Review Exercise Circle the probable fallacy of ambiguity in the arguments.

1. **Example:**
   The average salary of all nurses in the city in the last three years was $60,000 a year. Therefore, Mr. Smith's average salary as a nurse in the last three years was $60,000 a year.
   a. Equivocation
   a. Amphiboly
   b. Accent
   c. Composition
   (e.) Division

2. Mrs. Somas is giving a lecture on grizzly bears in the science room tonight. Since grizzly bears are dangerous, we'll certainly want to avoid the science room tonight.
   a. Equivocation
   b. Amphiboly
   c. Accent
   d. Composition
   e. Division

3. A flake of pepper is light and what is light cannot be black. So pepper cannot be black.
   a. Equivocation
   b. Amphiboly
   c. Accent
   d. Composition
   e. Division

4. My Hummer is safer on the whole than Hummers were ten years ago. So the wheels on my Hummer are safer than wheels on Hummers were ten years ago.
   a. Equivocation
   b. Amphiboly
   c. Accent
   d. Composition
   e. Division

5. Neutrons, electrons, and protons are odorless. Dogs and cats are made of neutrons, electrons, and protons. So dogs and cats are odorless.
   a. Equivocation
   b. Amphiboly
   c. Accent
   d. Composition
   e. Division

(Continued)

6. A student delivers a term paper late to the teacher, and the teacher says that she will waste no time in looking at it. So, the teacher will probably return the paper within the next day.
    a. Equivocation
    b. Amphiboly
    c. Accent
    d. Composition
    e. Division

7. We should not speak ill of our friends, but it's okay if Fred refers to them in disparaging ways.
    a. Equivocation
    b. Amphiboly
    c. Accent
    d. Composition
    e. Division

8. Some stamps in Daniel's collection are ten years old or older. So Daniel's collection is at least 10 years old.
    a. Equivocation
    b. Amphiboly
    c. Accent
    d. Composition
    e. Division

9. Ketchup is better than nothing, but nothing is better than a dinner cooked by Chef Danielle. So ketchup is better than a dinner cooked by Chef Danielle.
    a. Equivocation
    b. Amphiboly
    c. Accent
    d. Composition
    e. Division

10. Each atom in the sun is very small. So the sun itself is very small.
    a. Equivocation
    b. Amphiboly
    c. Accent
    d. Composition
    e. Division

Chapter 8 Quiz

Choose the best answer for each of the following questions.

1. This fallacy may occur when one concludes too quickly from one or more examples to a general conclusion about all such things.
   a. Division
   b. Equivocation
   c. False cause
   d. Hasty generalization
   e. Appeal to ignorance

2. An argument may commit this fallacy when it drags another issue into an argument that is irrelevant to and distracts us from the issue being argued.
   a. Division
   b. Equivocation
   c. False cause
   d. Hasty generalization
   e. Avoiding the issue

3. In this fallacy the meaning of a word shifts in the course of an argument and the persuasive force of the argument depends on that shift in meaning.
   a. Equivocation
   b. Amphiboly
   c. Accent
   d. Composition
   e. Division

4. An argument commits this fallacy when principles conflict and we justify our choice of action by appealing to the less plausible of two or more principles.
   a. Personal attack
   b. Accident
   c. Avoiding the issue
   d. Irrelevant conclusion
   e. Composition

5. This fallacy occurs when we unreasonably argue from either something true of a part or parts to the nature of the whole thing.
   a. Personal attack
   b. Accident
   c. Avoiding the issue
   d. Irrelevant conclusion
   e. Composition

(Continued)

6. This fallacious argument occurs when the arguer assumes that only two alternatives are available when in fact there may be several other alternatives that could be true.
    a. Begging the question
    b. Complex question
    c. Suppressed evidence
    d. False dichotomy
    e. Division

7. This fallacy occurs when we assume in the premises the very point we are trying to conclude.
    a. Begging the question
    b. Complex question
    c. Suppressed evidence
    d. False dichotomy
    e. Division

8. This fallacy is the reverse of the fallacy of composition. This fallacy occurs when we unreasonably argue from the whole to the part.
    a. Begging the question
    b. Complex question
    c. Suppressed evidence
    d. False dichotomy
    e. Division

9. Appeal to an authority is always a fallacious argument.
    a. True
    b. False

10. Since Personal Attack is a fallacious argument, we should never question what a person says.
    a. True
    b. False

11. All arguments from whole to part are fallacious.
    a. True
    b. False

12. Some arguments from part to whole are not fallacious.
    a. True
    b. False

13. Appeal to Force can be a relevant argument.
    a. True
    b. False

14. Arguments by analogy are always fallacious because no analogy can give a perfect similarity between two different cases or situations.
   a. True
   b. False

15. An argument from a sample of 25 polluted streams and rivers to a conclusion that probably most of the 50 streams and rivers in a state have polluted waters is necessarily a hasty generalization because not all 50 streams and rivers have been tested for water pollution.
   a. True
   b. False

Index

D

E

F

Invalid / invalid arguments, 133, 135-136, 140, 156, 166, 313-315, 319-321, 332, 334-335, 344-345, 369-371, 383, 422
  definition, 135
  and Venn diagrams, 332, 334-335, 344-345
Irrelevant conclusion, 507

L

Logically equivalent, ix, 265-269, 389-391, 394, 396, 399-401

M

Major premise, 150, 305, 312, 314-315, 321, 332-333, 358, 366, 371, 383, 404, 422
Major Term 305, 312, 314-315, 321, 332-333, 358-360, 365-371, 383, 404, 422
Material implication, 267-269
Mathematical evidence, 47, 63
Middle Term 150, 305, 312-313, 315, 321, 332, 358-361, 365-371, 422
Minor premise, 150, 305, 312, 314-315, 321, 332-333, 358, 371, 404, 422
Minor Term, 305, 312, 314-315, 321, 332, 358-360, 365-371, 404, 422
Mob appeal, 502
Modus ponens, 213
Modus tollens, 214

N

Negative premise and negative conclusion, rule, 319, 321, 365

O

Observational evidence, 47, 60
Obversion, 394-396, 400-401, 412, 422
Ockham's Razor, 471
Opinions, viii, 50
Ordinary language syllogisms, 358, 404-405, 408, 412-413, 422-423

P

Particular affirmative claims, 298, 301, 313, 320-321, 329, 341-345, 376, 381-382, 390, 395, 399, 404-405, 423
Particular negative claims, 298, 301, 313, 319-321, 329, 341-345, 376, 381-382, 390, 395, 400, 405, 423
Particular premise and particular conclusion, rule, 320, 321, 365, 382, 422
Personal attack (*Ad Hominem*, against the person), 506
Predicate Term, 150, 301, 305, 328, 358, 381, 383, 389, 394, 399, 404-405, 422
Premise(s), 115
Premise indicators, 119-120
Principle of parsimony, 471

Q

Quantifier, 301, 358, 396, 404-405
  complex quantifiers, 405
  nonstandard quantifiers, 405
  ordinary language quantifier, 404-405
  part of categorical claim, 301, 358
  reducing quantifiers, 405
Quizes, 45-46, 92-93, 130-131, 199-200, 291-292, 450-451, 487-488, 525-527

R

Random sample, 485
Reducing a categorical syllogism, 358, 404-405, 408, 412-413, 422-423
Rules for evaluating categorical syllogisms, 312-315, 319-321